Library of
Davidson College

STUDIES IN
NAPOLEONIC STATESMANSHIP

GERMANY

STUDIES IN NAPOLEONIC STATESMANSHIP
GERMANY

BY

HERBERT A. L. FISHER, M.A.

GREENWOOD PRESS, PUBLISHERS
NEW YORK

320.943
F533s

Originally published in 1903
by Oxford at the Clarendon Press

First Greenwood Reprinting 1969   74-137

Library of Congress Catalogue Card Number 69-13897

SBN 8371-1302-4

PRINTED IN UNITED STATES OF AMERICA

PREFACE

THIS book is a study in civil and administrative history. Its object is to describe the growth, to analyse the character, and to estimate the influence of the Napoleonic system in Germany. Of campaigns and battles it will say practically nothing; of diplomacy only so much as will enable the reader to understand how it was that by 1807 Napoleon had become the master of Germany. Personal descriptions will occur, for all systems are worked by men and moulded by those who work them. But the main purpose of the book is not to draw portraits of persons, but to show how the Napoleonic States in Germany were created and governed.

If Napoleon, as Mr. Gladstone held, was the greatest administrator in history, then his administrative work is a theme worthy of serious attention. Yet no complete history of the civil side of the Napoleonic Empire has yet appeared, and indeed, while so much material still remains unpublished and unexplored, it is unlikely that the great work will be accomplished in this generation. Nevertheless, there seems to me to be some value in a provisional account, however imperfect, if only as indicating fruitful lines of research, and I have begun with a volume upon Germany, in the hope that I may be encouraged to complete the work at some future date by further studies of Napoleonic statesmanship in France, Italy, Holland, and Belgium. My reason for beginning with Germany rather than with Italy or France is partly that the material is of a more manageable bulk, and partly that the way has been simplified by some excellent monographs, among which I would specially mention the names of Perthes, Rambaud, Thimme, Goecke, and Darmstaedter. At the same time I should not have ventured to approach the subject of the Napoleonic system in Germany without a fair working knowledge of the legal and administrative changes which came over France during the Consulate and the Empire; and I must ask my readers to believe that I have made myself acquainted with the essential authorities, Locré, Thibaudeau, and Fiévée, not to speak of more recent books such as those of Pérouse, Blanc, Rocquain, Taine, and Sagnac.

A distinguished French writer has spoken of '*la fureur de l'inédit*,' and I agree that the homage paid by historical scholars to unpublished documents, just because they are unpublished, often amounts to a disease. Yet in the history of any modern administration, research in archives is of high importance. Every member of the Civil Service is, no doubt, painfully conscious of the vast mass of correspondence, of the letters and memoranda, the petitions and inquiries, the reports and statistical tables which accumulate in his office. Little of all this may ever deserve to be published, but much of it may repay the swift reader, who takes up one transaction after another, until he becomes thoroughly acquainted not only with the affairs themselves, but with the principles upon which they are handled, and with the men who handle them. Impressions derived from such a course of study, from papers no one of which in itself may deserve publication, may only be represented by a paragraph, a phrase, or an epithet. But they are none the less worth having. They reproduce, for the author at least, the very atmosphere of the times.

The bibliographical notes appended to the chapters will indicate to the reader the authorities which I have personally found most useful. I have not felt it necessary to give exhaustive references to printed works. The *Correspondance de Napoléon*, with its supplements by Brotonne and Lecestre, is naturally the main authority, and perhaps second in importance comes the *Correspondance du roi Jérôme*, edited by Baron Ducasse. A serviceable bibliography of Napoleonic literature has been brought out by Kircheisen: and this, together with the excellent bibliographies contained in Lavisse et Rambaud, *Histoire Générale*; Fournier, *Napoléon I*; and Thimme, *Das Kurfürstenthum Hannover*, will put the student in possession of all that he is likely to require. It may perhaps be useful to remind such as may consult these bibliographies, of all forms of literature the most depressing, that in spite of the torrent of fresh-poured ink, no one can neglect with impunity the splendid apology of Thiers, the keen criticism of Lanfrey, or the facile story of Bignon, which, undertaken at the recommendation of Napoleon himself, sparkles in places with the glitter of 'things seen.'

A word may now be said as to the unpublished sources of material utilized in this volume. The French occupation of Hanover has been very thoroughly treated by Thimme, who has worked up the Hanoverian archives, but there is valuable additional material to be found in the Archives du Ministère des Affaires Étrangères, and some curious details in the reports of Sir Charles Gordon in the Foreign Office Papers in our Record Office. The very valuable Baden Correspondence published by Erdmannsdörffer throws a strong light upon Napoleon's diplomacy in Germany in 1804 and 1805, but must be supplemented by the papers of our own diplomatic agents which lie at the Record Office. There are few better chronicles of the last hours of the Holy Roman Empire than the despatches of Alexander Horne, our envoy at Ratisbon, unless it be the correspondence of General Hédouville, the French agent. The first of these authorities has not, I think, been previously used, while the second has been singularly neglected. Horne is to be found among the papers of the English, and Hédouville among those of the French Foreign Office.

For the history of the Grand-Duchy of Berg the student must go to the Archives Nationales in Paris and to the Staatsarchiv at Düsseldorf. The material at the Archives Nationales is extremely voluminous, but beautifully arranged and catalogued. I have read not all, but nearly all, that is to be found there. At Düsseldorf the mass of papers is even greater, and the cataloguing very rough. Much of the material, probably most of it, is a duplicate of documents transmitted to Paris; but nevertheless the archives repay a visit, and I regret that my stay was necessarily so short. There are a few papers concerning the grand-duchy at the Ministère des Affaires Étrangères, but they are of slight importance.

The Kingdom of Westphalia, far richer in printed authorities than the Grand-Duchy of Berg, is apparently less rich in unpublished material. There is nothing at the Archives Nationales, and copious selections from the most valuable correspondence of Reinhard, which are preserved at the Ministère des Affaires Étrangères, have been printed in the *Revue Historique* by Baron Ducasse. Little or nothing can be found at the

Landesbibliothek at Cassel, save some rare books and pamphlets. The archives of Marburg contain a great deal of interesting local material, illustrating the working of French administration in Southern Hesse, but unfortunately the accounts of the Royal Westphalian Treasury, which I was particularly anxious to see, have been removed to Berlin, where are also to be found the reports of the Prussian envoy, von Küster. The loss of Küster may be lightly borne, for his correspondence has been more than once used, and shows him to have been a dull fellow. But it would be worth while to check the picturesque statements of the *Secret History of Westphalia* and similar works by reference to the royal accounts.

For the history of Northern Germany the correspondence of Davoût is of primary importance. Most but not all of it has been printed by Mazade, and it is quite essential to have recourse to the *cartons A. F.* iv. 1654-7 in the Archives Nationales, containing as they do, not merely the correspondence of Davoût himself, but also all the letters and memoranda forwarded through Davoût to Napoleon. Of these enclosures the most interesting are the letters of Rapp and Poniatowsky. The Foreign Office and Colonial Office papers relating to Heligoland throw some interesting light on the continental blockade, and should be utilized by all who wish to write upon that subject.

For the Grand-Duchy of Frankfort I have been content to build upon the excellent monograph of Darmstaedter, who has used the archives of Frankfort and Wiesbaden to excellent effect. I have, however, supplemented his results by the correspondence of Hédouville, Bacher, and Dalberg, which is contained in the Archives du Ministère des Affaires Étrangères.

The history of the four Rhenish departments has still to be written, and I trust that M. Lévy-Schneider, the learned biographer of Jean Bon St. André, may see his way to write it. Assuredly there must be valuable material at Coblenz, some of which has probably found its way into local periodicals, to which I have been unable to obtain access. But a voyage of discovery to Coblenz was beyond me; and my chapter upon the subject adds nothing, save for some gleanings from the Archives Nationales, to what has been common knowledge to students.

My thanks are due to the French Minister of Foreign Affairs, who generously permitted me to consult the archives of the French Foreign Office, and to the numerous archivists, French and German, whose kindly help and unfailing courtesy have left a deep impression upon me. It is also a great pleasure to acknowledge the ever-ready assistance which has been given me by Mr. Hubert Hall, of the Record Office. To Mr. Calderon, of the British Museum, I owe some information gleaned from the principal Polish authority upon the Grand-Duchy of Warsaw. In conclusion, I wish especially to express my gratitude to Professor York Powell, a Delegate of the Clarendon Press, for the many valuable suggestions which he has made while the sheets were passing through the press. It is not by any means my first obligation to the Regius Professor, and I intend that it shall not be my last. Men so learned and generous as he must expect, like the Duke of Wellington, to be 'much exposed to authors.'

H. A. L. F.

April, 1903.

CHAPTER I

GERMANY AND FRANCE

'L'Allemand est une créature qui boit plus qu'elle ne peut porter, un tonneau qui contient plus qu'il ne paraît, et un homme qui sait plus qu'il ne dit : j'y ajoute, un homme d'honneur et de probité.'

OXENSTIERNA, *Pensées diverses.*

I

FEW problems are more interesting to the sociologist than the mutual interaction of different civilizations. What are the conditions which assist fusion, what are the subtle causes that arrest it, what historical medium acts as a conductor, what medium again is non-conducting, what elements of national genius, taste, and character are capable of exportation, what incapable, and why some characteristics are more easily assimilated or imitated than others, these and a host of other subsidiary questions will always arise when conquest, migration, or mere juxtaposition places two different races in a position where it is impossible for either to remain unaffected by the characteristics and ideals of the other. The collision between France and Germany during the revolutionary and Napoleonic age was far more than a shock of arms. It involved an attempt on the part of France to complete and extend the domination of her sentiment and her logic, of her lightest fashions and deepest thoughts, and above all of her most solid contrivances in the realm of politics. In this process the political map of Germany was transfigured, and the old ideas that had ruled the small German principalities went suddenly, painfully, and shamefully bankrupt. A new conception of the State was worked out in practical detail with the aid of Germans upon German soil. It was no mere superficial affair, for every cottage knew and felt the change, which indeed entered into the most intimate social relations, and included new laws touching divorce, inheritance, the civil marriage, the labour service, the right to take up a trade or handicraft. But this experiment, profound and important though it was, was carried out under conditions which ensured failure, though the effects of it, negative and positive, have been far reaching. The most adverse of these conditions was the fact that the newly formed States were caught up into the whirl of the Napoleonic wars.

Of the two countries with which we are concerned, one was humble and docile, while the other was proud and imperious. One already knew much of what the other had to teach, and had long looked upon her as spiritual mistress and guide, while the other had never realized that the pupil of so many generations had achieved intellectual manhood and was already feeling the charm and the spell of a new discipline. While Germany knew France and admired her, France was alike ignorant and contemptuous of Germany. 'Where are you going?' says an imaginary traveller in Baron Risbeck's Travels. 'To Germany.' 'To that horrid country? I have just been through it, but in truth there is nothing there which merits attention[1].'

The really remarkable thing in Germany escaped all French observers until the Revolution drove Charles de Villers, and the Empire drove Madame de Staël, to seek a refuge beyond the Rhine. It was the growing emancipation of the country from the intellectual domination of France. In the last quarter of the eighteenth century a national literature sprang up in Germany, deriving its inspiration, so far as that inspiration was derived at all, from the Elizabethan drama or the poets of ancient Greece, or from the literatures of primitive or mediaeval times.

'Scarcely,' wrote Schiller in 1794, 'has the cold fever of Gallomania left us, when a still hotter fever of Graecomania breaks out.' But the renascence of Hellenism—though its like had not been experienced since the fifteenth century diffused Greek knowledge among the scholars of the West—was merely one symptom out of many of a changed attitude towards literature and art. Among the debts the world owes to Rousseau the greatest perhaps is his protest against the complicated artifice of civilized life. But the conventions of literature were seen to be as complicated and as arbitrary as the conventions of politics, and in the light of Rousseau's teaching

[1] Risbeck, *Voyages en Allemagne*, i. 5, and Lang, *Memoiren*, i. 248.

the classical tradition of French literature, with its delight in logical coherence, its passion for abstractions, its pure colourless and attenuated vocabulary, its strict regard for the dramatic unities, and its time-honoured conventions of rhythm and rhyme, appeared to be contrary to 'nature' and therefore to be condemned. Lessing exposed the defects of the French drama and attempted to provide a German substitute. Herder argued that there was an essential difference between the imitation of Greek and Latin models, since the Greeks represented the natural and common element in civilization and could therefore be imitated with profit, while the Latin races, representing a specialized form of culture only appropriate to their own peculiar racial temperament, could not be copied without danger. Whatever may be thought of this particular argument, it was a sound instinct which led Herder to protest against the servile imitation of French models. In the realm of literature Germany had already learnt every lesson from France that she was capable of assimilating. She was now beginning to discover a soul of her own.

Of this profound movement France was almost wholly ignorant. A young German philologist who was in Paris in 1802 wrote that nobody knew Schiller, that a French friend who had been taking German lessons for seven years cited Hagedorn, Zachariae, and Gellert as the best German writers, and that the booksellers only remembered to have heard of some translations of a 'Monsieur Schéet,' who upon examination turned out to be Goethe[1]. The statement must no doubt be taken with qualifications, but in the main the impression conveyed by it is correct. A few bad translations—and the translations from the German into French made during the eighteenth century are said by those who have examined them to be uniformly bad—can never popularize a foreign literature, and with the single exception of *Werther*, and possibly also of Schiller's *Robbers*, which was adapted for the French stage and acted in Paris in 1792 and 1793, no work of German literature achieved anything like popularity in France. Of more serious books Lessing's *Dramaturgy* (translated in 1785) alone attracted some notice, for it brought principles of aesthetic criticism to bear upon

[1] J. F. Reichardt, *Vertraute Briefe aus Paris*.

French dramatic art. But that Germany either possessed or might possess a literature of her own was an idea which had never entered the French mind during the Ancien Régime, and the Empire of Napoleon had already been founded before a little band of writers—Stapfer, de Villers, de Gérando, Garat, and Malouet—attempted in the *Archives Littéraires de l'Europe* to give to France a true idea of the position of German poetry and German thought in the world of intellect [1].

If it was a rare thing for a Frenchman to have read a translation from a German work, the Frenchman who understood the German language was a still more singular phenomenon. Voltaire's countrymen regarded the tongue of Goethe as a barbarous and difficult *patois* which the polite society of Europe, Germany included, had agreed to neglect; nor could it be forgotten that Leibnitz, though praising the virtues of German as a medium for philosophical writing, had elected to publish his most important compositions in French, and that Frederick the Great had openly expressed his contempt for the language and literature of his own country.

But if the language of Goethe was almost unknown in France, there can have been few educated Germans, from the King on his throne to the merchant at his desk, unacquainted with French. French was the language of diplomacy and Court society; it was often the medium of erudite intercourse; it was the key to the most accessible polite literature in the world. When the Duke of Brunswick, who was a Prussian field-marshal, wrote to the King of Prussia, he wrote in French. At Herr Kiekhöver's house, a centre of musical society at Hamburg, the conversation, says Spohr, was almost entirely in French [2]. 'I was very much surprised,' said the French professor at the Karlsruhe Lycée in 1807, 'to hear at Meschede (in Westphalia) a man in the costume of an inhabitant of the country cite with accuracy Joinville, Brantôme, de Thou, and all our classics. He was a manufacturer of the neighbourhood [3].' Another traveller says: 'I doubt whether there are in France many towns whose

---

[1] Virgile Rossel, *Histoire des relations littéraires de la France et de l'Allemagne* ; Süpfle, *Geschichte des deutschen Kultureinflusses auf Frankreich.*

[2] Spohr, *Autobiography* (Engl. tr.), 17.

[3] *Lettres sur la Westphalie*, 1809.

libraries are furnished with German journals. In the first German town I visited I found the journals of all countries [1]. An official report prepared for the French Emperor in 1810 offers still more striking testimony to the capacity of Germans for reading foreign tongues and to the diffusion of reading habits among them [2]. 'There is scarcely an educated German,' it says, 'who cannot read French, Italian, and English, as well as Latin.' And it may be added that in the field of pedagogy Rousseau had no disciples so strenuous, so unquestioning, and so devoid of humour as the Germans [3].

The intellectual hegemony of France was indeed so clearly marked as to excite special investigation. In 1783 the Academy of Berlin proposed for competition the question, 'What is it that has made the French tongue universal?' and Rivarol gained the prize by dwelling pardonably upon the intrinsic merits of the language over which he exercised so delicate a mastery. But in truth many historical causes quite unconnected with philology had contributed to the diffusion of French: the dazzling magnificence of the Court of Louis XIV, which was specially impressive to the German princes who were just emerging from the havoc of the Thirty Years' War; the Revocation of the Edict of Nantes, which, by dispersing the Huguenots over Europe, provided every considerable city with needy and competent teachers of the French language; the wars of the seventeenth and eighteenth centuries, during which thousands of French deserters found a home in Germany; but above all the brilliance of the French classics, the elegance and wit of their lighter literature, and the attractive urbanity of French life and conversation.

The contrast between German knowledge of France and French ignorance of Germany is summed up thus by one of the few Frenchmen of the Revolutionary period who knew what Germany was like, Charles de Villers. 'Germany,' he

[1] Virgile Rossel, *Histoire des relations littéraires de la France et de l'Allemagne*, 153-4.

[2] Report of Cuvier and Noel, extracts of which are published in Gutsmuth's *Neue Bibliothek für Pädagogik*, 1812, 39 ff.

[3] Bernard Christophe Faust à l'Assemblée Nationale *sur un vêtement libre, uniforme et national à l'usage des enfans*. Aux dépens de l'auteur. 1792. Bueckeburg en Westphalie.

says, 'differs from France so profoundly that the contrast is hard to explain and the country difficult to know well. For us Frenchmen it is like the East, where everything is at first strange and unintelligible alike in thought and in expression. The Germans know us better in general than we know them. Of all Europeans they are those who are the best at observing and studying foreign peoples and who do most justice to them. We often see them forcing themselves to adopt our manner of speech, our idiom, to enter into our views; in a word, they will make themselves almost Frenchmen in order to facilitate our intercourse with them [1].'

This docile, laborious, and highly educated people was condemned to a kind of political paralysis. While in the realms of speculation, knowledge, and feeling Germany was during the seventies, eighties, and nineties achieving results which no other European nation could rival, her political system was so unreasonable, inconvenient, and cumbrous as to be destructive of the intelligent handling of public affairs. Nominally an Empire, Germany was in reality a federation of States, and, as Montesquieu pointed out, a very bad kind of federation. The units of which it was composed were unequal in size, various in constitution, and far too untrammelled in their political action. They could make war upon their own account, and hire out their armies to foreign powers without imperial consent. The map of Germany was a mosaic, especially in the centre, in Swabia, along the banks of the Upper Rhine, and in Westphalia, and the arbitrary intermixture of States was fatal to any effective administration of them. Nor were the imperial institutions capable of directing the multifarious atoms which composed the Germanic body. The Diet of Ratisbon was a mere congress of diplomatic agents who did not act, but did little more than register decisions separately taken by the States from which they were severally accredited. It was composed of three Colleges—the Electoral College which chose the Emperor, the College of Princes, and the College of Free Towns. A majority of two Colleges was required for a resolution or *conclusum* of the Diet. The preponderant influence belonged to the princes,

---

[1] *Coup d'œil sur les universités et le mode d'instruction publique de l'Allemagne protestante.* Cassel, 1808.

and among the princes to a small number of families, most of whom were Electoral. But so little interest was taken in the affairs of the body that absenteeism was rife. Thus in 1788 of the hundred voters inscribed in the College of Princes fourteen only came to Ratisbon, while of the fifty-one free towns, eight alone were represented.

The Circles of the Empire were doubtless of value in the sixteenth century. But their political organization, which had never been complete, had almost everywhere fallen entirely into desuetude. The Emperor was in reality only the honorary president of the confederation. His prerogatives had been whittled away by a series of imperial capitulations, the first of which was drawn up before the election of Charles V. He convoked the Diet, ratified its recesses, gave investiture of fiefs, received the homage of imperial towns, and had the right to send a commissioner to be present at episcopal elections. But an official document of 1764 stated his imperial revenue to amount to 13,884 florins and 32 kreuzers. The imperial army could not be collected without the order of the Diet of the Empire, and could not march without the consent of the diets of the Circles. The two courts instituted to judge cases reserved for the Emperor, that is to say, the imperial Chamber at Wetzlar and the Aulic Court at Vienna, were proverbial for their delays, and they had no means of enforcing their decisions against a prominent prince who chose to defy them.

Nor was this federation by any means a federation of equals. There were three hundred and sixty States in the Empire, representing every grade in the feudal hierarchy from the knight to the Emperor, and a day's journey might take a traveller through a free city, through the territory of a sovereign abbot, through a village owned by an imperial knight, through the possessions of a landgrave, a duke, a prince, and a king [1].

This political diversity would not necessarily have been injurious, though it would always have been inconvenient, if the multitudinous States of Germany had been animated by a common feeling of nationality. But such a feeling, though dimly present to some natures, had no weight in the counsels of German cabinets. The Reformation and the wars of religion

[1] Himly, *Formation territoriale de l'Europe*, 286 ff.

which proceeded from it, had left scars and divided memories in the least rancorous of peoples. The Protestants had enlisted Swedes and French, and the Catholic escutcheon was darkly stained by the brutalities of Spaniards and Croats. In the eighteenth century the savagery was diminished but the egoism remained. Every German Court pursued its own advantage regardless of the welfare of the Empire. Austria ceded Lorraine to France that the Hapsburgs might be strengthened in Italy, steadily plotted the partition of Bavaria, and negotiated for the cession of Luxemburg. Prussia seized Silesia in 1740, and with Saxony and Bavaria entered into a scheme for the partition of the Austrian dominions. The rivalry of the two leading German powers led to foreign intervention, and English, French, and Russians joined in the long quarrel which owed its origin to the greed of 1740 and was only terminated by the exhaustion of 1763. The first partition of Poland, nine years later, was the crowning triumph of politic fraud and greed unabashed.

With such examples before them it is small wonder if the secondary German princes eagerly sought to obtain an advance in dignity, to swell their armies, to fill their coffers, and to expand their frontiers at the expense of their weaker neighbours. The clerical principalities seemed marked out for the spoiler, and in the seventies and eighties men were already talking of secularization as an easy means of gratifying the lay appetite. 'The only desire which the duke clearly expressed to me,' says Mirabeau of Ferdinand of Brunswick in 1786, 'is the separation of the Electorate of Hanover from the English monarchy and the secularization of certain States which may one day contribute an equivalent for Saxony[1].' The traffic in souls and square miles was no invention of Napoleon. All through the eighteenth century it entered into the calculations of the German princes.

II

Every traveller in Germany remarked the contrast between the Catholic and Protestant territories of the Empire. The difference, says Risbeck, is like the difference between France

[1] Cf. Sorel, *L'Europe et la Révolution Française*, i. 460.

and Spain [1]. In one quarter you found ignorance, squalor, degrading superstition, in the other educational zeal, reading habits widely diffused, and free thinking. While Protestant Saxony was thriving and intelligent, in Catholic Bavaria ' superstition and poverty blended with distress ' were ' visible in every village and almost in every countenance [2].' In Protestant Germany crime was extraordinarily rare, but nowhere were gallows and wheels so much in requisition as in Bavaria, and the astonishing proportion which burglary bore to other forms of crime in that country was attributed to the badness of the schools and the habits of beggary encouraged by the Roman Church [3].

Whereas the Protestant Universities were flourishing, the Catholic Universities were in the lowest state of obscurantism and decay. When Soemmering, an able young anatomist, wrote a dissertation upon negroes for the University of Mainz, in which he argued that the negro was structurally more akin to the ape than to the white man, he was reprimanded at the instance of the Chapter of Cologne, which conserved the relics of the three Kings of the East, and was jealous of the honour of King Melchior [4]. Sailer, one of the few German Catholics of real spiritual power in the later half of the century, was expelled from his professorial chair at Dillingen, because it was only by expelling him that the Elector of Bavaria could obtain a loan from the Obwexer bank, which was then dominated by Jesuit influence [5].

Nevertheless during the later half of the century even the Catholic Church in Germany gradually became affected by the liberating influences of the time. New ideas arose respecting ecclesiastical organization, and a change began to come over the thought and spirit of many Catholics.

The eighteenth century has been called the age of enlightened despotism, and every German prince, whether enlightened or barbaric, was striving to acquire despotic power in his own dominions. In this enterprise the Catholic princes, less for-

[1] *Voyages en Allemagne*, i. 165 ; Mirabeau, *Royaume de Prusse*, i. 34.
[2] Wraxall, *Memoirs of the Courts of Berlin, Dresden, Warsaw, and Vienna in the years* 1777-9, ii. 199.
[3] *Durchflüge durch Deutschland, die Niederlande und Frankreich*, vii. 156, 174 ; Mirabeau, iii. 205.
[4] Mirabeau, i. 224.
[5] *Allgemeine Deutsche Biographie*, art. Sailer.

tunate than their Protestant neighbours, were brought into necessary conflict with the independent power of the Catholic Church. The power of the Pope directly challenged their territorial sovereignty. So long as this power lasted no Catholic prince in Germany was, or could be, master in his own house.

To the unuttered thoughts and desires of dissatisfied Catholics there came in 1763 a startling response in a work printed at Frankfort under the title *Iusti Febronii de statu Ecclesiae et legitima potestate Romani pontificis liber singularis ad reuniendos dissidentes in religione christiana compositus*. This book, first published in Latin, but speedily translated into German, was a direct attack upon the monarchical organization of the Roman Church. It argued that the Pope was subject to general councils: that he possessed no spiritual titles superior to those of the bishops. It pleaded for the conciliar government of the Church, and urged that if the Pope refused to summon general councils, national councils should meet after the French model, and that the Catholic princes and bishops should agree to stand together and to disregard any papal censures which might be provoked by their action.

Febronius achieved the kind of success which rewards the man who puts into formal shape a large inarticulate mass of feeling. His treatise became the textbook at Vienna; a University was created at Bonn to expound his doctrine; and there were few teachers of canon law in the Catholic Universities of Germany who did not teach some form of Febronianism. In Austria Joseph II carried out the precepts to the letter, submitting monks and bishops to State control, and even cherishing the thought of a complete separation from Rome. Nor was 'Josephism' confined to the Hapsburg dominions. The Archbishops of Mainz, Cologne, Trèves, and Salzburg met together at Ems in 1786 and drew up a declaration—the famous Ems *Punktation*—in which, while conceding to the Pope all the privileges which he could be proved to have exercised in the first centuries of Christianity, they denied all the claims based upon the spurious Isidorian decretals. No diocesans were to have recourse to Rome, no papal exemptions were to be permitted, monasteries were to be withdrawn from foreign superiors, and no papal bulls were to be regarded as binding until they had received the sanction of the bishop to whose diocese they were directed. The attempt to establish a national Catholic Church in Germany failed, but in few countries was there less of Ultramontanism, and it is doubtful whether the breach between the French Revolution and the Papacy sensibly affected the prestige of France among German Catholics [1].

The Roman Catholic system does not admit of free dogmatic criticism, and the German Catholics were but rarely tempted into intellectual indiscretions. Here and there a German bishop or canon would finger Voltaire and place a bust of Rousseau in his study, but the scepticism which was so common among the French abbés was rarely to be found. Nevertheless a more charitable and tolerant spirit gradually spread among the educated clergy. Works of Protestant theology began to find their way into Catholic libraries and to influence Catholic thought and speech [2]; in the See of Salzburg the singing of German hymns and the use of the German Bible were encouraged. In Würzburg and in Mainz Catholic prelates improved the elementary schools, and Karl Joseph von Erthal, Archbishop of Mainz, actually abolished some monasteries, applied their revenues to the University, and appointed Protestant professors to University chairs. The newer Catholicism was represented by an order of Joseph II of Austria, who directed that young clergymen should no longer be trained ' in dogmatic subtleties and scholastic nonsense,' but should rather be impressed with the points of agreement between the Roman Catholic and the other Christian Churches.

The two Protestant Churches of Germany were affected in a far higher degree by the double influence of Erastianism and rationalism. From the very first the Lutheran Church had been made a department of the State, and to this day it has never overcome the paralysing effects of this association. In

[1] Eilers, *Meine Wanderung durch's Leben*, i. 73 ; Hettner, *Geschichte der deutschen Litteratur*, ii. 306-13.

[2] Thus under the enlightened rule of Franz Ludwig von Erthal of Würzburg (1779-95), Catholic clergy were accused of free thinking, plain speaking, and converse with Protestants (*Bedenken in Hinsicht des Zustandes der Religion und Geistlichkeit*, 1792 ; quoted by Schmid, *Geschichte der katholischen Kirche in Deutschland*, 86).

the eighteenth century, when despotism was in fashion, the servility of the Lutheran clergy was a byword[1]. There was no act of authority which they were not prepared to applaud, and no adulation with which they would not bespatter a noble or a prince. The most popular preacher in Hanover, Consistorialrath Uhle, openly in the pulpit compared the Duke of Cambridge to the Son of God, who had come to redeem the sins of his people, and the congregation was not shocked[2].

Few passages in history are more difficult to explain than the sudden loss of spiritual force which befell the Lutheran Church after the death of its founder. An age of intense passion and inner conflict was succeeded by a period of the most arid theological controversy. A form of orthodoxy was developed hardly less strict than that from which the north of Germany had only just emancipated itself, and, moreover, utterly deficient in all those suggestions and appeals to the imagination that abound in the Roman system. There was little enough either of devotion or large-mindedness in the rule of the Lutheran pedants of the seventeenth century, and devotional natures sought refuge in various forms of pietistic exercise which lay outside the horizon of official worship. But no organization can long resist the insidious influence of the intellectual atmosphere which encompasses it, and the vigorous blast of rationalism which blew through the later half of the eighteenth century made rents in the stout old Lutheran fortress. The herald and the prophet of the new movement, Johann Semler, occupied the chair of theology at Halle from 1754-91. His piety, his elevation of character, his industry, his intellectual fearlessness combined with exceptional longevity to give him a commanding influence over theological studies in Germany. Thoroughly versed in Locke and the literature of English Deism, Semler applied himself to freeing religion from its dogmatic trammels. In his view theology was the product not of religion but of the Church, and being framed to meet transitory and local needs it possessed merely a transitory and local value. Religion was essential, personal, and moral, and implied the full and harmonious development of individual character. Every man

---

[1] Eilers, *Meine Wanderung durch's Leben*, 1856, i. 25.
[2] *Hannover wie es war, ist, und werden wird*, 1804, 34.

must have his own private religion, and private religions could only possess that measure of common agreement which subsisted between the characters of men. The appeal to the Apostolic Church was absurd because it could be historically shown that the Apostolic Church was full of the errors, the superstitions, and the crudities of the time. Nor could a more certain criterion of religious truth be found in Sacred Writ itself, for this too was composed under historical conditions, and while some of its teaching was of universal application, other parts of it were tempered to long-vanished Hebraic readers and to long-vanished Hebraic times [1].

This free spirit of inquiry, this search for the essence of religion, this application of scientific historical canons to Biblical studies spread like fire through Northern Germany. Mirabeau remarked in 1786 that almost all the Prussian clergy were infected. 'Already,' he writes, 'they openly proclaim that the Old Testament is a mass of fables mingled with the history of the Jewish people, which has no obligatory force for us; that the Apostles were not inspired, at least in details, and that they might easily have been deceived; that Jesus Christ was a prophet, a man sent by God to preach a new religion and to seal it with his blood, but not a universal redeemer who has paid all the debts of the human race [2].' A superintendent-general, issuing a direction to his subordinate clergy in 1781, remarked that the theologians of the new school avoided mentioning the name of Jesus in their sermons. He admitted that the common 'talk about the Lamb, the blood and the wounds' was 'phantasy,' but nevertheless the clergy were wrong in going to the opposite extreme. They should remember the virtues of this 'excellent man (*vortrefflicher Mann*), and seek to awake on every opportunity a feeling of love and gratitude for them [3].' In 1800 it was reported that religion was dead, and that 'it is no longer the fashion to be a Christian [4].' Nowhere was there

---

[1] Hettner, *Geschichte der deutschen Litteratur im achtzehnten Jahrhundert*, ii. 286-97.

[2] Mirabeau, i. 232.

[3] Eilers, *Meine Wanderung durch's Leben*, i. 81, and cf. Philippson, *Geschichte des preussischen Staatswesens*, i. 37.

[4] Eilers, i. 72, 75.

a greater abundance of natural piety, of simple domestic religion, than in Germany. But much of it was not enrolled in any of the great ecclesiastical regiments, and the 'drum ecclesiastic,' whether beaten by a Lutheran pastor or a Catholic bishop about the year 1800, would have had no power to thrill a single soul or to lead a single body into uncomfortable places. But in truth neither pastor nor bishop was cast in the heroic mould.

Such reflections may seem superfluous. But it is well to understand from the outset, that a force which in a nation largely composed of peasants may be often expected to inflame passions and to shape events, was in Germany singularly feeble. The pastors and priests of Germany had long been regarded as the spiritual police of the State. Schooled in obedience themselves, it was their duty to enforce the same discipline of obedience upon their flocks. State ordinances were read from the Prussian pulpits, and some of the men who read them were destined within a few years to give out from the same place the bulletins of Napoleon's armies. 'An insurrection of the *curés*' was impossible in Germany, nor did the Churches provide any tribunes of the people. Politics were the affair of the prince whose will and intelligence were guided by God—a theory as convenient to King Jerome of Westphalia as it had been to the Landgraves of Hesse-Cassel or the Kings of Prussia.

III

These political and intellectual conditions produced a spirit wholly unfavourable to the development of energetic character. The *Sturm und Drang* period of German history has indeed been not infrequently compared with the French Revolution. There was the same upheaval and effervescence of thought, the same glorification of nature, the same removal of traditional restraint, the same prodigal sentimentality in both movements. But there was a profound difference. The French enthusiasts created a new order of society; for the German it was sufficient to experience the vicarious violence of the stage. The one movement became fiercely practical; the other was merely an emotional fashion, which small men cherished and great men outgrew. When the fumes of this excitement had evaporated, Germany resumed her mood of bland and enlightened curiosity. Gustav Freytag has acutely observed that no German writers of the period knew how to depict a real man of action. Everywhere the speculative self-questioning temper clouds the will of their heroes. And in real life there was little to evoke and everything to impede the growth of practical enterprise. Commerce and manufacture were as yet too insignificant in volume to exercise a profound influence on national character. The age of mediaeval maritime enterprise had passed, that of modern colonial adventure had not begun. War is sometimes a useful school of practical energy, and the wars of Frederick the Great made Prussia. But there can be no worse influence in a State than unintelligent militarism, and the militarism of the German States was unintelligent, oppressive, and all-pervading. In those days the rules of war were formal, and the men pieces of a machine of whom little else was demanded save physical precision. There was scant occasion for brain or initiative when battles were decided by the push of bayonet or the impact of cavalry. There was little patriotic enthusiasm when soldiers of fortune passed from service to service, when choice recruits were kidnapped from neighbouring principalities and whole regiments hired out to the highest bidder. The army was one of the properties of despotism, together with the mistresses, and the kennels, and the well-filled stables. Only in Prussia had an army served a serious purpose, and Jena was to show that the military system of the great Frederick was as rotten and obsolete as the useless pomp of regiments that decorated the processions of an Elector of Mainz or a Margrave of Baden.

The reaction of all this militarism upon civil life was very serious, and it cannot be described with greater force than in the words of a remarkable book which appeared in 1759, 'The Master and the Servant [1],' by Friedrich Karl von Moser, whose life had been spent in the civil service of Hesse-Homburg and Hesse-Darmstadt. 'The despotism of several of our German masters,' he writes, 'their harsh treatment of their subjects, the

[1] *Der Herr und der Diener*, 45 ff.

frequency with which they violate the most sacred promises and the compacts which they have made with their Estates, their ignorance and wilful neglect of duty, their exaggeration of prerogatives reasonable and inviolable in themselves, for these, together with many other signs of evil times, we have mainly to thank the military method of government.' And then the writer introduces us to the prince who having spent his youth in the camp succeeds to his father's throne. He expects the same blind unquestioning obedience of his servants as the officer exacts from his men in the trenches. He plagues the treasury and the country with a thousand demands; he will not be denied or contradicted, and looks upon all with whom he has to do as his enemies. In time the despotic temper of the master communicates itself to all departments of the State. As the prince bullies and hectors his ministers so the minister bullies and hectors his inferiors, and the government, which should be all harmony and co-operation, becomes like a regiment in which each rank despises the rank below it.

Militarism, however, was not the only poison at work. It is indeed an error (refuted by the whole course of Greek history) to suppose that large and serious political issues cannot arise in small States, but when a system of small States is combined with a system of social privilege the cumulative effect is apt to be disastrous to political perspective. The petty cabals and the trivial occupations which consumed the energies of many a small German Court; the ceremony, the red tape, the aristocratic exclusiveness, the pestilential atmosphere of spite and selfishness, of vice and ignorance, have been depicted in many a caustic and diverting page [1]. The plethora of useless offices, everywhere a blot on German administration, was most apparent in the small State. 'A little territory,' writes K. von Moser, 'composed of a small town and four or five villages has a Chancery, a Consistory, a Treasury, a Court Marshal's office,

---

[1] The lively Wilhelmina of Prussia has cleverly satirized the loutish and spiteful courtiers of Baireuth who derived their amusement from the bottle and their instruction from the stable and the cow-house. The picture of the Court of Oetting-Oetting in Lang's *Memoiren* is almost equally mordant.

a Forest department, a Board of Works; and a case arose within my knowledge where five decrees were issued from the Treasury to mend some broken tiles on the castle roof. A word spoken to a builder would have been quite as efficacious [1].'

In the larger States there was more movement, and Prussia at least offered a career of public service not inferior in opportunities, as Stein was destined to show, to that of an intendancy or prefectship in France. Everywhere, however, initiative was lamed by the excess of central control, by the absence of fortifying external criticism, by the habit of referring all administrative questions to Colleges and Boards, by the vice of inordinate writing, and by the fact that the main avenue to the administrative career lay through the study and practice of the law. The effect of these interconnected causes may easily be imagined. Whenever an administrative problem offered itself, the first impulse of the administrator was to consider it upon its legal side, to search for precedents, to consult colleagues, to refer to a higher authority. The slowness and timidity of German administrators became as proverbial as the delays of the German law courts; and it is worth remarking that the only minister gifted with comprehensive vision who appeared in Southern Germany during the later half of the century was sprung from a Savoyard family and educated on French lines in a French school [2].

While the movement of philosophical opinion was untrammelled, the press was regarded with dislike and controlled with strictness. There was not a State in Germany but was prepared to punish the newspaper that printed unpleasing news or indulged in inconvenient political comment. A writer in the Gazette of Erlangen expressed during the Seven Years' War some sympathy for Austria. The King of Prussia ordered

---

[1] *Der Herr und der Diener*, 324.

[2] The popular prejudice against First Ministers was as strong in Germany as in England (Moser, *Der Herr und der Diener*, 214). The same author says that phlegm is the quality most generally prized in a minister (ibid. 246). A. W. Rehburg complains that the Prussian method sets 'half the inhabitants of a country protocolling' (*Ueber die Staatsverwaltung deutscher Länder und die Dienerschaft des Regenten*. Hanover, 1807).

a colonel to give him five and twenty strokes and to require a receipt[1]. When a paper appeared in Würtemberg which published news which, though true, was distasteful to Austria, the government of Vienna at once remonstrated with the Court of Stuttgart, and forbad the imperial post to distribute the offending organ[2]. The result was that the newspapers were few in number, poor in matter, and restricted in circulation. Saxony lived upon one political newspaper, and that an official organ. The *Diarium*, founded in 1703, sufficed for Vienna; and in Berlin, where, as Lessing remarked in 1763, freedom of speech meant only freedom to scatter gibes at religion, political journalism was confined to two meagre periodicals, the Gazette of Spener and the Gazette of Voss, containing half the interest which can be found nowadays in the humblest rural paper. A few dry facts as to the movements of the Court, an official decree or circular, talk of a forthcoming sale of horses, a notice of a book or two, half a dozen advertisements—such is the type of German newspaper in the eighteenth century. Timid, jejune, servile, plunging into the turbid morasses of science, literature, and theology in its efforts to avoid the surging and perilous waters of politics, it is powerless to instruct, to amuse, or to influence.

There was indeed some improvement during the last quarter of the century. Schlözer, a professor of the University of Göttingen and a Hanoverian subject, started, about 1770, a political paper, in which many acts of oppression and injustice committed by the smaller German despots were freely criticized. But there was an ample dose of discretion mixed with the valour of the professor. The editor took care never to attack his own government, which would have been suicidal, or the governments of Prussia and Austria, which would have been dangerous. The names of the contributors who supplied him with facts were carefully concealed, and their manuscripts recopied before they were sent to the press. The Hanoverian authorities, who may have enjoyed an exhibition of satirical artillery that would never be directed against themselves, replied to the representations of outraged princelets that the King of

---

[1] Lévy-Bruhl, *L'Allemagne depuis Leibnitz*, 208.
[2] Salomon, *Geschichte des deutschen Zeitungswesens*, ii. 42 ff.

England granted his subjects entire liberty of thought and writing [1].

But though political papers multiplied towards the end of the century, especially after 1789, the political press never became a power. The publicists either noisily croaked over a particular abuse in a neighbouring State or else smothered themselves in the clouds of abstract philosophical disquisition. Feeling was growing that political inequality must be absurd, but no one dared advocate far-reaching changes. The cumbrousness of the imperial constitution was a commonplace, but no newspaper undertook a campaign for its reform. Indeed, thirty years of peace seemed a sufficient answer to those who would plead the necessity of organic change [2].

In some territories the Landstände or Estates afforded a possibility of debate; but though these assemblies sometimes performed a useful office, acting as checks upon the autocratic power of the prince, they did not provide any real political training. They were for the most part highly aristocratic in composition, their powers were circumscribed, and their meetings were often intermitted for long periods of time, during which they were represented by a standing committee. No great reform was ever inaugurated, no great abuse was ever repressed by the Landstände. The Hessian Estates repeatedly sanctioned the traffic in Hessian soldiery. The provincial Estates of Hanover, despite the connexion of the Electorate with the free people of England, never supported the abolition of noble privilege or the emancipation of the peasantry. Indeed, the fashion of enlightened despotism, which prevailed in the forward German States during the later half of the eighteenth century, tended more and more to throw these bodies into the shade; and the more advanced and intelligent opinion of Germany condemned them as obsolete instruments of reaction, much as the Parliament of Paris was condemned by Voltaire and Turgot [3].

The extreme intricacy of the Germanic Constitution and the complication of territorial rights and claims gave a peculiar

---

[1] Lévy-Bruhl, 209-10.

[2] Erdmannsdörffer, *Aus den Zeiten des deutschen Fürstenbundes*, 10.

[3] Preser, *Der Soldatenhandel in Hessen*; Moser, *Der Herr und der Diener*, 103-4; Winkopp, *Der Rheinische Bund*, vi. 126.

colour to political activity. The qualities required in a public servant were rather those of the skilled solicitor who knows all the intricacies of a large and complicated family estate than those of the politician who has to gauge and direct popular forces or to devise remedies for popular discontent. Since, for the most part, the revenues of the State were derived from the private domains of the sovereign, the art of public finance was hardly known, and forestry, mining, and farm management became a branch of politics. A theory of administration, or Cameral Science, as it was called, was invoked to aid the State Treasury in its multifarious and domestic functions; and *Cameral Studies* formed the most valuable and substantial portion of German political literature in the eighteenth century. The economics of forestry were discovered by von Carlowitz; Süssmilch's theory of population expounded the political value of numbers to Frederick the Great; while Schlözer of Göttingen helped to create descriptive statistics.

The pursuit of technical studies at the Universities doubtless had some advantages, and it was only natural that, in a country wasted and depopulated by the Thirty Years' War, the theory of production should have outrun the theory of exchange. But an investigation of the phenomena of exchange in general would have been more fruitful and illuminating, and would have provided a better discipline to statesmen than the specialized and highly technical counsels of the Cameralists. The system of the French economists or physiocrats, however, was more theoretical and less immersed in matter than the Cameralistic Science; and, despite many fallacies, it had the supreme merit of preaching freedom of trade. It was received with enthusiasm in the German Universities, being made known chiefly through the *Éphémérides du citoyen,* published from 1767 onwards, and was only displaced by the victorious force of Adam Smith's *Wealth of Nations.* This great treatise, however, though it had been translated into German in 1776-8, had hardly left a mark upon opinion before the French Revolution. Nor can it be said that it had in any way affected the public policy of the German States [1].

---

[1] Roscher, *Geschechte der National-Oekonomik in Deutschland*; Higgs, *The Physiocrats*; *Dictionary of Political Economy,* art. German School of Political Economy.

GERMANY AND FRANCE

Yet nowhere was there stronger need for sound economic doctrine. Malthus, who travelled in Germany in 1799, said that there was no part of the country rich enough to support an extensive system of parochial relief, and though the remark is perhaps exaggerated, it testifies to the general impression of indigence left upon the mind of an acute observer [1]. The volume of trade was small, and impeded by the most absurd and harassing regulations. Industry was stifled by guilds, by State supervision, and by unwise taxes, while the agricultural population, weighted by feudal dues and services, was unable to turn the soil to the best advantage. The roads were few and bad; the towns decayed in numbers and prosperity; the population stationary, if not diminishing [2]. Thirty years of peace had done nothing to promote the economic prosperity of Prussia, simply through the unwise legislation of the Prussian government; and yet Prussia was in the van of reform [3]. It is a singular fact that Frederick the Great, who was so deeply impressed by the belief that the strength of States consists in population [4], should never have dreamt of establishing free trade in land, or of abolishing serfdom—the two surest methods for increasing the population and the resources of his kingdom. And where Frederick II was blind it was not vouchsafed that his successor should see.

'The Germans,' wrote Mme. de Staël, 'have much universality in mind, in literature, and in philosophy, but none in affairs. . . . They unite the greatest audacity of thought to the most obedient character [5].' The servile respect for authority, whether embodied in the person of a prince or in the parchment of an ancient document, had entirely obliterated the power of correct political vision in the whole nation. Though the study of

[1] *Essay on the Principle of Population* (reprint of 1890), 492.

[2] Before the Thirty Years' War the population of Germany was possibly 25,000,000. In 1816 it was reckoned at 24,830,000. Himly's figure for the eighteenth century (28,000,000 to 30,000,000) is too large. The total population of the free towns was at most 700,000 (G. von Schönberg, *Volkswirthschaftslehre*, i. 865-9; Himly, *Formation territoriale de l'Europe*, 290, 304).

[3] Philippson, *Geschichte des preussischen Staatswesens*, i. 444. Most of the Silesian towns were heavily indebted in 1789 (ibid. 445).

[4] *Antimachiavel*, c. 5.   [5] *De l'Allemagne*, liv. i, c. 13, § 2.

history and political economy was actively pursued, nobody seemed to understand the significance and drift of events. While Napoleon was revolutionizing their country, the publicists of Germany were applying their frigid erudition to the discussion of irrelevant and futile constitutional subtleties, and the most momentous period of German history only produced two political writers of talent. Bishop Butler once asked himself the question whether a whole nation can go mad. With some of the German periodical literature of this time in one's recollection, one is tempted to ask whether a whole nation may not grow blind[1].

The French Revolution supplied the electric shock which woke Germany from her lethargy. To the intellectual class the fall of the Bastille and the Declaration of Rights seemed to be the prelude of the golden age. Minds and characters so diverse as those of Kant and Fichte, of Goethe and Stolberg, were affected by something of the contagious enthusiasm. 'The 14th of July,' wrote Johann von Müller, the historian, 'is the finest day there has been since the fall of the Roman Empire.' The whole literary class was in ecstasies, for the cosmopolitan and humanitarian dreams upon which it had fed for more than a generation seemed destined at last to pass into the region of palpable things.

Yet there is in every nation a massive fund of unexamined sentiment which outweighs all the light sparkling coin of literary gentlemen. Germany had thought, dreamed, criticized, jested, but the last thing which could be said of German public opinion was that it was revolutionary. The peasantry was alike incapable of generalizing its grievances and closely wedded to ancient ways. There was the strongest attachment to the princely dynasties, there was a deep-rooted respect for birth and titles. The governments were despotic and for the most part reactionary. Though Kant had proclaimed that man should be treated as an end in himself, there was no readiness to apply

---

[1] Read the pedantries which appeared in Winkopp, *Der Rheinische Bund*, or Voss, *Die Zeiten*. Görres (with Gentz the only real German publicist of the period) is properly severe on German *Unklarheit* (*Politische Schriften*, i. 115–32). A similar complaint urged against Prussia is to be found in Massenbach, *Memoiren*, iii. 48.

GERMANY AND FRANCE

the doctrine to the economics of the village, or to liberate serfs after the quixotic manner of Joseph II of Austria or Charles Frederick of Baden. Goethe for four years held high office in the government of Weimar; he was in favour of freeing the peasantry from feudal burdens, and of multiplying peasant holdings, but he was totally unable to give effect to these amiable views, so great were the obstructions of the vested interests [1]. No one loved or appreciated the German country-folk more deeply than Justus Möser, the learned and fanciful historian of Osnabrück, but he defended serfdom and solemnly argued that unpropertied persons were not entitled to the benefits of the ordinary forms of law [2].

Again, the German was essentially pious. Unorthodox views of Biblical exegesis are happily consistent with that virtue. There was not, as in France, a passion to subvert a dominant priesthood, for the priesthood in Germany was never dominant. Nor was there a feeling, save for a short time in Bavaria, that the Church was a formidable enemy to freedom of thought. Indeed, the Lutheran divines 'thought' far too freely for the taste of their congregations, and the Catholic religion was at once more tolerant and more staid than in any other country in Europe. When Napoleon was at Weimar in 1808 he learnt that Wieland was described as the Voltaire of Germany. With a touch of malicious curiosity he summoned the veteran writer into the ball-room and tried to take the measure of his infidelity. 'Is there not,' he asked, 'good reason to believe that Jesus Christ never existed?' The old man streamed into rhetorical denials [3]. There were in truth many Semlers but no Voltaires in Germany.

If German society was ill-prepared to accept the French Revolution, still less prepared were the German governments. Some of them had been willing to initiate reforms, but they had no intention of capitulating to the mob. Prussia was now in the full tide of obscurantist reaction, and quick to take

---

[1] Goethe an Frau von Stein, April 2, 1782, and June 9, 1784; and cf. Roscher, *Geschichte der National-Oekonomik in Deutschland*, 477-9.

[2] *Werke*, ii. 14, v. 119, x. 155. For these references I am indebted to Hettner, iii. 383-4.

[3] J. von Müller, *Erinnerungen*, 251-2.

alarm at the least symptom of democracy. As early as the autumn of 1792 the government of Frederick William II prohibited all French publications in Prussia, and the strictest measures were devised to control the entrance of French emigrants into the Prussian dominions. In the same year Austria and Prussia declared war upon the French Republic. A peasant revolt in Silesia in 1793, supplemented by minor riots in other parts of Germany, still further emphasized the policy of repression. The Diet of Ratisbon, urged by Weimar, Prussia, and Saxony, formally prohibited students' associations, under the belief that they were specially productive of political ferment, and in 1797 the Prussian government instituted a permanent commission of professors in every University of the kingdom, charged with the duty of checking the political ebullition of the students. Thus a bridle was placed upon the only class in the community which possessed ideas and the spirit of reform [1].

Two conceptions of the State, one based upon autocracy and privilege, and the other based upon political freedom and equality before the law, were now brought into sudden conflict. The conquests of revolutionary France no longer permitted the question to remain in academic shadow. In 1794 the right bank of the Rhine was conquered and absorbed into the new system, and though in the following year Prussia made her peace with the French Directorate, and withdrew Northern Germany from the war, the contest between the old régime and the new still continued. Austria and England remained at war with France, fighting for Belgium, for the lost Rhenish Germany, and for the old incapable Bourbon dynasty. In 1796 French democracy swept into Northern Italy. A young general of the Directorate overran the Lombard plain, brushed away the Sardinian king, overcame the armies of the alien Austrians, and established new-fangled republican institutions upon the French model over the vale of the Po. If he should complete his conquest of Austria and make terms at Vienna, what might not be the fate of Germany? In September 1797 General Hoche had set up a Cisrhenane republic at Bonn. Would there then be

---

[1] Lévy-Bruhl, *L'Allemagne depuis Leibnitz*, 232-3 ; Philippson, *Geschichte des preussischen Staatswesens*, ii. 184.

a series of such republics, Cisalpine, Cisrhenane, Alemannian, Bavarian, forming an eastern vanguard for the new democracy? The future lay in the hands of Bonaparte the conqueror of Italy, but he stopped short in the full tide of victory and on October 17 made peace with Austria at Campo-Formio.

[1] CHIEF AUTHORITIES: Häusser, *Deutsche Geschichte*; Sorel, *L'Europe et la Révolution française*; Rambaud, *Les Français sur le Rhin*; Philippson, *Geschichte des preussischen Staatswesens*; Hettner, *Geschichte der deutschen Litteratur im achtzehnten Jahrhundert*; Lévy-Bruhl, *L'Allemagne depuis Leibnitz*; Mirabeau, *De la monarchie prussienne*.

CHAPTER II

BONAPARTE AND THE FIRST GERMAN REVOLUTION

I

CAMPO-FORMIO AND RASTADT

' C'est ici que se décide maintenant le sort de l'univers entier.'
METTERNICH, *Mémoires*.

It was during the negotiations leading to the Treaty of Campo-Formio that Bonaparte first came into contact with the political problems of Germany. Two great Austrian provinces, the Netherlands and the Milanese, had been conquered by France, and French diplomacy intended to retain them. A new State, the Cisalpine Republic, had been founded by Bonaparte in Northern Italy from the Milanese, from part of the Papal territories, and from the principality of Modena, and no peace would be concluded by France unless the Cisalpine Republic were recognized by the Court of Vienna. These demands, however, were far from exhausting the sum of the French claims. It was one of the secular ambitions of the Bourbon monarchy to extend the dominion of France to the waters of the Rhine. Henry II had acquired Metz, Toul, and Verdun, and the Treaty of Westphalia (1648) had legalized the acquisition of these bishoprics in Lorraine, and added to them Austrian Alsace. Under Louis XIV the Rhine frontier was more than a policy, it was a passion. First Aix-la-Chapelle and then Franche-Comté, and lastly Strasburg and the remainder of Alsace, passed from Germany to France. Under the later Bourbons the momentum of French arms was enfeebled, but the aims of French diplomacy were unchanged, and the most pacific of ministers managed to extract from the Polish War of Succession the reversion of the Duchy of Lorraine to the Crown of France. The Republic inherited the ambitions and completed the work of the Monarchy. French armies overran Belgium, revolutionized Holland, and sent the three Electors of Mainz, Trèves, and Cologne flying across the Rhine. But these conquests, though practically complete, had not yet been recognized by Diet or Emperor. It was accordingly part of the French scheme to extract from the Germanic body a formal cession of the conquered territories upon the left bank of the Rhine.

But to secure concessions of such magnitude it was necessary to find compensation for the House of Hapsburg. Bonaparte had astutely foreseen and made provision for the emergency. The Republic of Venice was weak and defenceless; it marched with the Austrian border; it offered a post on the Adriatic; it was invested with the glory of a great commercial and political tradition. On shameful pretexts its territory was occupied by the French army, and the form of its ancient constitution overturned. Such a bait was too tempting to be refused, and by the Treaty of Campo-Formio the Emperor accepted Venice, Istria and Dalmatia, and all the Venetian territory west of the Adige. In return he ceded Belgium, renounced Lombardy, and consented to the convocation of a congress at Rastadt (a small town in the Duchy of Baden) to settle the terms of peace between France and the German Empire. Yet the cool reason which dictated these provisions was supplemented by a startling touch of imagination. In the distribution of the spoils of Venice, France claimed Corfu and the Ionian Islands. It was the first overt hint of those oriental ambitions which exerted so powerful a fascination over the mind of Bonaparte. With characteristic versatility he had profited by the humiliations of Austria to lay stepping-stones towards the conquest of Egypt and of all that might lie beyond.

These were the public clauses of the treaty. The secret articles were more important for Germany, and revealed the indifference of Austria to the integrity of the Reich. The Emperor promised to help France to obtain almost all the German possessions west of the Rhine, save the three Prussian territories of Cleves, Meurs, and Guelders, a stipulation dictated by no love for the Court of Berlin, but solely that Prussia might be deprived of any claim to compensation. In return the French government promised to assist Austria to acquire the Bishopric of Salzburg and a section of Western Bavaria. For every acquisition France might make in Germany the Emperor was to receive an equivalent, and conversely France was to be compensated for any future extensions of Austrian power within the Empire. While the Emperor promised to urge the Diet to relinquish its suzerain and feudal claims over Italy, the two contracting parties agreed to 'unite their good offices' to secure adequate compensations for the princes and States of the Empire who should suffer loss either in virtue of the Treaty of Campo-Formio itself, or in consequence of the agreement hereafter to be made at Rastadt between the French Republic and the Diet. The Prince of Orange, who had been deprived of the Stadtholderate of Holland, was likewise to receive a territorial indemnity in Germany. Lastly, twenty days after the exchange of ratifications, the Austrian troops were to withdraw within the hereditary dominions of the Emperor, a measure which would leave Western Germany open and defenceless before a French advance, while by an additional secret convention Austria promised to take the diplomatic steps necessary to secure the cession of Mainz to France. All these undertakings were made by the head of the Hapsburg House, not as Emperor, but as King of Bohemia and Hungary.

'Never, for many centuries,' wrote Bonaparte to the Minister of Foreign Affairs, 'has a more brilliant peace been made [1].' The recognition of the regicide government of France by one of the most conservative Courts of Europe; the acquisition of Belgium and Mainz, of the Rhine frontier and the Ionian Islands; the acceptance of the Cisalpine Republic; the fresh dissension sown between Austria and Prussia, and between Austria and the Reich; the large place reserved for the French Republic in the assignment of territorial compensations in Germany—such were the results of Bonaparte's prowess as general and diplomatist.

The treaty marks a new epoch in the history of Germany. A serious blow was struck at the German Empire, which was condemned to lose the left bank of the Rhine, the Circle of

[1] *Napoléon Corr.* iii. 392, no. 2,307.

Burgundy, and all those ancient Italian rights which had been the object of so many a bitter contest ever since in the tenth century Otto I had marched his Saxons to Rome to claim the Imperial crown. The secularization of the ecclesiastical principalities was rendered inevitable, since it was decided that the German princes dispossessed on the left bank were to receive territorial compensations on the right. Foreigners—a Prince of Modena, a Prince of Orange—were to be imported into the Empire. And yet Austria, who consented to all this, who was willing to go hand in hand with France in the traffic of populations at the expense of the old territorial arrangements of the Empire, was to lose little or nothing herself. Though she had been defeated in five campaigns, she had contrived to cancel her penalties. Venice was more than adequate compensation for the Milanese, and the Inn quarter of Bavaria for the Netherlands, which Austria had always regarded as a useless encumbrance. The treaty in fact consolidated, unified, and rounded off her territories, and provided that Prussia, for all her timid subservience to France and jealously guarded neutrality, should gain nothing. Basle was avenged at Campo-Formio. As Prussia had abandoned Austria and the Empire in 1795, so Austria abandoned Prussia and the Empire in 1797. France was waiting to reap the fruit of their jealousies.

The air was full of ideas and apprehensions when the diplomatists of Germany gathered together at Rastadt. Shortsighted optimists believed that they were about to witness a new birth of the old Empire—an improvement in imperial justice, freedom of the press, religious toleration, the abolition of beggary, the protection of German manufactures. Other pamphleteers were frankly Gallican. A German patriot recommended the cession of Ehrenbreitstein, an alliance between France and Prussia, and a great neutral union of German princes. The venerable body of the Reich was made the butt of many frivolous jests and satirical brochures. The imperial titles, it was intimated by one writer, might be sold by auction to provide for the funeral of the defunct Empire. The army might go to the Elector of Hesse-Cassel, the Golden Bulls to the Pope, the archives to the chemists, and the revenues to the poor-house at Ratisbon, for it was clear that the French

Republic was the sole lawful heir of the left bank of the Rhine.

The clumsy mockery of the pamphleteers was amply deserved. Save the French Republic, hardly a power represented at Rastadt was not at once deceiving and deceived. The delegates of the Emperor professed to be anxious for the integrity of the Reich, which in the secret articles of Campo-Formio their master, as King of Bohemia and Hungary, had so completely betrayed. Austria believed that France, in pursuance of her promise, would assist her to procure part of Bavaria, but the government of the Directorate had no such intentions. She believed that France would neither take from Prussia territory on the left bank, nor give to her territory on the right, for this too had been promised in the Treaty of Campo-Formio. But France had already signed a treaty with Prussia (May 5, 1796) by which the latter power had been promised the Westphalian bishoprics as an indemnity for her losses on the left bank. The smaller German powers came to the Congress loudly protesting their fidelity to the Empire. But many of them had already entered into secret understandings with France, according to which they were to receive compensations at the expense of the German Church. The Landgrave of Hesse had even been promised the Electoral hat.

Upon this curious and sordid turmoil Bonaparte descended, as First Plenipotentiary of the French Republic. Leaving Milan December 17, 1797, he crossed Mont Cenis to Geneva, where three hours after midnight he caused the imprisonment of the banker Bontemps, who had been delated to him for an offence against the government of France. At Soleure he was received with suspicion, and his advice to the inhabitants of Berne to make a fourteenth Canton of the Pays de Vaud was rejected with pride. He stopped at Morat to visit the field of battle and deplore the faults of Charles the Bold. A guard of honour attended him from Geneva to Basle, and in the last-named city he was received with arches and acclamations. 'I will not compare you to Turenne or Montecuculi; I will only say Bonaparte is the greatest man of the universe,' is a phrase culled from one of the complimentary speeches delivered on the occasion. When the General sat down to dinner, respectable citizens acted as waiters in order that they might have a closer view of the conqueror of Italy. The honoured guest improved the occasion according to his custom. 'The men of Basle,' he said, 'like the Genevans, have in consideration of their democratic feelings a special claim on the friendship of the French Republic'; and again: 'If the enemy had been fortunate, Basle would have been made a fief of the Empire.' It was the pose of the destroyer of Venice to appear as the champion of the democratic party in Switzerland, and to link his own name with those of the Swiss heroes who had fought in the liberating wars against the House of Hapsburg. But there was little time to develop the theme. On the night of November 25, after a swift journey, he mounted to the quarters assigned to him in the florid old Castle of Rastadt, which had been built by that Margrave Louis of Baden who had acquired such fame in the Turkish wars of the seventeenth century [1].

It was not Bonaparte's intention to plunge deeply into the Serbonian bog of the compensations. He wished to exchange the ratifications of the Treaty of Campo-Formio, to hasten the signature of the military convention which was to cede Mainz to France, to impress upon the peace Deputation the necessity for speed, to terrify them by hints of force, to glitter for a moment at this famous Congress which his victories had called into being. He had not yet shown himself to the Germans, and indeed German problems had hardly occupied his brain except in so far as they were involved in the negotiations with Austria. But these negotiations had fixed a conviction in his mind. 'If the Germanic Body,' he wrote to the Directorate, May 27, 1797, 'did not exist, we should have to create it expressly for our convenience [2].' An ardent student of the life and campaigns of Frederick the Great, he could not fail to be acquainted with the main historical forces which were at work in Germany, but the moment for complete initiation had not yet come. Paris was calling for her Italian victor, and the

---

[1] Bailleu, *Preussen und Frankreich*, i. 178; *Napoléon Corr.* iii. 450, no. 2,379; Barras, *Mémoires*, iii. 99, 104; Ochs, *Geschichte der Stadt Basel*, viii. 246 ff.; *Moniteur*, nos. 76, 77; Lanfrey, c. x; Hueffer, *Der Rastatter Congress*.

[2] *Corr.* iii. 74, no. 1,836.

young general was anxious to enjoy a triumph in the capital, and to take the horoscope of its base and divided government.

Meanwhile it would be possible to get to know something more of German men and matters. It was reported that at Friesenheim the General had made exhaustive inquiries into the characters and dispositions of the Margrave of Baden and his ministers; and the Court at Karlsruhe received the flattering intelligence that 'Baden and Würtemberg are the German princes who realize expectations.' Soon after the arrival at Rastadt the General expressed a wish to see the members of the peace Deputation. They made their visits sometimes separately, sometimes in twos and threes, full of curiosity as to the appearance and demeanour of this wonderful man. They describe his yellow complexion, his thin body, his lively gestures and profound glance, his dress rich but careless, his bearing courteous but unconstrained by diplomatic forms. He held the ear of Georgii, a deputy from Würtemberg, as he walked him through two long saloons, cross-questioning him upon the affairs of the duchy, and appearing well content to learn that in the Estates of Würtemberg there was neither Tiers État nor Noblesse. Towards the Margrave of Baden, upon whose territory the Congress was held, and who presented him with a carriage and four horses, he professed to entertain feelings of special regard. It was noticed that he was peculiarly polite to the envoys of the free towns, to whom he would expound his own love of liberty, and the community of principle which should bind them to France. He did not conceal his disgust at the delay of the Austrian plenipotentiaries (the old fogies, *les ganaches*, as he called them) to appear at the Congress, and he uttered his mind with characteristic frankness upon the most important affairs of state. To the envoys of Baden he explained the importance of the future French garrisons at Mainz and Kehl for the princes of the Empire, who would thereby be protected by France against their natural foes Prussia and Austria. That Austria was the chief enemy of the Reich was the burden of many a discourse. The order issued by the Emperor to the deputies at Rastadt to respect the integrity of the Reich was, he explained, 'mere comedy,' since the integrity of the Reich had already been sacrificed at

Campo-Formio. He had in his possession 'two hundred letters and proofs' that Thugut had received bribes from the French at Constantinople, and if that Austrian statesman had thrown any further obstacles in the way of peace they would have been published to the world. To Albini, envoy of the Elector, he said brusquely, 'Where will the Elector reside when he has lost Mainz?' When the officers of the garrison at Rastadt came to pay their respects, he delivered to them a harangue upon the unimportance of Baden in the military world. Von Stadion, who happened to pay his call attired in the mantle of a Würzburg canon, received a lecture upon the position of the German clergy. ''The German bishops,' said Bonaparte, 'are spiritual rulers and men of war. How do these titles agree? How are they grounded in the Gospel? The Electors of Trèves, Cologne, and Mainz are always talking about Heaven, but their castles and riches are a hindrance to their getting there. Do you know that the Gospel says, "The rich shall not enter into the Kingdom of Heaven"?' With von Löben, the Saxon envoy, he talked of the Golden Bull, the Imperial Constitution, and the Deputation. When the envoy explained that both religious parties were equally represented at the Congress, Bonaparte remarked that for that they had specially to thank the Elector Maurice of Saxony and his struggles against Charles V. He spoke of the Imperial Constitution as a metaphysical body without coherence: one part waged war, another stood neutral, a third concluded peace. To Professor Martens of Göttingen, who was present as Councillor of the Hanoverian Deputation, he said, 'You teach public law; it must be modernized. How does the North-German line of demarcation agree with the precepts of the Constitution? I believe the learned men will have to make a good many changes in their Code. The small sovereigns, who now follow the Emperor and now Prussia, must feel that France is their natural protector, and make peace like Baden and Würtemberg.' Above all he insisted that there must be no delays, no second edition of the tedious drama of the Westphalian negotiations, for if the Reich did not accept the situation promptly, the French drums would be tapping in the Black Forest to bring Germany to its senses. These conversations were generally held as Bonaparte and his guests sat round the stove in the evening, when the darkness had blotted the western spurs of the Schwarzwald and the distant outlines of the Vosges [1].

It was in the same room—in the left wing of the castle—as that in which old Marshal Villars had slept when he came to sign another treaty sixty-five years before. A room of many memories! It was here, before the astonished old-fashioned diplomats of the Reich, with their stiff thoughts and formal manners and carefully powdered *perruques*, that Bonaparte first expounded his thoughts upon Germany, reeling them out with the verve of an Italian improvisatore, as a man might tell a ghost story or a fairy tale to act as a cordial against the chill November night.

Among the interviews of this memorable time there was one which attracted considerable notice. The King of Sweden, who had not recently troubled himself much about German affairs, had now waked up to the fact that both as Duke of Pomerania and as one of the guarantors of the Peace of Westphalia, he was entitled to take part in the proceedings of the Congress. In the latter capacity (as guarantor of the treaty) he now sent to Rastadt Count Fersen, a man who is famous in history as having been the Swedish ambassador in Paris during the French Revolution, and as one of the contrivers of the flight to Varennes. On the afternoon of November 28, Count Fersen called upon Bonaparte. His presence was extremely distasteful on three grounds. In the first place it conflicted with Article 20 of the Peace of Campo-Formio, which restricted the Congress to the envoys of the Republic on the one hand and of the Reich on the other. In the second place, if Sweden claimed to be represented as guarantor of the Treaty of Westphalia, Russia might equally claim to be represented as guarantor of the Peace of Teschen; and, thirdly, the personality of Fersen, a declared antagonist of the French Republic, was almost an insult. 'I cannot understand,' said the General, 'how the Swedish Court can send an ambassador whose person must be decidedly unpleasant to every French citizen. . . . No, sir,

---

[1] Vreede, *La Souabe après la paix de Bâle*, lxv; Erdmannsdörffer, *K. F. von Baden, Politische Korrespondenz*, iii. 13-20; Häusser, *Deutsche Geschichte*, ii. 146 ff.; Hueffer, *Der Rastatter Congress*.

the French Republic will not tolerate that persons, who are only too well known through their connection with the old kingly house, should come to insult the representatives of the First People of the Earth.' After a stormy interview Fersen was shown to the door. 'He changed colour many times,' wrote Bonaparte with satisfaction to the Directorate.

On the evening of November 28, the Austrian envoy Cobenzel arrived, and Bonaparte was able at last to get to business. The military convention, which arranged for the cession of Mainz to France and for the evacuation of the Venetian provinces by the French, was signed on December 1. To the proposal of Cobenzel to leave Germany as it was, and to provide compensations in Italy, Bonaparte would not give a hearing. He was not inclined to disturb the Cisalpine Republic, and he had seen enough of Germany to know that French interests lay in the secularization of the ecclesiastical territories, and in the attachment of the German princes of the west to French rule. Nor was he now inclined to reopen large questions of policy. Immediately after the signature of the convention, at 3 a.m. on December 2, he left Rastadt, abruptly postponing a promised visit to the Margrave of Baden, and summoned by a letter which he had caused Barras to write to him. The Austrian plenipotentiaries were told that he expected to be back again in a week's time. But sharp people thought that Rastadt had seen the last of him [1].

In Paris he was interviewed by Sandoz Rollin, the Prussian envoy, and to him made further discourse of German affairs. 'The Great Frederick is the hero whom I love to consult in everything, in war and in administration: I have studied his principles in the midst of camps, and his familiar letters are for me lessons of philosophy.' To the proposal that France should concert with both the Prussian and the Austrian Courts upon the principal objects to be submitted to the Congress, he replied hastily in the negative, saying that the secret articles

[1] *Corr.* iii. 452, no. 2,382; Hueffer, *Der Rastatter Congress*; *F. O., Germany*, 20. 'At a drawing-room held yesterday, His Majesty spoke to Prince Reuss with interest and much sensibility on the melancholy accounts which arrived from the Empire, and seemed piqued at the haughtiness of *ce Monsieur B.* and the other French plenipotentiaries at Rastadt' (Elgin to Grenville, Dec. 25, 1797.—*F. O., Prussia*, 46).

at Campo-Formio had been drafted to suit the Court of Berlin, and that it was regrettable that Prussian envoys had not been sent to Udine or Rastadt. He defended his method of treating with both powers separately, a method well calculated to prolong the German discord.

'The policy of Austria,' he said on another occasion, 'is to remove her possessions from the French Republic and to have no point of contact with her. This ought also to be the policy of Prussia. Our revolutionary principles should suit the one power as little as the other.' He protested against the idea of calling Russia and Sweden in to assist at the Congress; he said that Prussia was the natural ally of France, and that she would do well to recognize the Cisalpine Republic and 'to establish with it relations of the most intimate amity,' the surest way to embitter the relations between the Courts of Berlin and Vienna. The cession of the left bank of the Rhine had been agreed upon between the Court of Vienna and himself, and it should be carried into effect. Certainly the possession of Mainz, which the Emperor had abandoned to France 'in a deplorable manner,' and without compulsion, had given the Directorate the idea and afterwards the right (*l'idée et bientôt le droit*) of acquiring the left bank of the Rhine, a thing which otherwise could not have occurred to its mind. But his desire and that of the Directorate was that the King of Prussia should intervene in the Treaty of Campo-Formio, and induce the Electors of Saxony and Hanover to consent to the cession of the left bank before the Emperor compelled them to do so. Prussia would thus be taking upon herself some of the odium which would attach to Austria as the author of the dismemberment of the Empire, and thereby acquire a claim to larger indemnities. It was not obscurely hinted that if Prussia declined to depart from her passive neutrality she would have to witness the aggrandizement of Austria at the expense of Bavaria, and the overthrow of the balance of power within the German Empire[1].

It is hardly necessary to point out that these reasonings were disingenuous. The cession of Mainz had been forced on Austria; the idea of the Rhine frontier was as old as the sixteenth

---

[1] Bailleu, *Preussen und Frankreich*, ii. 164–9, 177, 184.

century; the partition of Bavaria had been agreed upon in the secret clauses of the Treaty of Campo-Formio, as also that Prussia was to obtain no compensation at all. But it was convenient to sow dissension between Berlin and Vienna, to prevent negotiations between Prussia and Austria about the compensations, and to involve both Courts in the common discredit attaching to a treaty which ratified the dismemberment of the Reich.

All the leading ideas which are to govern French policy in the future—the secularization of the ecclesiastical principalities, the pretended care for the smaller German princes, the playing off of Berlin against Vienna, the abolition of the old imperial polity, the domination of France in Western Germany, the pushing of Prussia and Austria eastwards, are represented in some shape or other in these early conversations of Bonaparte in 1797. These ideas were not born with him nor were they confined to him. They belonged to an old French diplomatic tradition; they had been revived by the conquests of the revolutionary armies; they were held by the Directorate. Even Germans were found to recognize that the Empire was obsolete, and that the Rhine was the natural frontier of the French Republic. Nor was Bonaparte intending to resume the threads of the German negotiation which he had dropped so precipitately at Rastadt. That Congress, as he shrewdly saw, would last long; and it was not one of the fields in which a man might reap a harvest of praise. He was now General of the Army of England, inspecting the harbours and fortifications on the Channel coast, and secretly preparing his Egyptian voyage. On the night of May 3–4 he suddenly left Paris to embark at Toulon for the East. Enough that for a brief moment he has contemplated Germany. He does not forget, and he intends to return [1].

[1] Rambaud, *Les Français sur le Rhin*, 294; Bailleu, ii. 162.

CHIEF AUTHORITIES: Koch et Schoell, *Histoire abrégée des Traités de Paix*, vol. v (contains a list of the older authorities); Garden, *Histoire générale des Traités de Paix*, vol. vi; Rambaud, *Les Français sur le Rhin*; Sorel, *Bonaparte et Hoche*; Hueffer, *Der Rastatter Congress*; Bailleu, *Preussen und Frankreich*; Erdmannsdörffer, *Karl Friedrich von Baden, Politische Korrespondenz*; Metternich, *Mémoires*, vol. i.

II

LUNÉVILLE AND THE ACT OF MEDIATION

'The common mass of the German States ... must be gathered into one by the violence of a conqueror.'—HEGEL, 1801.

Two years after his brief visit to Rastadt, Napoleon suddenly returned from Egypt, overthrew the Directorate, and made himself master of France. During his absence the Congress had been dissolved, and war had broken out again upon the continent. The Austrians and Russians had turned the French out of Italy; the English and Russians had made a descent upon Holland; and all the issues provisionally settled at Campo-Formio were again immersed in the boiling and weltering cauldron of Fate. We are not here concerned with the military events which alternately depressed and exalted the fortunes of France, with the capitulation of Alkmaar which freed Holland from the invading army, with the victory of Zürich which made France mistress of Switzerland, with Marengo which destroyed the Austrian dominion in Italy, or with Hohenlinden which shattered the imperial army in Southern Germany. Suffice it to say that by 1801 Napoleon could dictate his own terms, and secure the fruits of his masterly success. The Treaty of Lunéville, February 9, 1801, 'was nothing else than the Peace of Campo-Formio, a little aggravated for Austria, and leaving the Empire no illusions.' It gave France Belgium, Frankenstein, and the Frickthal. It recognized the Cisalpine Republic. It ceded, both in the name of the Emperor and in that of the Empire, the German territories of the left bank to the French Republic, a concession no longer, as in 1797, embodied in a secret article, but openly set forth in the seventh clause of the treaty.

The Treaty of Lunéville has been called the 'First Revolution' of Germany. By it a territory of 150,000 square miles, peopled by 3,500,000 inhabitants, and amounting to about a seventh part of the population and territory of the whole Empire, was definitely transferred to foreign non-German powers. To indemnify the dispossessed princes the principle of secularization was admitted, which was tantamount to undermining the foundations of the old Imperial Constitution. But if the German Empire were doomed to die, its end need not have been indecorous. The Diet of Ratisbon summoned by the Emperor to consider the situation agreed, on the motion of Brandenburg, to ratify the treaty on condition that it should co-operate in arranging the transfers of territory which the treaty necessitated. If there had been at that time any feeling for the good name and internal independence of Germany as a whole, this business of the compensations would have been arranged as a domestic matter by the Colleges of the Diet. But Germany was incapable of common action. In the Diet itself there were three parties—those who wanted no secularization at all, those who wished for a restricted secularization, and those who would have a complete and absolute secularization of all ecclesiastical property. The violent ecclesiastics—the Elector of Trèves, the Bishops of Spire and Worms—belonged to the first party; Austria, Saxony, and Mainz to the second; Prussia and the Protestant powers to the third. Nor was there any agreement as to the mode in which the Empire should proceed. Several States would have liked the Emperor to take upon himself the whole odium and the whole responsibility. The Emperor was willing enough to do this, but on his own terms, which meant restricted secularization, a prospect unpleasing to northern greed. Saxony proposed that the whole Reichstag should discuss the affair, but the lay princes, fearing that they might be swamped by the clerics, the small nobles, and the towns, opposed. The majority decided upon a system according to which the Emperor should act as reporter, while the Reichstag should discuss his proposals, but the Emperor declined with decision and irony. The jealousies of Austria and Prussia, each of which wished to secure the largest slice, added to the difficulty of arriving at an agreement. When, in September-October 1801, Austria caused an Archduke of Austria to be elected to the Electorate of Cologne and the Bishopric of Münster (the territory of all others which Prussia was coveting), the rupture between the two powers became complete, and it was clear that the question of German indemnities must be submitted to foreign arbitration.

Even before this incident the Diet had declared its bankruptcy. After futile discussions, lasting from February to October, it determined (October 2) to appoint a commission 'to discuss with the French government the questions reserved for a particular understanding by the Treaty of Lunéville.' But as the two leading powers represented in the commission were hopelessly at variance, this issue was likewise closed. The divisions of Germany were the opportunity of Bonaparte. He determined to intervene in conjunction with Alexander of Russia, and to settle for Germany the affairs she was unable to settle for herself.

'The right of France to intervene,' says a French writer, 'resulted not only from the interest which she had in the definitive organization of Germany, but from the treaties of Westphalia, from the special treaties which she had concluded with most of the German States, Prussia, Baden, Hesse, Würtemberg, and Bavaria, and lastly from the text of the Treaty of Lunéville. The right of Russia to intervene was more contestable. It proceeded from her participation in the Treaty of Teschen (1779), which had confirmed former treaties, and from the desire of the First Consul to share his responsibility with a great power [1].' But in truth it is misleading to speak of technical rights. Franco-Russian mediation was acceptable to the German powers because they could not agree among themselves, and it was offered by Napoleon because it served his interest. The obtuse and dilatory diplomacy of Vienna gave to the First Consul an opportunity which he was quick to improve. When Austria proposed to the Court of Munich that Bavaria should cede certain territories to the Hapsburgs on her eastern border in exchange for compensations, Bonaparte explained to the Elector with masterly clearness that such a step would be fatal to the interests of his house [2]. It is no wonder that the princes spontaneously appealed to him, for an eye so clear, a hand so firm, a judgement so prompt, were not to be found in Germany. With serene self-confidence the French Foreign Office was prepared for the emergency, and had drawn up a plan of compensation immediately after the signature of the Treaty of Lunéville [3].

---

[1] Rambaud, *Les Français sur le Rhin*, 336.   [2] *Corr.* vii. 284, no. 5,796.
[3] Erdmannsdörffer, iv. 40.

LUNÉVILLE AND THE ACT OF MEDIATION 41

In the Franco-Russian note presented to the Diet the two mediating powers explained their position. They had been compelled to act by the delays and divisions of Germany; they were 'perfectly disinterested'; they would proceed with 'rigorous impartiality.' Their joint object was so to arrange the compensations as to 'establish the equilibrium which existed before the war between the principal houses of Germany[1].'

We now reach the most degrading page in the history of Germany. The secular princes, eager for the spoils of the Church, sent their envoys to Paris to treat with Talleyrand, the French Minister of Foreign Affairs, who handled the map of Germany with a freedom little short of being complete. The base obsequiousness of the German envoys was only equalled by the timorous greed of their impatient masters, and the favours of the First Consul were supplicated in terms that would not have been exceeded for abjectness in Byzantium. The house of Talleyrand became the mart in which so many square miles, peopled by so many souls, could be acquired for so many snuff-boxes, and so many francs, and so many attentions to Madame Talleyrand's poodle. Princes and dukes, princesses and duchesses, paid huge sums to be comprehended in the indemnities. Some of the money was intercepted by swindling agents: much found its way into the long purse of Talleyrand, whose enormous fortune was largely built out of the complimentary gifts which he received for his services upon this occasion[2]. The First Consul wisely kept himself aloof from the open traffic, but behind the scenes he was scheming restlessly: plan after plan for the reconstruction of Germany was drawn up by his own hands, and then thrown into the fire. Maps would be specially prepared, and then crossed out: now he would have Austria near, now he would have her far; his subordinates were in despair, and doubted whether he was in earnest, but it was his policy which really guided events. To isolate

---

[1] Garden, *Histoire générale des Traités de Paix*, vii. 147 ff.

[2] A lively picture of all this is given in H. von Gagern, *Mein Antheil an der Politik*, i. 110 ff. For the presents made to the French see Erdmannsdörffer, *Politische Korrespondenz*, iv. 195, 202, and the curious letter of Hirsinger to Maret, quoted p. 62, n. 1.

Austria; to satisfy Prussia so far as possible and to attach her to France, without permitting her to extend over the centre of Germany or in the direction of the French frontier; to make separate treaties with the small princes; to build up the secondary States of Germany, such as Bavaria, Würtemberg, and Baden, into a buffer against the House of Hapsburg; and in all this to make such concessions to Russia as might flatter her pride without in the least impairing the interests of France, —these were the main ideas of his policy [1].

Everything did not fall out exactly as Bonaparte would have wished. He would have given Mecklenburg to Prussia, and transplanted the two Houses of Schwerin and Strelitz to Franconia. By such an arrangement the Hohenzollerns would have been prevented from obtaining their compensations either in the centre or in the west of Germany. They would be thrown northward and burdened with a large tract of barren and backward plain, their weight in European affairs would not be increased, and their political interest would shift from the Main and the Rhine to the Baltic. The two dukes, however, proud of their ancient Slavonic descent, refused to move, and even had they consented, Russia would probably have opposed the exchange. But the main objects of the First Consul's policy were attained. Prussian compensations lay partly in the west —Westphalian abbeys and bishoprics—and partly in the centre, Erfurt and Eichsfeld [1]. The coveted Baireuth and Würzburg went, not to Prussia (as she had hoped), but to Bavaria. Separate treaties were signed with Baden, Würtemberg, and Hesse-Cassel, promising each territorial gains and the Electoral dignity. Osnabrück was to go to Hanover, the old Duchy of Westphalia to Darmstadt; a new ecclesiastical Electorate at Aschaffenburg was designed for Dalberg, Coadjutor of Mainz: the number of free towns was to be reduced from fifty-two to eight. All this was done by a series of separate treaties and conventions between France on the one hand, and the German princes or towns on the other.

These treaties and conventions made up the French plan, which, having received Russia's assent, was presented to the Diet, accompanied by the insulting but necessary provision that

---

[1] Von Gagern, *Mein Antheil an der Politik*, i. 110.

it must be accepted in two months. Still further to emphasize the nullity of that ancient body, France authorized her clients to occupy provisionally the territories assigned to them. The speed with which this authorization was acted on was the reverse of edifying, and gave rise to much legitimate outcry. Meanwhile the peace Deputation of the Diet pursued its examination of the Franco-Russian plan amidst a storm of recriminations from all who believed themselves injured. The Deputation, to save its own dignity, wished to approve the acceptation of the act of indemnity *en bloc*, while reserving to itself the power to make necessary amendments. But Bonaparte refused to accept a resolution that might have opened the way to insidious changes, and, so long as the Peace of Amiens lasted, he held out against any modification of his plan. But the outbreak of the war with England, and a coolness with Russia, made him disposed to be more accommodating to Austria, who had the most powerful reasons for being discontented with the Franco-Russian plan. Concessions were made to Francis, who withdrew his opposition, and on February 25, 1803, the Diet began to discuss the amended plan. Their decree ratifying the territorial changes proposed by France and Russia changed the face and the structure of Germany.

The number of German States was reduced by about one-half by the absorption of the ecclesiastical principalities, in itself a great and salutary simplification. The old organization of the Circles was completely broken up. Of the fifty-two free towns six finally remained: Hamburg, Bremen, Lübeck, Frankfort, Augsburg, Nuremberg. Of the three ecclesiastical Electors, one only survived, and he was transplanted from Mainz to Ratisbon, and endowed with an artificially constructed state and revenue composed of the Bishopric and Principality of Ratisbon, the town and county of Wetzlar, the Principality of Aschaffenburg, and a charge of 600,000 florins on the Rhenish octroi. The Grand Masters of the Teutonic Order and of the Order of St. John represented all that was left of the thirty-four ecclesiastical votes in the Diet. In the College of Princes the majority passed from the Catholics to the Protestants, from the south to the north, from the party of Austria to the party of Prussia. In the distribution of territory the claims of the small princes and knights—the Austrian garrison in the west—were either wholly or partially disregarded.

All the distinctive features of the Holy Roman Empire were in fact either modified or completely obliterated. The Emperor, whose prestige had been already shattered by the French victories, was forced to look on while Bonaparte and his Russian ally arranged the map of Germany to suit their convenience. While the ascendency of the Hapsburg House received a fatal blow by the weakening of the Catholic element of the Diet, by the destruction of the ecclesiastical principalities, by the surrender of the interests of the knights and smaller princes, but above all by the strengthening of Prussia and the intermediate powers, Bavaria, Baden, Würtemberg, the disappearance of most of the free towns, and of all the ecclesiastical principalities save one, showed that Germany was at last nearing the end of her mediaeval constitution. The whole internal balance of power was in fact overturned. Prussia, which had only lost Cleves, Meurs, Guelders, some cantons in Frisia, and some customs on the Meuse and the Rhine, received territories which in population and area were three times and in revenue four times as considerable as those which she had been compelled to relinquish. She was awarded the Westphalian Bishoprics of Hildesheim and Paderborn, the town and part of the Bishopric of Münster (one of the richest sees in Germany), six Westphalian abbeys, Erfurt and the Thuringian territories which had belonged to the See of Mainz, and the free towns of Mülhausen, Nordhausen, and Goslar. Nor was this all. A small State, containing a population of one hundred and twenty-six thousand souls, was created for the Stadtholder of Holland out of the Bishoprics of Fulda and Corvey, the imperial town of Dortmund and three scattered abbeys, and destined to revert to the Prussian crown in the event of the extinction of the Orange line.

Bavaria obtained even greater favours. While she had lost in the Duchy of Deux-Ponts and other scattered principalities and possessions on the left bank 580,000 inhabitants and 4,000,000 florins, she was now presented with 854,000 inhabitants and a revenue of 6,607,000 florins. But these figures only inadequately represent the value of her new possessions. She acquired the better part of the Bishopric of Würzburg, and the whole of the

Bishopric of Bamberg, two of the richest and most civilized territories in Germany. She obtained the Bishoprics of Freising and Augsburg, part of the Bishopric of Passau, the Priory of Kempten, twelve abbeys, and seventeen free towns. Instead of being scattered in widely dispersed fragments and studded with municipal and ecclesiastical *enclaves*, Bavaria was now a compact and continuous State, nor was it a slight advantage that her territory with its poor and backward population should be united to others which had long felt the stimulus of energetic and enlightened rule.

Baden, which had lost about 25,000 inhabitants and 240,000 florins on the left bank, received benefits on a similar scale from France. She gained the Bishopric of Constance, together with the territories on the right bank which were formerly attached to the Sees of Spire, Strasburg, and Basle, the towns of Heidelberg and Mannheim, ten abbeys, seven free towns, and other possessions, in all 237,000 inhabitants and 1,500,000 florins, or about ten times as much as she had lost. In addition to this the Grand Duke of Baden received the Electoral hat.

The Duke of Würtemberg and the Landgrave of Hesse-Cassel were likewise made Electors and obtained large territorial acquisitions. Hesse-Darmstadt, for the loss of 40,000 subjects, was recompensed by the gain of three times as many. Hanover received the Bishopric of Osnabrück; Mecklenburg a claim on the octroi of the Rhine. The recipients of these favours were under no delusions as to the source from which they were derived. They had bargained for them in Paris, and it was well understood that the consent of the Reich was a pure formality. For the two years during which the compensations were being discussed, the influence of Bonaparte was predominant in Germany, veiled though it was under diplomatic fictions. The princes who sent their ambassadors to Paris, and their backsheesh to Talleyrand, were in reality doing their first acts of obeisance to the new Charlemagne. Silently but surely the bases of a new Germanic Confederation were being laid, a confederation which looked not to Austria but to France for leadership, protection, and (we must add) for plunder. The externals of the Empire indeed still existed—the Diet at Ratisbon, the Court of Wetzlar, the Electoral hats. But no one respected them, no one cared when they were to go or how soon, except a handful of interested or disinterested pedants. The German Revolution had not been accomplished without exciting passions, but they were the passions of envy and greed. It had helped to consolidate and to unify Germany, to make its structure more reasonable and more modern. But it had not excited enthusiasm, it had not kindled a spark of patriotism, it had not even fired the imagination of intellectual men as something tending to higher things. The people of Germany had no part in this revolution. The guns of Marengo and Austerlitz gave the signal for it; Russia and France presided over its course: the fruits of the change were enjoyed not by the people but by the despots who ruled them. Its first result was to enslave Germany to France.

One person all the while had been watching this sordid process of dissolution with keen and restless interest. It was more than five years since Bonaparte obtained his first glimpse of German men and German affairs at the Congress of Rastadt. Then he was merely the First General of the Republic, and in no position to dominate or control the internal rearrangements which resulted from the treaty his arms had wrung from Austria. Then he was merely a spectator, but now he was a master as well. *Les gros lots s'arrangent en secret*, and Bonaparte is the final arbiter. To the disappointed Germans he repeats a formula, *Il faut étouffer les regrets*. If he affected to believe that politics are propelled by their own momentum, and that human will is only important in war, it was because he wished to veil his own interposition [1]. But none the less he has learnt many things in the course of this passage of diplomacy. The map of Germany, the resources and population of the German States, are now familiar to him. He knows by heart all the secret ambitions, all the historical traditions, of the German princes, how many men they can put into the field under the old dispensation, and how many men they can command under the new [2]. Projects large and small, wise and sober, shoot through the brain which has been kindled by these inquiries and discussions. Why should not part of Hanover

---

[1] Von Gagern, i. 112.
[2] Erdmannsdörffer, iv. 192, 444.

LUNÉVILLE AND THE ACT OF MEDIATION

go to Denmark, and Sweden take Norway[1]? That would change the whole face of the North. Or why should not a league or leagues of German princes be formed under French protection, to serve as a barrier against the ambitions of Prussia and Austria? The idea occurs to others as well. On Aug. 29, 1803, several of the smaller princes and counts of the Empire entered into a union at Frankfort for the purpose of obtaining the protection of France[2]. On Sept. 20 a plan was drawn up for a League of Princes at Cassel. In November the Houses of Furstenburg, Hohenlohe, and Oettingen decided to form a union after the pattern which had been set at Frankfort, and to send a resident to Paris to protect their rights and prerogatives, 'finding themselves perhaps unduly disadvantaged by the new plan of indemnities.' 'The direction of public opinion,' said Massias the envoy at Karlsruhe to Talleyrand, Feb. 17, 1804, 'seems to me to tend more and more every day to the partition of Germany[3].'

[1] Erdmannsdörffer, v. 76.
[2] Hardenberg, *Denkwürdigkeiten*, ed. Ranke, ii. 37.
[3] Erdmannsdörffer, iv. 438-9, 452, 462.

CHIEF AUTHORITIES : Koch et Schoell, *Histoire abrégée des Traités de Paix*, vol. vi ; Garden, *Histoire générale des Traités de Paix*, vol. vii ; Häusser, *Deutsche Geschichte* ; Rambaud, *Les Français sur le Rhin* ; H. von Gagern, *Mein Antheil an der Politik*.

CHAPTER III

HANOVER

'L'Angleterre ! Voilà la racine des discordes européennes ; aussi me tiendrai-je sans cesse prêt à tout événement.'—NAPOLEON.

THE early years of the Consulate stand out in all French history as a period of brilliant legislative achievement, and in the Constitution which centralized authority, in the Concordat which healed religious strife, and in the Code which harmonized the discoveries of democratic jurisprudence with the ripe and tested wisdom of the legists of the Monarchy, we have the most durable monument of Napoleon's genius. It is difficult for posterity to realize the delighted rapture with which the majority of the French nation watched the swift unrolling of this splendid pageant of civil history. Such boldness of design, such grandeur of scale, such swift and accurate execution seemed to reveal a new art of politics, compared with which the contrivances of other times and other nations appeared paltry and outworn. Guided and inspired by a mind so potent, France felt herself fit to rule the world[1].

During a portion of this brilliant period in her annals France was at peace with all the powers of Europe. Her two inveterate enemies, Austria and England, had been compelled, the one at Lunéville in 1801, the other at Amiens in 1802, to come to terms with Napoleon, and it was only in the distant island of St. Domingo that French armies were still engaged in warlike operations. It is idle to conjecture what might have been the course of history if this peace had been prolonged for ten years, and if Napoleon had continued to concentrate his splendid energies upon civil and colonial enterprise. But the sane and temperate character of the Roman was wanting to the modern Caesar, and England took reasonable alarm at his

[1] The early writings of Roederer are the best reflection of the jubilant enthusiasm of these times.

restless ambition. It is indeed as probable that Napoleon did not intend to provoke war, as it is certain that his actions were calculated to provoke it. He annexed Piedmont, gave a constitution to Switzerland, and made no secret of his designs on Egypt. The government of Addington may have violated technicalities, but no government of spirit and forethought would have acted otherwise. In May 1803 the short-lived Peace of Amiens was at an end.

This English war lasted till 1814, and is the master-key to the later history of Napoleon. All his wars with Austria and Prussia, with Spain and Russia, which acted with such solvent power upon the old fabric of Europe, rose out of the war with England, and are connected with it. To conquer England, as Napoleon himself said, it was necessary to conquer the continent. The occupation of Hanover, the confederation of the Rhine, the formation of client principalities and kingdoms in Germany, the exclusion of English and colonial wares from the continent, all these acts of policy flowed from one source, the dogged antagonism of the English people.

When, in the spring of 1803, diplomatic relations between France and England showed signs of strain, Napoleon at once turned his eyes to the German possessions of the British sovereign. It is true that the Electorate of Hanover, being a member of the Holy Roman Empire and only bound to England by a personal connection, was not necessarily involved in English quarrels. Moreover, Hanover had been expressly included among the powers neutralized at the Peace of Basle in 1795, and the English diplomatists argued that if the King of England went to war with France, he went to war as King of England and not as Elector of Hanover. Any violation of Hanoverian territory would, according to this view, be a wanton violation of North German neutrality and of treaty obligations entered into by France herself. Such a theory had not commended itself to the Prussians in 1801, and it was little likely to commend itself to Napoleon in 1803. In 1801 the Prussians who had joined the Armed Neutrality of the North marched an army into the Electorate, occupied it for half a year, and left it impoverished by twenty million thalers. Why should not Napoleon do likewise? It was ludicrous to speak as if Hanover and England were two separate entities, when Hanoverian soldiers had fought in the English wars, and when the Hanoverian forests might supply timber to the English fleets. The occupation of Hanover by the French armies was a legitimate move in the game of war; it was also the only direct and immediate way in which Napoleon could strike at his rival [1].

On March 30, 1803, Napoleon took the first step towards active intervention in Germany. A despatch of that date orders Citizen Lacuée, aide de camp to the First Consul, to make a thorough inspection of Holland, and thence to travel into Germany. 'You will go to Emden at the mouth of the Ems, to Bremen at the mouth of the Weser, you will go to Hanover, Osnabrück, Nimeguen. . . . You will estimate the strength of the Hanoverian army, and the obstacles which may be opposed to an invasion [2].' Meanwhile troops were being massed upon the Channel coast, and on April 18, 1803, General Monbrichard was ordered to collect at Nimeguen, under the command of Brigadier-General Frère, six infantry battalions, six squadrons of cavalry, and a division of eight pieces of artillery. 'It is indispensable,' ran the instructions, 'that this gathering should be formed without noise or ostentation [3].' By the beginning of May, some 25,000 troops had been collected in the north of Holland, under the command of General Mortier, ready to descend upon the Electorate whenever the expected ultimatum should be delivered.

The prospect of a French occupation of Hanover was highly displeasing to the Court of Berlin, since it would involve not only a violation of the neutrality of Northern Germany, of which Prussia was the chief guarantor, but also a blockade by the English of the mouths of the Weser and the Elbe, with all its consequent drawbacks to Prussian trade. Under these circumstances there was one course, and one only, which Prussia could have pursued with credit to herself and with a reasonable

---

[1] The advantages which Napoleon contemplated from the occupation are summed up by Lucchesini, and expounded by the Emperor himself in an interesting conversation (Bailleu, ii. 201, 215, 216).

[2] *Corr.* viii. 261-2, no. 6,658. On March 22, Duroc warned the Prussian Court that Hanover would be occupied by the French in the event of war (Bailleu, ii. 129). [3] *Corr.* viii. 283, no. 6,695.

prospect of success. At the first shot fired in the Channel, Frederick William should have thrown his troops into Hanover, and kept it as a deposit till the end of the war. But the King of Prussia had not the courage to accept the bold counsels of Haugwitz, and resorted to the slow medium of negotiation. He first addressed himself to the Court of St. James's, offering to take the Electorate under his charge, provided that England should oppose no obstacle to the free navigation of the Elbe and the Weser under the Prussian flag. A curt refusal from London diverted the supplications of the weak king to Paris. But while the precious hours were wasted in entreaty, the French troops were advancing in forced marches upon Hanover [1].

Imagine a flat and sandy waste, here and there relieved by tracts of thriving forest and arable land, and only on its southern boundary by rolling pine-clad hills; with a few small towns, the largest, Hanover, containing but 16,500 souls; with little trade or commerce; with no political journals; its roads bad; its villages collections of miserable huts; its peasantry, save in the Elbe marshes and in Hadeln, subject to onerous feudal services; its politicians all aristocrats supported by Court offices, and therefore timorous and dependent; its towns governed by narrow and domineering oligarchies; its University learned but obsequious; its industries stifled by guilds, and uninformed by mechanical or chemical knowledge; its government, local and central, a chaos of disparate and independent institutions grown together by accident and the lapse of time; its law antique, barbarous, chaotic—such was the Electorate of Hanover, a country inhabited by a population more insular than the English, and long sunk in the lethargy which is the product of a bad political and social constitution, of consistent neglect, and of the absence of large national hopes. Under George II something had been done to rouse the country. The king was a frequent visitor to Herrenhausen, and the quiet gabled streets of Hanover were enlivened by the wigs, the uniforms, and the equipages of the royal Court. The University of Göttingen, founded in 1737 through the zeal of the learned Münchhausen,

[1] Bailleu, ii. 133, 145 f., 158, 160; Hardenberg, *Denkwürdigkeiten*, ii. 18.

was a more solid contribution to the welfare of the country, and did something to civilize a singularly ignorant aristocracy as well as to provide a training for the statesmen and administrators of Germany. But the reign of George III was an epoch of stagnation, though some slight impetus was given to farming and horse-breeding by the foundation of an agricultural society and a royal stud at Celle. The king, whose boast it was that he was born and bred a Briton, never once set foot in his German dominion, which was left to be governed by a series of councils. As there was no general assembly for the whole Electorate, and as every province save one (Diepholz) possessed its own provincial Estates, which had to be consulted upon all important questions, administrative celerity was impossible. Aristocratic bodies are proverbially tenacious of ancient rights and privileges, and the provincial Estates of Hanover were aristocratic and obstructive. In the absence of the Elector the supreme governing body, the *Geheime-Rats-Kollegium*, had not the power to override the sinister interests of these local assemblies, whose opposition was sufficient to thwart any serious effort to secure reforms.

Indeed it would have been difficult to construct a piece of machinery more perfectly calculated than the Hanoverian Constitution to defeat progress. The *Geheime-Rats-Kollegium*, recruiting itself by co-optation from a select circle of aristocratic families, was not only devoid of personal eminence, but also paralysed by the extreme subdivision of political power. The domains, forests, mines, rivers, tolls, and licences, were controlled by a separate council (the *Kammer-Kollegium*) responsible only to the Elector, military arrangements being left to be haggled over by a commander-in-chief who wanted to spend money, and a civilian war-chancery bent upon economy. Again, certain parts of the Electorate, Stade, Ratzeburg, Osnabrück, although nominally controlled by the *Geheime-Rats-Kollegium*, were in reality almost autonomous, possessing their own special governments. True, members of the Supreme Council presided over the Chambers that administered the domains and also over the war-chancery, and some slight reforms in the direction of increased centralization were made in 1801 and 1802. These circumstances, however, did not alter the fundamental character of the government. There was no Prime Minister, there was no tradition of Cabinet ascendency, the members of the government represented nobody but themselves. The smallest crisis was sure to reveal divided aims, flurried counsels, and paltry ambitions.

This diversified and divided administration was, so to speak, stained and coloured to a single hue. It was a bureaucracy of aristocrats, worked for the benefit of the most exclusive aristocracy in Germany. All valuable posts in the State, military and civil, were monopolized by the nobles. The provincial Estates, without whose assent no new tax could be imposed, were everywhere dominated by the nobility, who took good care that none of the burden of taxation should fall upon themselves. Hence, although every province had its own peculiar fiscal system, all systems were agreed upon one point, that the burgher and the peasant should contribute most. Luckily the government was mild and its needs were small, and the peasantry, helped by frequent remissions of taxation and by some domestic industries, was generally able to make ends meet. The condition of the agricultural population seems, however, to have been the reverse of prosperous. In Osnabrück the peasant was still a serf, and when the serf died the lord claimed half of his movable property. Insecurity of tenure, feudal dues, inequality of taxation, patrimonial courts (not to speak of the high corn-prices that had prevailed in the country since 1780), were more general influences operating to check the prosperity of the rural poor. The movement of commerce, impeded by internal customs duties, by guilds, and by the predominance of English imports, was not sufficiently brisk to attract the clever young countryman into the towns. The nobles brought over their luxuries from London, and it is with some reason that Hanoverian writers complain that the commercial prosperity of the Electorate was sacrificed to the English connection.

The repercussion of the French Revolution was felt but faintly in this sleepy quarter of the world. A few voices were, however, raised against the régime of aristocratic privilege and the personal union with England. In 1793 the Hanoverian government, becoming conscious of the unpopularity of a poll-tax, allayed the brewing storm by some concessions to the principle of fiscal equality. A little blood was even shed at Osnabrück, and then all seemed to relapse into the accustomed calm. But questions had been raised and minds exercised, and there was a growing discontent with absentee rule. In Bremen and Verden, old possessions of the Swedish Crown, men said that it was better to be ruled from Stockholm than from London. And though elsewhere the loyalty to the Guelphic House remained intact, a feeling was growing up that the Electorate should be separated from England and transferred to the Duke of Cambridge, youngest son of George III, who in the early months of 1803 was serving as inspector of infantry and cavalry in the Hanoverian army.

Such in brief was the condition of the Electorate when the news came to Hanover of the rupture of the Peace of Amiens.

The Hanoverian ministry had been expressly told that England could do nothing for them, but they had made no preparations, still vainly relying upon assistance from Berlin. On May 22, people positively asserted in the streets of Hanover that Prussia was determined to defend the Electorate from the French. Two days earlier the feeble and undecided government had ordered a *levée en masse*; two days later, alarmed by the unpopularity of the measure, they explained that they had no such intention, but merely wished to add 15,000 recruits to the army. But so raw and undisciplined were these hasty levies that after a week's probation they were dismissed to their homes[1]. The army which General Mortier was leading into Hanover was composed of seasoned troops, but its numbers did not exceed 17,000 men. With 22,000 regular troops at his command, half of them experienced veterans, and a park of over fifty guns, the Hanoverian field-marshal ought to have given a good account of himself. At best he might expect to fight on even terms against a force numerically inferior, dangerously short of ammunition, far weaker in the artillery and cavalry arms, and operating in an enemy's country[2]. At worst

---

[1] 'Without uniforms, without discipline, without drill, and incapable of the commonest movements which require precision, of what use can they be to us?'—*A Hanoverian English officer a hundred years ago. Memoirs of Baron Ompteda*, 128.

[2] Dumas, *Précis des évènements militaires*, ix. 187–8; Mortier to

he might have expected to make good his retreat to Stade, whence his army might be safely trans-shipped to England. But the Hanoverian field-marshal was Johann Ludwig von Wallmoden, an elderly gentleman of seventy-seven, courtly, well-informed and cultured, but totally lacking in decision and military promptitude. The son of that Mme. von Wallmoden who as the mistress of George II has been immortalized in the memoirs of Lord Hervey, John Louis had owed his promotion rather to Court favour than to ability. He had seen something of the camp in the Seven Years' War, and again in 1794, but his name is not illustrated by a single action of daring or of skill. As the owner of two fine houses and the best picture-gallery of the Electorate, Wallmoden occupied a position of social distinction, from which he looked down with some contempt upon the civilian members of the Supreme Council. He was the last man to unite the country, to inspire enthusiasm, or to lead a forlorn hope.

Rumour swelled the numbers of the advancing Frenchmen to 40,000 or 50,000, and the Hanoverian army on the Weser, which had been carefully dispersed into four separate detachments, might reasonably feel uneasy at the impending shock [1].

On June 1 a small skirmish was fought at Vechtsdam, in which a dragoon and two horses were wounded, and immediately the Hanoverian general Lensingen fell back upon Suhlingen. Meanwhile three emissaries from the Supreme Council were, with the consent and acquiescence of Wallmoden (so it would appear), treating with Mortier in the French camp. The government had decided to capitulate before a blow was struck, and the commander of the army actually endorsed their decision.

Napoleon, June 3, 1803 : *A. F.* iv. 1594. The reports of Sir Charles Gordon are also very instructive (*F. O., Frontiers of Holland: Secret Communications,* 7). Gordon says of the French, 'They had not a piece of artillery above an eight-pounder; not a single pontoon; and but three companies of artillery of about sixty men each, with not enough ammunition between Holland and the Weser for an action of two hours' time.'

[1] It is said that the Hanoverian army was commanded not to fire, and to ' use the bayonet only in the most pressing necessity and with moderation ' (*Lebensbilder aus dem Befreiungskriege,* i. 202).

On June 3 a convention was signed with the French at Suhlingen, which stipulated that Hanover and its forts should be occupied by the French army; that the Hanoverian forces should retreat behind the Elbe, and engage not to bear arms against the French army and its allies so long as the war between France and England should last; that all munitions of war were to be given up to the invaders; that a French army of occupation, clothed, supported, and provided with the necessary remounts by the Hanoverians, was to occupy the Electorate; that all the revenues of the Electorate were to be put at the disposition of the French, who were also to fix a war-contribution for the support of their army; that all endowments, save those of the University, and all properties belonging to the English king were to be sequestered, and all English soldiers and agents to be taken to France. The general commandant-in-chief reserved to himself the power of making such changes as he should judge suitable in the Hanoverian administration, and it was agreed that the existing government of the Electorate should abstain from exercising authority in the country occupied by the French troops[1].

This convention was signed by Mortier, 'saving the approbation of the First Consul,' and to the First Consul it was submitted. But while the ruler of France was gratified with the ease and celerity with which the Electorate had been occupied, he was unwilling to ratify the Convention of Suhlingen until the British government had given their ratification and consented to exchange captive French sailors for the Hanoverian soldiers who had pledged themselves to take no further part in the war. For Napoleon the seizure of Hanover was merely a move in the game against England. He wanted timber for his ships, horses for his cavalry; he saw an opportunity of molesting British commerce, of controlling the mouths of the Weser and the Elbe, and of destroying some British shipping. Not least, in the capitulation of Suhlingen, there appeared to be a chance of an exchange of prisoners such as would reinforce the depleted crews of the French navy. In order to prevent the possibility of any evasion of the convention, he ordered the Hanoverian

---

[1] Dumas, *Précis des évènements militaires*, ix. 392 ff.

troops into the Bishopric of Osnabrück, and sent thither General Dessole with three half-brigades to help Mortier in the task of supervision. Until the decision of his Britannic Majesty was known, the Hanoverian army was not to be permitted to retreat across the Elbe [1].

As the Cabinet of St. James's declined to ratify the convention, Napoleon ordered Mortier to disarm the Hanoverian army, to dismount the cavalry, and to send cavalry and infantry alike as prisoners of war into France [2]. Provisions were running short in the Hanoverian camp, and though 11,000 of his men were eager to contest the passage of the Elbe, Wallmoden determined to treat [3]. It might be argued in defence of this resolution that since the army had already agreed to abstain from any further participation in the war with France, there was not much harm in going a step further and consenting to be disarmed and disbanded. The general feeling of the country was against fighting, and the Landstände declared that they would no longer pay the troops if they were foolish enough to offer a patriotic resistance to the invaders. Considerations of the pocket were more potent than the dictates of honour, and when Mortier withdrew the proposal that the men should be sent into France as prisoners of war there was no difficulty in coming to an agreement [4]. By the Elbe Convention, sometimes called the Convention of Artlenburg, which was signed July 5, 1803, the Hanoverian army was dissolved, its horses, guns, and arms ceded to France, and its officers put under pledge not to leave the Continent [5]. About a thousand men of a higher spirit than their comrades escaped to Stade, where they were taken up by some British ships and transported to England. This was the origin of that Hanoverian Legion which earned such high distinction in the Peninsular War.

'Citizen Lieutenant-General Mortier,' wrote Bonaparte on July 11, 1803, 'I approve of the convention which you have made, since it fulfils my political object, and spares the blood of a great number of brave men. I recommend you to

---

[1] *Corr.* viii. 357-8, no. 6,821-2.
[2] Ib., 363, no. 6,835.   [3] *A. F.* iv. 1594.
[4] Ompteda, 159-63 ; Dumas, ix. 219.
[5] Dumas, ix. 395-7.

be inflexible in its execution, not to suffer in any manner the introduction of mails, couriers, or English merchandise into the country which you occupy either in the Elbe or the Weser. . . . Send us horses into France, especially for the heavy cavalry. If there are two or three hundred for the guard, send them to Paris. Take care to disarm the country; and shut up all the arms in strongholds until you can get them sent into France [1].'

Baron Risbeck, writing in 1780, describes Hanover as the most miserable country in Germany; 'I cannot conceive,' he says, 'how our troops can have lived in this country during the last Silesian war [2].' Nor had the lapse of a score of years materially altered the situation. The revenue of the Electorate all told only amounted to twelve million livres, and of this sum half was devoted to the payment of the army and the interest on the debt. There seemed to be no fresh economies to be practised, no fresh sources of wealth to be explored. The income derived from the private domains of the Elector had been wholly expended upon public objects within the Electorate, and the separation from England did not in consequence bring an extra penny into the Hanoverian exchequer. Two French naval officers inspected the forests, and reported that the wood was too tender to be used in ship-building. The subordinate officials were perhaps over-numerous, but the French had to admit that their salaries were small, and that the accounts of the Electorate were signalized by the greatest order and by a general spirit of economy. For the government of the Elector the French came to entertain a certain respect. 'Hanover,' writes the Intendant-General of the Grand Army, 'resembles a family submitted to feudal but paternal regulations, rather than a State governed by laws of constraint.' The hospitals were pronounced excellent; the prisons 'sanitary'; the prisoners well fed; 'the régime very humane.' Specialists reported that the forests were admirably managed. There was hardly any crime or litigation, and, though the technical rights of the landlord were extensive, the French admitted that they were softened in practice by clemency and good feeling. It was remarked that ' an hereditary

---

[1] *Corr.* viii. 398, no. 6,904.
[2] *Voyages en Allemagne,* iii. 114.

probity' was a general characteristic of Hanoverian officials, and the observer was inclined to attribute this pleasing feature to 'the beneficence of the government, to good examples, and to domestic education.' A few timid and obsequious remarks at the beginning of the French occupation seem to have led some Frenchmen to believe that the English connection was universally unpopular, but the error was profound and soon dissipated. The Hanoverians were patient; ' we cannot reproach them with any complaint, any murmur, any act,' says an official report in 1807, 'but they maintain an attachment to their government which they do not dissimulate. They are obedient to the conqueror, but they sigh for peace, and hope that it will restore them to their Elector [1].'

It was not the intention of the First Consul to take over the government of the country or to present it with a new legal and institutional equipment. So long as Hanover supported his army of occupation, so long as it was closed to the English merchant and the English recruiting sergeant, he was content to allow the old machinery to creak along its accustomed grooves. But to obtain the required supplies it was clearly necessary to construct a new wheel in the administration which should revolve alike more rapidly and more obediently than the rusty engines of the Electoral polity. A small Executive Commission, consisting of Hanoverians conversant with the finance of the country, was formed by General Mortier, and entrusted with the task of extracting the necessary supplies. The orders of the general to the Executive Commission were transmitted by a government commissary, C. F. Durbach by name, who had been an administrator in the Rhenish districts, and was acquainted with both the French and German tongues. Not a penny could be expended by the Executive Commission without Durbach's sanction, and measures were taken to prevent any possible source of taxation from lying hid. It was Durbach's duty to take stock of all the revenues of the Elector, the Estates and the bailiwicks, of all British property, of all taxes, charges, and possible resources, and to report upon the relative wealth of the different districts

---

[1] *Affaires étrangères, Correspondance politique: Brunswick et Hanovre*, 54.

of the Electorate. He was to render a daily account of his operations to the general; he was empowered to attend and to preside over the Executive Commission; and he was charged to transmit all sums received to the *payeur général* of the army. By this contrivance Mortier obtained an independent estimate of the resources of the country, a supply of well-instructed Hanoverian advice, and a complete control over the revenue and expenditure of the Electorate. All else was allowed to pursue its ancient course.

It is difficult to know whether to applaud or to condemn the bovine acquiescence of the Hanoverian population under the French yoke. Mortier's soldiery, despite the fly-leaves sold in the London streets, appears to have been well in hand, and we believe that there were few outrageous breaches of discipline[1]. Both Mortier and Bernadotte (who succeeded him in the command) were naturally humane, and did what they could to apply emollients to the wound. But the malady of military billeting and financial extortion remained persistent and exasperating. A small landowner in the county of Hoya, with a rent-roll of some 10,000 francs, found himself obliged to entertain a colonel, an officer, ten horses, and three servants, at a monthly charge of 960 livres. The town of Hanover had a garrison of more than 4,000 men, an addition equal to nearly a fourth of its civilian population, and it must have been difficult to look on to the street of any Hanoverian town or village without catching sight of a French uniform. In the first three years of the French occupation, according to the unimpeachable evidence of a French statistical survey, the Electorate had paid into the army chest 67,230,000 francs and increased its debt by 22,000,000, and all this time the ordinary sources of revenue were drying up. The product of the customs had diminished by a third, owing to the interruption of commerce. Agriculture was half paralysed by the withdrawal of horses, carts, and cattle for military purposes, and by 1807 the total yield of taxation had

---

[1] This is confirmed by Gordon, who speaks in high terms of the conduct of the French soldiers (*F. O., Frontiers of Holland: Secret Communications*, 7). The atrocities of the *Annual Register* are borrowed from an imaginative fly-sheet.

fallen from twelve to nine millions, 'and,' says a French report, 'it cannot be increased.'

The difficulties of the financial situation were so glaring, and the good faith of the Hanoverians was so obvious, that it was clear either that the army of occupation must be reduced or that fresh sources of supply must be obtained outside the Electorate. But to reduce the army of occupation was the one thing to which Napoleon would not consent. 'It must consist,' he wrote to Mortier (August 4, 1803), 'of from thirty to thirty-five thousand men, and must be nourished for a long time by the country.' The Hanoverian envoys in Paris vainly protested, mingling base assurances of hostility to England with their pleas. The First Consul gave them fair words: he did not wish the unfortunate people to be ruined; he would 'withdraw his troops and make the country feel the effects of his protection and his clemency.' But no substantial reduction was ever made. The army of occupation averaged from 25,000 to 30,000 men, more than twice as many as the revenues of the country would support. And in addition there were large requisitions of horses for the use of the artillery [1].

There remained the expedient of a loan. The credit of the Executive Commission, necessarily slight, was diminished by the fact that several members of the old Regency had taken refuge in the neighbouring Duchy of Mecklenburg, and fostered a belief in an approaching Guelphic restoration. But the property of the King of England in the Electorate was valued at 200,000,000 livres, and it was suggested to the Minister of War that a loan issued upon this security and backed by the name of the First Consul would be readily taken up by the Hanseatic towns or by the neighbouring princes [2].

The three Hanseatic towns, Hamburg, Bremen, and Lübeck, had preserved their ancient independence through the critical

---

[1] *Corr.* viii. 443, no. 6,981; *Affaires étrangères, Corr. pol.: Brunswick et Hanovre*, 54, and *Hamburg*, 118. Bernadotte wrote to Napoleon (July 20, 1805): 'If the army could be reduced to 15,000 men with staff in proportion, then by means of great economy and a loan of two millions a year it would be possible to make the two ends meet.'

[2] Léopold Berthier to the Minister of War, Sept. 22, 1803. *Affaires étrangères, Corr. pol.: Brunswick et Hanovre*, 54.

years immediately following the Peace of Lunéville, when so many free cities of the Empire had been forced to part with their political sovereignty. Rumour said that the miracle had been accomplished not without large *douceurs* to Talleyrand and to the officials of the French Foreign Office concerned with the affair of the German compensations[1]. Certainly to the three towns themselves the object would have seemed fully worth large pecuniary sacrifices. The Hanseatic cities were proud of their traditions, and rightly jealous of an independence dating back to the days of the Hohenstauffen Emperors. Nowhere was public spirit stronger or the art of municipal government more fully understood than in Hamburg. The commercial glory of Lübeck had indeed departed, and Bremen had not yet begun to participate in the advantages derived from a line of steamers to the North American shore, but judged by the standard of the times the three cities were prosperous, cultivated, and well governed. While the French conquest of Belgium and Holland during the revolutionary wars had temporarily eclipsed the prosperity of Antwerp and Amsterdam, the opulence of Hamburg rose by leaps and bounds. Though the streets were unlighted and unpaved, the feasts of the merchant-princes were worthy of Lucullus. It was currently said that you should breakfast in Scotland, sup in France, but *dine* at Hamburg, and that nowhere else in Europe could you order thirty-two wines from your merchant and have them all good[2]. The Commentaries of a critic of genius will not permit us to forget that the first experiment of a national German theatre was made at Hamburg, and the visitor who gazes upon the loaded barges, the grim warehouses, and the dark and tortuous canals of this Northern Venice, may feel that Lessing's onslaught on the classical canons of French dramatic art is not inappropriate to the Teutonic genius of the place.

The outbreak of the war between France and England was

[1] 'At Paris M. Abel presented to M. de Talleyrand and to M. Markoff a box *en émail* containing 24,000 francs in notes, &c.'—Hirsinger to Maret, Oct. 5, 1804. *A. F.* iv. 1706 b.

[2] *A Journal of the Defence of Hamburg*: London, 1832. The population of the three cities at this time was as follows:—Hamburg, 115,000; Bremen, 45,000; Lübeck, 40,000. *A. F.* iv. 1706 b.

a serious blow to communities whose prosperity largely depended upon the carrying trade. The blockade of the Weser and the Elbe by the English was answered by the French, who threatened to confiscate all English wares transmitted to the fairs of Frankfort and Leipzig. Yet the Hanseatic burghers, realizing that loss was inevitable, hoped by strict economy and a conscientious preservation of neutrality to avert the ruin that had swept over the neighbouring Electorate. But if they expected to be let alone by the French, their disappointment must have been great, for not only did the French occupy Cuxhaven (which belonged to Hamburg) but they proceeded to demand a loan [1].

Of all forms of investment which could have haunted the mind of a Hanseatic burgher in November 1803, none was likely to have been more distasteful than a loan for the support of the French army of occupation in Hanover. The security was dubious and the purpose was hateful. But Hamburg was left no choice. 'General Berthier,' wrote an English agent, 'said that he was no diplomat, that he must have an immediate answer—yes or no,' and the Senate of Hamburg lent the three million marks at the point of the bayonet [2]. The First Consul was indignant that a loan should have been contracted by French military officers without his authorization, and the terms of the convention were so compromising that he insisted upon its revision. 'This loan is badly made,' he wrote; 'it did not belong to French dignity to send a general to make this loan; that degrades the character of a general. If the loan was to be made openly, an officer of inferior rank should have been sent, accompanied by an agent of the treasury. But it would have been much better that the loan should have been made by the Estates (of Hanover) and in their name, and that General Mortier should only have ostensibly intervened as a guarantor [3].' Accordingly the order went out

---

[1] *Corr.* viii. 425, no. 6,956. 'Cuxhaven restait un objet de discorde qui eût compromis Hambourg si les Anglais avaient su y entrer et s'y comporter avec l'arrogance qui les caractérise.'

[2] Rumbold to Hawkesbury, Nov. 13, 1803. *F. O., Hamburg*, 24. A mark was 16*d.* sterling.

[3] *Corr.* ix. 120–1, 123–4, nos. 7,336, 7,340–1.

that the Estates of Hanover should be the contracting party, and that the loan should be hypothecated solely upon the domains of the King of England. If the Estates refused, France must have recourse to war impositions upon the Electorate.

To mortgage the private domain of the King of England was as repugnant to the Hanoverian Estates, as the issue of a loan based upon the mortgage was distasteful to Hamburg, but circumstances were imperious, and it was an ill season for the punctilios of loyalism. The Estates borrowed and Hamburg lent, and the French army consumed. In this way a violent situation was regularized in the eyes of diplomatic Europe.

When Bernadotte succeeded to the command of the Hanoverian army in July 1804, he found the pay of the soldiers four months in arrear, and no more than 200,000 francs in hand. It was necessary again to demand money from outside. Vainly did Hamburg plead her deserted quays, her emptied storerooms, and point to the fact that the first loan had only been covered by the forced advances of her wealthier burghers [1]. When Bremen grumbled and haggled, such of her merchants as happened to be travelling in the Electorate were arrested and their goods confiscated by the French soldiers, and when this device failed Bernadotte informed the Senate that if at the end of twenty-four hours it had not sanctioned the loan, every citizen of Bremen found upon Hanoverian territory would be treated as a spy and shot [2].

It was not sufficient that these sovereign towns should be forcibly compelled to lend money to a foreign aggressor upon doubtful security. They were placed under the strict supervision of the French police. 'In a town like Hamburg,' wrote Bonaparte, December 26, 1803, 'the police ought to have not one spy but ten [3].' The agent of the French Republic,

---

[1] Bernadotte to Talleyrand, July 11, 1804. Answer of the Senate of Hamburg, July 27, 1804. *Affaires étrangères, Corr. pol.: Hamburg*, 118.

[2] Reinhard to Talleyrand, Aug. 4, 1804, and Sept. 2, 1804. Reinhard, the French agent, speaks of the 'ridiculous and inconceivable obstinacy' of Bremen. *Affaires étrangères, Corr. pol.: Hamburg*, 118.

[3] *Corr.* ix. 173, no. 7,428.

M. Reinhard, a Würtemberger by birth but a Frenchman in sympathy, was to be entrusted with the duty of enforcing the rigorous *neutrality* of the Hanseatic towns. It was his duty to delate Englishmen and *émigrés*, and to *command* the suppression of papers and pamphlets offensive to the First Consul. The Senates of Hamburg, Bremen, and Lübeck knew too well the kind of sanction which underlay the representations of the French minister, and it must be confessed that Bonaparte encouraged no diplomatic illusions. 'Recommend M. Reinhard,' so he wrote to Talleyrand, August 18, 1804, 'to be more active in suppressing the insolence of the towns of Bremen and Hamburg. It is with regret that the Emperor will find himself obliged, if they continue to manage their police so ill, to send 8,000 or 10,000 men to manage it for them.' The answer to this threat was the prompt suppression of an offending journal, coupled with the punishment of its unfortunate printer [1].

The French men of business might well be alarmed at these high-handed proceedings, for at that time no less than one-sixth of the foreign trade of France was done with the Hanseatic towns, who distributed through Central and Eastern Europe the wines, the brandies, and the silks of the Republic. Since, with trifling exceptions, all this trade was carried on by Dutch or German vessels, it would be at once interrupted by English cruisers, if the free cities were forced by Napoleon to abandon their attitude of neutrality. But considerations of this frigid type had little or no weight in the policy of the Consulate. One day before the breach of the Treaty of Amiens, Napoleon observed with a smile to the Council of State, that the First Consul was not like the kings by the grace of God. Their power was assisted by ancient habits. With him it was the opposite. Ancient habits were so many obstacles. 'The French government

[1] *Corr.* ix. 476, no. 7,943 ; Reinhard to Talleyrand, September 7, 1804, *Affaires étrangères, Hamburg*, 118. At the baths of Travemünde, in the territory of Lübeck, a certain Count von Bodmer called upon the musicians to strike up ' God save the King.' Reinhard intimated to the Senate that if this happened again, he would get Bernadotte to send a French sergeant *afin de mieux maintenir la neutralité*. Reinhard to Talleyrand, July 20, 1804.

to-day has nothing in common with the government of yesterday. It has need of action, of brilliance, and consequently of war[1].'

[1] J. H. Lasalle, *De la neutralité des villes anséatiques*, 1803 (Brit. Mus., R. 300); Marco de Saint-Hilaire, *Napoléon au Conseil d'État*, i. 154-5.

PRINCIPAL AUTHORITIES : Thimme, *Die inneren Zustände des Kurfürstenthums Hannover unter der französisch-westphälischen Herrschaft* ; A. W. Ward, *Great Britain and Hanover* ; Havemann, *Das Kurfürstenthum Hannover unter zehnjähriger Fremdherrschaft* ; Ompteda, *Memoirs* ; Bailleu, *Preussen und Frankreich* ; Dumas, *Précis des évènements militaires*.

CHAPTER IV

THE CONSPIRACY AND THE RAIDS

'Est-ce que vous croyez, citoyen ministre, que parce que je suis à Malmaison, je ne sais rien ? Je ne me repose pas sur la police moi ! . . . Je fais ma police moi-même, et si la vôtre veille, comme vous le dîtes, moi aussi je veille, et souvent jusqu'à deux heures après minuit.'

NAPOLEON.

MASTER of Belgium and Holland, of the Rhine provinces and Hanover, and real though informal head of a client group of German princes, the First Consul began to regard Germany as annexed to his system. In the war which had broken out between France and England, Germany must show unequivocal devotion to French interests. English intrigue, English goods, English emissaries must be excluded from the continent, and Great Britain must be exhibited to the world as the outlaw race, violating the law of nations, both by land and sea, and unworthy of honest or respectable friendships. It is possible to discern all the lineaments of the continental system in the policy pursued by Napoleon in 1804.

The English government had from the first proclaimed its devotion to the cause of the Bourbons, and it made no secret of its desire to overturn the Consulate and restore the ancient monarchy of France. Not only were the Count of Artois, the Duke of Berry, and the Prince of Condé living in England, but England was still the asylum of those royalist *émigrés* who had not yet been erased from the lists of emigration and permitted to return to France. Just as the First Consul tried to stir up sedition in Ireland, so the government of George III paid money to assist in fomenting disturbances in Brittany and the Vendée. Napoleon wrote to the Pope to ask him what means of influencing public opinion in Ireland might be at his disposition. The English government relied upon royalist and Jacobin conspirators. Neither government would have stooped to encourage assassination, but it was considered fair at that time for belligerent powers not only to acquire all possible information through spies as to the plans and intentions of their adversaries, but also directly to foster insurrection and civil war in the dominions of their foe [1].

The rupture of the relations between France and England fanned the hopes of the exiles into sudden flame, but their plans now assumed a shape which was at once more promising and more criminal than those in which they previously had indulged. The Vendée and Brittany were exhausted, the south was pacified, there was no hope of any general royalist rising. But a blow might be struck in Paris itself and at the person of the First Consul. It was known that there was a Jacobin party in the city which deeply resented the suppression of republican liberties, and it was believed that the whole network of Jacobin influence through France was still extant and capable of being used for royalist ends. 'Jacobinism,' wrote Bertrand de Moleville, one of the most fanatical of the exiles, 'is the first instrument of the counter-revolution. We must restore general disorganization and the kind of chaos from which the Revolution issued.' In this unnatural alliance between the two extremes of political thought it was hoped that General Moreau might be included. The victor of Hohenlinden was the most popular soldier in the army: he was known to cherish republican memories, and in his sulky retirement at Grosbois he made no effort to conceal his jealousy and his chagrins. It was believed that he could be induced, through the solicitations of his former friend Pichegru, to enter into the plot, or at any rate that he could be hopelessly compromised. His great name would win the army. The crucial undertaking, however, was not to be left to the accomplishment of Jacobin or republican hands. A bold Breton desperado, Georges Cadoudal, with a band of hardy Chouans, was to attack the First Consul and his escort and to vanquish them in fair fight. In this struggle Bonaparte would be killed or

---

[1] 'It is the acknowledged right of belligerent powers to avail themselves of any discontents existing in the countries with which they may happen to be at war.'—Circular note of Lord Hawkesbury, April 30, 1804. *Annual Register*, 1804, 215.

THE CONSPIRACY AND THE RAIDS 69

captured. Two Bourbon princes, the Count of Artois and the Duke of Berry, would then appear in France to direct the royalist movements. In the wilds of Brittany men would have already descended to stir the old white furies, and with the French Cromwell down and dead, would not Moreau step out of the shadow to play the part of Monk? Such were the outlines of the conspiracy.

There was a certain villain who had acted as secretary to the Commune and is said to have been concerned in the September massacres, by name Mehée de la Touche. This man, who had been imprisoned by the Consular government as a Jacobin, arrived in England in February 1803, representing himself as an enemy to Bonaparte, and was received into the counsels of the royalists. It was he who inspired their hopes of Jacobin help, and it is probably to him that the conspiracy owed much of its actual shape. But while plotting with the royalists in London Mehée was also in the pay of the French police, and through him Napoleon was made aware of the details of the plot. We need not blame the First Consul for regarding it as outrageous and wicked. We need not question the reality or appropriateness of his indignation. It was in truth flat murder thinly disguised; had it been successful it must have led to the utter disorganization of France. That the plot of Georges should have received the full sanction of the Prince of Artois is an indelible blot on the reputation of the Bourbon House, and it is deeply to be regretted that £3000 of English money should have been expended in subsidizing the rising in the west, which was a subsidiary feature in this criminal enterprise [1].

Napoleon, once aroused, pursued the trail of conspiracy with the zest of a practised sleuthhound. His letters to Régnier and Fouché are full of directions that So-and-so should be watched, So-and-so imprisoned, So-and-so banished. He dictates instructions to Mehée, for the plot is a plant of great political promise, which must be watered, encouraged, and allowed to develop to maturity. The Bourbons must be exposed, the English government implicated, and a blow struck to teach Europe manners. *Ces misérables Anglais nous por-*

[1] J. H. Rose, *The Life of Napoleon I,* i. 451-2.

tent la corruption sur toute la côte, he writes, March 12, 1804[1]. English spies at Genoa, English intrigues in Munich, an 'inundation' of English spies and agents in Hanover, *émigrés* at Frankfort and Hamburg, an Anglophile paper in Holland, one English agent plotting an insurrection in the four departments, another brewing evil with a French abbé at Stuttgart, 'a subterranean working at Brest and Boulogne, which in two towns so far apart can only be the work of English agents'—he sees, or professes to see, perfidious Albion everywhere spinning her treacherous and all-embracing nets[2].

Meanwhile the plot ripened. On August 21, 1803, Georges with the first detachment of conspirators disembarked at Biville, and his men found their way by separate routes to Paris. A second detachment followed in December, a third in January. In September and October a few accomplices had been arrested, but there was no certain evidence against them. They were interrogated, but revealed nothing. On January 21, 1804, the First Consul determined to bring the men before a military commission, and one of them, Kerouelles, turning craven on the place of execution, made a clean breast of what he knew, and declared that Georges was in Paris. Immediately afterwards one Troche, on being arrested by the police, announced that a fourth detachment was about to land, headed by a Prince of the Bourbon House, and Savary, in disguise, was despatched to watch the coast. Indeed every piece of fresh evidence seemed to implicate the Princes, and to reveal a conspiracy more formidable than had been expected. A mysterious person about forty years of age and disguised in a long cloak used to visit Georges, so ran the report of some Chouans who were arrested on February 9. Surely he must be a prince? A man called Bouvet de Lozier, one of Georges' lieutenants, attempted suicide, failed, and with broken nerves confessed the whole story to Réal—how Georges and Pichegru had disembarked, how Monsieur (the Count of Artois) was to come to Paris, how Moreau had met Pichegru and Georges by moonlight in the Boulevard de la Madeleine. It was time to strike. On

---

[1] *Corr.* ix. 285, no. 7,614.

[2] Ib. 190, no. 7,462 ; 272, no. 7,594 ; 274, no. 7,598 ; 299, no. 7,633 ; 329, no. 7,690 ; 354, no. 7,739.

February 15 the warrant for Moreau's arrest was signed. On February 28 Pichegru was betrayed. On March 9 Georges was taken after a desperate struggle. The *Moniteur*, March 10, declared that Georges had confessed that his mission was to assassinate the First Consul.

All the principal conspirators, save the Princes, were now in the hands of the First Consul, yet on the theory of the police the rôle assigned to the Princes was hardly less important than that of the Jacobins and the Chouans. It was in vain that the coast was watched. The Princes did not land, could not be found. The depositions were disappointing, for it was clear that Moreau was barely compromised, and Georges stoutly and persistently denied that the plot was one of assassination. The First Consul was determined to put a stop once and for all to these detestable dealings. On March 10 he wrote to Berthier ordering the seizure of the Duc d'Enghien.

This young man, the grandson of the Prince of Condé, was living at Ettenheim near Strasburg, a place in the territory of the Grand Duchy of Baden. He had served in the emigrant armies, was in receipt of a pension from England, and had requested permission to join an English regiment, but he was probably ignorant of this conspiracy and entirely unconnected with it. His residence at Ettenheim was well known to be caused by an attachment to a lady—Princess Charlotte de Rohan—to whom, in fact, he was secretly married, and also by the neighbourhood of the Black Forest, which afforded him facilities for sport. The ingenuity of the French police had, however, woven his name into the fatal web. On February 28 Mehée told Réal that some general officers of the army of Condé had come to Offenburg, a village in the neighbourhood of Ettenheim, to concert measures with the Duc d'Enghien. Accordingly the prefect of Strasburg, acting on instructions from Paris, sent a non-commissioned officer of *gendarmerie* named Lamothe to watch the Prince. Lamothe reported that the Prince was at Ettenheim in the company of Dumouriez and a Lieutenant Smith, recently arrived from England, and that he was corresponding actively with Offenburg, in which place there was a number of *émigrés*. Shee, the prefect of Strasburg, forwarded this report to Réal in a covering letter which stated that the Duke had made frequent visits to Strasburg and Benfelden, and expatiated on the intrigues of the *émigrés* of Offenburg and of their directress the Baroness von Reich. A certain Lévidant, arrested as a Chouan in Paris, avowed that he had seen a young man about thirty, well-clad, with distinguished manners, visit Georges at Chaillot. He had immediately supposed that the young man 'might well be the Prince of whom he had heard speak.' Combining these scattered clues, the police arrived at the theory that the Duc d'Enghien had paid a flying visit to Paris to direct the plot.

Maria Eleanora Cecilia Reich von Platz had corresponded with Pichegru, and was the centre of a little coterie of *émigrés* who lived at Offenburg. It was said, too, that she served as intermediary between Condé and Fauche Borel, a well-known royalist conspirator. From the beginning of March she had been under close observation. French gendarmes in disguise were lodging in the town, changing their names and their quarters every two days. On March 7 Régnier, the Grand-Judge, drew Napoleon's attention to the conspirators at Offenburg, and recommended a demand for their immediate extradition, and on March 10 Talleyrand wrote to Edelsheim, the minister of Baden, enclosing a copy of this report, and formally demanding 'that the individuals who composed this committee at Offenburg should be arrested and delivered with their papers to French officers, charged to receive them at Strasburg.' The French Minister of Foreign Affairs further required 'that by a general and irrevocable measure all the French *émigrés* should be removed from the countries which compose the Electorate of Baden,' explicitly basing his order on the first article of the Treaty of Lunéville, which provided that 'No help or protection shall be given either directly or indirectly to those who may wish to injure one or other of the contracting parties.' 'It is evident,' he remarked, 'that they (the *émigrés*) are a class of persons who, according to the terms of the Treaty of Lunéville, ought not to find asylum or protection in the Germanic States. Their exclusion is then a matter of strict right.' Whether the words of the treaty will bear this interpretation may be a matter for discussion [1]; but in truth all argument

---

[1] 'Il ne sera donné aucun secours et protection soit directement soit

THE CONSPIRACY AND THE RAIDS 73

was something of a superfluity. On the very day on which Talleyrand wrote the letter to Edelsheim, Napoleon took the question of the Baroness von Reich into his own hands. Without waiting for the answer of the Court of Baden, he ordered General Caulaincourt to surround the town of Offenburg, and to seize her and the other agents of the Britannic government.

Rarely has a more complete insult been offered to a friendly power. The territory of Baden was suddenly, without warning, invaded by a little army of 800 men, provided with food and ammunition for four days. Two towns belonging to the Elector were surrounded in the dead of night, and several persons forcibly carried off into France without any formal act of extradition. A French agent assumed the uniform of Baden to create the impression that the government of Karlsruhe was a consenting party, and assisted the operations at Offenburg. At Ettenheim two native officials presumed to expostulate with the French commanding officer, and to ask the cause of this extraordinary violation of neutral territory. General Ordener replied that he did not know himself, that it was an affair of State, and that his Serene Highness of Baden had been informed of the movement the evening before. He added, said these officials, 'that we were to keep quite quiet, for he had three guns with him, and at the least uprising would immediately order them to open fire on the burghers[1].' The Duc d'Enghien, a lieutenant of the Condé regiment named Schmid, the Baroness von Reich, General de Thumery, Colonel von Grünstein, and eight other persons were driven away across the border. On March 20, after a perfunctory trial before a military tribunal, the Duke was shot in the moat of Vincennes[2].

Thirty-four hours after the event the government of Karlsruhe received the news of this astonishing raid. The Elector indirectement à ceux qui voudraient porter préjudice à l'une ou à l'autre des parties contractantes.' The French ministers in Germany had orders to demand the expulsion of *all émigrés*, which implies that every *émigré* was a conspirator. Erdmannsdörffer, v. 21.

[1] Id., v. 10.
[2] Lamothe had confused Thumery with Dumouriez, but Napoleon was aware of the error before d'Enghien's execution. Boulay de la Meurthe, *Les dernières années du duc d'Enghien*, 203-20.

was an old man with an amiable philosophy of life, and a rooted disinclination to navigate rough waters. He had corresponded with the elder Mirabeau upon economics, and even carried out in his own margraviate an interesting experiment in physiocratic finance. The historians of Baden wax eloquent when they describe the beneficent intentions and the enlightened rule of Charles Frederick, whose chief aim had been to exemplify in his own government and person the ideas of the reigning French philosophy. He was now, after taking part in the wars against the French Revolution, at peace with the Consulate, and no act of subservience to Napoleon was too abject for him or his timid ministers [1].

All that the French demanded was granted. No sooner was Talleyrand's letter received than a decree was issued banishing all French emigrants from the territory of Baden. 'This document,' says a Dutch diplomat who then happened to be in Paris, 'closed the mouths of the defenders of the Elector.' The only reproach the government of Charles Frederick dared to make was confined to a statement in the preamble of the decree, to the effect that the arrests had been carried out unexpectedly and without its knowledge. In the *Moniteur* the text of the decree was altered, so that the Elector might appear to be a consenting party to the raid. The minister of Baden in Paris, the Baron von Dalberg, attempted to redress the error, but no journalist was bold enough to contradict the organ of Napoleon. Nor did the Baron inform his Court officially of the raid till March 20, and then in language which suggested a source of embarrassment rather than a crying scandal. The Court of Karlsruhe, instead of protesting bravely, apologized with baseness, and Talleyrand, mingling mendacity with arrogance, told Dalberg that the raid had been undertaken 'to save the Elector from embarrassment,' and complained of the 'incredible things' which were said at Karlsruhe. So terrified was Charles Frederick at the wrath of the French that he 'highly disapproved' of the 'licence' with which his

---

[1] Drais, *Geschichte der Regierung und Bildung von Baden unter Carl Friedrich*; the biographies of Kleinschmidt, Nebenius, and Vierordt; *Carl Friedrich's brieflicher Verkehr mit Mirabeau,* edited for the 'Badische Historische Commission' in 1892.

subjects treated the theme. When the King of Sweden, Gustavus IV, who was the son-in-law of the Elector, and at that time living at Karlsruhe, openly expressed his abhorrence, certain persons of the Court came to the French agent, and prayed him to convey to the First Consul that 'the sojourn of the King of Sweden at Karlsruhe was in many respects a burden to his Electoral Serenity.' The Emperor of Russia, who was chivalrous, powerful, and distant, lodged an energetic protest (May 6) with the Diet of Ratisbon against the violation of the territory of Baden. But the Elector of Baden, instead of hailing such a pronouncement with joy, was struck dumb with terror. He thanked Russia for her excellent intentions, but at the same time supplicated the Diet, in terms prescribed by Talleyrand himself, to drop the subject in the interests of European peace. He had received, so ran the memoir, 'sufficiently tranquillizing information.' 'The knife was at our throat,' wrote Dalberg, who drafted these hollow words; 'how could we refuse what they required of us?' As Napoleon remarked, 'It was for the sovereign of Baden alone to complain, and he has not done so.' The First Consul also freely said that the sovereign of Baden had been warned, and that the arrests had his consent.

The other German powers emulated though they could not surpass the fulsome acquiescence of Baden. Berlin society was indignant, but the cowardly government did not dare to protest. Austria was not in a position to fight, for her finances and army were alike disorganized, and the Archduke Charles was in favour of peace. She refrained from influencing the German Diet, declined to notice the protest of Louis XVIII, and expelled the French *émigrés* from Swabia and the Breisgau. 'If you are not pleased with my ministers,' said Francis to Champagny, 'let me know, and I will dismiss them.' But, nevertheless, behind this loudly advertised complaisance, the House of Hapsburg was reforming her relations with England and Russia [1].

If such was the conduct of the great powers, what could be expected of the small ones? It was not for them to uphold the dignity of the Reich when Baden acquiesced and Prussia and Austria thought well to be silent. An incident shortly revealed

[1] Erdmannsdörffer, v. 1-124.

in the clearest light the subservience of Germany. The English envoys who happened at this time to be accredited respectively to the Courts of Munich, Stuttgart, and Hesse-Cassel, were Francis Drake, Spencer-Smith, and Brook Taylor. These three gentlemen were not only using their positions to procure information as to the internal condition of France, and the plans of Bonaparte—which would have been legitimate—but were also actively engaged in intrigues with royalist conspirators. There is no evidence that any one of them had knowledge of an assassination plot; indeed, Drake expressly denied having had such knowledge. But they wished to promote active disaffection, especially in the army, against the person and government of the First Consul, and Drake's instructions, as given in the *Moniteur*, are scarcely creditable to his employers.

Napoleon was aware of these foolish and culpable proceedings. The British ministers at the Courts of Munich and Stuttgart had allowed themselves to be involved in a compromising correspondence with the agents of the French police; and the notorious Mehée, his imagination quickened by the careful promptings of the First Consul himself, extracted from Drake some written indiscretions, which, together with the secret instructions of the British government, were printed in the *Moniteur* on March 25. A long report from the pen of the Grand-Judge Régnier accompanied these documents, and held up the British government to execration. It was represented that the true object of Drake's mission to Munich was to 'recruit agents of intrigue, of revolt, of assassination, to make a war of brigandage and murder against the French government, and to injure the neutrality and dignity of the government to which he was accredited,' and a copy of the Drake correspondence was addressed to every member of the diplomatic corps, accompanied by a note upon the profanation of the sacred character of ambassador [1].

The Duc d'Enghien had not lain in his grave for a week when Napoleon made this solemn appeal to the law of nations. But though it demanded little intelligence to perceive, it would have argued some degree of courage to indicate the irony of the

---

[1] For Napoleon's instructions to Mehée, see *Corr.* ix. 73, no. 7,240; 216, no. 7,497; 291, no. 7,620; *Moniteur*, March 25, 1804.

THE CONSPIRACY AND THE RAIDS

situation. It is not therefore surprising that the imperial manifesto was met by exaggerated assurances of horror from the timorous Courts of Germany. The Bavarian minister had no words too strong to condemn 'the disgraceful and criminal proceedings of Mr. Drake.' Count Beust, the envoy of the Elector of Ratisbon, professed 'profound indignation,' while Abel, the agent of the free towns, spoke of the plot as having been principally directed against the person of the First Consul, 'whom all the inhabitants of the free towns of the Empire regard as the generous protector who has saved their independence, and for whom they are penetrated with the highest veneration and the most perfect attachment[1].'

Meanwhile Napoleon had ordered Talleyrand to demand the immediate expulsion of Drake from Munich, the seizure of his papers by the Elector, and the arrest of the Bishop of Chalons, and of two other royalist conspirators who had been mentioned in the Drake correspondence. Three months before, the Elector had informed the British minister that no one abhorred Jacobinism or the conduct of the French more than he did, but a cloud in the sky was not more unstable than the will of this timid sovereign. Without even awaiting explanations from England, Baron von Montgelas, the Bavarian Prime Minister, was commanded to tell Drake that the Elector could neither communicate with him nor receive him in his palace, and that his mission was terminated. On these tidings, the British minister, fearing that he might be involved in the fate of the Duc d'Enghien, made an abrupt and somewhat ignominious flight, attributed by the *Moniteur*, which adds several fanciful details, to the 'disorder of his conscience communicating itself to his mind[2].'

Soon afterwards, on April 11, a second report was published by Régnier, in which the First Consul was solemnly informed that Drake was not the only English agent implicated in vile

[1] *Moniteur*, March 28, 1804.
[2] Drake's correspondence, *F. O. Bavaria*, 26, 27; *Annual Register*, 1804, 220 ff. and 283 ff.; Montgelas, *Denkwürdigkeiten*, 87, 88; *Moniteur*, April 11, 1804. The methods of Drake were objectionable, though sanctioned by usage. He suborned two clerks in the office of the Bavarian Prime Minister to betray secrets. Drake to Hawkesbury, April 14, 1803. *F. O. Bavaria*, 26.

intrigue. Mr. Spencer-Smith, who was accredited to the Court of Würtemberg, was declared to be guilty of similar misdemeanours. Not a single letter of Spencer-Smith's was included among the papers annexed to the report, but the lacuna was filled by the narrative of a certain Captain Rosey, who, acting under instructions from Mehée de la Touche, and representing himself to be a royalist emigrant, had obtained some oral and written communications with the British agent. The Court of Würtemberg, alarmed by the fulminations of the *Moniteur*, at once ordered the recall of Spencer-Smith, but the English envoy, anticipating his fate, had left Stuttgart a week before the *dénouement*. Indeed, his position in that city had long been intolerable. The government of the Duchy had actually decreed that all French travellers and all strangers not invested with any public character, civil or military, or travelling without passports, should be brought before M. Didelot, the representative of France, upon their first entry into the capital. From the moment of his arrival the British envoy was shadowed as if he were a murderer or an anarchist. 'I had generally,' he wrote home, 'two or three police-sergeants in sight from my windows, and not infrequently the French secretaries of legation (of whom there were three or four attached to the mission of Stuttgart) relieving one another like regular patrols, particularly when a carriage was at the door. I could not send a person out on an errand who was not dogged out and at home, nor walk about myself without eternally meeting the same inquisitive faces.' It is little wonder that under the circumstances Mr. Smith kept a pistol handy, for as he explained to Captain Rosey, the Elector of Würtemberg would give him up without a word of warning, if Bonaparte should demand his arrest[1].

There remained Mr. Brook Taylor, the somewhat guileless representative of British interests at the Court of Hesse-Cassel. On July 30, 1803, Taylor wrote to Lord Hawkesbury enclosing

---

[1] Spencer-Smith to Hawkesbury, June 3, 1802, *F. O. Würtemberg*, 3; *Moniteur*, April 13, 1804, piece ii; *Annual Register*, 1804, 285. Smith, on his return to London, gave an account of his conversations with Rosey which is at variance with that given in the *Moniteur*. The reader should compare the *Annual Register*.

communications from a body which styled itself the General Council of the Cisrhenane Confederation. There was a letter to George III, a letter to the British Cabinet, and a table of the 'effective strength' of the Confederation on July 15, 1803. According to the story of the conspirators, the Confederacy had been formed in the later part of 1800, with a view of freeing Belgium and the Rhenish provinces from the intolerable oppressions of the French. A general rising had been concerted for the night of February 1–2, 1801, but the plan fell through, and before a blow could be struck the Peace of Lunéville dashed the hopes of 120,000 men. Now, however, the renewal of the war had revived the activities of the plot. In the matter of men the Confederacy was stronger than ever, for it numbered over 172,000 scattered through the eastern *arrondissements* from the Vosges to the Channel. But in money it was weak. To be precise, a sum of £20,000 was urgently required of the British government. With a viaticum so modest the leaders had little doubt of success. Ten days after the rising 300,000 Rhinelanders would join the standard, not to speak of the Unistes, a widely ramified and powerful secret society in France, with which they had already entered into relations. Such a force would make but short work of the 8,000 men who garrisoned the conquered provinces, and when success had been achieved, it was intimated that the conspirators, respectable men and mightily adverse to republics, would establish a Cisrhenane monarchy, placing the crown upon the head of the 'Prince of York,' whose 'sublime qualities' had already made an ineffaceable impression on their hearts [1].

Further research may perhaps be able to determine the exact significance of these wild proposals. Was it merely the clumsy attempt of a knot of needy Germans to replenish their purses? Was it a subtle concoction of the French police? Or was there a basis of truth in the story of this gigantic conspiracy hatched by the malcontents of Belgium and the Rhine provinces? Two facts, however, are certain. The British government declined to have anything to do with the chiefs of the Cisrhenane Confederation, and somehow or other the Taylor correspondence found its way into the pigeon-holes of the French ministry of

[1] The *Conseil-Général* to George III. *F. O. German States*, 12.

police¹. It was not until May 8, 1804, that the First Consul determined to utilize his information. 'See,' he wrote to Régnier, 'that all the documents relative to Mr. Taylor and the insurrection which he wished to cause in the four departments of the Rhine, be sent to you at once and put in order, so as to get this minister driven out of Hesse-Cassel².' Yet the documents were not published till November 18, and then they were not printed in their entirety, for the long list of the conspiring communes was omitted. Was it that Napoleon was contemplating a voyage to the land of 172,916 bogus members of a bogus Cisrhenane Confederacy? And did he reflect that it would be unwise to publish aspersions upon the loyalty of provinces recently annexed to France, through which he was proposing to make a triumphal tour? But however this might be, Brook Taylor was driven from Cassel.

Meanwhile a great event had occurred in France, for on May 18, 1804, the Senate adopted a new constitution which transformed the Consulate into the Empire. It was a change not only of internal structure, though in this respect it was of the greatest moment, discarding, as it did, the last forms of republicanism; but it also marked a new step in the development of Napoleon's European ambitions. They were now indeed patent to all men. 'The *arrière-pensée* of the man,' wrote Dalberg, the minister of Baden at Paris (April 27, 1804), 'is the domination of the world, and his mind is struck with the idea that destiny calls him to the rôle of Alexander and Charlemagne³.' But it was a needless refinement to speak of *arrière-pensées*. 'If I am forced to make a continental war,' observed the new-made Emperor to his marshals, 'I will change the face of Europe⁴.'

Upon the acceptance of the Empire there followed a tour of inspection and triumph through the Rhenish provinces, the object of which was alike military and political. The new Emperor, who was aware that Germany might once more

---

[1] Taylor to Hammond, Dec. 28, 1803, *F. O. German States*, 12: 'I have informed the chiefs of the Cisrhenane Confederation that H. M.'s government has come to the determination not to encourage any insurrection under the present circumstances in France.'

[2] *Corr.* ix. 354, no. 7,739.

[3] Erdmannsdörffer, v. 56, 126.   [4] Id. v. 114.

THE CONSPIRACY AND THE RAIDS 81

become the battle-field of Europe, was anxious to strengthen his frontier on the German side, and to prepare a rapid mobilization. It was well also that he should be reassured of the pliancy of the German princes of the south; that he should learn from their own lips, if possible, and if not, from the lips of their ministers, the amount of assistance that they would be able to afford in the case of a war with Austria; in a word, that he should lay the foundations of a German Confederacy under French protection. At Aix-la-Chapelle he received an envoy from the Court of Vienna, sent to recognize formally his assumption of the imperial crown. The head of the Holy Roman Empire, Francis II, had already (August 11, 1804) taken the new title of Emperor of Austria, but there was nevertheless a small but studied humiliation conveyed in the choice of the capital of Charlemagne as the place in which the successor of the Carlovingians should recognize the usurper's title. From Aix-la-Chapelle Napoleon proceeded to Mainz, where it had been arranged that he should meet a great assemblage of subservient Germans.

The famous city of Mainz still bore the scars of war. One whole quarter was in ruins, and others presented a sad spectacle. But while the evils of war are temporary and may be remedied, the city was suffering a more durable hardship in the shape of the French customs regulations. The Mayençais had the mortification of knowing that in Germany articles of luxury could be purchased at two-thirds of the price which they were compelled to pay for them on the left or French bank of the river. They complained that their commerce was ruined and their trade destroyed, and they hoped that the visit of the French Emperor would put a term to their misfortunes. Bonaparte held colloquies with the merchants while an anxious or curious crowd collected round his house, but he was not come upon a commercial errand[1]. His first care was to inspect the fortifications of a city which would clearly play an important part in any German campaign, and for two days he spent eight hours on horseback, surveying bridges, walls, and cannon. His next object was to sound the loyalty and to ascertain the views of his German *clientèle*. The assemblage was not indeed

[1] Erdmannsdörffer, v. 134.

all that he had intended. On one excuse or another the Electors of Hesse, of Würtemberg, and of Bavaria, as well as the Landgrave of Hesse-Darmstadt, absented themselves from the meeting, and sent their agents instead to convey compliments to the French Emperor. But there were two persons whose presence it was peculiarly necessary for Napoleon to secure, and these two persons came. The first of these was the old Elector of Baden, whose territory had been violated by the capture of the Duc d'Enghien, and the second was Freiherr Karl Theodor Anton Maria von Dalberg, Arch-chancellor of the Empire and Archbishop of Ratisbon, who had been evicted from the See of Mainz in consequence of the French annexations. Of all German princes these two had most reason to complain of Napoleon, and their attendance at Mainz would most signally demonstrate the Emperor's influence. There was no difficulty in securing Charles Frederick: he had been effectually cowed by Talleyrand's hectoring diplomacy, and, as one of his ministers remarked, 'the guns of Strasburg commanded the policy of Baden.' But the Arch-chancellor made a feint of resistance. It would be, he represented, extremely painful to him to come to Mainz, a city associated with his ancient glory. Might he not pay his respects at some other place on Napoleon's route? The Emperor, however, was inexorable. To Mainz he must come, and to Mainz he came[1].

It is worth while to dwell for a moment upon the singular character and career of Karl von Dalberg. His birth made him the peer of the most noble and ancient families of Germany. In the twelfth century a Dalberg had been Archbishop of Cologne; a Johann von Dalberg, Bishop of Worms, had been a famous patron of letters in the fifteenth century, and was the recipient of many dedications from German Humanists. But it was at the imperial coronations that the pride of the Dalberg family was most conspicuously exhibited. At this high festival, attended by all the princes and nobles of Germany, the herald would at a given moment cry out three times, 'Is no Dalberg there?' And if a Dalberg were present he stepped out of the throng fully armed and accoutred, the first of all the chivalry

[1] Erdmannsdörffer, v. 129, 131, 133; *Corr.* x. 1, 2, nos. 8,066-8; *Moniteur*, 1804.

THE CONSPIRACY AND THE RAIDS 83

of the Empire to receive the honour of knighthood from his newly elected sovereign. The traditions of old imperial and ecclesiastical Germany, destined so soon to pass away, seem to be specially embodied in this Rhenish house which had given a president to the imperial Chamber of Wetzlar, a prince-abbot to Fulda, archbishops to Mainz and to Cologne, and a long series of chamberlains and councillors to the prince-bishops of the Rhine. Yet there was nobody in Germany whose temper was less mediaeval than Karl von Dalberg. Though from the age of ten onwards he had held posts connected with the Church, his mind was singularly liberal and free from prejudice. His education had been broken and somewhat desultory, a combination of law, theology, and painting against a background of travel, fortified by excellent introductions. But his intelligence was quick, his sympathies open, his affections warm. He entered public life at a happy moment, after the last fiery spurts of the Seven Years' War, when even prince-bishops began to think of setting their houses in order after the model of the great and victorious Frederick of Prussia. His master, Emmanuel Joseph, Archbishop of Mainz, was a man cast in the new mould of despotic philanthropy, and Dalberg proved as apt and zealous a pupil, as high birth combined with a sentimental and dilettante temperament would permit. In 1772, when twenty-eight years of age, he was made Statthalter at Erfurt, a position which gave him the opportunities of a proconsul. His rule was mild, tolerant, and beneficent. He abolished torture, started a chemical laboratory, stimulated useful economic inquiries, and organized the wits and savants of his Saxon proconsulate into an Academy. The praise of this amiable young person was on all men's lips. Goethe sent him the manuscript of his *Farbenlehre*, and treated the Dalbergian comments with respect. Twenty years after he had quitted Thuringia the natives would speak of the 'Coadjutor's time' with gratitude and regret. Schiller received subsidies from the Dalbergian purse, as well as an indifferent picture from the Dalbergian brush on the occasion of his wedding. Wieland prized his warm and respectful letters. Young Wilhelm von Humboldt thought him charming, and lauded the elevation of his views and the excellence of his character. He governed his people, shot his pheasants, flirted platonically with his female friends, gave charming dinners, read papers innumerable to his Academy, lectured on the principles of aesthetics, and published *Contemplations on the Universal*. There was no subject, from a kitchen stove to a scheme of penal law, upon which he was not prepared to dash off some well-intentioned, high-sounding, and ill-considered effusion. He was one of those expansive and prosperous persons who are blind to differences and dividing lines, and have not the grit to think unpleasantly. When the news came to Erfurt that Louis XVI had been brought back from Varennes, he walked out on to the balcony with a lady friend, Karoline von Beulwitz, and, looking up at the moon and stars, said in full round tones, 'What are the events of this little Earth in comparison with the immeasurable Heaven? A king and a queen fleeing their realm, what is that beside the world above us?' Men with such powers of spacious self-consolation easily adapt themselves to circumstance, and often fall into moral disaster unconsciously, while bestowing upon their own dubious actions the most handsome epithets. Dalberg posed as a high-priest of Nature and humanity, but a political rôle was forced upon him. A conflict of allegiances at once arose, calculated to perplex an honest judgement prepared to face facts. The Elector of Mainz belonged to the Fürstenbund, and the object of the Fürstenbund was to thwart the plans of Joseph II of Austria. Dalberg was an imperialist if he was anything; he heartily admired Joseph as a statesman and revered him as the head of the Empire. But, on the other hand, he was made Coadjutor of Mainz in 1787 by Prussian influence, and as coadjutor he was member of the Bund. A strong man would have gone into the whole situation, and then taken his side. He would have argued either that the increase of Austrian power in Germany was good or that it was bad; either that Prussia represented the true course of German development or that she did not. But Dalberg did neither the one thing nor the other. In a series of vague and verbose epistles he tried to represent to his imperial friend that the Fürstenbund, so far from being aimed against the Hapsburgs, was in reality but a step towards the unification of Germany under their control, and salved his conscience with many pious aspirations to that desirable end. We are inclined to think that he may have deceived himself. But if so, he must have been the only dupe.

The French Revolution found him still vague, benevolent, and patriotic. As a priest and a German he deplored, as a man of letters and an optimist he was inclined to palliate, the effervescent actions of the conquerors. Meanwhile a rich crop of ecclesiastical pluralities came to ripeness for him, the Bishopric of Constance in 1800, the Archbishopric of Mainz in 1802. No more golden harvest was offered to the advancing scythe of secularization, and Dalberg was compelled to take precautions. Already in 1797 the Court of Mainz had made up its mind to accept the principle of secularization, and to drive the best bargain which the circumstances might permit. At Rastadt its representative, Baron Albini, pleaded that though bishoprics and abbeys might be thrown to the hungry, the Electorate at least should be spared. But the question was not settled then, and five years succeeded, ominous with menace. It was clear to Dalberg that he could hope for little support from Austria or Prussia, for in his efforts to please both powers he had earned the gratitude of neither. So he turned to the rising sun, and sent Count Beust to Paris to save as much as might be of his spiritual dignity. The step was successful, and amid the plentiful mowings of 1803 he was left, not indeed uninjured, but still erect, and sole survivor of the race of ecclesiastical Electors. The dioceses of Ratisbon and Mainz, of Trèves and Cologne, or rather those parts of them which lay west of the Rhine, were placed under his spiritual supervision, and a small secular State with Ratisbon for capital was constructed to maintain his temporal dignity [1]. Such was the man who was now to serve as an apt instrument in Napoleon's unsparing hand.

The meeting of so many princes, princesses, and ambassadors excited the liveliest curiosity in the Courts of Europe. That there was some political design behind these sumptuous festivities was obvious, but it was not clear what that design precisely was. Lucchesini, who was Prussian ambassador in Paris, told his master (November 26, 1804) that the Emperor and the

[1] Beaulieu-Marçonnay, *Karl von Dalberg und seine Zeit.*

Arch-chancellor were discussing the plan of a union between the Electoral Courts, adding that so inordinate was the Emperor's ambition that he might some day wear the imperial crown in Germany. In a later letter (December 21) further details were added. The plan of a German federation under French protection was mooted by Dalberg, and warmly supported by Hesse-Cassel, in the presence of Bonaparte himself. Electoral Saxony and Baden had not concurred, and the Bavarian envoy told Lucchesini that his own Court was ignorant of any such plan. It was represented that the French Empire, having secured its natural limits on the side of Germany by the Rhine frontier, had no interest in further aggrandizement; that the Court of France was consequently 'the natural friend and impartial protector' of the German Empire against the Courts of Vienna and Berlin, who would naturally seek to enlarge their boundaries at the expense of the smaller princes. According to another account, Napoleon spoke very strongly against Russian influence in the Reich, and advocated the necessity of a third power under French protection, which could hold Prussia and Austria in check, thrusting aside the objections of the Arch-chancellor with 'Good! if the princes do not desire my protection, I will give their lands to the man who shall aid my plans.' Another report says that he urged Dalberg to appoint a coadjutor, and thus settle the succession to his important post. 'It will never do,' he said, 'for an Austrian prince to get the place; that house can never be given the head and tail of German affairs, the initiative and the ratification[1].'

Nothing, however, was decided. It was enough for the Emperor to have supervised the fortifications of the town, to have received the homage of the princes and envoys of Germany, and to have thrown into the timid minds of his audience the seeds of so vast a political idea as the Confederation of the Rhine.

Some scraps of Bonaparte's talk have been preserved. He

---

[1] Rechberg's despatch of October 15, 1804, quoted by Sicherer, *Staat und Kirche in Bayern*, 108–9. For the schemes and conversations at Mainz and Paris, Bailleu, *Preussen und Frankreich*, and Erdmannsdörffer's collection of the Baden correspondence have been utilized.

asked the envoy of the Elector of Würtemberg whether the intestine war between the father and son would soon finish, and said that a term must be put to it. The agent of Bavaria was questioned as to the disposition of the troops in Munich. Were they in camps or in cantonments? It was remarked that although Bonaparte did not return the visit of the Electors, he yet specially singled them out for distinction, and the tempting prospect of the Breisgau was hung out before the Princes of Baden.

Some of the acolytes of Mainz reappeared in Paris later on in the year, for the ceremony of the imperial coronation by the Pope. The Elector of Baden, whose government coveted the Austrian possessions in Alsace, sent his son and his grandson to offer the 'homage of his profound veneration on the important occasion,' and the Arch-chancellor and the Hereditary Prince of Hesse-Darmstadt also attended to pay their homage. Never was Dalberg more serene or self-important. At a dinner-party, at which the Pope was present, the Emperor declared that he would not admit the pretensions of the cardinals to rank above the German Electors, saying, 'I treat you as a sovereign and brother; the cardinals are my cousins.' When the conversation turned on the ecclesiastical reconstruction of Germany, his Imperial Majesty said that the proposed plan for a German Concordat, a scheme much favoured by Dalberg, had a 'particular interest' for him, and even used threats to the cardinals who were throwing obstructions in its way. 'How do you dare,' he asked, 'to refuse longer when it depends upon me to make you canons of Rome, and the Pope a bishop?' And indeed it was to the interest of France that the Pope should sanction the changes resulting from the political rearrangements of 1803.

In the intervals of the festivities all kinds of political schemes were broached. Hints were thrown out that a new Congress might meet in some German town, such as Ratisbon, to settle the Concordat, to reorganize the Circles, and to arrange disputes as to the debts of the princes who had received compensations in 1803. His Majesty, receiving the Electoral Prince of Baden in the most obliging manner, let drop in conversation that his territory (which was in the direst financial straits) might well maintain ten thousand troops. Margrave Louis of Baden was told that it had been a mistake to leave the Breisgau in the hands of Austria. 'We cannot,' said Napoleon, 'tolerate it any longer.' The Hessian plan of an Electoral union leaked out and became matter for open discussion. Dalberg formally proposed to the Count von Bunau, the Saxon minister at Paris, that his Court should join the union, but the French Ministry of Foreign Affairs professed the most complete indifference, and denied all knowledge of plans for changing the Germanic Constitution. The Foreign Office was even for the time inaccessible to the solicitations of German princes. It was clearly the Emperor's object to profess the utmost loyalty to the existing constitution of the Reich, while stimulating the princes to the discussion of subversive schemes. In the approaching struggle with Austria he would raise the banner of the Holy Roman Empire, and when victory had been secured, the Germans themselves should help him to destroy it.

The amenities of the coronation were hardly concluded when Germany was startled by a fresh and unexpected outrage.

The free town of Hamburg had already suffered from the invasion of Hanover. It had been compelled to advance a loan to the French at the mouth of the pistol; but it was now to experience an insult, no less direct than that inflicted on the Grand Duchy of Baden by the seizure of the Duc d'Enghien. 'Immediately after the Drake affair,' wrote Bonaparte to Fouché, October 7, 1804, 'Lord Hawkesbury had the imbecility to issue a circular to justify the conduct of that minister before the cabinets of Europe. In order to expose the absurdity and atrocity of the principles he then advanced, my intention was to send to the same cabinets the circular with an answer[1]. I have thought better of it since. I wish the English minister

[1] *Corr.* x. 17, no. 8,100. Lord Hawkesbury's circular note (April 30, 1804), after disclaiming 'the unfounded and atrocious calumny' that his government were 'parties to any project of assassination,' proceeds to lay down the principle that 'a minister in a foreign country is bound by the nature of his office . . . to abstain from all communication with the disaffected in the country to which he is accredited . . . but he is not subject to the same restraints with respect to those countries with which his sovereign is at war' (*Annual Register*, 1804, 215–17).

THE CONSPIRACY AND THE RAIDS 89

at Hamburg to be carried off, together with his papers, and immediately afterwards I will cause this abduction to be notified to the Courts of Europe, justifying it by Lord Hawkesbury's note. They assure me he is lodged near the river. It will be easy for General Bernadotte to get him carried off. Write to him in this sense and consult M. Lachevardière, who is, I believe, in Paris, and who ought to know this minister's house. Two boats, full of infantry, and twelve or fifteen disguised gendarmes would suffice for this expedition. We should find some interesting lights in this correspondence.'

Sir George Berriman Rumbold, the British agent at Hamburg, against whom Bonaparte was plotting this design, was a robust Gallophobe. His correspondence shows him to have been an honourable man, but not a very discreet one. He hated the French, expected other powers to do the same, and was, perhaps, too ready with the epithets 'pliant' and 'pusillanimous,' when describing in an official despatch the conduct of a friendly power. As Hamburg was naturally friendly to England, Rumbold was the centre of a large and active Gallophobe colony. He seems to have been in regular correspondence with many of the foremost *émigrés* at that time residing in Germany, and it was his function not only to represent British interests in the most important of the free cities of the north, but also to transmit intelligence to his government and to encourage resistance to French aggression. But not a particle of evidence can be found in the correspondence now lying in the National Archives of Paris to implicate either Sir George Rumbold or Lord Hawkesbury in any plot against the life of the First Consul [1]. There are, in fact, in this litter of washing bills and tailors' bills and draft despatches to the Secretary of State no 'lights' which would have seemed 'interesting' to Napoleon or his police.

Bernadotte threw himself with zeal into the congenial task

---

[1] *Archives Nationales*, F^7. 6,448-50, and *F. O., Hamburg*, 25. 'I have never received commands from your Lordship to engage in operations of a confidential or secret nature. I have therefore confined myself to endeavours to obtain information of what our enemies were preferring against us.'—Rumbold to Hawkesbury, April 20, 1804.

of capturing a British envoy in a neutral town. No sooner had he received Fouché's letter than he sent the chief of his staff, General Berthier, to inspect the fortifications of Hamburg. That officer reported that the town gates were shut every evening at seven, and that on no pretext were they opened before 6 a.m. at the earliest. The keys of the gates were during the night deposited in the Senate-house, troops guarded all the issues day and night, and sentinels were posted on the ramparts. On the river-side the town was defended by great chains and two bodies of watchmen. It would be quite impossible to carry off Rumbold with any secrecy if he happened to be in the town. 'In that case,' wrote Bernadotte, 'your Majesty will perhaps judge that a man who has put himself outside all laws ought to be seized wherever he may be, and that if we have no other means of carrying him off, I ought to march a battalion or more by night from the fortress of Lauenburg so as to be at Hamburg when the gates open. I shall take care to send the day before some men in disguise, who will surround the house of Rumbold at break of day and enter to secure his person. These men will then resume their uniforms and execute the orders they have received. The general officer commanding the troops at the gate will give a solemn assurance to the Senate that we have only come to seize a chief of assassins who wishes to plunge our country into mourning. He will also declare to the Senate that its conduct in this matter will determine the good or evil dispositions of France towards it[1].'

It did not, however, come to this. Adjutant-Commandant Maison, who was sent into Hamburg by Bernadotte, reported that the British minister was residing not in the town itself, but at Grindel, his country residence, a mile and a half off. This made all comparatively easy. The night of November 25 was fixed by Maison for the execution of the plot. General Frere, commanding the French troops at Hamburg, supplied a hundred men, and the detachment was disembarked punctually at midnight at Hamburgerburg, between Altona and Hamburg. The town was shut up, and there was nothing to fear. Two carriages were waiting at the bank. Maison jumped in with about

---

[1] *Archives Nationales*, A. F. iv. 1,594.

THE CONSPIRACY AND THE RAIDS 91

a dozen men and drove off rapidly to Rumbold's house, leaving the remainder to follow on foot. Placing a man to watch every door and window, Maison waited for Frere's detachment. He was certain that Rumbold was within, for at four o'clock on that very afternoon he had been found at home by Maison's young German brother-in-law, Weigott, who had been sent for the precise purpose of spying out the land. When it was clear that Frere could not be far off, Maison ordered a German named Steck (provided by Marshal Bernadotte) to knock at the door and to announce himself as a courier come from Tonningen with despatches. A servant called out, 'Hand the papers through the window.' Steck insisted that he must speak with Rumbold, but an entrance was denied him. Then Maison gave orders for the door to be forced. The French burst into the house and found Rumbold in bed. They ordered him to rise and dress, and seizing all the papers in the house, made their way back to the river. At 6 a.m. they were embarked with their prey. If the tide had not been contrary they could have started two hours earlier [1].

A coach strongly guarded conveyed the unfortunate British envoy to Hanover, and thence to Paris, where he was lodged in the Temple Prison, fearing not unnaturally that he might be called upon at any moment to meet the death of the Duc d'Enghien. But Napoleon had overstepped the limit. The British agent was accredited not only to the free town of Hamburg, but also to the Circle of Lower Saxony, of which the King of Prussia was Director. The whole of Germany was profoundly moved by so flagrant a violation of international right and courtesy. The Senate of Hamburg met at 7 a.m., and sent a deputation to the French minister to protest against the violation of their neutrality; the French minister denied having had any knowledge of the transaction. The Senate sent a circular letter to all the Courts informing them of the event. The King of Prussia energetically espoused the cause of the British agent, and demanded his release. 'I am compromised,' he wrote, 'and I am compromised in the most sensible manner,' alike as Director of the Lower Saxon Circle, as a friend of France, and as the protector of the neutrality of Northern Germany. The Emperor

[1] F. 6,448, no. 9,497, printed in *Revue Rétrospective*, June 1901.

was not prepared at this juncture to sacrifice the friendship of Prussia. Rumbold was released on November 11, but not before he gave his parole never to come within a distance of fifty leagues of the posts occupied by the French army so long as the war lasted. The *Moniteur*, commenting upon the event, remarked that if the case of this 'worthy *confrère* of Drake, of Spencer-Smith, and of Taylor,' had been brought to a termination, '*précis* quite as curious as those of his rivals would have offered themselves.' There was no one to contradict the assertion, and with this parting shot the disgraceful episode came to a close [1].

[1] *Gentleman's Magazine*, 1804 ; Bailleu, ii. 307 ff.; *Revue Rétrospective*, June 1901; *Moniteur*, November 11, 1804.

PRINCIPAL AUTHORITIES : Nougarède de Fayet, *Recherches historiques sur le procès et la condamnation du duc d'Enghien* ; Welschinger, *Le duc d'Enghien* ; Boulay de la Meurthe, *Les dernières années du duc d'Enghien* ; Erdmannsdörffer, *Karl Friedrich von Baden, Politische Korrespondenz* ; Correspondence of Drake, Spencer-Smith, Taylor, and Rumbold at the Record Office ; Rumbold's papers in the *Archives Nationales* ; Papers printed in the *Moniteur* and *Annual Register*.

CHAPTER V

THE CONFEDERATION OF THE RHINE

' Culbuter le corps d'Allemagne, c'est perdre l'avantage de la Belgique, de la limite du Rhin ; car c'est mettre dix ou douze millions d'habitans dans la main de deux puissances dont nous nous soucions également.'—
NAPOLEON, May 26, 1797.

THE war with Austria came in August 1805. Napoleon had foreseen it and had worked for it. In January he told his Council of State that it was to this end solely, and not for the purpose of invading England, that he had kept his army on a war footing for two years. The English descent was a mere pretext, but the camp of Boulogne would give him twenty days' start of his enemy [1]. It was a falsehood to say that the Boulogne flotilla was never seriously meant ; it was both seriously meant and anxiously contrived. But there was, nevertheless, an element of truth in Napoleon's statement. In two years of assiduous military preparation he had fashioned a splendid army, capable of giving effect to his will, of making and of maintaining new conquests for the Empire. He had harangued these men and inflamed them with the prospects of new laurels and new wealth, speaking to the generals of an ' Empire of Europe,' and indicating glorious destinies that might recall the times of Alexander. Germany, Italy, the Balkan peninsula, the ancient monarchy of Spain, were all weak and helpless, as he knew. Why should he not revive, nay extend the Empire of Charlemagne, or rather superadd to the rôle of Charlemagne, limited to that old Europe in which nothing was to be done, the more glorious and romantic rôle of the Macedonian? He was a man of many schemes, and he pursued them conjointly. As early as May 1804, he declared to the Italian chargé d'affaires that it was hardly suitable that he should continue to be Emperor, and at the same time President

[1] Miot de Melito, *Mémoires*, ii. 258 ; and cf. Metternich, *Mémoires*, i. 39.

of a Republic, and that the Consulta of Milan had better reflect upon the situation and submit its proposals. It was equivalent to an invitation that the Cisalpine Republic should be converted into a monarchy or annexed to France, prospects, as Napoleon knew, equally alarming to the Court of Vienna. Still the plan was persisted in, and in September Austria was informed that Joseph, the eldest of the Bonapartes, would be invited to assume the crown of Italy. But it was necessary to keep within the four corners of the Treaty of Lunéville, and the Hapsburgs were assured that the Italian kingdom would be entirely separate from the French Empire, and that Joseph, in the event of his accepting the proffered monarchy, should renounce his right of succeeding to the throne of France. Immediately after the coronation in December the discussions of the Italian plan were resumed, and the kingdom, offered successively to Joseph and Louis, was finally taken by Napoleon himself. How could Austria be expected to acquiesce in such an act? She was indeed assured that the arrangement was temporary, and that there was no intention of definitive incorporation. But she was condemned to watch the sumptuous progress of Napoleon through Lombardy, the solemn coronation at Milan, the upstart alien usurping those ancient forms with which the Emperors of the Holy Roman Empire had been wont to receive the iron crown. She saw in prospect the doom of Venetia and of Naples, and she combined in a coalition with England and with Russia. When, in February 1804, the English Parliament was asked for five and a half millions of secret service money, the situation was made clear to Napoleon. That money could only be required for a Russian or Austrian subsidy. He knew then that a war with Austria would come, and he felt that, when it did come, it would make him master of Germany and Italy. When and how depended on the waves and the weather. If he could once elude the British fleet, march to London, raise the *canaille* and dethrone George, he reckoned that Austria would be too wise to stir. If on the other hand there was hindrance in the Channel, then he would force on the war with Austria, conquer Central Europe, and defeat the sea by the land.

In this war he intended to have the South German princes on

THE CONFEDERATION OF THE RHINE 95

his side, and the success with which this intention was achieved is one of the momentous influences in German history, colouring the whole subsequent development of the south, and explaining movements apparently very distant, such as the curious constitutional agitations which shook the Swabian mind in the second and third decades of the nineteenth century. Of these South German alliances the most important was the Bavarian, not only because Bavaria was the largest and most concentrated principality in the south, but also for its military tradition and proximity to Austria; and as early as July 1804 Napoleon mooted the idea of a marriage alliance between some member of his house and the reigning family at Munich. By November 8 the scheme had solidified into a secret negotiation, and the most stringent pressure was being applied to the Bavarians. 'A refusal and even marks of repugnance,' wrote Talleyrand to Otto, the French minister at Munich, 'is the thing in the world most impossible to palliate or repair.' How, it was intimated, could the Elector decline an alliance with the 'first Empire in Europe' and the 'first sovereign in the world'? Nevertheless the affair was allowed to drag, until in March 1805 Otto received instructions to propose to the government of Munich an offensive and defensive alliance with France.

This decision, felt at once by all to be tragic and momentous, was forced upon a dismayed and divided Court. The Elector, Maximilian Joseph of Zweibrück, an amiable but nerveless prince, had before the Revolution served as the colonel of a French regiment. He considered France as his adopted country, he admired Napoleon, he believed that the French alliance might bring him aggrandizement and prestige, he remembered the ancient enmities of Austria, and her present support of the Imperial Knights—a tooth gnawing at his dominion. His Prime Minister, Montgelas, a Savoyard penetrated by French influence, was carrying out in Bavaria the same work of enlightened centralization which had been accomplished in France by the Revolution and the Consulate. But the Electress was sister of the Empress of Russia and the Queen of Sweden. She hated the Revolution, and she hated Napoleon, and threw the fires of her passionate and ardent temperament into the whirl of politics. Primed by the ministers of Russia and Sweden, Caroline boldly pressed their views upon her weak and distracted husband. She proposed that Montgelas should be dismissed, and that a close alliance should be formed with the Court of Vienna.

By August 1805 Napoleon had made up his mind as to the particulars of the alliance which the unfortunate Elector was to be compelled to accept. The Emperor's stepson, Prince Eugene, was to marry Augusta, the eldest daughter of the Elector, and Bavaria was to be bound to France by an offensive and defensive alliance. It was no obstacle to Napoleon that the Bavarian princess was already betrothed to the Prince of Baden, and that both families were anxious to carry out the arrangement. With prompt decision Napoleon swept away the pleas and protests, and forced the aged Charles Frederick to renounce the marriage he had devised for his son. It was, however, a more difficult task decisively to compromise Maximilian Joseph, whose territories would be the first to suffer from an Austrian war. The Elector implored Napoleon to allow him to remain neutral, at least till the arrival of a French army, and then that the alliance should not be signed till the Austrians had violated his territory. 'In the name of God,' he cried to Otto, the French minister, 'do not fight against the whole world,' for it appeared to him that Prussia too would certainly join in the fray. But Napoleon would permit no delay. The unlucky Prince was obliged to authorize his minister to sign a provisional treaty on August 24, but no sooner had he taken this step than his mind was beset with fresh doubts and terrors. On September 6 Austria summoned him to join forces with her army on pain of being treated as an enemy. The Prince wrote an autograph letter to Francis, imploring the Emperor to let him preserve the appearance of neutrality until his son, who was travelling in France, had returned. 'I am the most unfortunate of men,' he wrote to Otto, September 8; 'do not be angry. God knows that I am not false. . . . If you could have seen what I have suffered these two days you would have pity on me.'

Otto saw that the Elector was wavering. He came to the palace, told him that he must leave Munich immediately, and place himself under the protection of the advancing French army. The miserable man consented, and on the night of September 8-9 left his capital, and, accompanied by the *Corps diplomatique*, fled to Würzburg. Here the struggle of the powers for the body and soul of Maximilian Joseph began afresh. At one moment, stirred by the recollection of his predecessor, Charles VII, who had lost his dominions owing to a French alliance, he resolved to treat with the Austrians, now in possession of Munich, but Otto averted this danger by sending extraordinary couriers to Bernadotte and Marmont, whose divisions were rapidly advancing on the Main. The arrival of the French troops decided the day, and on October 12 the Elector ratified the provisional treaty. With signal duplicity Otto, acting on the authorization of Talleyrand, altered the date of the treaty from August 24 to September 23. 'From this most important change of date it becomes evident,' remarks Otto, 'that the Elector has only concluded an alliance after having been driven from his capital, and that his Majesty the Emperor only commences the war in order to restore his ally, and to avenge the injury which has been done to him[1].'

The old Elector of Baden had already been exposed to so many humiliations that the Treaty of Ettlingen, signed on September 2, 1805, can have surprised no one familiar with the Court of Karlsruhe. By this arrangement the House of Baden was bound to furnish 3,000 men to the Grand Army, and the same number was demanded from the Landgrave Louis of Hesse-Darmstadt. 'My intention,' wrote Napoleon to Talleyrand, 'is to comprise Darmstadt in my Germanic Confederation, composed of Bavaria, Darmstadt, Würtemberg, and Baden. In a word, I must have 3,000 men from Darmstadt or the Landgrave will renounce my protection for ever, and suddenly break off the expectation to which an alliance of 200 years entitles him.' Louis, who in his youth had frequented the society of freemasons, savants, and philosophers, had been one of the princes who had received most benefit from the territorial

---

[1] Talleyrand to Otto, Nov. 8, 1804. Otto to Talleyrand, Feb. 6, March 12, March 20, Aug. 12, Sept. 2, Oct. 9, 1805. *Affaires étrangères, Corr. Pol.: Bavière*, 180; Lang, *Memoiren*, ii. 117-20; Pelet de la Lozère, c. xi; *Souvenirs du Général Thiard*; Lefebvre, *Histoire des Cabinets de l'Europe*, ii. 122-6.

rearrangements of 1803. But for his political direction he looked to the Court of Berlin, and his hesitation to furnish a contingent, prolonged until the battle of Austerlitz, provoked a stinging rebuke from Napoleon [1].

No historian has ever had many good words to spare for Frederick II of Würtemberg. That he was able, prompt, and endowed with a certain spaciousness of vision may be conceded. But a ruffianly and suspicious temper made him intolerable alike as ruler, husband, and parent. It would have been possible to ridicule his preposterous obesity and inordinate self-importance if these defects had not been combined with cruelty and caprice, if he had not bullied his wife, maltreated his sons, and misgoverned his people. Having served as an officer in Prussia and Russia, he had seen the manners and customs of many men, and imbibed an enthusiasm for progressive despotism as a type of government. The ways of Old Würtemberg were to him alien and senseless, for he first set foot in the country in 1797, when he was thirty-six years of age, so that he was quite untroubled by sentimental considerations. He meant to make himself autocrat, to break the Chamber and its committees, to cow the nobles, to form a standing army, to encourage agriculture and the University, and to extract from the general situation of Europe as many square miles as possible for his duchy.

There had never been any real danger that a west wind would drive revolutionary fire from Paris across the pines of the Black Forest. The Swabian is a pleasant fellow, often dreamy and thoughtful, losing himself in cloudy abstractions or feeding upon the sober diet of memory, but rarely inflamed to violent action. The land of Hegel and Schelling and Schiller produced at this time some rhetorical journalists but no serious political movement. A few busy creatures talked and dreamt of an Alemannian Republic and of a union with the Swiss, but after the careful siftings of a vigilant police the number of dreamers reduced itself to six. The real obstacle which Frederick had to encounter was not the democratic aspirations of a

---

[1] *Corr.* xi. 272, no. 9,307; 539, no. 9,671; 544, no. 9,680; *Affaires étrangères, Corr. Pol.: Hesse-Darmstadt,* 3. M. Rambaud points out that Louis was the last German prince to abandon France in 1813 (*L'Allemagne napoléonienne,* 37–8).

THE CONFEDERATION OF THE RHINE 99

people, but the opposition of the Lutheran pastors and town magistrates who sat in the Chamber and served on its standing committees. These men were no democrats; they were Old Würtembergers, representing all the cherished prejudices of that ancient stronghold of southern Lutheranism. They were against a standing army, for Old Würtemberg had never had one; they were against new taxes, regarding indeed all taxation as exceptional, and only to be levied in times of utter need. Their tradition of diplomacy—a tradition sanctified by long usage among the small independent German towns—was to buy neutrality from the larger powers. When the Duke sent envoys to Rastadt or to Vienna or to Paris, they were confronted with the agents of the Estates, charged to promote a separate and generally an opposite policy. The inner Committee of the Estates kept a secret treasure of its own, and was in fact the real sovereign in the land. Yet, though Frederick was active and domineering, he did not dare, without external support, to overturn an ancient constitution which had been guaranteed as late as 1770 by Prussia, England, and Denmark.

Napoleon had watched Frederick from afar, and fathomed his aims. Though the Elector was fluent in the language of Voltaire, having received his early education at Lausanne, he was understood to detest France and all her works. His wife was English or rather Hanoverian, a daughter of George III; his nephew was Alexander of Russia; he had joined hands with Austria in the last war, and was even now in the summer of 1805 proposing to Bavaria, Baden, Hesse-Darmstadt, and Prussia, the formation of a system of armed neutrality, in order to exclude the troops of the belligerent powers from passing over their respective territories. Napoleon knew all this, and had taken his precautions. Two years earlier the Electoral Prince of Würtemberg had confided to the French legation at Stuttgart the story of the brutal ill-treatment which he had received from his father. 'I thought,' wrote Didelot, the French envoy, 'of the importance which it might be to us to have in the very bosom of the family of the Elector a man who should necessarily be devoted to our interests.' Considerations so obvious as these were not neglected. The young man was honourably received in Paris, and while the Emperor relieved his necessities by an ample loan, he may have reflected that if the worst came to the worst, an obnoxious parent in Stuttgart might be relieved of his duties by a grateful and subservient son[1].

It did not, however, come to this. On August 30, 1805, the Electoral Cabinet, assured that neutrality was out of the question, consented to the defensive and offensive alliance with France. 'I must,' wrote the Elector, August 29, 'take part either against France or for her,' and such being the nature of the alternative, Frederick's decision is no matter for surprise. He knew that Austria could not defend his territory from the French; he knew that the French could defend his territory from Austria. Yet he was reluctant to cast the die, and the terms of the treaty were still under discussion when the French troops crossed the border, and Ney, pointing his guns on Stuttgart, forced an entry into the Elector's capital[2].

On October 11 the news reached Frederick that Napoleon had crossed the Rhine. An aide de camp was immediately sent to invite the Emperor to Ludwigsburg, where the Court of Würtemberg was then assembled. At Pforzheim the guest was met by the High Chamberlain and the Chief Equerry, and as he proceeded further on his route by Prince Paul of Würtemberg. Bonfires blazed at set intervals along the high-road, and a salvo of a hundred guns saluted the entrance into Ludwigsburg. Though the night was well advanced—it was ten o'clock—the Court was assembled at the foot of the palace-stairs. A thousand lights coruscated 'Welcome,' and there was a cheerful rattle of guns to salute the master of the Legions. It was the first occasion on which the Emperor of the French had received hospitality from one of the old European dynasties.

He desired at once to be presented to the Electress, divining in this well-instructed and conscientious Hanoverian the bedrock of resistance. To her he spoke much of the excellent qualities of the English and of their admirable literature, and the woman was conquered. On the next day he addressed

---

[1] *Affaires étrangères, Corr. Pol.: Würtemberg,* 40 ; Alombert et Colin, *La Campagne de* 1805 *en Allemagne,* i. 66 ; Pfister, *König Friedrich von Württemberg und seine Zeit,* 1–159; Masson, *Napoléon et sa famille,* iii. 134; Treitschke, *Deutsche Geschichte,* ii. 297 ff. ; Spohr, *Autobiography* (Eng. tr.), 107–8.

[2] Häusser, ii. 578–9 ; Dumas, xiii. 341 ; *Corr.* xi. 273, no. 9,310.

himself to the cross-grained tyrant, an interview lasting four hours, from which the Elector emerged exhausted but enthusiastic, saying that he had never met such eloquence save in Frederick the Great, and that the two men had the same *tournure d'esprit*. It may be surmised that threats were mingled with cajolery. 'If I had resisted the Emperor,' said Frederick a few days later, 'my States would have been divided up, and my house would have had to live upon the pity of foreign Courts.' But there was certainly a copious supply of imperial blandishments, and a 'flattering picture,' to use the Elector's own phrase, was drawn of the benefits which would accrue to Würtemberg from the French alliance. One boon, conveyed in language of coarse but congenial brevity, was specially precious. As Frederick paraded the intractable opposition of his Estates, Napoleon told him to 'get rid of the beasts.' So on October 8 the treaty was signed, by which France promised to aggrandize Würtemberg, while Würtemberg promised in return to furnish ten thousand men for the coming war. And meanwhile it is clearly understood that the 'beasts' may be safely abolished. Subservience abroad, despotism at home, such is the true nature of the Würtemberg contract [1].

If Baden and Würtemberg expected to be treated with courtesy and consideration by the armies of their new ally, they were soon undeceived. The first town Napoleon entered in the territory of Baden was Kehl, opposite Strasburg. Despite the prayers of the inhabitants, he ordered most of the houses to be pulled down and the town to be fortified with all speed. At Rastadt there was an outcry against the licence and the requisitions of the French troops. 'What would you have?' said the Emperor to one who expostulated; 'the Frenchman is gay, especially when he marches to battle.' 'Greater violence,' said an official, 'was not even exercised in the year of misfortune 1799, and could not be practised by the most declared foe.' Complaints from all sides flowed in to Frederick

---

[1] *Affaires étrangères, Corr. Pol.*: *Würtemberg*, 39-41; C. G. de Wreede, *La Souabe après le traité de Bâle*; Häusser, *Deutsche Geschichte*, iii. 230; Schlossberger, *Politische und militärische Correspondenz Friedrichs von Würtemberg mit Napoleon I*; L. von Wolzogen, *Memoiren*; Eugen von Würtemberg, *Memoiren*; Lévy, *Napoléon et la Paix*, 326-41.

of the French pillaging in Würtemberg. 'Now our bailiffs,' said the Elector, 'or other civil servants are maltreated for having refused requisitions which their duty does not permit them to furnish. Now our subjects, after having shared their bread with the French troops, are not only pillaged and deprived of their clothes, linen, and cattle, but mishandled and even wounded.' Such was the practice of the great ally. It remains to consider the theory of the alliance [1].

Before his series of treaties had been completed, Napoleon had promulgated the official justification for the campaign. When the French army crossed the Rhine, October 1, a proclamation was issued in the following terms:—'Soldiers, the war of the Third Coalition has begun; the Austrian army has crossed the Inn, violated treaties, attacked our ally, and driven him from his capital. You yourselves have had to hurry with forced marches to the defence of our frontiers. We will not stop until we have secured the independence of the German Empire, succoured our allies, and confounded the pride of our foes [2].' To Frederick of Würtemberg he wrote, October 2: 'Your Highness can no longer conceal from yourself the fact that the House of Austria does not disguise its intention of getting hold of the Germanic Body (*s'emparer du Corps Germanique*) and of destroying all the sovereign houses [3].' Germany, in other words, was given to understand that the Emperor of the French was marching to Vienna in order to uphold the dignity and integrity of the Reich.

The new allies sang in chorus to this strange melody, adding variations of their own. Max Joseph warned his people against the treacherous plans of Austria, who wished to compel Bavaria to fight for a cause foreign to her own interests. Frederick issued a manifesto enumerating all the grievances of Würtemberg against the Court of Vienna—arrears of compensation, meddlesome interference in the affairs of the Swabian Circle, and the protection of the Imperial Knights, grudges ever ready to crystallize round the seed of imperial prerogative [4].

---

[1] Erdmannsdörffer, v. 242, 349; *Affaires étrangères, Corr. Pol.: Würtemberg*, 41.

[2] *Moniteur*, Oct. 2, 1805.   [3] *Corr.* xi. 273, no. 9,309.

[4] Häusser, iii. 577 ff. The Bavarian army is represented by the

THE CONFEDERATION OF THE RHINE 103

If there was one body which might have been expected to detect the hollowness of Napoleon's professed loyalty to the Empire, it was the Diet at Ratisbon. But the Diet closed its eyes, and accepted without protest the French assurances that the war was undertaken in the interests of Germany. Not a single voice was raised to protest against so transparent a fiction. Posts placed round the city of Ratisbon proclaimed the neutrality of the territory in Latin and French inscriptions. The Diet declared itself neutral, it declined to mention the Empire of Germany, it received bulletins from the French camp announcing 'the prodigies which have avenged the Germanic Empire for the invasion of one of its principal members,' it refused to entertain the complaints of the Imperial Knights whom the princes of South Germany and the allies of Napoleon were now vigorously plundering of their rights. The sanctimonious Dalberg uttered pious wishes for the preservation of the Reich and the union of all German hearts [1].

The triumphal progress of the French arms was saluted by the dithyrambic enthusiasms of the South German press, and the Bavarian journalists affected to believe that the victory of Ulm would restore the ancient independence of the Bavarian race [2]. Meanwhile the diplomatists of Munich and Stuttgart, of Karlsruhe and Darmstadt, were anxiously calculating the possible profits of their latest political speculation, and filling their respective chanceries with paper reconstructions of Germany. The princes having once taken a side, were determined to lose no chance for lack of zeal, and pursued the conqueror with professions and compliments, with suggestions and inquiries.

The correspondence between the Emperor and his new ally Frederick of Würtemberg during the campaign of Ulm and Austerlitz reads like a fragment of a piquant comedy. Napoleon

Moniteur (Oct. 2, 1805) as 'burning to measure itself against the oppressors of the country,' and a good deal of capital is made of the Austrian requisitions in Bavaria (ib. Oct. 3).

[1] Häusser, iii. 583-4.
[2] Id., iii. 599. Otto was instructed (Oct. 4, 1805) to inform the Elector of Bavaria that Napoleon would not lay down arms until he, the Elector, was placed in a position in which he might keep up an army of 50,000 men, and be entirely independent of Austria.

asks that Prince Paul of Würtemberg may be sent to join him at Munich, since the army of Würtemberg is not sufficiently considerable to afford the Prince adequate lessons in the art of war. 'It is better that he should serve under my orders in the French army.' The Elector felicitates the Emperor on his victories, 'which assure the political existence and the tranquillity of the south of Germany'; he perfectly appreciates the honour which is destined for Prince Paul; but circumstances will not permit him to accept it. The young man has a delicate chest, and his brother, the Electoral Prince, a scapegrace, has just announced his return to his duties and his father. When the Emperor sends 'his brother' a present of six Austrian guns, the Elector replies that he will always conserve this precious monument of his Imperial Majesty's glory; that the Electoral Prince has returned; that he flatters himself 'that the example of his father will impose upon him the duty of being faithful to the protector and the august ally of the House of Würtemberg.' At the same time he takes the liberty of reminding his Imperial Majesty that the time is rapidly approaching when Austria will be compelled to sue for peace, and that his Majesty, 'occupied with the great interests of Europe,' may not be able 'to enter into individual details' concerning the interests of his German allies. Has not the moment come when the Elector of Würtemberg may send one of his ministers to his Imperial Majesty 'to recall to those whom he shall appoint for the purpose, several subjects which will require local discussion and knowledge'? 'I strongly approve,' answered the Emperor from his camp at Reich, 'that you should send a minister to me. . . . In the instructions which you give to your minister, you must determine what portion of Germanic usage must be abolished. . . . I mean first the Aulic Council, and a great part of the attributions of the Diet of Ratisbon, which in truth is no more than a miserable monkey-house (*n'est plus qu'une misérable singerie*).' The Baron de Norman was accordingly sent as extraordinary envoy to consult with Talleyrand upon the affairs of this Germanic Empire which both parties intended to treat so cavalierly. At the same time the Elector, in return for the Grand Cordon of the Legion of Honour, transmitted the decoration of the Order of Würtemberg to Napoleon.

THE CONFEDERATION OF THE RHINE 105

'The annals of my house,' he wrote, 'will glory in daring to count you in the number of those who have accepted this honour.'

On November 16, Napoleon, who was writing from the imperial palace at Schönbrunn, began to be explicit. 'I can only,' he wrote, 'reiterate to you my firm intention to execute my promises, and to this end I shall receive your notes with pleasure. I think that you ought to do everything you can. For instance, you might arrange with the Elector of Baden to establish your own postal system. You might also get hold of the equestrian order while declaring that your intention is not to take its property, but to destroy a kind of sovereignty which depends on Austria and incommodes the Electors. If you think it would be useful to you to get hold of the Teutonic commanderies so as to endow your own order, I don't see what's to prevent you. . . . If there is anything else you can do, let me know, so that I can advise you, and so that in a treaty of peace one can say in a word, "Everything which has been done by the Electors is recognized." If you can manage to send two or three hundred carriages here, I will send you the artillery which may have belonged to you, and which Austria may have taken from time to time, also the guns, of which I have a great quantity. . . . It would be perhaps the moment for you to send some one to St. Petersburg to your sister, in order to make her feel that having projects so advantageous for her house, it would be singular that Russia should be so strongly opposed to them; that this is even advantageous to Russia, since it would weaken Austria; and that it is not very advantageous to France, since France could retain what she is giving to others. An adroit man might turn to good account the circumstances and the discontent which the Emperor of Russia feels towards Austria. I think that a mother imploring her son for the splendour of her house would produce a good effect, and it would be possible so to turn and draft the treaties that Russia's vanity would be flattered by your aggrandizement. What I tell you, then, isn't a thing of great importance, but you will feel that it also may have its degree of utility. Why should not a mother obtain from her son a letter of recommendation for her house? It is all very well to be the mother of an Emperor of Russia, but one ought not to forget the house from which one springs.' The uses of Würtemberg are now sufficiently clear. The Würtemberg influence is to detach Russia from the Coalition, and to help to recommend Napoleon to the Diet. In all things he will be acting on the advice of the Electors, Electors enriched with the spoils of the imperial nobility, who are, so to speak, the Austrian garrison in Germany, and alienated from the Hapsburgs by the acceptance of Austrian guns, and by participation in the war which brings Napoleon to Schönbrunn.

The battle of Austerlitz broke the armies of Austria and Russia, and diminished the utility of fraternal injunctions from Stuttgart. The Frenchmen were showing fine sport, and Frederick's blood was up now that the hounds were close upon their quarry. He hears that the Bavarian troops have occupied the Tyrol. 'Might it not,' he asks, 'be appropriate for me similarly to order the occupation of that portion of the possessions of the house of Austria which is found included (*enclavée*) or interlaced with my territories?' The Teutonic Knights and the immediate nobility—whose lands had been seized by the Princes—had raised an outcry, and the Elector Archchancellor was about to present their complaints to the Diet of the Empire. It was quite sufficient to convert Frederick to the unceremonious view of that ancient institution which his august protector had not hesitated to profess. 'My satisfaction,' he writes, alluding to the victory of Austerlitz, 'is too great to permit me to fatigue you to-day, Sire, with these petty annoyances (*tracasseries*) of Ratisbon, of this Diet which you have so aptly termed a monkey-house, and in which I am now recognizing the ridiculous characteristics as well as the malice of these animals.'

But that the Arch-chancellor should play 'the great German patriot' was as unpleasing to Napoleon as to his correspondent. 'My minister,' he answered (December 13, 1805), in reference to the affair of the knights, 'has orders to declare that what you have done is under my guarantee, and that if the least attempt to disturb it be made by the Germanic Body, so far from maintaining that institution, I shall help to procure its dissolution.' 'I dare flatter myself,' replied Frederick, 'that the lesson which you have given, Sire, to the Elector Arch-

THE CONFEDERATION OF THE RHINE 107

chancellor will calm his patriotic zeal and shelter us from his boastings[1].'

By treaties concluded at Brunn and Pressburg (December 12 and 26, 1805), between the Emperor Napoleon and the Elector of Würtemberg, the promises of the interview of Ludwigsburg are translated into fact. The Elector becomes a king: his territory is doubled: he is no longer pestered by imperial rights, or imperial enclaves. And all was due to Napoleon. Though his kingdom was the smallest in Europe, the joy of the new sovereign was overflowing, and the Empress of Russia was called upon to sympathize with dignities which had been acquired through the defeat and humiliation of her son.

As the battle of Austerlitz decided the campaign, so the Treaty of Pressburg (December 26, 1805) sealed the humiliation of Austria, excluding the House of Hapsburg alike from Italy, Switzerland, and the Rhine. The Tyrol and the Vorarlberg—that great mountain barrier which commands the connection between Italy and the Danube—was given to the Elector of Bavaria, who received in addition the Principality of Eichstätt, the remaining portion of the Bishopric of Passau, the town and territory of Augsburg, the Bishoprics of Trent and Brixen, the town of Lindau, the Margraviate of Bingen, and other lordships of less importance. The Electors of Würtemberg and Baden divided between them the remaining Austrian possessions in the West, and the only compensations which Austria received for these huge sacrifices were the Electorate of Salzburg, which in 1803 had been adjudged to the Archduke Leopold (now transferred to the Principality of Würzburg), and the right of appointing an Austrian archduke to the post of Grand Master of the Teutonic Order. By the fourteenth article of the treaty the domains of the Imperial Knights situated within the territories of Bavaria and Würtemberg were mediatized. An advance in title and dignity was secured to the Napoleonic allies and recognized by Austria. Bavaria and Würtemberg were henceforth monarchies; the Elector of Baden and the Landgrave of Hesse-Darmstadt took the title

---

[1] *Corr.* xi. 332, no. 9,391; 347, no. 9,412; 370, no. 9,444; 418, no. 9,501; 474, no. 9,567; Schlossberger, *Politische und militärische Korrespondenz*, 1–36.

of Grand Duke. But perhaps the most important concession for the sovereigns of Bavaria, Würtemberg, and Baden was the declaration in the fourteenth article, that they should enjoy complete and undivided sovereignty over their own States. This clause practically shattered the links of dependence which bound the three Courts to the chief of the Empire.

Yet, momentous as is the Treaty of Pressburg, there is nothing to cause surprise in its stipulations, which indeed only carry out the lines pursued by French diplomacy ever since the first breach with Austria in 1792. Nay, to exclude Austria from Germany and Italy,—is there not an old-world ring about that policy? Its lineaments would have been familiar to Francis I, to Richelieu, and to Chauvelin. But it was not, for all that, the inevitable, perhaps it was not the wisest policy which Napoleon could have pursued. Talleyrand, the shrewdest head in the French Empire, advised another course, believing in the value of the old Franco-Austrian alliance which had been the work of Bernis and of Kaunitz. His view was that Austria should be given the Turkish provinces of Moldavia and Wallachia, that the Republic of Venice should be re-established, that the kingdom of Italy should be decisively separated from the French Empire, and augmented by no accessions of territory. Austria would thus be more than compensated for her losses in Swabia. The apple of discord would be thrown between Vienna and St. Petersburg, and England would no longer find allies on the continent, for while Austria joined hands with France, the Muscovite Empire, excluded from the Balkan peninsula, and condemned to satiate its enormous ambitions in the East, would be brought into inevitable collision with the rulers of India [1].

This scheme Napoleon rejected. Perhaps he reflected that the Prussian alliance would be more valuable to him as a weapon against England, for through Prussia he could enforce the continental blockade on the North of Europe. Perhaps too he felt that Austria would not accept the Danubian principalities with the certainty of giving umbrage to her late ally, and the very knowledge that such an offer had been made would render the breach between France and Russia irreparable. The scheme of Talleyrand was indeed conceived in a modest key,

---

[1] Bignon, *Histoire de France*, v. 19 ff.; Lefebvre, ii. 235-6.

THE CONFEDERATION OF THE RHINE 109

little consonant with Napoleon's ambitions. He determined to cripple Austria once and for all, and by the arrangements of the Peace of Pressburg thought that he had effected his object.

The German Confederation had indeed been expressly recognized in this treaty, but there was a general feeling in the air that some large change was impending. In political pamphlets, in diplomatic despatches, in the chatter of Ratisbon, a new Constitution for Germany was a familiar topic, and when Napoleon arrived in Munich on December 30, speculation and curiosity became acute. The main purpose of the Emperor's stay in the Bavarian capital was to celebrate the marriage between Eugène and Augusta, to arrange the disposition of the French army in Southern Germany, and to sound-opinion as to the constitutional settlement of the German Empire. For this last purpose it was necessary to interview the French agent at Ratisbon, and General Hédouville was exhaustively cross-examined upon the trend of German opinion in that city and upon the sentiments of the Arch-chancellor. Then Napoleon gave audience to Dalberg. What passed in the hour's interview has escaped record—all but the fact that the Arch-chancellor came out 'penetrated with admiration.' We cannot, however, doubt that Dalberg seized the opportunity of ventilating his favourite project of a German Concordat, and that a picture was drawn of a Church disorganized by secularizations, of vacant bishoprics, insufficient sees, and unsettled diocesan frontiers [1]. At this particular moment such words would chime in unexpected concert with Napoleon's policy, for he had broken out into violent quarrel with the Pope, who resented the French occupation of Ancona. Dalberg suggested alike an argument and a threat which Napoleon was not slow to insert in a correspondence of recrimination. 'The Romans complain,' he wrote to the French ambassador at the Curia, 'that I have managed the affairs of Italy without them. Ought it then to have happened as in Germany, where there

---

[1] Krämer's eulogistic and uncritical biography represents Dalberg in an heroic light. He was roundly abused by Napoleon for his independence, and retorted with spirit and wit. (Krämer, *Carl Theodor, Reichsfreyherr von Dalberg*, 1817; Gams, *Geschichte der Kirche Christi im neunzehnten Jahrhundert*, i. 394; Hédouville to Talleyrand, Jan. 3, 1806, *Affaires étrangères, Corr. Pol.: Allemagne*, 731.)

are no longer any solemnities, any sacraments, any religion? Tell them that if they do not stop, I will show them to Europe as egoists, and that I will establish the affairs of the Church in Germany with the Arch-chancellor and without them[1].' Nothing could have been more pleasing to Dalberg than such a prospect. He seemed to have made the Emperor a convert to his ideas. Did not Napoleon recommend despatch in the matter of the Concordat, saying frequently that owing to the delays of the Curia souls were perishing? Then, too, the Arch-chancellor was invited to celebrate the royal marriage. In a paroxysm of enthusiastic gratitude he wrote a memoir urging the French Emperor to undertake, like Charlemagne, the regeneration of the Empire. But he was still attached to that venerable edifice, the *confusio divinitus conservata*, and would not willingly have it destroyed. Napoleon tranquillized his misgivings. He told the Arch-chancellor that he had abandoned his first idea of a general overthrow of the Reich, and with this hollow assurance the vain and fatuous old gentleman returned to Ratisbon [2].

There ensued a period of rumours and suspicions, surprises and suspense. The Diet understood as early as February that the fate of the Empire was to be decided, and all its members anxiously looked forward to the 'development of the grand crisis.' Secret intelligence came from Munich, that the lesser States of the Empire were to be preserved, but that the feudal nexus with the House of Austria was to be dissolved, and that though Bavaria, Franconia, and Swabia might continue to send envoys to the Diet, they would no longer address themselves to the Emperor or to the imperial Courts. But while the Arch-chancellor was deliberating the organization of the Chapter of Ratisbon and the election of a coadjutor, everybody knew that the big business would be transacted in Paris [3].

[1] *Corr.* xi. 529, no. 9,656.

[2] Horne to Hammond, Jan. 20 and 23, 1806; *F. O., Bavaria,* 31. For Dalberg's note (Jan. 17, 1806) on the Regeneration of the Germanic Nation, see *Affaires étrangères, Corr. Pol. : Allemagne,* 731 : ' *Que l' Empire d'Occident renaisse en l' Empereur Napoléon tel qu' il était sous Charlemagne, composé de l' Italie, de la France et de l' Allemagne.*'

[3] Horne to Hammond, Feb. 20, 1806 ; Horne to C. J. Fox, March 14 and 23, 1806 ; *F. O., Bavaria,* 31; Dalberg to Hédouville, March 19, 1808 ; *Affaires étrangères, Corr. Pol. : Allemagne,* 731.

THE CONFEDERATION OF THE RHINE 111

It was the habit of Napoleon, when large political changes were impending, to invite memoranda and plans from his ministers and their subordinates, and the spring of 1806 was fertile in schemes. In February a memoir was drawn up in the French Foreign Office, doubtless in accordance with the Emperor's instructions, upon 'States to be formed in Westphalia and along the Rhine[1].' The writer pointed out that as long as Prussia preserved her provinces in Westphalia and especially East Frisia, all French plans against the British Cabinet would fail; that Emden had replaced Hamburg as continental distributor of British wares, and that measures must be taken to close every port or quay to England from the coasts of Holland to the mouths of the Elbe. The writer concluded by suggesting the outlines of one or two States, whose territory was to stretch from the Electorate of Baden to the North Sea. This precious scheme, though conceived in the Napoleonic vein, was too extravagant to suit the needs of the hour. It would have involved instant war with Prussia, and for this the Emperor of the French was not prepared. A more modest craft was launched upon the waters. In March the world was informed that Prince Joachim Murat, the Emperor's brother-in-law and the Grand-Admiral of France, had been intruded into the circle of the princes of the German Empire as Grand Duke of Berg, a small Bavarian territory on the Rhine ceded by treaty to France. The intelligence was regarded as reassuring at Ratisbon. Surely, it was argued, Napoleon would not have made Murat a Prince of the Holy Roman Empire, if the Holy Roman Empire was forthwith to be destroyed. But men who argued thus had still all to learn about the restlessness of Napoleon's mind and the uncertainty of his plans. Even as late as the middle of April, letters came from Paris announcing that the 'new Carolingian Code,' as it was then called, was still in the greatest confusion[2].

Meanwhile a fresh cause of perturbation arose from a new

---

[1] *Mémoire sur les États à former en Westphalie et le long du Rhin*; *Affaires étrangères, Mémoires et Documents: Allemagne*, 118.

[2] Horne to Fox, March 30 and April 20, 1806; *F. O., Bavaria*, 31. Bacher to Talleyrand, April 15, 1806; *Affaires étrangères, Corr. Pol.: Allemagne*, 731.

and utterly unlooked-for quarter. The Arch-chancellor's head, never very strong, had been completely flustered by the Munich visit. Napoleon and he, he and Napoleon, were entering upon an era of constructive statesmanship, and while it was for Napoleon to execute, it was for Dalberg to suggest the reforms needed by Germany. He would begin, for instance, with the formation of a Metropolitan Chapter for Catholic Germany. It should be composed of twelve counts of the Empire, and twelve doctors in the Canon Law, together with the Canons of Mainz and Ratisbon. But a more important object was the selection of a coadjutor, and Dalberg submitted three names for Napoleon's approval. It was a gross betrayal of German independence to refer a question of this kind to a foreigner, for the coadjutor would succeed to the Arch-chancellorship, and the Arch-chancellor was the conservator of the laws of the Empire, and the representative of the Emperor in the Diet. But Dalberg was now determined to take no step without Napoleon's authority, and the names of the Count of Stadion, the Count of Sternberg, and Baron Wessenberg were sent to Hédouville to be transmitted to Paris on April 19. Whether from contempt, accident, or policy, no answer was forthcoming to these paltry communications. Dalberg began to feel uneasy. At the beginning of April he received a hint from some quarter that his town of Ratisbon had been demanded by Bavaria, and his Principality of Aschaffenburg by Hesse-Cassel. The treachery of Bavaria stung his confiding heart with peculiar bitterness. Had not the Bavarian King given him in writing the strongest assurances of friendship only a few days before? Whither could he turn for protection in a lawless and treacherous world? Then a happy thought flashed into his head: he bethought him of Cardinal Fesch.

His Eminence Cardinal Fesch, Archbishop of Lyons and Primate of the Gauls, was the uncle of the Emperor of the French. He had speculated successfully in land and pictures, and was reputed to possess one of the finest art collections in Paris. A learned scholar has said that he united the greed and vanity of a Corsican with the obstinacy and heaviness of the Basle bankers, from whom upon his paternal side he was derived. Though by no means destitute of ecclesiastical zeal, he hunted fortune with the versatile tenacity of the Bonaparte family. He had been in turn a seminarist, a constitutional priest, an inspector of carts, a speculator in Church lands, a picture-dealer, an archbishop, and a cardinal. He was now, having amassed an enormous fortune, ambassador of the French Empire to the Court of Rome. But to Fesch the Eternal City was almost as distasteful as Tomi was to Ovid or Macedonia to Cicero. Though he was conceited enough to imagine himself a diplomatist, he quarrelled with everybody at the Papal Court and pined to be permitted to spend part of the year at least among the more familiar luxuries of Lyons and Paris. At one point only had he been brought into connection with Germany. Bavaria was anxious to make a special Concordat with the Pope, and the influence of Fesch had already been enlisted in the promotion of this object [1].

The future was now luminous and hopeful to Dalberg. Fesch alone could maintain the religious and political constitution of Germany. With Fesch as coadjutor during his life, and Arch-chancellor after his death, all would be serene: the Concordat which would organize the Catholic Church in Germany under the control of the Archbishop of Ratisbon; the maintenance of the Electoral dignity and the Electoral State; the Pontifical confirmation of the Statutes of the Chapter of Ratisbon; the conservation of the German Empire itself. On April 14 he broached the scheme to Hédouville, and five days later emitted to Napoleon the following effusion:—

'The estimable Germanic nation groans in the misfortunes of political and religious anarchy. Sire, be the regenerator of the Constitution! Here are some wishes dictated by the state of affairs! Let the Duke of Cleves become an Elector! Let him obtain the octroi of the Rhine over the whole right bank! Let the Cardinal Fesch be my coadjutor [1].'

[1] The correspondence of Fesch with Napoleon during the Roman Embassy is printed by Ducasse, *Histoire des négociations diplomatiques relatives aux traités de Mortfontaine, de Lunéville et d'Amiens*, i. 13 ff. Cf. also Consalvi, *Mémoires*, ii. 131-5; Lyonnet, *Vie du Cardinal Fesch*, i. 495-539, ii. 24-30; Masson, *Napoléon et sa famille*, ii. 204-11, iii. 351-64, iv. 413-32. Fesch's letter on the Bavarian question is unprinted (Fesch to Talleyrand, Aug. 7, 1805, *Affaires étrangères, Correspondance Politique: Bavière*, 181). Cf. Sicherer, *Staat und Kirche in Deutschland*, 76-110.

It so happened that, on the very day upon which this letter was despatched, Napoleon wrote to the Pope to withdraw his ambassador from Rome. Nothing therefore could have been more timely than the proposal of Dalberg. Yet the imbecility and vagueness of his proposals provoked a reply at once arrogant and precise. On April 26 Tallyrand wrote to Hédouville that he had not thought fit to put the Arch-chancellor's suggestions before the Emperor. If, however, the Arch-chancellor was willing to sign a convention in virtue of which, while the Emperor guaranteed his States and revenues on the one hand, the Arch-chancellor engaged on the other to cause Cardinal Fesch to be received and recognized as coadjutor within a month, then Hédouville was at liberty to sign on his part. Dalberg was horrified at the crudity of the French. Such a convention, he said, would be simoniacal, contrary to canon law, a stain on his honour; he had wished to treat directly with Cardinal Fesch; he would never sign. But his counsellors advised him to submit, and on May 7 the secret convention received its signatures. 'I could not help,' wrote Hédouville, May 8, 'hurting the delicacy of the Elector by sounding him to-day as to what he wanted for his family. The relation who interests him most is his nephew, the minister of Baden at Paris[1].'

On May 28 the nomination of Cardinal Fesch was announced to the astonished Diet. His ancestors had in the fifteenth century, so ran the official recommendation, distinguished themselves in Basle, and the force, the intelligence, and the great influence of the eminent prelate rendered him admirably fitted to discharge the office to which he would eventually be summoned. It is needless to say that nobody was deceived, and that nobody in the Diet had the courage to protest. And yet in the natural course of events a Corsican *parvenu*, knowing little of Germany, possessing no German, would come to be the Arch-chancellor and senior Elector. He would preside over the imperial elections and over the Diet, and it was in his custody that the seal and the archives of the Empire would be kept.

---

[1] *Corr.* xii. 375, no. 10,240; *Affaires étrangères, Corr. Pol.: Allemagne,* 731. Napoleon wrote to inform Fesch, May 16. Ratifications were exchanged, May 22. Dalberg wrote to inform the Pope, May 24, and to inform Fesch, May 28.

THE CONFEDERATION OF THE RHINE 115

In the opinion of the English envoy Germany had now received a Stadtholder who, like Schimmelpenninck in Holland and Melzi in Italy, was simply to be the passive transmitter of the mandates of the Emperor of the French. At the special demand of Fesch and with the consent of Napoleon, the bulls of institution permitted the new coadjutor to retain, with his German offices present and prospective, the Archbishopric of Lyons and the Primacy of the Gauls [1].

Meanwhile 'the new Carolingian Code' was being slowly elaborated in Paris. On April 10 the Emperor wrote to Talleyrand his views upon the small German princes whose territories lay in the sphere of influence possessed by the sovereigns of Bavaria, Würtemberg, and Baden. 'If they are left their independence, they will vote against France, either because they are Austrians or because they have too many relations with Austria, and because these little princes cannot be reconciled with the sovereigns of Bavaria, Würtemberg, and Baden. The true interest of France is that the German Empire should only be able to reorganize itself by the aid of a strong and powerful direction. France has an equally real interest in seeing the only three princes who since the Revolution have frankly made common cause with her amply recompensed. I should therefore be disposed to think that it would be expedient to conclude a secret convention with the three sovereigns whom I have just named, and to augment their States by 150,000 or 200,000 souls without any direct intervention on my part: in a word, to let them do it between themselves, and to prevent them from pronouncing my name. In this way the College of Princes would be deprived of some Austrian votes, and a new difficulty would arise in the way of establishing an equilibrium of votes between Austria and Prussia. The three princes would be much more at my discretion than they are at present, because, having failed to receive public sanction for their operations, they would find themselves

---

[1] Horne to Sir Francis Vincent, May 28, 1806, *F. O., Bavaria*, 31; Lyonnet, ii. 30, 620. Hédouville writes of Dalberg, May 29, 1806: '*La seule chose qui l'ait un peu affligé, a été l'idée de plusieurs personnes qui ont pensé que sa démarche lui avait été suggérée par la France.*'—*Affaires étrangères, Corr. Pol.: Allemagne*, 731.

in a violent situation; and as their usurpations could only be legally sanctioned by the imperial authority of Germany, it would result that they would always be obliged to recur to my support, and that I should consequently dispose of three Electoral votes. German opinion would thereby be more divided, which is all in favour of France[1].'

According to this scheme, then, the Empire is preserved, but the small princes of the south are sacrificed secretly to the three allies of France. Talleyrand, who was assailed on all sides by the petitions and complaints of the German envoys, drew up a plan by which the petty sovereignties were to be distributed among seven princes, the Kings of Bavaria and Würtemberg, the Electors of Baden and Hesse, the Landgrave of Hesse, the Prince of Nassau-Usingen, and the Duke of Berg. In vain did the Foreign Minister entreat his master to settle the map of Germany once and for all[2]. Napoleon's restless mind was the despair of his subordinates. Scheme after scheme was devised, corrected, torn up, and thrown into the fire. On April 24 the Emperor wrote a note dividing Germany into eight States, four of which, Bavaria, Baden, Würtemberg, and a new State to be formed out of Berg, Cleves, Hesse-Darmstadt, with Hanover, Hamburg, Bremen, and Lübeck, were to represent French interests. 'After this division,' he continued, 'suppose that one should destroy the Germanic Constitution, and annul the little sovereignties for the profit of the eight large States, one must make a statistical calculation to know if the four States which are in the interests of France will lose or gain more by this destruction than the four States which are not.' A month later the destruction of the Empire is a settled thing. 'There will be no more Diet at Ratisbon, since Ratisbon will belong to the Empire[3].' All kinds of unexpected side-winds came to perplex the current. At one time the Emperor took it into his head that the Prussian alliance would never be very

---

[1] *Corr.* xii. 266-8, no. 10,071.

[2] A. F. iv. 1,706 b. '*Assailli de toutes parts*,' concludes the writer, '*soit de réclamations et de plaintes, soit de demandes que la raison et la modération n'ont pas dictées, j'ose dire à V. M. que j'ai une sorte d'intérêt personnel à ce que le sort de toutes ces petites souverainetés de l'Allemagne soit une fois et irrévocablement fixé.*'

[3] Napoleon to Talleyrand, May 31, 1806; *Corr.* xii. 416, no. 10,298.

THE CONFEDERATION OF THE RHINE 117

useful, since Prussia could never command the Sound. That being so, why should not Hanover be restored to England, and Prussia compensated in Central Germany? Then granted that the Empire was to be dissolved and a new Confederation founded in its place, who were to be the members of the new body? In the Rue de Grenelle the pale black-haired hypochondriac Labesnardière toiled away with the learned Pfeffel—the chief authority in German affairs in the French Foreign Office—at the elaboration of draft after draft. At first it was proposed that the Kings of Naples, Italy, and Holland were to be included, and that crowns should be distributed to the rulers of Baden and Darmstadt, Berg and Hesse-Cassel. This was grandiose and Carolingian, but it presented difficulties, and Talleyrand no doubt exerted his influence in favour of a more modest scheme. Meanwhile the old disgraceful scenes of bribery and corruption were re-enacted in Paris. Hamburg bought its independence for several million marks. The Duke of Mecklenburg presented the French minister with a *douceur* of 80,000 Friedrichsd'or. It is needless to continue the shameful catalogue. Bavaria, Würtemberg, and Baden, who had all served in the war and had some claims on the consideration of the Emperor, were permitted to discuss certain questions with the agents of the French Foreign Office. But their envoys were not allowed to see the whole act until it was finally submitted for their signature. On the night of July 6–7 Talleyrand surprised Von Gagern, the envoy of the Prince of Nassau, by reading out to him the fateful document. But the news was not yet common property, nor were any copies of the act allowed to pass out of the French minister's hands. It was necessary first to secure the military position of France in Southern Germany, and Napoleon wrote to Berthier ordering concentration so that he might 'have in line and almost in Vienna 232,000 men [1].' Such a demonstration would silence all protests and ease the exchange of ratifications. On July 17 it was judged that Berthier was ready, and the Treaty of the Confederation of the Rhine was signed in Paris. The act was laid before each envoy separately, and the princes were given twenty-four hours in which to choose between acceptance and mediatization. Of the princes named in the act,

[1] Napoleon to Berthier, July 11, 1806; *Corr.* xii. 533, no. 10,479.

only one—the Prince of Lichtenstein—refused to accept. Rather than abandon his post in the Austrian service he resigned his territory to his son.

Fifteen princes of the Empire joined the league—the Kings of Bavaria and Würtemberg, Charles of Dalberg (Arch-chancellor of the German Empire), the Elector of Bavaria, the Duke of Cleves and Berg (Prince Joachim Murat), the Landgrave of Hesse-Darmstadt, the two Princes of Nassau-Usingen and Nassau-Weilburg, the two Princes of Hohenzollern-Sigmaringen and Hechingen, the two Princes of Salm-Salm and Salm-Kirburg, the Prince of Isenberg-Birstein, the Duke of Ahrenburg, and the Count de la Leyen.

These fifteen sovereigns declared themselves separated for ever from the territory of the German Empire, and united by a special confederation under the name of Confederate States of the Rhine. The common interests of this Confederation were to be treated in a Diet convened at Frankfort, and composed of two Colleges, the College of Kings and the College of Princes. It was given to the Arch-chancellor to prepare a 'fundamental statute' which should determine when and how these bodies should deliberate. The College of Kings was to be composed of the Kings of Bavaria and Würtemberg, of the Elector Arch-chancellor, who by this act received the additional title of Prince-Primate, and of the Princes of Baden, Berg, and Hesse-Darmstadt, now promoted to the Grand-Ducal rank, and accorded the privileges and prerogatives attaching to royalty. The nine other confederates were to form the College of Princes. When the two Colleges of the Diet sat together the Prince-Primate was to preside, when they sat apart the Duke of Nassau would preside over the princes, and the Prince-Primate over the kings. The Emperor of the French was Protector of the Confederation, and enjoyed the right of nominating the successors of the Prince-Primate.

Then followed certain provisions to promote a simplification of German territory. Frontiers were rectified in order to obviate the inconveniences resulting from *enclaves*; all the confederates renounced once and for all any and every pretension they might have had upon one another's territory; the free towns, small dukes, counts, and princes, whose territories were

THE CONFEDERATION OF THE RHINE 119

intermingled with those of the confederates, were mediatized and forced to descend from the position of sovereign to that of subject. Thus the King of Bavaria obtained Nuremberg, two commanderies of the Teutonic Order, and twelve or thirteen other principalities. The free town of Frankfort went to the Prince-Primate, and twenty principalities were absorbed by Würtemberg. It is unnecessary here to give all the details, but there was not a member of the Confederation who did not receive some substantial share of the plunder.

Yet some protection was afforded to the unfortunate princes who saw themselves so suddenly deprived of their ancient sovereign rights. Their patrimonial property was reserved to them, together with all those seigneurial and feudal rights which were not essentially inherent in sovereignty, and they were allowed to possess all the privileges which the confederate princes themselves enjoyed on their own domains [1]. In criminal cases they could only be tried by their peers, and their property could never be confiscated. They were free to reside wherever they liked, provided that it was in one of the States which were members or allies of the Confederation of the Rhine, and their functionaries were either to pass into the service of the new princes or to receive a pension. Finally the confederate princes were empowered to possess in full sovereignty the lands of the Imperial Knights situated within their several States.

By these masterly provisions the political map of Germany was simplified, and more was done for the cause of good government in the valleys of the Danube, the Neckar, and the Main, than had been effected by all the policies of the eighteenth century. It is idle to weep over the lot of a Prince of Oettingen or a Count of Fugger. These petty Courts, full of picturesque anomalies, deserved to disappear. They were fatal to the interests of administrative unity; they choked the growth of large political ideas; they were the hotbeds of tiny and contemptible intrigue. Yet little sympathy can be extended to the larger powers who cringed and clamoured for their extinction. They were alike traitors to a great historic tradition, and blind to

---

[1] Some dispute arose as to the scope of these concessions (art. 27), especially in connection with the phrase '*basse et moyenne justice*.' It was generally taken to mean justice in first and second instance.

the higher things of the future. It was one of those moments in history when vulgar greed is made the instrument of social and political improvement.

It was a great occasion for Napoleon. He was an artist in affairs, and revelled in the excitement of political composition. Many years before he had said that if the German Empire had not existed, it would be necessary to create it. Yet now he was destroying all that was confused, all that was obsolete, all that was obscure and inimical to progress in that 'vast and mysterious Germany,' which had so long lain helplessly swathed in her mediaeval bandages. Waste, perplexity, ineffectiveness, were indeed abhorrent to his clear and classical spirit of order, but in this matter he was not actuated by altruistic motives. If he made his German confederates masters and lords in their own homes, it was in order that by this very mastery they might more effectually serve the master and lord of France. This, indeed, is the main purpose of the Confederation of the Rhine, and the subject of some important provisions which must now be summarized.

It was first stipulated that the princes of the Confederation should not take service of any kind, save in the Confederate States or with the allies of the Confederation. Secondly, it was provided by article 35, that 'there should be between the French Empire and the Confederate States of the Rhine, collectively and separately, an alliance in virtue of which every continental war, in which one of the contracting parties might be involved, would become immediately common to all the others.' Thirdly, the contingent of soldiers to be furnished in case of war by each of the allies was fixed. France must supply 200,000 men, Bavaria 30,000, Würtemberg 12,000, Baden 8,000, Berg 5,000, Darmstadt 4,000, Nassau and the small princes 4,000, and these armaments were to be put on foot only in pursuance of an invitation addressed by the Emperor to each of the allied powers. Lastly, the Confederation was not closed: it was to be open 'to all other princes and States of Germany whom it shall be found to the common interest to admit.' Although the tenor of this clause would seem distinctly to imply that the confederates would be consulted as to the admission of new members, there is no instance in which this was done. The admissions were regulated by Napoleon alone, and in the end all Germany passed under the common yoke.

The French government had, as we have seen, taken careful precautions against resistance in Germany. 'I send you to-day,' wrote Napoleon to Berthier, July 16, 1806, 'a treaty which I desire you to keep to yourself, and which I wish to have sanctioned before my army repasses the Rhine; by this means I shall have no dispute upon this point[1].' The mandate went out to Berthier that the ratifications were to be exchanged at Munich on July 25, and the French general possessed in a numerous and well-equipped army the most solid of arguments for despatch. Yet the treaty aroused many misgivings in the Chancelleries of Munich and of Stuttgart. The King of Bavaria saw 'with pain' the elevation of the Prince of Lichtenstein; he objected to the College of Princes; he was suspicious of the Federal Council, and trusted that it would not take cognizance of any affairs relative to the internal interests of the several States except upon the formal demand of the parties directly interested. Both Bavaria and Würtemberg objected to the French protectorate, and to the right claimed by the Emperor of naming the Arch-chancellor[2]. But what was the use of drafting notes? It was well understood that unless the princes swallowed the whole document, the French army would not recross the Rhine. On July 27 the ratifications were exchanged, and the South German States had sold themselves into slavery[3].

The text of the treaty reached Dalberg on July 24, and plunged him in 'veritable desolation.' General Hédouville reminded him that the new order of things was but the accomplishment of the wishes which he himself had expressed in his two notes of January 17. 'The Arch-chancellor cried out with pain that he had not meant to abolish the Germanic

[1] *Corr.* xii. 547, no. 10,502.
[2] *Affaires étrangères, Corr. Pol.: Bavière*, 182.
[3] ' *Quoique les échanges n'ayent pu avoir lieu le 25, cette date sera conservée dans tous les procès-verbaux.*'—Otto to Talleyrand, July 29, 1806. Würtemberg made a formal protest against the cession of Tuttlingen to Bavaria which Berthier refused to accept. Otto prevented Bavaria from protesting on an equally trivial point. Otto to Talleyrand, August 3, 1806; *Affaires étrangères, Corr. Pol.: Bavière*, 182.

Constitution, but on the contrary to consolidate it, and to assure to it the most powerful protector by lawfully placing the crown of Germany upon the august forehead of His Majesty the Emperor Napoleon.' On the 25th he declared that he would abdicate, retire to Paris, and ratify in the name of Cardinal Fesch, for never would he consent to the spoliation of the orphan and the widow. On the morning of the 26th, however, this effervescence had passed away, and he allowed himself to be persuaded to sign. Four days later he was even enthusiastic over the new order of things. 'He is already recompensed,' wrote Hédouville, 'by the sweetness of being able to console a great number of interesting individuals whose lot depends on his, and especially by the hope of seconding the intentions of the august monarch whose protection will bring order, calm, and happiness to this part of Germany.' By July 31, he was planning schemes for the organization of the Assembly at Frankfort, and looking forward to the hour when he should go there to proclaim the august Protector of the Confederation [1].

On August 1 the Baron d'Albini, on behalf of the Prince-Primate, communicated the treaty to the Diet of Ratisbon, the text accompanied by an important and characteristic declaration. In this the Emperor of the French declared that he 'no longer recognized the existence of the German Constitution, while acknowledging the entire and absolute sovereignty of each of the princes whose States at present compose Germany.' He had accepted the title of Protector of the Rhine, but only 'with a view to peace, and in order that his mediation, constantly interposed between the most feeble and the most strong, should avert all manner of dissension and trouble.' The document concluded with asserting that His Majesty had declared that he would never extend the boundaries of France beyond the Rhine. To that promise he had been faithful. Now his sole desire was to employ the means which Providence had confided to him to free the seas, to liberate commerce, and to assure the repose and happiness of the world [2].

[1] Hédouville to Talleyrand, July 26, 30, 31, 1806; *Affaires étrangères, Corr. Pol.: Allemagne*, 732.

[2] The text of the Dictatum Ratisbonae is printed in Winkopp, *Der rheinische Bund*, i. 48 ff.

THE CONFEDERATION OF THE RHINE 123

The members of the Diet, delegates for the most part of the conspiring and confederate States, openly approved the doom, nor was there a stir of arms in Vienna. On August 6 Francis formally renounced his imperial title, and the Holy Roman Empire was at an end.

CHIEF AUTHORITIES : Häusser, *Deutsche Geschichte* ; Alombert et Colin, *Histoire de la guerre de* 1805 *en Allemagne* ; Lefebvre, *Histoire des Cabinets de l'Europe* ; Martens, *Histoire des Traités* ; Schlossberger, *Politische und militärische Correspondenz Friedrichs von Würtemberg mit Napoleon I* ; *Preussische Jahrbücher*, xiv. 577–616 ; Winkopp, *Der rheinische Bund* ; H. von Gagern, *Mein Antheil an der Politik*.

CHAPTER VI

THE FALL OF PRUSSIA

'Il faut que cette guerre soit la dernière et que ses auteurs soient si sévèrement punis que quiconque voudra désormais prendre les armes contre le peuple français sache bien avant de s'engager dans une telle entreprise quelles peuvent en être les conséquences.'—NAPOLEON.

HARDLY had the federation of the Rhine been formed when it was called upon to receive the baptism of fire, for in September 1806 war broke out between France and Prussia. The effects of this war were so momentous, leading as it did to the establishment of French hegemony in Northern Germany, that it will be necessary here to indicate the circumstances out of which it arose.

Ever since the Peace of Basle in 1795, the House of Hohenzollern had managed to preserve its neutrality. While the Southern States had been overrun with French and Austrian armies, Prussia had pursued a policy of peaceful and inglorious self-aggrandizement. Her finances were unflourishing, her king was timid, and upon a narrow view of Prussian interests there was something to be said for the lucrative friendship of France. Nations are slow to unlearn a diplomatic tradition, when once it has been blackened by powder; and Prussia had been too long accustomed to find her arch-enemy in Vienna, to make researches in other quarters. She still remembered the long series of Silesian duels, in which the greatest of her kings, pitted against overwhelming odds, had achieved the reputation of his country. The contest over the Bavarian succession and the keen rivalries over the partitions of Poland were of more recent date, and the jealousy of threescore years flamed out anew over the squalid turmoil of the indemnities. The allies of Austria were England and Russia, and with these countries the Court of Berlin had fewer points of antagonism. Yet if the Prussians had forgotten the English desertion of Frederick the Great in the Seven Years' War, they conceived that there was reason to fear the commercial and maritime ascendency of our country. The instability of Russian policy, so frequently disturbed by revolutions of the palace, had passed into a proverb, nor could it be forgotten that Russian armies had twice in recent times pierced into the heart of Brandenburg, and that the splendid military machine of the Great Frederick had been shattered by a Russian victory. Colonel Massenbach was an intelligent and patriotic officer, with more than the usual allowance of political imagination. He served the Prussian government with pen and sword, and was not afraid to speak his mind. But he never ceased to maintain that Austria was the natural and immortal enemy of his country, and that the true interests of Prussia lay in a close alliance with France.

The Court of Berlin gradually awoke from its slumbers to realize that peril might arise in the west. In 1803 the French occupied Hanover, seized Cuxhaven, blocked the Elbe and the Weser; in 1804 came the execution of the Duc d'Enghien and the abduction of Rumbold. A war-party grew up in Berlin, headed by the beautiful and spirited Queen Louise, supported by the Duke of Brunswick and the Prince of Hardenberg, by Beyme and Lombard among the ministers, by Blücher and Ruchel among the generals. Two policies were now face to face, peace or war, freedom or servitude, the coalition or Napoleon. The year which ended in Austerlitz was the crowning year of torture and indecision. On the one hand Russia and Austria were arming against Napoleon, but on the other hand France was offering to Prussia the bait of Hanover. As the balance was trembling, the King of Prussia heard that French troops were marching upon the Danube, through the Prussian territories of Anspach and Baireuth. That news was decisive. Turning to Hardenberg he said, 'Things are reversed,' and threw himself into the arms of Alexander of Russia. There was an interview at Potsdam, a famous oath at the tomb of the Great Frederick, and Prussia, fortified by the friendship of the Czar, mobilized her army to give effect to an ultimatum which Napoleon would never accept. Rarely has a great transaction been more wofully mismanaged.

The Prussians loitered, though they had everything to gain by speed; the Austrians and Russians hurried, though they had everything to gain by delay; and Austerlitz was fought and won before Haugwitz, the Prussian envoy, had presented his ultimatum.

The Emperor of the French plumbed the situation to its depths, and overwhelmed the miserable ambassador and his hollow congratulations in a scene of studied sarcasm and violence. A far-sighted and spirited statesman would have resented these insults, and urged his government to throw their army upon the long line of the French communications. But Haugwitz, cowed by Napoleon, and believing that war would spell instant disaster, permitted himself to sign the Treaty of Schönbrunn, which gave Hanover to Prussia in exchange for three small and widely-scattered territories, Anspach, Neufchatel, and Wesel. It would have been difficult to construct a treaty which in appearance so favourable, was in reality so damaging to the good name of Prussia. The Court of Berlin had guaranteed the neutrality of Hanover in 1795, and fallen short of her duty in permitting it to be occupied by the French in 1803. While Haugwitz was toiling over the wintry roads towards Vienna, the Prussians were eagerly counting upon English friendship and English subsidies in the event, which then seemed inevitable, of a breach with Napoleon. Indeed, Hardenberg had solemnly assured the Russian minister that Hanover should never pass from English hands without the consent of the Court of St. Petersburg. Yet all obligations of honour were now thrown to the winds. Napoleon required of Prussia that she should rob England, and Haugwitz consented to the transaction.

When the terms of the treaty became known in Berlin there were general and loud expressions of indignation, so loud that an order was issued to the officers of the garrison to abstain under severe penalties from alluding to the state of public affairs[1]. But since the rejection of the treaty would bring war, and the acceptance of it disgrace, it was resolved to find salvation in amendments. Prussia proposed that she should

---

[1] Cölln, *Vertraute Briefe über Preussen,* i. 160; Jackson to Fox, March 22, 1806, *F. O., Prussia,* 71.

THE FALL OF PRUSSIA

not take Hanover at once, but that she should keep it as a deposit till the conclusion of a general peace. The solution was ingenious, for it seemed to harmonize appetite and honour: but Napoleon would not hear of it. Indeed Haugwitz was compelled to return to Berlin with a treaty even more disadvantageous than the terms of Schönbrunn, for it explicitly bound his government to exclude England from the mouths of the Elbe and the Weser. If the Prussian army had still been in its cantonments in Upper Saxony and on the Main, harnessed and accoutred for the fray, it is possible that Napoleon would not have pressed, and that Frederick William would not have conceded the points in dispute. But in an access of pitiable economy, the heads of the war and finance departments in Berlin advised the reduction of the army to a peace footing, and in the very midst of a critical negotiation Prussia demobilized her forces. From that moment, as the British envoy Jackson remarked, 'the hopes of obtaining any remission of the terms imposed at Vienna became very faint[1].' Indeed, the new and more onerous treaty was accepted at once by the feeble government of Frederick William, though it brought in its immediate train a breach with England and the loss of one-fourth of the Prussian revenue by the closure of the ports.

The formation of the Confederation of the Rhine later on in the summer added to the disquietude of Berlin. But Napoleon had no desire to force on hostilities, and proposed that a confederation of the North might be formed under Prussian hegemony. He would acquiesce absolutely, so Frederick William was assured, 'in all the measures which the King of Prussia might judge to be agreeable to his interests,' and it was even suggested that the House of Hohenzollern should assume the imperial rank[2]. These proposals were flattering to Prussian vanity, and if the negotiations for the Northern league had gone smoothly, war might perhaps have been postponed. But the whole scheme, as Napoleon possibly divined, proved to be illusory. Saxony disliked the thoughts of a Prussian Emperor, and had no fancy for a close union with Berlin. The Elector of Hesse-Cassel aimed at forming a league of his own, small

---

[1] Jackson to Fox, April 3, 1806 ; *F. O., Prussia*, 71.
[2] Bailleu, *Preussen und Frankreich*, ii. 488-99.

and neighbourly, with himself for Protector. The two Mecklenburg dynasties were Slavonic, and held aloof. The Duke of Oldenburg was a relation of the Czar, a circumstance productive of difficulty, and Napoleon refused to permit the absorption of the Hanseatic towns into the Prussian system [1].

Alarming rumours, borne on every wind, mingled with this irritating trickle of diplomatic disappointments. It was rumoured that Fulda, which belonged to the Prince of Orange, the brother-in-law of the Prussian King, had been offered to Hesse-Cassel in order to draw him into the Confederation of the Rhine; that Bavaria was to have Baireuth; that the French army was mobilizing in the south; that the Landgrave of Hesse-Darmstadt was to be King of Westphalia; that the county of Mark was to be wrenched from Prussia and given to Murat, and that French troops were pouring into Wesel. The Prussian army, which had been mobilized in 1805 and then demobilized, was restless, dissatisfied, and burning for the fray [2].

Napoleon did not want war with Prussia, but if the Prussians wanted war with him, well, they should have it. He had just consolidated the imperial system at home; he had placed Louis on the throne of Holland and Joseph on the throne of Naples, and he was embroiled with the Pope. A Calabrian revolt, fostered by the English, who held Sicily, was threatening the unsettled foundations of the Neapolitan throne, and Napoleon's eye was fixed upon Calabria. At the same time he had opened out negotiations with the ministry of Fox, which had come into power in England in the month of April. If Sicily were ceded to the Neapolitan kingdom, Napoleon would be prepared to restore Hanover to the Guelphs. In the interval of peace he would build a navy, and then what might he not accomplish? Constantinople, Egypt, India—these were dazzling visions.

On August 6 the news came to Berlin that Napoleon had offered Hanover to England; Hanover, concerning which Talleyrand only a month ago had reassured the Prussian envoy 'in the most positive manner and at the express order of the

---

[1] *Preussische Jahrbücher*, xiv. 577–616; *Archiv für sächsische Geschichte*, vi. 36 ff.; Flathe, *Geschichte des Kurstaates und Königreichs Sachsen*, ii. 633.

[2] Bailleu, ii. 489, 93, 504.

Emperor.' The cup of disillusion was filled. To obtain Hanover Prussia had undergone anguish, humiliation, and material loss; it was the one compensation for insults accepted, shipping destroyed, commerce intercepted. And now Hanover was coolly offered to England. It seemed obvious at Berlin that Napoleon had a settled plan for the ruin of the one solid unconquered German power. Had not the French ambassador urged Prussia into war with Sweden, in order that, seizing Pomerania for herself, she might relinquish the county of Mark to Murat, the new Grand-Duke of Berg? Were not French troops pouring into Wesel? Was not Murat's lawless conduct a standing threat of war? There were rumours that the French troops had occupied Würzburg and were advancing on Saxony and Prussia. On August 8 the King appealed to the Czar. 'He intends to destroy me,' he wrote; 'will you see this, Sire, with indifference[1]?' On the 9th the orders were issued for the mobilization of the Prussian army. Alexander, too, was ready to fight.

In the period of heated suspense before the actual outbreak of hostilities an event occurred which caused the most intense indignation throughout Germany. On the very day, so it would appear, upon which the ratifications of the act of the Rhenish Confederacy were exchanged at Munich, the Bavarian government was required to discover the authors of two treatises, one of which bore the significant title 'Germany in her Deep Humiliation[2].' It will be remembered that after the battle of Austerlitz the French army remained cantoned in Southern Germany, and that its presence was a material factor in securing the prompt acceptance of the act of Confederation. This army lived on the land, sucked it dry, and was guilty of some gross outrages. To the indignation which resulted the pamphlets in question gave vigorous expression. It was represented that since the days of Tilly and Wallenstein Bavaria had seen nothing so bad; that during the last six months she had suffered as much through the French occupation as if she had had to maintain an army of 200,000 men for several years at

[1] Bailleu, ii. 509.
[2] Otto to Talleyrand, July 28 and August 24, 1806; *Affaires étrangères, Corr. Pol.: Bavière*, 182.

the ordinary rate of pay; and that Napoleon was clearly attempting to enslave Germany.

The authorship of these pamphlets was not discovered, but some booksellers were arrested and brought before a French military court at Braunau, an Austrian town still in French occupation. Six were condemned to death, and of these one, Palm of Nuremberg, was executed (August 25) as the publisher of 'Germany in her Deep Humiliation.' The man was known to be an upright, simple, God-fearing burgher; a citizen of an ancient city, once free and imperial; condemned to death by the verdict of seven French colonels in time of peace for a pamphlet written in Vienna which he had never read. All Germany was thrilled with indignation at this outrage on civic liberty, and with the emotion still vivid upon her Prussia plunged into war. Never was an army or a people more confident of success.

The end of Prussian vainglory came with surprising quickness. Swiftly marching through the gorges of the Thuringian forest, Napoleon won a decisive victory over the Prussian army at Jena and Auerstädt on October 14, and a fortnight later he was in Berlin. In a proclamation of November 12 he said with perfect truth, 'The whole of the Prussian monarchy is in my power,' and indeed, save for 15,000 men in Silesia and some garrisons in the Baltic fortresses, the Prussian army was dispersed or destroyed. It remained to utilize the victory and to remould the political conditions of Northern Germany.

Among the allies of Prussia in the Jena campaign was the Elector Frederick Augustus of Saxony, an elderly, pacific, and unambitious prince, whose little army of 21,000 men was no match for the big battalions of his nearest neighbours, Austria and Prussia. The Saxons had been drawn against their will into the crusade against revolutionary France, but once successfully extricated in 1796, had no mind to renew the hazards of war. But though it was wise to be unambitious, it was fatal to be unintelligent, and the policy of Dresden lacked intelligence. 'If automatic regularity could be a solid basis for States,' said a young Austrian envoy destined to be the most famous statesman in Europe, 'Electoral Saxony would have

THE FALL OF PRUSSIA

been invulnerable[1].' There were three possible lines of action open to the Elector. He might make a formal treaty with Prussia, he might join the French connection by entering the Confederation of the Rhine, or he might proclaim and emphasize his independence. The French government skilfully intimated that it would acquiesce in either of these alternatives, and would gladly see the Elector assume a higher title. Wavering between these policies, on the one hand tempted by France but loathing her principles, on the other hand urged by Prussia but suspecting her power, the ministers of Frederick Augustus wasted the precious moments in futile proposals. When war broke out in October 1806, it found them still undulating in indecision. The Elector, while sending pacific assurances to Napoleon, allowed the Prussian troops to enter his territory.

Circumstances forced him into war. The Prussian troops were at hand while Napoleon was far off, and the Elector must either aid Prussia or fight her. In this crisis he acted with signal feebleness. He ordered his army to effect a junction with the Prussian troops, while at the same time he assured Napoleon that he would not permit it to pass the Saxon frontier. But if the Elector proposed, the Prussian generals disposed, and the Saxon contingent was swept along into the Thuringian gorges, where it experienced heavy losses at Schleitz and Saalfeld.

Napoleon had accurately gauged the situation of Saxony. He remembered that the Electorate had been invaded by Frederick the Great, and made the cockpit of a desperate war; he knew of old the rivalries of Dresden and Berlin; he saw that with a completely open frontier on the Prussian side, and a small army, the Elector was unable to resist the Prussian invasion. There had been no formal alliance signed between Frederick Augustus and Frederick William; there had been no formal declaration of war from the Court of Dresden, and the Saxon representative still continued to reside in Paris. Napoleon determined to spare the Elector, to detach him from Prussia, and to convert an unwilling foe into a useful ally. On October 3, while staying with Dalberg at Aschaffenburg, he

---

[1] Metternich, *Mémoires*, i. 33.

invited the Arch-chancellor 'confidentially to inform the Elector of Saxony that his best course in case the arms of His Majesty should triumph in his country would be not to leave it, and then he would not be treated as an enemy [1].' On October 7 he declared in his message to the Senate that 'Saxony was invaded, and that the wise prince who governed it was forced to act against his will, and the interest of his peoples.' Even as his armies were pushing through the depths of the Thuringian forest, he issued a proclamation to the peoples of Saxony in the following terms:—

'Saxons, the Prussians have invaded your territory. I enter it to deliver you. They have violently dissolved the bond which united your troops' (alluding to the fusion of a Saxon with two Prussian battalions), 'and have united them to their army. You must pour out your blood not only for interests foreign to you, but even for interests contrary to you. Saxons, your lot is now in your hands. Will you hesitate between those who put you under the yoke, and those who wish to protect you? My success will assure the existence and independence of your prince, of your nation. The success of the Prussians will impose on you eternal claims. To-morrow they will ask for Lusatia, and the day after for the Elbe-bank. But what do I say? Have they not demanded everything? Have they not for long tried to force your sovereign to recognize a sovereignty, which, if it were imposed on you, would efface you from the rank of nations? Your independence, your constitution, your liberty will then only exist in recollection, and the masses of your ancestors would be indignant to see you reduced without resistance by your rivals to a slavery prepared for so long, and your country sunk to be a Prussian province [2].'

After the battle of Jena some 300 Saxon officers and 7,000 men fell into Napoleon's hands. He summoned the officers round him in the hall of the University of Jena, told them that he had only taken up arms to assure the independence of the Saxon nation; that their sovereign, whose qualities he recommended, had shown extreme feebleness in allowing the Prussians to enter his territory; that the Saxons must join

[1] *Affaires étrangères, Corr. Pol.: Allemagne*, 732; Senfft, *Mémoires*, 12.
[2] *Corr.* xiii. 315, no. 10,949; 334, no. 10,978.

the Confederation of the Rhine under the protection of France, a protection which was not new, since for 200 years, without French aid, they would have been invaded either by Austria or by Prussia. The prisoners were then sent home, after giving their parole that they would never again serve against France. On October 21 the Emperor wrote to the Elector from Halle, saying that he had ordered a cessation of hostilities against the Saxons, that he would send a minister to settle the terms of peace, and that he was looking forward with pleasure to making the acquaintance of His Highness and the Electress.

Saxony, then, was to be saved, but not without punishment. On the day after Jena she was sentenced to a war contribution of 25,375,000 francs. All her cannon, munitions of war, shoes, military clothing, salt, and magazines, were appropriated to the use of the Grand Army, and before the French occupation came to an end, the military requisitions had mounted to 32,000,000 francs. The capital was held by a Bavarian garrison and governed by a French officer, and the furniture of the English embassy was packed up for Paris. A decree of October 23, 1806, divided the Electorate and the small Thuringian States which adjoined it into four *arrondissements*, and the civil and military administration of these districts was lodged in the hands of French intendants until the close of the war.

Meanwhile negotiations went on at Berlin for the conversion of the armistice into a peace. From these discussions it was clear that Napoleon was seeking not only to rivet Saxony to France, but also to embroil her permanently with Prussia. He therefore insisted that she should accept a fragment of the territory of her late ally, and that the whole Saxon army should forthwith join forces with the French and share the rest of the campaign. These harsh demands, though preserved in essence, were somewhat softened in detail, when the treaty came to be signed at Posen on December 11. The Electorate, converted into a kingdom, and drawn into the circle of the Rhenish Confederation, was bound to France by a strict offensive and defensive alliance, and saddled with the obligation of furnishing a contingent of 20,000 men. For the present war, however, it was sufficient if 6,000 Saxons only joined hands with the French in thrashing the Prussians and the Russians. In return for this concession the new King should pay a subsidy in cash, which ultimately came to be fixed at 25,000,000 francs. An article stipulated for the transfer of the Circle of Cottbus from Prussia to Saxony, and another for the admission of Catholics to the same civil and political rights as were enjoyed by the Lutherans of Saxony. It was stated in the treaty that His Majesty the Emperor and King made a special condition of this object. Since the sovereign House of Saxony was Catholic, though the population was Lutheran, some surprise may be felt at Napoleon's solicitude. But the French agent at Dresden had written home not long before that the Lutherans of Saxony were wont to look to Prussia for protection against their Catholic Court. His Majesty the Emperor and King, who had already required the dismissal of two Saxon ministers, may have desired to weaken the Prussophil element in the Cabinet of Dresden by opening high office to the Catholics; nor should we forget that while the Treaty of Posen was being discussed, he was fanning the flames of national feeling in Catholic Poland[1].

If Saxony was saved, reconstituted, aggrandized, it was because the Elector was known to be an unwilling client of Prussia, and because his alliance could be supremely useful to France. But there were other clients of the Hohenzollern House, the Elector of Hesse-Cassel, the Duke of Brunswick, and the Prince of Orange, who did not fare so well.

William VIII, Landgrave and first Elector of Hesse-Cassel, was a grandson of George II, a Prussian field-marshal, and a bigoted foe of revolution, liberalism, and enlightenment. His admiration for the Prussian army was unbounded. 'It's the finest corps of officers extant, and they're all nobles, sir,' he said to the French ambassador. Cherishing two passions only, soldiers and wealth, he earned the reputation of being at once the greatest miser and one of the richest princes in Germany. His soldiers were hired out to foreign powers, and his vast fortune, acquired partly by these military speculations and partly by loans issued to his own subjects, was managed with probity, zeal, and brilliance by a Hebrew banker, the founder of the Rothschild fortunes. Yet even bad governments breed

[1] *Corr.* xiv. 60, no. 11,427; de Clercq, *Recueil des Traités,* ii. 196; Bonnefons, *Un allié de Napoléon,* 176-226.

THE FALL OF PRUSSIA

special virtues, and the Hessian peasantry felt for their rubicund and niggardly tyrant emotions of loyalty, gratitude, and respect.

Napoleon had long been uncertain of Hesse-Cassel, and in the negotiations with England in the spring and summer he had even contemplated giving Hesse to Prussia, in case it were necessary to restore Hanover to the British Crown. The Elector on his side was no enthusiast for Napoleon, but neither was he willing to be the cat's-paw of Prussia. Still, after many months of tergiversation he ordered (August) his minister, Baron Waitz, to draw up a treaty of alliance with the latter power. But he was only a fair-weather friend, and when he saw that war was imminent he drew back and refused to sign. It was in vain that Frederick William offered him the command of the armies of Westphalia and Hanover, and prayed that Prussian troops might occupy some posts upon the river Fulda. The Elector replied that he had determined to observe a strict neutrality.

Unfortunately the Hessian army was put upon a war footing. The action was ambiguous. Did the Prussian field-marshal intend to fall upon the French rear or flank as they were advancing on Berlin? Was it his purpose to sell his army to the highest bidder, or was he merely determined to contest the right of French and Prussian troops to cross his territory? It is no wonder that Napoleon required a clear and instant statement of the Elector's intentions. He sent word to Cassel that Hessian neutrality could only be respected upon two conditions. The army must be demobilized, and not a single Prussian soldier must tread the soil of the Electorate.

William was probably honest, but the conduct of Hessian affairs lent itself to misinterpretation. During the critical first week of October the Elector visited the head quarters of the Prussian army, and in his absence a Prussian corps led by General Blücher entered Hesse, and was received in Cassel by the Electoral Prince attired in the uniform of a Prussian lieutenant-general. A few days afterwards the Prince suddenly fled from the capital, and joined the Prussian army. For these untoward circumstances the government of Cassel offered apologies and explanations. The Elector had visited the Prussians to plead for recognition of Hessian neutrality; the entry of Blücher was unauthorized; the flight of the Prince was the result of a quarrel with his father. But the time for apology had gone by—Hesse-Cassel was fatally compromised [1].

On October 25 Napoleon wrote from Potsdam to the Elector recapitulating his grievances, and announcing the military occupation of the country. 'My intention is,' he wrote to Mortier, 'that the House of Hesse-Cassel should cease to reign, and be effaced from the number of powers [2].' The inhabitants of Hesse were informed that their religion, their laws, their customs, their privileges would be respected, and that discipline would be maintained. 'Have confidence,' proceeded the proclamation, 'in the great sovereign upon whom your lot depends. You can experience nothing but improvement.' Two plenipotentiaries from Cassel hurried to Berlin with proposals from William. The Elector would contribute 12,000 men to the French army, levy an extraordinary contribution, and allow the French to remain in occupation of Rinteln, Hanau, and Marburg. The Emperor seemed tempted. He put Bignon, the young French minister at Cassel, some questions as to the Hessian troops and the qualities of the Elector, and spoke for a few minutes as if he were prepared to accept the propositions. Then suddenly pulling himself up, and with a brusque change of tone, he said, 'Bah! Brunswick, Nassau, Cassel, all these princes are essentially English, they will never be our friends,' and so saying strode out of the room [3].

Two days later (November 4, 1806), there followed the famous twenty-seventh bulletin announcing the deposition of the Electoral family [4]. 'There is not a House in Germany which has been so constant an enemy of France. For many years it sold the blood of its subjects to England to make war upon us in the two worlds, and it is to this traffic in his troops that the Prince owes the treasures he has amassed. This sordid avarice has brought with it the catastrophe of his House, whose existence on our frontiers is incompatible with the security of France. The English may still be able to corrupt some

---

[1] Bignon, *Histoire de France*, v. 435 ff.; Rambaud, *La domination française en Allemagne*, 101–27.

[2] *Corr.* xiii. 394–8, no. 11,061.   [3] Bignon, vi. 35.

[4] *Corr.* xiii. 470–3, no. 11,167.

THE FALL OF PRUSSIA

sovereigns with gold; but the loss of the thrones of those who receive it will be the infallible consequence of the corruption. . . . The people of Hesse-Cassel will be happier. Relieved of these immense military *corvées*, they will be able to surrender themselves quietly to the cultivation of their fields. Relieved of a portion of their taxes, they will also be governed by generous and liberal principles, principles which direct the administration of France and of her allies.' On November 1 the French troops made their entry into Cassel, and the Elector had but just time to escape in the novel and uncongenial attire of a civilian.

The fall of the House of Brunswick, decreed more promptly, aroused general regret in Germany. No German prince was more liked and respected than the aged Charles William Ferdinand, field-marshal in the Prussian army, who received a mortal wound on the field of Auerstädt. As Electoral Prince he had won his spurs in the Seven Years' War, and his gallantry had evoked the tribute of an ode from his august uncle Frederick II. Famous in war, he was also an excellent ruler in times of peace. A heavy debt bequeathed by an extravagant predecessor was reduced, if not extinguished, by the wise economies of a Court remarkable in all Germany for its naturalness and simplicity. At the same time the poll-tax was abolished, the excise diminished, and the lot of the peasantry improved by the reduction of tithes and feudal dues. While Leisewitz was reforming the poor law, and Campe carrying out educational experiments, the Duke was feeding his restless energy upon all the details of administration. 'A prince,' he used to say, 'must not live in his Court, but in history.' And as he chatted Platt-Deutsch with the country folk, or drafted the rotund preamble of some beneficent decree, he felt that the eye of history was upon him. 'He was adored by his subjects,' says a French administrator who was sent into the duchy in 1806; 'his acts of charity were not reckoned up, for it would have made an endless repetition. Intelligence, probity, devotion to the public good were titles to his favour, and at a time when the Jews were shamefully persecuted in Germany he placed a merchant named Jacobson on his Council of State, a devout Jew, a virtuous man and a philanthropist.' The strict economy of the government was unfavourable to the development of the arts and sciences, and the libraries, museums, and picture-galleries of the duchy were permitted to starve. Charles Ferdinand was neither learned nor a patron of letters. But he had seen Rome with Winkelmann, he corresponded with Voltaire, and he cherished a personal friendship with Marmontel. Though his dull English wife preferred her game of ombre to the music of Spohr or Nardini, the Duke was a genuine musician, and practised his violin until middle life. No prince in Europe was a more finished gentleman or a better linguist. Yet this versatile and accomplished nature was not devoid of grave defects : a somewhat clouded intelligence, a will beset by swarms of misgivings, an over-tender care for the great reputation of his youth. A certain morbid self-consciousness grew on him with years. While the world was expecting him to act and to lead, he was anxiously interrogating the looking-glass of public report [1].

It is no wonder that Charles Ferdinand seemed to be the incarnation of all that was hostile to the Napoleonic system. He was a Guelph and the son-in-law of an English king; he held the bâton of a Prussian field-marshal; his signature had been unfortunately attached to the manifesto of 1792, which threatened Paris with ruin if Louis XVI were not restored to liberty and power. To the French mind the name of Brunswick had come to be synonymous with all the forces of aristocracy and reaction, and it was believed that his influence had been largely instrumental in provoking the present war. Yet in truth no German prince was so genuine an admirer of France as the nominal leader of the monarchical crusade. 'He delights greatly in France,' said Mirabeau in 1786, 'and is exceedingly well acquainted with it.' Indeed, so notorious was his attachment that early in 1792 he received an invitation from the ministry of Narbonne to take over the supreme command of the French armies [2].

Borne off the field of Auerstädt mortally wounded and blinded in both eyes, the venerable commander still hoped for

[1] Pockels, *Wilhelm Ferdinand, Herzog in Braunschweig*; Massenbach, *Denkwürdigkeiten*; Heinemann, *Die herzogliche Bibliothek zu Wolfenbüttel*, 195; id., *Geschichte von Braunschweig und Hannover*, iii. 298 ff.; Beugnot, *Mémoires*; Spohr, *Autobiography*; Fitzmaurice, *Charles William Ferdinand, Duke of Brunswick*.

[2] Mirabeau, *Secret History of the Court of Berlin*, i. 18–21; *Revue historique*, i. 157 ff.

THE FALL OF PRUSSIA

kindly consideration. 'I know the French,' he said to the minister who counselled flight from Brunswick, 'better than you do. They will respect an old general wounded on the field of battle. The officers will give a ball, and go to the comedy, and flirt with the girls. See to their lodgings and that they lack nothing.' A letter was sent to recommend the duchy to the clemency of the Emperor.

Brunswick's anticipations were disappointed. Napoleon, already decided to dethrone the dynasty, broke out into fury at the receipt of the despatch. 'If I were to have the town of Brunswick demolished so as not to leave a stone standing, what would your prince say? Does not the law of retaliation permit me to do to Brunswick what he wished to do in my capital?' Then after insulting the Duke's strategy in the plains of Champagne fourteen years before, Napoleon accused him of having caused the war. 'How worthy of blame is this man, who with a word might have averted disaster, if, like Nestor, raising his voice in the midst of the councils he had said, "Inconsiderate youth, be silent; women, go back to your spindles, and return to the interior of your households."'

This would have been a strange allocution for a Prussian field-marshal to address to his queen, but Napoleon was not the finest judge of etiquette. 'Tell *General* Brunswick,' he said, 'that he will be treated with all the respect due to a Prussian officer, but I cannot recognize a sovereign in a Prussian general.' He was even more outspoken to the Chancellor of the Duke of Weimar. 'You see what I have done to the Duke of Brunswick. I intend to send these Guelphs back to the Italian marshes from which they sprang. I mean to crush them and to destroy them like this hat' (throwing his hat to the ground), 'so that they shall no longer be remembered in Germany [1].'

The third of the minor victims was William Frederick of Orange, brother-in-law to the Prussian King, who having been turned out of his hereditary dominions in consequence of earlier French victories, was compensated in 1803 by a small principality in the heart of Germany consisting of the secularized lands of Fulda and Corvey, the imperial town of Dortmund, and some abbeys in Swabia. There was a touch of irony in the fate

[1] F. von Müller, *Erinnerungen aus den Kriegszeiten*, 62.

which sent this revolutionary young Lutheran to govern one of the most bigoted Catholic provinces in the Empire. William Frederick had been impressed by the methods of Joseph II, and the little principality hardly knew itself under his stirring rule. A gay Court enlivened the sleepy capital accustomed to the ponderous ways of canons. Strange Dutchmen were reported to hold various offices. The University was turned into a Lyceum, and contaminated by the presence of Protestant professors. There was an end of many monasteries, and the Prince aimed at depriving the clergy of educational control. A workhouse built for the most part from monastic funds was an insult to the Roman theory of benevolence, while an ordinance that Catholics and Protestants might be buried in the same churchyard was regarded as a gross outrage on religious decency. The Catholic mind of Fulda was even beginning to effervesce into seditious sermons and pamphlets when Napoleon removed the well-meaning but unpopular Prince. Frederick William had fought under the Prussian flag, he was wounded at Auerstädt and taken at Erfurt. 'The Prince of Orange will no longer reign at Fulda,' wrote Napoleon to Mortier on October 17 [1].

The deposition of the Prince of Orange from a principality he had only ruled for three years and which thoroughly disliked him was a step not likely to cause any grave commotion of opinion in Germany. But it was far otherwise with the expulsion of the Houses of Hesse-Cassel and Brunswick. No one indeed was prepared to shed tears over the Elector of Hesse-Cassel, who had been too timid to fight and too irresolute to make peace. He had met little more than his deserts. But his House was ancient and popular, and deep in the German nature was the instinct of reverence for a family at once old and princely. And if this was the sentiment with respect to Hesse-Cassel, the fall of the House of Brunswick aroused a still keener feeling of pity and resentment. The tragic end of one of the most venerable and honoured figures in German history, blinded, wounded, and dying in exile, stirred the sentimental hearts of his compatriots. The expulsion of the Guelphs meant the snapping of a great historical tradition, a tradition of

---

[1] *Corr.* xiii. 366, no. 11,023; Darmstaedter, *Das Grossherzogthum Frankfurt,* 58 ff.

a thousand years, blended with memories of ancient emperors and many heroic, famous, and factious deeds. That the Houses of Brunswick and of Cassel should have been punished for their conduct during this campaign was to be expected. But a military execution was one thing, and the subversion of two ancient dynasties was another. The policy or impolicy of the deed would have to be judged by the results, by the quality of the new governments it would be necessary to set up in place of the old. Would they be German or French, conservative or progressive, strong or feeble, free or bound, lenient or tyrannous? The army bulletins announced to Hessians and Brunswickers a golden age. But who was to play the part of Astraea?

Napoleon was now master of Northern Germany from end to end. But in this conquest he had acquired more than the immediate material gain and addition to his military prestige: he had obtained a weapon against Great Britain. In the autumn of 1802, when relations were becoming tense between France and England, Napoleon, dictating instructions to Otto in London, said that if England insisted on stirring up war on the continent, she would compel the First Consul to conquer Europe. Appreciating his own naval weakness, he felt that the conquest of the island was dubious, perhaps impossible. But he believed that the wealth of England was fictitious and destructible, ignoring the profound workings of the English industrial revolution and the deep-set foundations of her commercial greatness. Like all strong-willed men he was apt to overrate the power of legislation to counteract natural forces, and the opinions of the physiocratic school which contended for free trade were dismissed with contempt as pestilent 'ideology.' It was his firm conviction that England and English obstinacy were at the bottom of the coalition and that the fountain could be dried at its source. The nation of shopkeepers could be reduced to beggary by persistent exclusion from the continental market. He could 'conquer the sea by the land [1].'

[1] '*Bonaparte du reste et toute son administration faisaient profession du plus grand mépris pour le commerce. On lui avait persuadé que l'esprit commercial était anti-monarchique; qu'il n'y avait pas d'honneur dans un pays commerçant et qu'il fallait que la France fût seulement militaire et agricole.*'—Pichon, *De l'état de la France sous la domination de Napoléon*, 158-9.

On November 21, 1806, a decree dated from Berlin declared the Britannic Isles in a state of blockade. All commerce and correspondence with them was forbidden. Every British subject found in any country occupied by the French troops or those of their allies was to be made a prisoner of war, and all English merchandise and property was declared good prize. No ships coming from England or English colonies were to be received in any continental port. Letters and packets addressed to an Englishman or written in England were to be seized by the post. Great Britain was to be cast out of the community of civilized nations.

To execute a measure such as this it was necessary for Napoleon to keep a tight hand upon Germany. 'In this new position,' he explained to the Senate, 'we have taken as the invariable principles of our conduct not to evacuate either Berlin or Warsaw or the provinces which the force of arms has thrown into our hands before a general peace is concluded, the Spanish, Dutch, and French colonies are restored, the foundations of the Ottoman Empire reaffirmed, and the absolute independence of this vast Empire, the first interest of our people, irrevocably consecrated.'

While these proud words were being written, the French army was enduring the horrors of a winter campaign in Poland. The military power of Russia, though it had been severely checked at Austerlitz, was still formidable in numbers and courage, and it was aided by the mud, the cold, and the desolation of the plains of Poland. It was still possible that Austria might rejoin the fray and throw an army over the Bohemian defiles upon the right flank of Napoleon. In such an event the position of the French would indeed be desperate. But Napoleon was equal to the emergency, and never in his whole career did he display a greater abundance of diplomatic resource.

CHIEF AUTHORITIES: Bailleu, *Preussen und Frankreich*; Oncken, *Das Zeitalter der Revolution des Kaiserreichs und der Befreiungskriege*; Lefebvre, *Histoire des Cabinets de l'Europe*; Häusser, *Deutsche Geschichte*; Bignon, *Histoire de France*; Rambaud, *Domination française en Allemagne*; Bonnefons, *Un allié de Napoléon*; Fitzmaurice, *Charles William Ferdinand, Duke of Brunswick*; Massenbach, *Denkwürdigkeiten*; L. Müller, *Aus sturmvoller Zeit*; Thiébault, *Mémoires*.

CHAPTER VII

TILSIT AND THE SETTLEMENT OF NORTH GERMANY

'Nous viendrons à bout de l'Angleterre ; nous pacifierons le monde, et la paix de Tilsit sera, je l'espère, une nouvelle époque dans les fastes du monde.'—NAPOLEON.

A SECRET despatch from Paris sent to the British government on June 4, 1805, contains the following passage : 'Bonaparte desires to avenge himself for the opposition which he has experienced from Russia and to annul her influence in Europe. *The re-establishment of the Kingdom of Poland is his favourite plan*[1].' The French Emperor had long followed the fortunes of Poland, and saw that this indolent, fiery, and unfortunate people might be of value in his political combinations. Polish exiles swarmed in the ante-rooms of the French minister at Dresden, shed their blood for the French cause in Italy, and poured the story of their wrongs into the sympathetic ears of Paris. The heroes of the War of Polish Independence clustered round Napoleon in Berlin and received his encouragement. 'Show yourselves worthy of your forefathers,' he said to a Polish deputation; 'they ruled the House of Brandenburg, they were the masters of Moscow, they took the fortress of Widdin, they freed Christianity from the yoke of the Turks. In Warsaw I will openly declare your independence[2].' As the Grand Army, accompanied by Polish legions and the patriot Dombrowski, moved into Warsaw, it was received with cries of welcome and triumphal arches. The hated Prussians, who had taxed brandy and musical instruments, who had disbanded the Polish army, allowed Polish officers to starve, filled all the civil offices with their creatures, lent money at usurious rates to needy landlords, striven to extend the dominion of the dreary Lutheran religion and the hateful German tongue—these Prussians had had their

[1] *F. O., France,* 72.   [2] Cölln, *Vertraute Briefe,* ii. 4.

way. Under a Catholic Emperor the ancient glories of the Polish kingdom would revive.

If Napoleon had wished to reunite the forces of Austria and Russia, no more effective plan could have been devised than the restoration of the Polish kingdom. Both powers had shared in the partitions and were determined to guard their spoils. By conceding then to the full measure of Polish aspirations Napoleon would have committed the supreme folly of making peace with Russia impossible and war with Austria certain. But every day spent in the Polish mud was pointing to the necessity of peace. The indecisive and costly battle of Eylau had dashed the spirits of the Grand Army and diminished Napoleon's prestige, nor could the continental blockade ever be made effective until Russia had been brought to terms.

Napoleon therefore, while studious to encourage the warlike propensities of his valuable allies, declined to commit himself to any definite assurance which might compromise the future diplomatic situation. He had never, so he said, recognized the partitions of Poland; he declared that he was touched by the melancholy fate of the country and by the passionate national sentiment which exhibited itself everywhere. The future, however, he would only indicate in cloudy and solemn declamation. 'Will the throne of Poland,' so it was written in the thirty-sixth bulletin, 'be re-established, and this great nation resume her existence and her independence? From the depths of the tomb will she be born again unto life? God alone, who holds the combinations in His hands, is the arbiter of this great political problem.' The Emperor was modest, for he too would have something to say to the solution.

At last the decisive victory came (June 1807) at Friedland, marked by huge Russian losses, and inspiring a quick impulse of despair. Alexander determined to treat for peace, and the French and Russian Emperors arranged to liquidate the unsettled affairs of Europe upon a raft on the Niemen. The main outlines of the scheme were already fixed in Napoleon's mind. Alexander would recognize the French conquests and the French vassal kingdoms, would offer his mediation to England, and in the event of its being declined would undertake to join the continental blockade. Napoleon on his side would offer his mediation to Turkey, and if this were refused, would assist his ally in the partition of the Balkan peninsula. Napoleon would be master of the West, Alexander of the East.

But if the large lines were settled, the details were floating and uncertain. The first plan submitted upon the French side provided for a strong unbroken chain of French power from the Rhine to the Niemen. Napoleon was to keep Hanover, the Hanseatic towns, the coasts of Mecklenburg and Swedish Pomerania, in other words the whole of the North German littoral, while Danzig was to be a free town. Besides this, five principalities influenced by France and firmly attached to the French system were to stretch across Northern Germany: first Berg, swelled by the Westphalian possessions of Prussia; then a State formed out of the territories of Hesse, Brunswick, and Nassau; and, thirdly, the new Kingdom of Saxony, which had already, as we have seen, been compelled to join the Rhenish Confederation. Silesia, the prize of so many efforts, would be wrested from the Hohenzollerns and given to a French prince; while, lastly, a principality would be formed out of the Polish lands which had been acquired by Prussia since 1772 [1].

The generosity of Alexander, whose conscience accused him of desertion, modified some details in this ruthless scheme, and Silesia was saved for the Hohenzollern House. None the less the open and secret treaties of Tilsit, which were signed between France and Russia July 7, 1807, dealt a crushing blow to the monarchy of Frederick William. On the east and west alike Prussia was stripped of her most precious possessions. On the east the Polish provinces were made into the Grand-Duchy of Warsaw and handed over to the King of Saxony, who was given a military road across Prussian territory to connect his new with his old dominions. By article 9 of the treaty a small strip of Prussian territory east of the Niemen was transferred to Russia, nominally to establish the 'natural limits,' but in reality to instil a drop of venom into the relations of St. Petersburg and Berlin [2]. The navigation of the Vistula was

[1] Hardenberg, *Denkwürdigkeiten*, iii. 492; Vandal, *Napoléon et Alexandre*, i. 88.

[2] According to Oginski (*Mémoires*, ii. 377), Napoleon offered the whole Duchy of Warsaw to Alexander.

to be free, an advantage which would be appreciated by the new Saxon and Polish vassals of the Emperor, but Danzig, which commanded this great estuary of Polish commerce, though nominally a free port under the joint protection of Prussia and Saxony, was garrisoned and continued to be garrisoned by French troops. If the Duchy of Warsaw was to be composed of the spoils of Prussia in the east, the Kingdom of Westphalia was to be created out of the provinces ceded by the King of Prussia on the left bank of the Elbe, together with other territories then in possession of Napoleon. Alexander agreed to recognize the Emperor's youngest brother Jerome as King of Westphalia, and despite the entreaties of Queen Louise the important fortress of Magdeburg was added to his dominions. It was also stipulated that the ports of the Duchy of Oldenburg and Mecklenburg should continue to be occupied by French garrisons until the ratifications of a definitive treaty with England had been exchanged [1].

When in the course of the negotiations Alexander expressed a desire that Prussia should have 200,000 souls on the left bank of the Elbe, Napoleon objected on the ground that the Prussian State would be interlaced with the Confederation of the Rhine. 'In so great an epoch,' he wrote, 'the most important thing is properly to define relations and limits. One must remember the evils produced by intermingled States: witness the passage over the territory of Anspach.' But to meet the Russian contention an article was inserted into the secret treaty to the effect that if Hanover were to be united to the Kingdom of Westphalia, Prussia should receive a compensation amounting to 400,000 souls on the left bank of the Elbe [2].

A treaty with Prussia was signed on July 9, in which that unfortunate kingdom notified its acceptance of these terms. But this was not the end of Prussian humiliations. A large French army was in occupation of the kingdom, and there was not a stronghold in Prussia which had escaped the burden of a French garrison. By a convention signed at Königsberg July 12, 1807, it was now arranged that the French troops

[1] The treaties of Tilsit are printed in Vandal, i. App. 1.
[2] *Corr.* xv. 384, no. 12,849.

TILSIT AND NORTH GERMANY 147

should be gradually withdrawn, but only when the war contributions demanded by Napoleon had been fully paid up. As the amount of these contributions had not yet been fixed, the country was faced with the appalling possibility of an indefinite military occupation.

Napoleon said long afterwards that probably the greatest mistake of his life was that he did not dethrone the King of Prussia when he could so easily have done so. 'After Friedland, I should have taken Silesia from Prussia, and abandoned this province to Saxony. The King of Prussia and the Prussians were too humiliated not to seek vengeance on the first opportunity. If I had acted thus, if I had given them a free constitution, and had delivered the peasants from feudal slavery, the nation would have been content[1].' But if such had been his action, would he ever have made peace with Alexander, and would he not almost inevitably have been faced with a combination between Austria and Russia ? After Eylau, peace was a necessity to Napoleon. The slaughter had been immense, the army was profoundly discouraged, the conditions under which warfare was waged were gloomy and dispiriting. All Napoleon's diplomatic powers were required to avert a fresh catastrophe. To have dethroned the King of Prussia would have been as fatal a step as to have made a King of Poland. And though Napoleon's ambitions were exorbitant, they were still mingled with a dash of prudence.

In the negotiations of Tilsit the name of Poland was not even mentioned. But while Napoleon refrained from reviving the ancient kingdom of the Poles, he did not wish to lose the support of a gallant and enthusiastic people. The creation of the Grand-Duchy of Warsaw, a small State of 1,850 square miles, and numbering something over two million inhabitants, seemed to be the wise compromise. It ensured order, it sustained patriotism, it humiliated Prussia, it gave France a sure bastion on the east. At the same time it was essential to show that the new grand-duchy was not intended to be the nucleus for the revival of the ancient kingdom. When Alexander suggested

---

[1] O'Meara, *Napoleon at St. Helena*, i. 346. Champagny in 1810 advised the destruction of Prussia on the ground that Prussia was the centre of anti-French influence in Germany. Senfft, *Mémoires*, 132–3.

that the Grand-Ducal crown should be offered to Jerome, Napoleon was tempted, but declined. For a moment it flashed into his mind that Jerome might be married into the Saxon House, so as to link Warsaw to Dresden and Cassel. 'Saxony joined to Westphalia,' he said to Frederick Augustus, 'that would make a fine kingdom.' But the objections to the plan were quickly apparent. It would bring France into dangerous and unpleasant contact with Russia, and involve the two nations in all the thousand and one altercations which arise between contiguous States. Accordingly he assured Alexander that it was not his intention to extend the sphere of direct French influence beyond the Rhine. 'The countries situated between the Niemen and the Elbe will form the barrier which will separate the great empires, and deaden the pin-pricks which between nations precede the cannon shots[1].' If the Duchy of Warsaw was not to be French, it was undoubtedly adroit to offer it to the King of Saxony. His loyal and lymphatic rule would calm Russia and please the Poles. Two Saxon Electors had already sat upon the throne of Poland, and the Diet had offered the crown in 1792 to Frederick Augustus himself. The new monarch spoke the Polish language, and professed the Roman Catholic religion, nor was there any likelihood that one of the slowest administrators in Germany would thwart the habits or violate the sentiments of a nation which, like the Irish, disliked the normal Teutonic views of progress. 'Under a Saxon, eat, drink, and loosen the belt,' so ran the Polish proverb of the eighteenth century. But if Napoleon offered the Grand-Ducal throne to Saxony, he was careful to reserve the essentials of power for himself. By the Convention of Dresden, July 22, 1807, the Emperor of the French was alone permitted to have a resident at Warsaw, and the Grand-Duke bound himself to support a contingent of 30,000 men who were to be placed under the immediate control of Marshal Davoût. Limited on the military side by the French marshal, and on the political side by the French resident, the sovereignty of Frederic Augustus was reduced to a sham. To render it effective it would have been necessary to appoint a resident Saxon viceroy in Warsaw, and the Court of Dresden

---

[1] Bonnefons, 221 ; Senfft, 30 ; *Corr.* xv. 384, no. 12,849.

suggested the name of Prince Anthony. But since a Saxon viceroy might have eclipsed the importance of the French resident, the scheme met with obstacles which Frederick Augustus was too languid to overcome.

While he was yet at Tilsit, Napoleon summoned some Polish magnates to help in the drafting of a constitutional statute for the new duchy, and the work was completed in Dresden. Every line in this document, which indeed is closely fashioned on the French model, bears the imprint of Napoleon. The Roman Catholic religion was declared to be the religion of the State, but all forms of worship could be fully and publicly exercised. A brief clause declared that serfdom was unconditionally abolished, and that all citizens were equal before the law, and the whole fabric of French jurisprudence and of French judicial organization was to be transplanted to the 'solitudes of Poland,' from which the French soldiers looked back so regretfully to the 'smiling landscapes of France.' Every two years a Diet, consisting of a life Senate of 18 and a Chamber of 100 members, was to meet at Warsaw for the discussion of bills relating to finance, currency, civil and criminal law. But the old tendencies to anarchy were to be repressed with a strong hand. The sessions of the Diet were limited to fifteen days, and the right of speech confined to members of these standing commissions and of the King's council. If the King should quarrel with his assembly, it was specially provided that he could carry on the finances without it. There was no danger that the Chamber would be swept by sudden waves of passion, for one-third retired by rotation every year, and the electoral lists were carefully made up and revised by government officials. As for the Senate, it was nominated by the King. Indeed extreme centralization was the key-note of the constitution in the Grand-Duchy of Warsaw no less than in France. The prefects, the sub-prefects, the burgomasters, the municipal counsellors were all to be named by the absentee monarch in Dresden. A few touches were borrowed from the famous constitution of 1791, to which the Poles looked back with affectionate regard, and the presence of bishops in the Senate recalled the days of King Stanislas. But though both constitutions agreed in strengthening the executive, they differed widely in an essential respect, for while the constitution of 1791 granted a large measure of political liberty, but hardly touched the fabric of social privilege, in the statute of 1807 social equality was decreed, and political liberty practically extinguished.

That this Napoleonic constitution contained within itself the seeds of political regeneration for Poland cannot be doubted. It cured what no Polish ruler would have dared to cure, and what the Prussian law had not attempted to cure, the cancer of noble privilege. The deep barriers between class and class, between the miserable down-trodden peasantry, the outcast traders of the Ghetto, the indolent and profligate nobility, were cast down with a powerful hand. The constitution of 1791 had ventured a timid protest against the noble who broke a contract which he had made with his peasants. The Prussian law had permitted marriages between nobles and the higher rank of burgesses in rare and special cases. But Napoleon with one gesture decreed the freedom of the village, and made peasant, Jew, and noble the equal citizens of a common State.

The legislation of the Saxon sovereign—*le médecin malgré lui*, as he was termed in the witty *salons* of Warsaw—filled in the cursory outlines of the Polish Lycurgus. By a decree of December 21, 1807, the peasant was permitted to quit his holding, and the free transfer of land facilitated by the abolition of the distinction between noble and peasant property. An end was made of the fearful punishments which had hitherto disgraced the law and the practice of the country, and after March 18, 1809, no criminal could be racked on the wheel, flogged in public, or burnt alive. A central committee was formed in 1810 to draw up a plan for elementary education, to draft a school code, and to take measures preliminary to the selection of elementary school-books. Sanitary administration, the very idea of which was unfamiliar in Poland, was entrusted to the supervision of a central medical council; and by the formation of a commercial college, of a law school at Warsaw, and of a school of administrative science, an attempt was made to open the eyes of intelligence among the governing class of the duchy.

It was not, however, to be expected that reforms so revolutionary as these would be altogether welcome. The spirit of Poland was aristocratic, Catholic, and anarchical; the spirit of the constitution was egalitarian, secular, and centralized. Though the higher clergy of Warsaw, who may have been more intelligent or more servile than their brethren, consecrated the Civil Code in the cathedral, and listened to an eloquent sermon upon its merits, yet its introduction was felt to be an humiliation and a national disaster. The Commons were unable to understand the laification of marriage and the interference with paternal authority; the nobles, especially the Lithuanian nobles, detested the abolition of slavery, and we have it on the word of Davoût, that if the power of the clergy had not already been broken by the Prussians, there would have been a Polish edition of the Vendée, directed against some of the institutions of the Code. It is a sufficient illustration of the barbarous character of the country that Lubienski, the Minister of Justice, who was responsible for the introduction of the French judicial system, was generally suspected of wishing to make himself master of all the fortunes of the country by his ascendency over the law courts, nor was the design considered to be illegitimate. It was the prevalent opinion that a judge who decided against the interests of his own family had failed to perform his duty [1].

To acclimatize the principles of a modern civilized State in an atmosphere so strange and uncongenial would have required force, time, and good will. But the King of Saxony was only an occasional visitor, and his Polish ministers were either incompetent or secretly hostile to the French system. Napoleon had advised Frederick Augustus not to 'burden his finances with the Prussian employés who were in the duchy,' or, in other words, to reserve all State employments to the Poles. So the great names in the patriotic annals of Polish history were

[1] Mazade, *Correspondance du Maréchal Davoût*, ii. 74, 230; Senfft, 117-8; Skarbek, *Dzieje Xięstwa Warszawskiego*, i. 140, 141, 188, 192-7. The *Moniteur*, Aug. 15, 1810, gives a curious account of the consecration of the Code in the Cathedral of Cracow, when it was extended to the four Galician departments which had been added after the war of 1809. After the office the Bishop thundered out the *Te Deum* and the *Salvum fac Napoleonem*, and then proceeded to the consecration of the Code.

promoted to places of honour, and while Malachowski, head of the patriotic party in 1791, was made President of the Council, Joseph Poniatowski, nephew of the last King of Poland, became Minister of War. But while this measure secured for the administration a certain air of popularity, it was not without immediate drawbacks. The Poles were unaccustomed to office hours, suspicious of Western novelty, and divided by cabals, and to the punctual French mind the Cabinet at Warsaw presented a distressing spectacle. Nor was it possible to repress the effervescence of a people in whom the habit of discussion and invective had been strengthened by centuries of aristocratic anarchy. The Polish deputies endured the ennui of their official parliament for the stipulated fifteen days, but when once the Marshal had declared this assembly to be dissolved, they continued their sessions informally and loaded the ministry with abuse. The debates, lately so arid, now became passionate and tumultuous, and Poland was gratified by a spectacle which recalled the good old days of liberty and disorder. Under these circumstances it is not wonderful if some features in the Napoleonic programme were altered or obliterated. While the government of Dresden was far from brave, the Polish aristocracy was a military asset which might be squandered by undue harshness or by misplaced philanthropy, so the peasant continued to perform *corvées* and to pay dues, and the Hebrew population, though admitted to civil, was, with some exceptions, jealously excluded from political rights [1].

It must be remembered that at the time of its creation the Grand-Duchy of Warsaw was lying waste and desolate. Some liberal provisions for the material welfare of the inhabitants, some compensation for the losses which they had suffered from the war, would have gone far to commend the new institutions, and to infuse a spirit of hopefulness as to the future of the country. This, however, was not the course

---

[1] Bignon, *Histoire de France*, x. 378; Laube, *Gesetzsammlung*, ii. 143 ff., iv. 120 ff. The preamble of the decree of Jan. 29, 1812, freeing the Jews of the duchy from the conscription on payment of 700,000 gulden, is characteristic. It is based on the fact (1) that they are not citizens, (2) that they are unworthy of the noble profession of arms, (3) that they cannot be trusted.

which commended itself to Napoleon. So far from helping Poland along the road of prosperity, he plunged her deeper and deeper into the morass of destitution. He reserved domains to the value of 26,582,000 francs to serve as dotations for his marshals and generals. The duchy was not only burdened with the support of a large army, but compelled to repay the sums which Napoleon had advanced to his Polish allies during the war. By a treaty concluded at Bayonne in 1809, the King of Saxony was forced to make a ruinous bargain with the Emperor, buying for a sum of 20,000,000 francs the right which France claimed to have inherited from Prussia of recovering private debts to the amount of 45,000,000 from the bankrupt proprietors in the duchy. Nothing was a source of greater weakness to the Court of Dresden than the attempt to recover these miserable Prussian debts. It made the Saxon name odious among the Poles, and produced incessant friction with the Court of Berlin.

From first to last, then, the Duchy of Warsaw presented a lamentable spectacle. The burden of an army, French and Polish, which in the autumn of 1807 amounted to 86,000 men, the ruin of the export trade in corn owing to the continental blockade, the remorseless rigour with which first the agents of the French and then the agents of the Saxon government pursued the creditors of Prussia, created uneasiness, discord, and distress. As early as September 1807 rumours were flying that it was the Emperor's intention to ruin the country and then abandon it. Though the King of Saxony, with rare generosity, refused to touch a penny of the Civil List allotted to him as Grand-Duke, there was a deficit of 21,000,000 in the budget of 1808. Napoleon, indeed, so far yielded to the complaints of the inhabitants as to take 8,000 Poles into French pay, and to summon them to France. But the country was never able to attain financial equilibrium, despite the introduction of novel and rigorous forms of taxation. In 1810 the expenditure was almost double the revenue; in 1811 the duchy was practically ruined. The pay of the troops in October of that year was eleven months in arrear; the soldiers had no boots or winter trousers; there was neither coin nor credit, and the contractors refused to advance.

'The dissolution of the Polish army,' wrote Poniatowski, 'seems almost inevitable.' Indeed, since the creation of the State, the revenues had never reached two-thirds of their estimated value. 'Nothing,' says de Pradt, who went to Warsaw in the summer of 1812, 'could exceed the misery of all classes. The army was unpaid, the officers were in rags; the best houses were in ruins, and the greatest lords were obliged to leave Warsaw from the want of money wherewith to provide their tables [1].'

'This languishing and almost agonizing body,' as Davout described the Grand-Duchy of Warsaw in 1808, was kept alive by the hope that some day or other Napoleon would restore the ancient Kingdom of Poland in its ample dimensions. For this end the patriots of Warsaw endured the conscription, and, what was even worse, the incessant and harassing inquisition of Davoût's spies. Though the miserable and distracted ministers were liable to have their papers visited by the French police, their conduct reprimanded by the French resident, and their subordinates dismissed and banished at the word of the French general; though every letter which passed through the post was read by a spy, and every paragraph which appeared in the newspapers was submitted to a censor, still the government laboured on. The one hope of all the patriots was a new war, and the one school of civic discipline was the army. Indeed, the megalomania of the Poles, which no misfortune could quench and no experience could temper, was the sole spiritual force which united the duchy to France [2].

Even before the formation of the Duchy of Warsaw, Napoleon had taken steps towards the organization of his conquests in Western Germany. On October 23, 1806, soon after Jena, a decree was issued establishing five military governments in the States which formerly belonged to Prussia, Brunswick, Hanover, and Orange-Nassau. General Loison was named Governor of Mark, Münster, Tecklenburg, and Osnabrück; General Gobert of Minden and Paderborn. General Bisson was sent to Brunswick, General Thiébault to Fulda, and General Clarke to Erfurt.

[1] Mazade, ii. 48, 115; Poniatowski to Eckmühl, Oct. 12, Nov. 22, Dec. 14, 1811; A. F. iv. 1656-7; de Pradt, *Ambassade à Varsovie*.

[2] Mazade, ii. 26, 107, 182, 391.

TILSIT AND NORTH GERMANY

On the same day Mortier was ordered to occupy Hesse, and to appoint General Lagrange military governor of the country; while, finally, by the end of November Hanover was again in French hands, and formed a seventh military government under Marshal Mortier.

It is important to remember the existence of these military governments, for they formed an essential part of the Napoleonic system, and some of them lasted for several years, as for instance Hanover, which remained under military rule till 1810, and Erfurt, which never obtained anything better. There were therefore a good many Germans whose impressions of French rule were mainly derived not from the fully organized *studied* principalities, like Westphalia or Berg, but from the unorganized rudimentary unstudied military governments, like Fulda or Hanover. Then again some of these rudimentary governments were afterwards superseded by organized Napoleonic States. There was, so to speak, a military preface, often not very amiable in tone, to the new State or to some part of it, but whether amiable or harsh these military preludes could not be without influence in the sequel, and thus they deserve a passing word.

To enforce the continental blockade, to spare the French taxpayer the cost of the war, to cement the loyalty and to refresh the courage of marshals, generals, or civil servants, to retain in the power of France provinces which might be used as objects of compensation in any peace negotiations, such were the main motives which underlay the military government. The structure of these governments was extremely simple. The province would be allowed to retain its old laws and customs, but it would be governed by a French military officer, held down by a French military force, and compelled to contribute dotations to the marshals, contingents to the army, and contributions to the treasury of France. In each government the general would be assisted by an inspector or sub-inspector of reviews, whose duty it was to control the finance, and to submit daily reports upon the financial situation to the inspector-in-chief, and this financial expert was assisted by a receiver who was subordinate to the receiver-general of the contributions of the Grand Army. Nor was this the sole limitation to the power of the military proconsul. Apart from the very vigilant supervision of Napoleon himself, who systematically encouraged the habit of delation among the officers, and exhibited a most marked and well-grounded distrust of French military probity, the soldier-rulers in Germany were in 1808 placed under the immediate control of Davoût or of Bernadotte. Frequently changed from place to place, they were unable to acquire any durable influence. But all the watchfulness of the Emperor could not prevent embezzlement and peculation [1].

Of the military governments established in Germany in 1806, that of Hesse was perhaps the most respectable. Here the two chieftains, Lagrange the general, and La Martillière the intendant, though not above pecuniary temptations, were capable and on the whole well-conducted [2]. Lagrange in particular was conspicuous for his humane temper, his excellent political judgement, and his soldierly bearing. The province which he was called upon to govern presented peculiar difficulties. It regretted its old Elector, it was full of a population trained in the use of arms, it was covered with wooded hills not ill-suited to guerilla warfare. The orders of Napoleon were accordingly stringent, precise, and exasperating. 'Destroy the fortifications of Marburg from top to bottom. Blow up the fortifications of Hanau, so that the place is as flat as my hand. Transport to Mainz all the artillery, all the magazines, all the furniture, statues, and effects of the palaces of the Court. Disarm the country strictly. Do not leave a cannon or a gun. Execute my orders, and arrest and send to France the colonels and the officers. Send an intendant and a receiver of contributions to collect the revenues of the Prince. For the rest, you may treat the country gently, but if there is the least movement anywhere make a terrible example. Let the first village which stirs be pillaged and burnt; let the first assemblage be dispersed, and its chiefs brought before a military commission. Let no prince of the House of Hesse, not even the women, be allowed to stay in the country. Give them their passports. Dismiss all the servants. Do this with exactitude, with firmness, but with all the French good nature, and with

---

[1] Some interesting light is thrown on Napoleon's attitude to the army by Gustave Canton, *Napoléon antimilitariste*.

[2] Brunner, *General Lagrange als Gouverneur in Hessen-Cassel*, 30, 31.

all the regard due to the sex. . . . If there is anything to be done which can be useful to this population and content it, such as the suppression of some onerous duty, let me know [1].'

Such then are the main principles. The country must be disarmed, repressed, pillaged of its art treasures, but compensated for these evils by some popular reforms, such as do not compromise the principles of authority. It is no wonder that the initial measures of Lagrange produced a revolt. The old soldiers of Southern Hesse, resenting disarmament, and being commanded upon pain of death to report themselves in their barracks, in order to be enrolled in the army of the French Empire, broke into insurrection. Many of their officers, who had refused to serve under the French colours, were already immured in the fortress of Mainz, and it was believed that a plot was on foot to capture and exile the whole Hessian army. For a moment it seemed as if the affair would be serious, for the castle of Marburg fell into the hands of the insurgents, and small French detachments were put to rout at Hersfeld and Smalkalden. But the men were ill-led, ill-combined, and half-hearted, and the effervescence soon subsided as General Barbot's troops poured in from the south. In spite of the Draconian orders of Napoleon, Lagrange handled the situation with judicious clemency. When the revolt first broke out, he issued proclamations promising a general amnesty to those who would return to their duty by a certain date. There were no holocausts of towns or villages, and hardly more than ten of the insurgents suffered the extreme penalty of the law. The clemency of General Barbot at Hersfeld was equally statesmanlike, but it was both stimulated and rewarded by the bribes of the inhabitants [2].

The province of Fulda—poor, hilly, sylvan, ignorant, without industry or manufacture—was, as we have seen, allotted to General Thiébault. His intendant reported great administrative confusion as a result of the frequent changes under the Orange régime. There was difficulty in getting information about the domains; the forests were not surveyed; there was no administration of princely gardens or fisheries, and here as elsewhere in

[1] *Corr.* xiii. 479–80, no. 11,174.
[2] Von Müller, *Aus sturmvoller Zeit.*

Germany the French mind was shocked by the dearth of exact statistics [1]. The military contribution laid by Napoleon upon this little district amounted to about a million francs, and as, besides this, the province had to contribute to the support of the governor and the government, not to speak of miscellaneous military requisitions, the scrutiny of the intendant was doubtless minute and unsparing. The memoirs of the lively general, however, show us some of the more pleasant as well as some of the worst features of the French rule. While the finances of the country were crippled, the governor realized 212,500 francs in 144 days. He organized concerts, brought a pastry-cook from Cassel, and 'added to the productions of the country the finest fish of the Rhine, the pheasants of Bohemia, and the pâtés of Strasburg.' A battalion of light infantry was raised for the Emperor's service, and there was no difficulty in finding volunteers. Since it was a point of honour with a French proconsul to denude his province of its choicest treasures, it was necessary for Thiébault to explore all the possibilities of loot. The Prince-Bishops of Fulda had not been patrons of the arts, and even if they had converted their tithes into Rembrandts or Raphaels, it may be suspected that the French general would have been an undiscriminating admirer. But in default of pictures there were three tons of the best Johannesberg vintage in the cellar, a chamois incarcerated in a wooden cage and said to be the only specimen of the kind taken alive, and a hundred and twenty chests containing the library of the defunct abbey of Weingarten. The mercurial governor settled with avidity upon these miscellaneous trophies. A travelling-cage was constructed for the beast, the precious fluid was bottled under the eyes of the satrap and despatched to the Emperor and to influential friends, while the rarest manuscripts from the monastic collection found their way into the Imperial Library in Paris.

General Thiébault intimated that he was fortunate in succeeding an unpopular and Protestant prince. The inhabitants of Fulda frequented the levées, appreciated the dinners, and admired the piety of a Catholic ruler; the old councils and the old stiff ceremonial remained as before, nor was there

[1] *Affaires étrangères, Mémoires et documents: Allemagne,* 137.

any change in the men who carried on the civil business of the province. But the weight of the contributions was appalling. A native, after two years' experience of French rule, wrote the following words: 'All the veins of the province have been opened, and it will bleed to death [1].'

The second military occupation of Hanover was characterized by exactions which were equally pitiless. 'The Hanoverian Estates,' wrote Napoleon to Berthier, October 19, 1806, 'have been shameless enough to offer me 300,000 francs a month from the revenues of their country; they must pay 1,200,000 francs a month, and 10,000 thalers a week.' The French officials upon the spot, General Lascalcette and Intendant Belleville, formerly prefect in the department of Loire Inférieure, were humane and sympathetic, and did everything which lay within their power to alleviate the burden of their subjects. Daru, informed by Belleville, submitted a report to the Emperor which painted in true and terrible colours the financial exhaustion of the country, its revenue diminished from 15,000,000 to 9,000,000, its debt increased during the French occupation by 22,000,000, while the increase on the total expenditure was estimated at over 67,000,000. The Hanoverian officials would not help to raise the taxes, and it would be impossible to replace them by Frenchmen who did not know the locality. A loan was out of the question, for the Estates had no credit, and if the Estates and the domainial chambers were dissolved, the French administrators would be obliged to 'seize the threads of a complicated and little-known administration.' Daru consequently advised that the imperial demands should be abated, and that 600,000 francs a month should be exacted in money, besides contributions in kind. Perhaps also an extraordinary revenue of 2,000,000 might be raised by the sale of forest timber. But even these demands were far too exorbitant, and met with the strongest protests from the standing commission of the Hanoverian Estates. The payment of 600,000 francs could at most be made for five months, and the sale of forest timber would destroy the capital resources of the country. As it was, the country was being plundered by six different French officials. There was Marshal Brune in the Hanse towns. Recruits

[1] Darmstaedter, *Das Grossherzogtum Frankfurt*, 66-7.

were marching through Hanover to join Marshal Mortier in Mecklenburg and Pomerania. At Hameln, General Treilhard required the construction of a hospital for 12,000 men, and the support of 6,000 invalids. From Erfurt Lemarquant was making requisitions for the building of magazines, not to speak of the cost involved by the new military roads. Since the French troops had entered the country, no less than 304,438 thalers had been expended on their service.

The remonstrances of the Hanoverians were by this time familiar to Napoleon, and he had a short way of dealing with them. 'I have ordered,' he wrote, March 23, 1807, 'that the States of Hanover should pay so much a week. They must pay it.... Make the States understand that if they do not pay one day or other, we shall take extraordinary measures to compel them [1].' In April two Hanoverian ministers were expelled the country, but still there was no money. In September the Estates were dissolved, and five of the most prominent members were imprisoned. Yet, despite the *coup d'état*, the old difficulties still persisted. Two members of the new government commissions formed by General Lascalcette, Meding and Von Münchhausen, were pronounced opponents of France, and offered a passive resistance to French proposals.

Yet, exorbitant as those proposals were, they were based upon principles of rational finance. Belleville declined to recognize the old provincial fiscal distinctions, and swept away all the aristocratic fiscal privileges. For the first time in the history of the Electorate a single tax was levied over its whole surface; for the first time the Hanoverian nobility were dosed with the bitter but salutary medicine of progressive imposts. But more was demanded than could ever be forthcoming from the normal methods of taxation, and the intendant was compelled to resort to violent measures. On December 25, 1807, Belleville demanded a forced loan of 10,000,000 from the wealthy. The loan was to be paid within three terms of twenty days. If the first third was not paid before the expiration of the first term, at least five soldiers and one non-commissioned officer would be quartered in the house of each delinquent. If within twenty days these measures were

[1] *Corr.* xiv. 504, no. 12,131.

not effective the proprietor was to be driven from his house, and his movables and if necessary his immovables sold by auction. Yet harsh measures cannot force money out of empty pockets, and by September 8, 1808, only 3,575,000 francs had been paid in to the French receiver, despite the fact that a supplementary loan had been raised from the poor. It was not half the original sum demanded.

It is unnecessary to pursue the details of Hanoverian fiscal history during the French occupation. Two observations may, however, be made. In Hanover, as in all the other 'reserved' provinces in Germany, the domains were separated from the other branches of revenue, and released from all charges save those connected with their own administration. The obvious source therefore from which the Hanoverian deficit could be diminished was cut off and diverted for the benefit either of the marshals and generals who had received dotations, or else for the benefit of the French exchequer. In the second place, the extreme difficulty which Hanover experienced in meeting the fiscal demands of the Emperor, led to the exercise of a strict control over the general expenditure on the part of the French intendant. He was obliged to insist that no money should be expended upon any purpose, central or local, without his leave, and eventually he went so far as to allocate a monthly sum of 500 thalers for the current expenses of government. The repercussion of the French occupation was thus felt in every sphere of life. The payments to magistrates and officials were curtailed; the members of the Estates no longer received their salaries; arrears of interest on the debt and arrears of pensions due to Hanoverian officers were simply repudiated—in a word, the whole civil service of the country was starved. By the end of 1809, the French occupation had probably cost the electorate between 40,000,000 and 50,000,000 francs, and Belleville represented that the French army alone had swallowed up four times the amount of the gross income of the country.

Meanwhile, Napoleon's control of Germany was complete. Austerlitz had confirmed his supremacy in the south, Jena had given him the command of the north, Tilsit secured him from danger in the east. Prussia lay crushed and mutilated, deprived of her fairest provinces, occupied by a foreign army, condemned to pay a huge contribution, and to witness the downfall of her three client dynasties, Brunswick, Hesse-Cassel, and Orange-Nassau. The Houses of Bavaria, Würtemberg, and Baden were now united to the family of Bonaparte by ties of marriage. Saxony and the smaller Saxon princes had joined the Confederation of the Rhine, and French troops watched the southern coast of the Baltic from the Trave to the Vistula. Of the conquered tracts some were being organized as vassal States, while others were placed under military government until their destiny should finally be determined. But in all, half the revenue from the domains was reserved for Napoleon.

'I saw the Emperor, that world-soul, ride through the city to reconnoitre,' wrote Hegel during the campaign of 1806, and many other fine Teutonic intellects shared the fascination. To some honest minds it seemed as if a new era was opening for Germany, as if the work of destruction was now ended, and the ground cleared for an imposing piece of political architecture. The pedants were at work upon the constitutional law of the Rheinbund, and prophesied brilliant things for that institution, while to others it seemed as if the most valuable lessons in political practice and philosophy would be derived from a study of the separate Napoleonic States. How far these prognostications were justified, and how far they were deceived, will be the theme of the remaining portion of this volume. In the history of political experiments there should be few passages more instructive.

CHIEF AUTHORITIES : Vandal, *Napoléon et Alexandre I* ; Bignon, *Histoire de France* ; Bonnefons, *Un allié de Napoléon* ; Mazade, *Correspondance de Davoût* ; Senfft, *Mémoires* ; Potocka, *Mémoires* ; *Bulletin des Lois du Grand-duché de Varsovie* ; *Gesetzsammlung des vormaligen Herzogthums Warschau, aus dem Polnischen übersetzt von S. G. Laube* ; Lublinier, *Correspondance entre le Code Civil du royaume de Pologne et le Code Civil français* ; F. Müller, *Aus sturmvoller Zeit* ; Thiébault, *Mémoires* ; Thimme, *Die inneren Zustände des Kurfürstenthums Hannover unter der französisch-westphälischen Herrschaft*.

CHAPTER VIII

THE CONSTITUTION AND THE CONCORDAT

'Le temps des institutions n'est pas encore venu. Elles suivront la paix générale.'—NAPOLEON.

THE disappearance of the Holy Roman Empire and the formation of a new political federation excited in Germany the most lively regrets and expectations. It was now remembered that an institution, which had long been the butt of ridicule, had performed a useful function as the protector of the weak against the strong, and as a safeguard of traditional rights against the despotism of the princes. The knights and the mediatized nobles had lost their historic champion, and even those whose material interests were unaffected could not regard the annihilation of an institution so old, so picturesque, so interwoven with the whole course of German history, without a pang of regret. Even in East Frisia the schoolmaster would tell the villagers that a great calamity had befallen them [1].

The task of drawing up a fundamental statute for the new Confederation had been assigned to Dalberg, and no commission could have been better calculated to enlist the support and tickle the vanity of that impetuous and incompetent politician. Perhaps also the selection shows that the proposed constitution for the Rhenish Confederacy was not very seriously regarded by Napoleon. Dalberg attacked the problem with characteristic zeal, and on August 5, 1806, a plan was on its way to Paris. The Diet of the Confederacy was to be convoked by the French Emperor and by the French Emperor only, and its session was to be limited to a period of fifteen days. His Imperial Majesty was to initiate, to veto, to sanction the laws, and to name the presidents of two permanent commissions constituted respectively for the preservation of public peace and the preparation of legislative measures. The language of the debates was to be

[1] Eilers, *Meine Wanderung durch's Leben*, i. 94.

German, and the officials of the Diet were to be German also. Further than this the scheme did not go [1].

The question of the Diet was far too delicate to be solved in so trenchant a manner. If Dalberg's scheme had been carried out, the Confederacy, instead of being a loose military union, would have taken upon itself the legislative and police functions of a State. Dalberg's lurking desire was in fact that the Rhenish Confederation should be a new edition of the ancient Empire, under French instead of under Austrian hegemony. Nor was he unwilling to see the imperial power fortified at the expense of the independence of the princes, for the princes had not only devoured the patrimony of the ecclesiastics, of the small nobles, of the knights—the classes in which he was specially interested—but their ecclesiastical policy was diametrically opposed to his own. While it was Dalberg's ambition that a single concordat should be made between the Pope on the one hand and himself on the other, as head and representative of the Catholic Church in Germany, the princes were anxious to make separate arrangements for their own several territories. It was natural, then, that the Arch-chancellor should desire to restrain and abridge their pretensions.

Such, however, was not the view of the French government. The essence of the compact with the German princes was that their foreign and military policy should be guided by Napoleon, while they should be given complete mastery of their own dominions, and at a time when France was drifting into war with Prussia it was specially important to regard the susceptibilities of the German confederates. Talleyrand accordingly drew up a clear statement of the position of his government, to emphasize the fact that the Emperor was protector, not sovereign, of the Confederation, and that every member of the league was endowed with the attributes of independence and sovereignty. 'The Diet in which they meet to discuss their common interests cannot,' he wrote, 'be compared to the legislative power of a separate State, or to the ancient Diet of the German Empire. It should, properly speaking, be nothing but a kind of political congress, where equals with common interests discuss those

---

[1] *Projet d'un statut fondamental*, Aug. 4, 1806 ; *Affaires étrangères, Corr. Pol.* : *Allemagne*, 732.

THE CONSTITUTION AND THE CONCORDAT 165

interests amicably, and agree upon measures for the common utility. Since the discussions which the confederates may have with their subjects cannot be brought before a foreign tribunal, the Confederation should not have courts. It is a court itself, but a court of conciliation, that is to say, it can only declare which of two parties is in the right [1].'

All schemes, then, for a further organization of a Confederate legislature fell to the ground. 'That man,' said Napoleon to Metternich, in 1807, as Dalberg left the room, 'is a numskull. He keeps tormenting me to reconstitute what he calls "*la patrie allemande.*" He wants to have his Ratisbon, his imperial Chamber, with all its traditions of the old German Empire. He has just been trying to talk this nonsense to me, but I cut him short. "Monsieur l'Abbé," I said, "I will tell you my secret. The small people in Germany want to be protected against the big: the big want to govern according to their fancy; now as I only want a federation of men and of money, and as it is the big people and not the small people who can give me the one and the other, I leave the former in peace, and the latter must get on as best they can [2]."' Three years later he was still of the same opinion. 'You know my principles with relation to Germany,' he wrote to Champagny. 'I attach no importance to the Confederation as a confederation, but I attach an importance to each prince separately, and I wish that all should enjoy their independence [3].' So the Diet of Frankfort never met, Bavaria and Würtemberg insisting that before it could even be summoned, the several members of the Confederation must accept the fundamental statutes [4]. Indeed, in view of the temper of Germany, such a gathering might have had its perils even as early as 1806 [5].

---

[1] *Affaires étrangères, Corr. Pol.: Allemagne*, 732; *Archives nationales*, A. F. iv. 1706 b. It does not appear that this memoir was transmitted to Dalberg, who was still permitted to enjoy the delights of his constitutional cloud-castles. Thus on Sept. 26, 1807, he submits an '*esquisse d'un statut fondamental pour la Confédération Rhénane.' Affaires étrangères, Corr. Pol.: Allemagne*, 733.

[2] Metternich, *Mémoires*, i. 58-9.   [3] *Corr.* xx. 269, no. 16,339.

[4] Bacher to Talleyrand, Oct. 17, 1806; *Affaires étrangères, Corr. Pol.: Allemagne*, 732; ibid., *Bavière*, 182.

[5] Otto to Talleyrand, Nov. 10, 1806: 'The diplomatic agents of the

Just as there was to be no constitution, so too there was destined to be no concordat for the Rheinbund.

The great bulwark of Roman Catholicism in Germany, 'the Catholic Spain,' as it has been called, was then, as it is now, Bavaria. Ever since the days when the first Protestant martyrs suffered in the Falcon Tower in Munich, the Bavarians had been the militant force of the papal cause in Germany. From them sprang the Catholic League and the counter-reformation, and it was the alliance of their princes with the Hapsburgs which once and for ever rolled back the Lutheran tide, and settled the question whether Germany was to be one or divided in creed. The devotion of the Wittelsbachs to the Pope brought many material advantages to their House, help against the powerful and 'immediate' Bishops of Bavaria, the Electoral rank, and last but not least the splendid appanage of Cologne, which for hard upon two hundred years was continuously ruled by Bavarian princes. In return they kept their country untainted by heresy and unillumined by knowledge, standing aside from the rest of Germany in a curious kind of somnolent isolation, at once infantile and patriotic. For a brief period during the reign of Maximilian III an irregular shaft of light pierced the darkness, and the secret and fashionable society of the Illuminati made war against the obscurantists of the Church. But this movement, full of unripe fancies, and accompanied by much that was silly and extravagant, perished abruptly under the persecutions of the succeeding ruler, Carl Theodor, and it was not until the accession of Maximilian Joseph of Zweibrück, in 1799, that a new era was really begun. Then all the old traditions of Bavaria were suddenly reversed. Not only was there a new ruling dynasty from the west—an Elector who had been a French officer, an Electress who was a heretic—but the country itself had been changed by the gifts of Napoleon. It was no longer the old Catholic peasant electorate, but a monarchy enriched by a constellation of ancient cities, and

allied Courts take no joy in Jena. A foreigner would say that they belonged to the conquered party. Can one not conclude that the union which has just been established will only last till an occasion offers for breaking it off?'—*Affaires étrangères, Corr. Pol.: Bavière,* 182; and cf. Müller, *Erinnerungen,* 182.

THE CONSTITUTION AND THE CONCORDAT 167

holding sway over 1,200,000 Protestant subjects. The new King was neither able nor industrious, but he had the good sense to see that the old ways were no longer possible, and he was well served by the ruthless and cynical intelligence of Montgelas. Through the energies of that minister the State was modernized in all its branches. The Protestants received toleration, the monasteries were abolished, and education was transferred to lay control[1].

But in a Catholic country, however modern, the Papacy can never be a negligible force, and the ministry of Montgelas wished to negotiate with the Curia whose spirit and traditions it had so rudely offended. For a whole century the Court of Munich had been striving to obtain a territorial Church, or in other words, to free itself from the metropolitan authority of the See of Mainz. But to win such an object a concordat with the Papacy was necessary; nor was it less essential, if the revolution of the last two years was to be commended to the minds of the ignorant, the scrupulous, and the devout.

There seemed to be only one way of overcoming the natural reluctance of Rome to sanction changes such as these. In 1802 the Pope had been forced by Napoleon to accept the French Revolution, and a concordat was signed in Paris for the settlement of the Catholic Church in France. Why should not a word from Bonaparte expedite the ecclesiastical affairs of Bavaria also? Accordingly the Elector applied for the mediation of the First Consul, and a scheme was submitted by the Court of Munich which Talleyrand thought to be reasonable (July 1802). Suggestions from a possible ally were always welcome, and Bonaparte wrote to the Pope to ask what the Curia was prepared to do for the Prince of Bavaria[2].

The Curia was not prepared to do anything. The more she had been forced to grant to France, the less she was inclined to grant to Germany. A papal Brief was issued on February 12, 1803, condemning the reforms of Montgelas, one of which, the granting of civil rights to non-Catholics, was

---

[1] Treitschke, *Deutsche Geschichte*, ii. 323 ff.; Sicherer, *Staat und Kirche in Bayern*; Otto Meyer, *Zur Geschichte der römisch-deutschen Frage*; d'Haussonville, *L'Église romaine et le Premier Empire*.

[2] *Corr.* viii. 7, no. 6,273.

specially abhorrent to the Roman tradition. To Bonaparte came a long and obscure reply, from which the First Consul was able to gather that his intervention was distasteful, and indeed on June 4, 1803, the Curia formally rejected the French mediation.

Meanwhile, on February 28, the Diet had issued the famous decree which ratified the territorial changes consequent upon the French conquest of the left bank of the Rhine. A new series of ecclesiastical problems now awaited solution. A fresh division of dioceses and provinces, a competent endowment for dispossessed bishops, a reorganization of such capitular bodies as had been affected by the secularization, these and other questions required prompt treatment. The terms of the decree clearly indicated that arrangements were to be made by the Curia in concert with the Diet, and as the Diet was supposed to be under Austrian influence the Pope determined to treat with it. In other words, there were to be no separate concordats, but one concordat for the whole Reich, and from February 6 to March 21, 1804, negotiations were carried on at Ratisbon to effect this object.

To the Arch-chancellor, who aspired to be Patriarch of Germany, nothing could be more distasteful than the policy of territorial concordats. To Bavaria nothing could be more odious than the claims of the Arch-chancellor. The Court of Munich again appealed to the First Consul, and for a second time Bonaparte intervened. As he was uncertain of the temper of the Diet, but anxious to conciliate Bavaria, he instructed his ambassador at Rome to support the Bavarian claims, and Cardinal Fesch orated upon the dangers of a possible Austrian Arch-chancellor. Both negotiations ended in failure. The Pope asked too much at Ratisbon, the Bavarians asked too much in Rome. In 1804, when Pius came to Paris to crown the Emperor, the question was still undecided and the Pope declined to discuss it. The Curia was adroit enough to understand that everything was to be gained by delay.

The quarrel of Napoleon with the Pope over Ancona in 1805, the Treaty of Pressburg which acknowledged the sovereignty of Bavaria, Würtemberg, and Baden, and the abolition of the Holy Roman Empire caused a change in the attitude of Rome.

THE CONSTITUTION AND THE CONCORDAT 169

If in 1804 the Pope was more willing to negotiate with the Arch-chancellor than with the princes, in 1806 the situation was reversed. In 1804 the Arch-chancellor was still the representative of an ancient and Catholic Empire, while the most important of the Catholic princes was supported by Napoleon in a policy destructive of ignorance, superstition, and intolerance. In 1806 the ancient Empire had been swept away, and it was only too probable that the Prince-Primate would be encouraged by the Protector of the Rhenish Confederation to claim independence for the German Church. The sensitive tentacles of papal diplomacy closed round the very objects which had previously been most repulsive to it, and separate negotiations were entered into with the Courts of Munich, Stuttgart, and Carlsruhe.

Immediately after the conclusion of the Peace of Tilsit Napoleon determined to take up the affairs of the Church, and forwarded through Eugène (July 22, 1807) a sharp and menacing letter to the Pope. He spoke of the immense services which he, the Emperor, had rendered to religion in France, in Italy, in Germany, in Poland, in Saxony. There was not a corner of the world in which the true faith had not been promoted by the Emperor and impeded by the Pope. He threatened that if the Pope tried to denounce him to the world, he would separate his people from all communication with Rome and 'establish a police.' Did the Pope take him for Louis le Débonnaire? But indeed the papal neglect of religion was of no recent date. Had not the Court of Rome, despite his solicitations, allowed the Church of Germany to perish and to remain in a dreadful anarchy? He was ready to unite the Gallican, the Italian, the German, and the Polish Churches in a council to arrange matters without the Pope and to secure his people from the priests of Rome. He would always be the Charlemagne, never the Louis le Débonnaire of the Church[1].

This curious fulmination was soon afterwards followed by a letter from Champagny, then Foreign Minister, to Cardinal Caprara. After representing that the Emperor was clothed with 'a priesthood which imposes on him the duty of defending

[1] *Corr.* xv. 441 ff., no. 12,942.

the Catholics of the Oder, the Vistula, and the Rhine, against the influence of Protestants and Lutherans,' he proceeded to press the conclusion of the German concordat. It must be dealt with at once and under the Emperor's 'own eyes,' on pain of an appeal to a General Council. Caprara, Bayane, and the Nuntio della Genga were named as the negotiators acceptable to Napoleon [1].

It would be inconceivable to imagine a demand couched in more peremptory language, and Dalberg, summoned by Napoleon himself to conduct the negotiations on the German side, came to Paris with lively hopes. Professing to represent the views now of all, and now of a great number of German bishops, he drafted some vague and magnificent aspirations in a petition to the Emperor. After demanding civil and political rights for all Catholics, a guarantee for existing Catholic property, an adequate endowment for cathedrals, seminaries, and chapters in the secularized States, and a settlement of diocesan limits and revenues, he went on to ask that the Primate of the German Church, the successor of St. Boniface, should exercise 'the functions of that dignity' over the whole of Germany, and that his mandates should be executed everywhere as soon as they had obtained the assent of the Diet and the approbation of the Protector [2]. But again the Papacy, its will steeled by a great ideal, its wits quickened by a long tradition of diplomacy, eluded the pressure of its foes. Caprara astutely suggested that the sovereigns of the Confederation who had Catholic subjects should be invited to send plenipotentiaries to the conference, and under that single drop of corrosive acid all the Arch-chancellor's hopes withered away. Dalberg's plan of a German patriarchate under Napoleonic control would be as abhorrent to the German princes as it was to the Curia. To the Papacy the pretensions of the German metropolitan had long been insufferable, and now they were presented in a form even more concentrated and dangerous than was the Ems punctation. But in truth there were many other causes of bitterness which divided the Pope from the Emperor, and when

---

[1] Champagny to Caprara : d'Haussonville, ii. 418 ff.

[2] *Projets pour les moyens d'obtenir un Concordat pour les États qui composent la Confédération Rhénane.*

THE CONSTITUTION AND THE CONCORDAT 171

on December 2, 1808, Pius recalled his envoys, the negotiations for the German concordat were at an end.

Napoleon does not appear to have followed these operations with interest, and granted Dalberg but one short and formal interview. In France the concordat was a necessity, a primary condition of social peace and a valuable instrument of empire. But in Germany Napoleon had nothing to gain by thwarting the territorial policy of the princes. There were no loose unregistered spiritual forces to be curbed, there was no revolutionary land settlement to be sanctioned. Josephism triumphed throughout the land. 'The German princes,' wrote Dalberg to Napoleon[1], 'insist upon State commissioners accompanying the bishops on their visitations, and no bishop can issue an order without obtaining the consent of his sovereign. When your Majesty wishes that a political event should be mentioned in the services of the Church, the order is given to the bishops. The German princes address their orders generally to the *curés*, and often prescribe the terms of the prayers.' This situation of affairs was altogether satisfactory to the Protector of the Rhenish Confederation. He had no mind to enter the arena as an episcopal gladiator against the laymen of Germany; he had taken the measure of Dalberg. There were things more pressing than German dioceses. He was content to insist that all powers joining his Confederation should admit Catholics to civil and political rights, and when he suspected that Catholics were not receiving fair treatment he came down with a heavy hand. It was convenient to figure as the Protector of the true faith in Germany, and over and over again in his anti-papal manifestoes we learn that the Church is perishing, that sees are unfilled, that the Pope is betraying Germany to the Protestants[2]. Yet when at last, in 1813, a new concordat was made with the Pope, there was no succour afforded to the 'perishing Church.' And so the grand German concordat was permitted to slide into oblivion, *chimaera bombinans in vacuo*, joining, somewhere in the regions of the inane, the fundamental

---

[1] Note on the ecclesiastical affairs of Germany, Aug. 13, 1807 : *Affaires étrangères, Corr. Pol. : Allemagne*, 733.

[2] *Corr.* xv. 506, 561 ; xix. 15 ; xx. 112 ; xxi. 352, 481-3 ; xxii. 111, 258.

statute which was never passed, and the Diet which was never summoned, and the courts of the Confederation which were never created [1]. Yet solemn and learned treatises were composed upon the constitutional law of the Rheinbund [2].

[1] An elaborate plan for the judicial organization of the Confederacy was submitted by Champagny to Napoleon, Feb. 28, 1808: A. F. iv. 1706 b; and cf. Pelet, *Mémoires*, i. 83-4.

[2] e. g. Klüber, *Staatsrecht des Rheinbundes*, Tübingen, 1808, hardly to be equalled for conscientious futility.

CHAPTER IX

THE FOUNDATION OF THE GRAND-DUCHY OF BERG

'Cette administration doit être l'école normale des autres États de la Confédération du Rhin ; c'est quelque chose que cela.'—NAPOLEON.

AMONG the reputations of the Grand Army there was none brighter than that of Joachim Murat. The sixth son of a small yeoman innkeeper, Murat was born on March 25, 1767, at La Bastide-Fontanière, near Quercy. Serving by turns in the fields or in his father's inn-yard, he learnt to ride horses, to tend them, and to break them in. His intelligence was active and supple, and, being destined by his parents for the Church, he rapidly acquired the elements of an education at the College of Cahors and the Seminary of Toulouse. His early letters show him to have possessed a rare power of facile and passionate expression, such as only proceeds from sensitive temperaments, and the letters written in later life to his little daughter unfold a tender and charming trait in his nature. He was tall and limber, with masses of silky black hair, an aquiline nose, blue eyes, the sunburnt skin of the southerner, an open mouth with full lips, and a frame of iron. It was clear that he would never do for the Church, and the passage of a cavalry regiment through Toulouse decided his fate. He enlisted, and in the turmoil of the Revolution he rose to the front, never doubting but that he was destined for great things. 'At my age,' he wrote in 1792, ' and with my courage and military talents I can go still further. God grant that I may not be frustrated.' At Vendémiaire the prayer was answered, and Murat attracted the favourable notice of Bonaparte. Henceforth his reputation was made. Aide de camp to Bonaparte in Italy, he demonstrated his powers as a leader of horse more than once, at Roveredo, at Bassano, at Rivoli. On the march to Cairo he commanded the rearguard ; at Salahieh he charged at the head of the Third Dragoons ; in the Syrian campaign at the battle of Aboukir he displayed intelligence, ingenuity, and courage. Hitherto he had not by any means been the servile adherent of Bonaparte. He was quarrelsome, he was ambitious, he looked rather to Barras than to Bonaparte for advancement. But Egypt made up his mind, and on the nineteenth of Brumaire he manifested his devotion. Then, as a reward for his loyalty, he aspired to the hand of Caroline, the beautiful sister of the First Consul. 'I had other views,' said Bonaparte; 'who knows the alliance I could have procured for Caroline?' But Josephine was on the side of the suitor, and at every objection the First Consul was reminded of Aboukir and Brumaire. At last the suppliants gained their will, and on January 18, 1800, the marriage-contract was signed. Murat, however, was not one of those men whose ambitions are quenched by matrimonial success. The Marengo campaign brought him fresh distinction and a sword of honour, and every day of good fortune inflated his insolence and aspirations. He thrashed an octroi official who demanded payment of him at the barrier of Paris; he declined indignantly the command of the army of the West; and, technically subordinated to Brune, he refused to receive orders from any one save the First Consul. Circumstances were favourable to his ambitions and his greed. The Neapolitans unwisely attacked Siena, and Murat, seizing a chance of independent action, moved into Tuscany. Foiled of a profitable campaign against Naples by the intervention of the First Consul, the greedy Gascon enriched himself at the expense of the Pope. Marching his army to Foligno in the heart of the Papal States, he demanded and obtained a hundred thousand crowns as the price of his retirement. The contract signed, the French general honoured His Holiness with a visit, and with six of his officers was entertained at the expense of the Apostolic Chamber in the Palazzo Sciarra. 'My visit,' he wrote, describing an audience with the Pope, 'has given him consideration and aplomb. He needed it.' It may be added that it was productive of more substantial benefits to the visitor, among which may be numbered a valuable Raphael. A Neapolitan campaign might be fruitful in similar gratifications, but the First Consul would not hear of it. Nevertheless the spoils of Italy sufficed to purchase one of the finest hotels in Paris, a country house, and an estate, at a total cost of twelve hundred thousand francs.

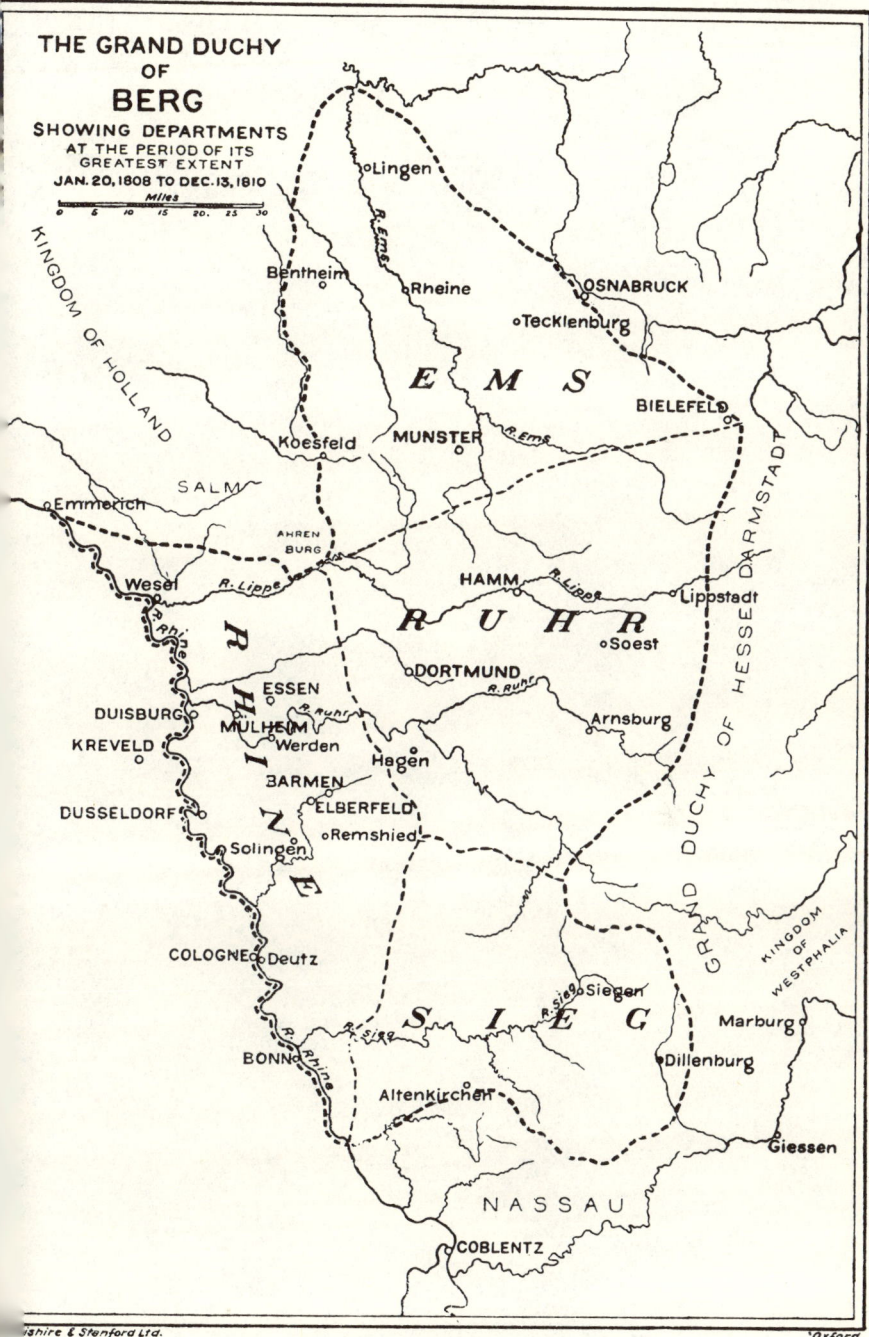

THE GRAND-DUCHY OF BERG

When in 1802 an Italian republic was founded, with Count Melzi, a wealthy and honourable Milanese, as vice-president and acting governor, Murat returned to Italy to command the French army of occupation. His conduct was abominable, and his rapacity the common talk. He entered into an open struggle with Melzi, was corruptly interested in a company of contractors, and did everything in his power to bring the administration into contempt in order that the republic might be annexed to France. It speaks well for Bonaparte that he consistently supported Melzi in this irritating contest. Nevertheless, when Murat returned to France in August 1803, he only found fresh honours awaiting him. He became a deputy to the Legislature, was made Governor of Paris, and received a marshal's bâton and a hundred thousand francs. Later he was created Grand Admiral, Prince of the Empire, and Senator. His income was enormous, his cook the best in Paris, his Court at the Hôtel Thellusson almost rivalled the Tuileries. But yet neither he nor Caroline were satisfied. They engaged in a campaign of calumny against Louis and Hortense, whose son had been named to succeed the Emperor, and were in covert opposition to Bonaparte. While Eugène was made Viceroy of Italy; while Joseph, a dull man without military talent, was sent to rule Naples, and Élise became Princess of Lucca and Piombino, Murat and Caroline were left in Paris, opulent but craving. Yet in the war of 1805 it was Murat's ruse which seized the bridge of Vienna, Murat who won the fight at Hollabrunn, and Murat again who helped to storm the plateau of Pratzen which was the key to Austerlitz. As he rode into action, his long black hair waving in the wind, his great white plumes in a clasp of brilliants, his body clad in a light blue velvet tunic embroidered with gold, a sash of light blue silk fringed with gold at the waist, his legs adorned with white breeches and the big yellow boots of the Thirty Years' War, he must have looked like some glorified circus-rider. But nevertheless, as the husband of Caroline and the first leader of horse in the French Empire, he aspired to be the ruler of a State, to frame laws, and to conduct an administration [1].

[1] *Correspondance de Murat,* ed. Lumbroso ; Masson, *Napoléon et sa famille,* ii. 38–54, 190, 204 ; iii. 47, 53, 269–93 ; Francesco Melzi d'Eril, *Memorie, documenti e lettere,* ed. G. Melzo ; de Sackow, *Mémoires.*

The campaign of Austerlitz brought into Napoleon's possession two small territories on the Lower Rhine—the Duchy of Cleves and the Duchy of Berg. The first had been the property of Prussia; the second was ceded by Bavaria in exchange for the Margraviate of Anspach, which Napoleon had wrung from the Court of Berlin. In both cases it was part of the formal stipulation that the duchies should be handed over to 'a prince of the Holy Roman Empire who should be designated by the Emperor Napoleon.' Nothing in appearance could be more reassuring. The dimensions of the new State were modest, and it was clearly destined for a German, who, as a member of the Reich, would owe homage and fealty to the head of the German Empire.

But all inferences drawn from the written word of treaties were delusive. As to the homage, that, as Napoleon wrote to Talleyrand, must remain in the greatest obscurity. 'I will decide in course of time,' said the Emperor, 'if the duchies are to be fiefs of the German Empire or of my Empire.' To predict any finality as to the size of the new State would be equally hazardous. Created as a makeweight to Prussia, it must be increased with every augmentation of Prussian territory. If, for instance, Prussia were detached from Holland and the Lower Rhine, and given compensation in the north, one might extend the States of the new prince, give him Münster, Hesse-Darmstadt, and their appurtenances, as, for instance, Hamburg or some other Hanseatic or mediate town [1].' In other words, the new principality, which is to be 'included either by family or geographical relations within the system of France,' will admit of indefinite extension. Formed out of the humiliation of Prussia, and created at a period of great tension between Paris and Berlin, it is designed primarily as a check upon Prussian influence. It is a buffer between Prussia and the Rhine; it places a bridle upon Hesse-Cassel to the east; it facilitates the supervision of Hamburg in the north; it gives to France the first stages on the road to Berlin. In the spring of 1806 these military considerations were all-important. On March 8 it was announced to Prince Joseph that the Duchies of Cleves and Berg were to go to Murat. 'The Prince Murat,' said Napoleon

[1] *Corr.* xi. 562, no. 9,716.

to the Senate, 'is to be charged with an important part of the frontiers of the Empire.' A soldier was summoned to do a soldier's work.

On March 15 a decree conferred upon Prince Joachim Murat the Duchies of Cleves and Berg, to be transmitted in order of primogeniture to his male descendants lawful and natural, and in default of heirs to pass successively to the heirs of the Emperor, to those of Joseph, and to those of Louis. Yet in no case were the duchies to be united to the Crown of France. The heir-presumptive was to be styled Duke of Cleves, and the dignity of Grand Admiral of France was to be hereditary in the ducal family, and to descend with the duchies. 'You must not,' wrote Napoleon to the new sovereign, 'put up the French arms anywhere [1].' But however carefully the new principality was discriminated from France, it was clear that Murat was to remain a French prince, and that his policy was to be shaped by his brother-in-law. 'Your rank in my palace,' wrote Napoleon, 'is fixed by the rank which you have in my family, and your rank in my family is fixed by the rank of my sister.' The Prussian government was fully justified in its expostulation against so flagrant a breach of the spirit and letter of the Treaty of Schönbrunn.

On March 25 the Duke of Cleves and Berg made his entry into Düsseldorf, the capital of his dominions, and a city whose name he was at that time unable to spell. 'At the moment,' says the *Moniteur*, 'that His Highness stepped upon the flying bridge, the music of the guard of honour struck up, and the sounds of instruments mingled with acclamations conveyed to the Prince while he was crossing the stream the first expression of the transports which burst out as he descended upon the territory of Berg.' At the gate of the palace the new sovereign was received by the Estates, the Privy Council, and the Regency. When the members of these bodies had been severally presented to him, he conferred long with them upon the industrial interests of Berg, 'gaining all hearts by the grace of his discourse, and the announcement of the benefits which he would bring to the State.' In the evening he went to the theatre, and was received with tumultuous enthusiasm. At the Hôtel de

[1] *Corr.* xii. 191, no. 9,975.

Ville 'two escutcheons sustained by a genius' were displayed on a transparency. On the first was traced '*Vive l'Empereur Napoléon*,' and below the second the triumphs of Joachim, *Victoire de Wertingen, Victoire d'Ulm, Passage du pont de Vienne, Victoire d'Austerlitz.*

On the next day the Prince, attired in a costume of the greatest magnificence, received the oaths of the members of the Estates, and of the executive and judicial authorities. He was then conducted by the clergy to the church, where he heard a solemn mass. 'The crowd,' says the *Moniteur*, 'was immense; it is impossible to paint the enthusiasm,' and, indeed, Murat wrote to Napoleon that the welcome surpassed all his expectations.

But if Düsseldorf was pleased with Prince Joachim, Prince Joachim was by no means pleased with Düsseldorf. 'Tell me, if you know, when you think that I can hope to return,' he wrote to Talleyrand three days after the solemn entry, when he had made research into the finance of the duchy, and found that it left 'hardly anything at the disposition of the prince.' On the same day he dilated to Napoleon on the smallness of his budget, the poverty of his people, and his inability to raise two regiments of 1,800 men apiece. He insisted that he must have more elbow-room, and a wider area of resource. The territories of the abbeys of Essen, Werden, and Elten had been acquired by Prussia in 1803; they contained rich coal-fields, and properly should belong to the Duchy of Cleves. But Murat was not content with demanding these abbeys. He must also have the County of Mark, which was 'indispensable,' and 'earnestly desired' by the inhabitants of his dominion. Nor did he confine his energies to paper. On March 28, the very day upon which these complaints were penned, French troops were sent to occupy the territories of the abbeys. It so happened that a Prussian force was in possession, and that the French were driven off. The spirits of the Duke of Cleves rose at the news. 'While I await the orders of your Majesty, your Majesty may count that the Prussians will not impose on me. Command me to chase them from Westphalia.' Murat, in fact, saw with some penetration that a Prussian war was an antecedent condition of the growth of his principality, and busily set himself to create friction. Napoleon at last burst out into

THE GRAND-DUCHY OF BERG 179

indignant rebuke. 'You must not turn all Germany against you. You act so precipitately that you will infallibly be bound to recede.... It is not my policy to annoy the King of Prussia. You must not show yourself such a restless neighbour. I recommend to you prudence and tranquillity [1].'

Meanwhile Napoleon had pursued the new sovereign with letter after letter of precise instruction as to the conduct which he should pursue in the duchies. On March 23 he wrote, in reference to some hasty proposals as to the organization of the country:—

'You must not take any decisive step now, because it will be convenient to give both countries the same organization. You will order that the octroi of the Rhine shall be paid in the same manner and on the same footing as under the Prussian régime. You may seize all the property of the immediate nobility at Berg and in the whole duchy. You must dismiss as soon as possible the employés of La Tour and Taxis from the postal service. At Wesel there are none of them, but they are always to be found in the Duchy of Berg. It was an imperial fief, and it was thus that the Emperor was kept informed of everything which was going on in Germany.... Nominate natives to the postal service, who will be attached to the country. Appoint on the spot people from Berg to the posts of Cleves, and people from Cleves to the posts of Berg.... In general you should put more confidence in the Bavarians than in the Prussian agents. When you have got to the bottom of the situation of affairs in your new States, you will see that it is impossible that a population of 300,000 souls should bring in so little as you say. The ordinary calculation is seven florins per soul, which would give a revenue of 2,000,000 florins or 4,000,000 francs. That does not mean that you are to be less economical, for you will want a small army both to occupy the youth of your country, and for the dignity of your State. According to the French usage, troops cost too much; according to the Bavarian usage, they are much cheaper.'

On April 4 follows another batch of directions:—

'I think you must form a regiment of four battalions, each battalion of eight companies, so as to be able to put 2,400 men

[1] *Corr.* xii. 291, no. 10,107.

into the field, with a company of artillery and six pieces of cannon. But you must take care not to form them too hastily. You must follow the economic manner of the country: German troops cost less than ours do. You must also pay great attention to the choice of officers, and appoint many landed proprietors.

'I am much surprised to learn that the principal people of the Duchy of Cleves have not wished to take the oath: let them swear within twenty-four hours; and if they don't, arrest them, imprison them, and confiscate their property.

'I have re-read with attention the project of organization which you have sent me. It is incomplete and bad. I have dictated to M. Maret some articles which he will send you by the same courier, not as anything definitive, but to show you how the thing ought to be done. Do not hurry. If the country of Berg and Cleves is to receive a good constitution, you must give yourself time to observe and see. Collect all the information; then it will be possible to arrive at an organization which shall suit the inhabitants and yourselves, and which may render your neighbours envious of forming part of your dominions. That is especially the end which you should propose to yourself.

'Three ministers are enough. 6,000 francs apiece is a suitable salary. Eight Councillors of State, at a salary of 2,000 apiece, seem sufficient for the country. As to the Estates, one cannot form an idea until one knows how they are composed. As to Justice, one must also know how it is formed and paid at present. Probably appeals went in the last instance to Munich, or even before the courts of the Empire. This must be abolished, and the highest Court of Appeal must be at Düsseldorf. As to property, seize the goods of the Order of Malta, of the Teutonic Order, and of the monks. All that together ought to increase your domain. What with the land and that portion of the revenue which will be reserved to your uses, you should have an income of 2,000,000 francs, so that you may maintain your State without having need of anything further. The troops, canals, debts, and other public purposes should be defrayed from the treasury funds, of which you have the administration [1].'

[1] *Corr.* xii. 211, no. 10,009; 258-9, nos. 10,054-6.

THE GRAND-DUCHY OF BERG

It would appear that in May there was an unpleasant scene between Bonaparte and the Murats. Caroline and Joachim had asked for Holland, which neither Louis nor his wife were anxious to take. When their petition was declined, 'the ambitious sister,' as she was called at St. Cloud, complained bitterly of the small lot which she had received on the right bank of the Rhine. On this she and her husband were threatened with permanent exile to the Duchies of Cleves and Berg, and, scared by so dreadful a prospect, threw themselves into the arms of the Talleyrands [1]. The French Minister of Foreign Affairs was at that time addressing his adroit intelligence to the organization of Western and Southern Germany, and in the arrangements of the Rhenish Confederacy the claims of the Murats were not forgotten. The Grand-Duke Joachim, Prince of the French Empire and Admiral of France, received a seat in the College of Kings; the territory and population of his duchy was practically doubled by the acquisition of the Duchy of Nassau and the Principality of Dillenberg, and finally the postal monopoly of Northern Germany, which had belonged to the House of Thurn and Taxis ever since 1615, was placed in his hands. In return for these advantages he was required to furnish a military contingent of 5,000 men.

Still Murat was dissatisfied. The grand-duchy, though doubled, was paltry when compared to Holland or Naples; its population only 590,000, its revenues insufficient. The County of Mark and the Westphalian provinces of Prussia lay in tempting proximity, and the Grand-Duke had 10,000 French troops under his command. If he could only push the Emperor into war with Prussia there would be more room. A pretext was not wanting. Certain territories which were to pass under his control were occupied by Prussian troops, whom, as he explained to the Emperor, it would be easy to expel. 'Veritable madness,' answered Napoleon with heat, on August 2. 'I cannot describe the pain with which I read your letters. You are desperately precipitate [2].' Yet there was a method in Murat's madness; and, despite the lectures of the Emperor, he continued his policy of goading the government of Berlin.

[1] Bailleu, ii. 461-2. [2] *Corr.* xiii. 33, no. 10,587.

One more assault upon the proprieties of international intercourse was committed by Murat previous to the outbreak of hostilities. On September 1, 1806, he convoked his Estates, nominally to vote the budget but in reality to decree the abolition of all fiscal privilege. To the twenty-seven nobles and twenty burgesses of the assembly it was explained that the properties and domains of the dispossessed princes in the duchies must contribute *pro rata* to the exchequer; but though in itself the principle was admirable, its application to the duchies violated rights which had been expressly guaranteed not two months before by the act of the Confederation of the Rhine, and by the Emperor of the French. But Murat was not burdened with constitutional scruples, and Napoleon could not afford to quarrel with his lieutenant on the eve of a war.

Many brilliant exploits are recorded of Murat during the Prussian campaign. He displayed himself a born leader of cavalry, and as he was not prone to underestimate his own merits he expected a great reward. At the interview of Tilsit he was for appearing in a Polish uniform, as a hint that he deserved the Polish crown. 'Go and put on your general's uniform,' said Napoleon, 'you look like Franconi.' That ambition then was slain, and Murat had to relapse upon his dull little duchy, the resources of which had been considerably depleted by the requisitions of the army of the King of Holland. A negotiation, lasting five months and seventeen days, then ensued as to territorial adjustments. The crux was the town of Wesel, which Napoleon regarded as one of the most important fortresses of the Rhine, and which he had from the first been determined to retain in French hands. Murat made himself ridiculous by some wild talk. He said that he would throw himself with his army into Wesel and defend the town. One would see whether the Emperor would have the face to besiege him before the eyes of Europe, and as for him, he would hold out to the last. But all the same the instrument was signed on January 20, 1808. Wesel was ceded to France, and incorporated in the French Department of the Ruhr. In return the grand-duchy was augmented by the Prussian County of Mark with the town of Lippstadt, the Prussian portion of the Principality of Münster, the Prussian County of Tecklenberg, and by the County of Lingen which had been inherited by the House of Brandenburg in 1702 from the House of Orange—an addition of 146 square miles and 362,000 inhabitants.

The Grand-Duchy of Berg had now reached its maximum development [1]. It contained a population of 120,000 souls, and was about a hundred and fifty miles long by ninety to fifty-seven broad. Since the country had not been ruled by any long succession of sovereigns, it was not deeply attached to any particular dynasty, and the public spirit was reported to be good, that is to say, well affected towards France, the aristocracy to be reasonable and the middle class to be numerous. Every canton, says Beugnot, had its peculiar characteristics, moulded by religion, government, and topography [2]. Münster, an old Catholic ecclesiastical fief, retained the manners of the seventeenth century. The capital was controlled by a bishop, and filled with religious houses and the winter residences of the feudal nobility. 'At Münster the palaces are spacious rather than commodious; the servants are numerous, the old etiquette severely retained, the furniture and plate of a heavy richness.' A refractory servant was punished by being made to sit upon the *chevalet*, a kind of wooden horse, which it was painful to bestride. The patriarchal authority exercised by the lords over their servants and their serfs was wielded with mildness and charity, and the rural population, which was bound to the soil, received assistance in sickness and old age. The peasantry of this old-fashioned province is described to us as being in general religious, sober, and laborious, while the nobility were generally charitable and often dignified and well informed. 'When,' said Beugnot, 'I visited this old country, my Germania in hand, I recognized the truth of the great painter's colours, and I no longer believe that his pictures are

---

[1] On Jan. 22, 1811, the portions of the duchy north of the river Lippe were united to the French Empire and went to form the Departments of Lippe and Ems Supérieur. This, like all other sudden readjustments of territory, caused considerable administrative and financial difficulty. A. F. iv. 1865, 1886 a.

[2] Beugnot, *Mémoires*, i. 290 ff.

imaginary[1].' The neighbouring County of Mark presented a striking contrast. This province, hilly and unfertile, conserved the traces of the long and attentive administration of the great Frederick. It had, in fact, profited by all his good laws, while escaping his fiscal avidity. There was not a watercourse which had not been utilized, not a profitable line of communication which had not been opened, no advantageous commercial relations which had not been established. Under the capable administration of M. Eversmann, the County of Mark had become one of the most active industrial centres in Germany. The population is described as enterprising, often irreligious, often unscrupulous, but strong, and determined not to acquiesce in defeat. Under the French rule they dreamed of vengeance, and made no secret of it[2]. And the old Prussian administrators fostered the sentiment. The County of Nassau-Siegen was the ancient patrimony of the House of Orange, which has given a dynasty to Holland and to England. The inhabitants of this picturesque district still showed the oak under which Maurice was seated, when a deputation of the Beggars of Holland came to invite him to lead them to liberty. Yet they were now forced to pass to an alien power, and their last native prince surrendered the home of his race in response to a demand conveyed to him with incredible brutality[3].

The Duchy of Berg itself had been an appanage first of the Palatine, and then of the Bavarian House. Its capital, Düsseldorf, a pleasant and well-built town upon the Rhine, had been the seat of a polished Court, and owing to the marriage of a Prince Palatine to a lady of the Medici House, possessed one of the finest picture-galleries in Northern Europe, the treasures of which were, however, removed to Munich when the duchy passed into

[1] The sympathies of the ecclesiastics and gentry of Münster were strongly Austrian. '*Le tout est autrichien, on y rêve la domination d'un archiduc.*' The canons are described as a '*milice autrichienne.*' It would be well, says an official of the duchy, to introduce some *hussards* into the town. '*Avec ce moyen ce pays sera civilisé en moins de deux années.*'— *Bulletin du Grand-duché de Berg* (March 1809) ; *A. F.* iv. 1225.

[2] Beugnot's statement is fully confirmed by contemporary correspondence ; cf. *A. F.* iv. 1225.

[3] Beugnot, *Mémoires*, i. 300.

French hands. The ducal castle of Bensburg, built in the Italian style, has been much admired, and the influence of the Court diffused through Düsseldorf and its immediate neighbourhood that soft and docile temperament which finds easy satisfaction in official posts. Further east, however, in the valleys of Barmen and Elberfeld, and in the cantons of Ronstorf, Remscheid, and Solingen, there was a vigorous and independent industrial population.

The constitution of the Duchy of Berg was regulated by two decrees of 1672 and 1675, which confirmed a custom still more ancient. According to these documents the country was represented by a Diet consisting of two colleges, the College of Nobles and the College of Towns, which must be convoked at least once a year. The College of Nobles consisted of thirty-eight members; and it was necessary to possess sixteen quarterings of nobility, and one at least of 160 specified manors, to be entitled to a seat. The College of Towns consisted of eight members drawn from four boroughs. The Diet was bound to secrecy, and exerted but a nominal control over affairs, since the assent of one of the colleges was deemed sufficient authority for the executive, and the sovereign could always dominate the College of Towns. Further, many legislative acts had been published without any communication with the Diet at all. Yet year by year this assembly had solemnly met, voted the taxes which were demanded of it, addressed a statement of grievances to the government commission, and receiving a formal and insignificant reply had quietly accepted dismissal.

For purposes of local government the duchy was divided into eighteen bailiwicks, each of which was presided over by a grand bailiff, who was always a noble and generally an absentee. In every bailiwick there was a receiver of domains, a receiver of contributions, inspectors of public works, and foresters, all of whom were dearly paid and insufficiently controlled. There was, it would seem, much miscellaneous plunder of the inhabitants by the functionaries, and this malignant spot in the body politic was aggravated by the custom according to which the servants of the State received part of their remuneration in the shape of corn, hay, and other products from the domains. Another serious defect was the absence of a clear division and definition of administrative functions. 'The administration,' complained Murat, 'is a chaos which I have great difficulty in clearing up. There was never a less regular organization. A portion of the revenues belonged to the King of Bavaria, a portion to the Duke of Bavaria, his brother-in-law. A portion was deemed to belong to the country itself, and was appropriated to certain branches of expenditure. But all this was administered without any kind of order. There was a royal regency, a ducal regency, a privy council, a commission, . . . no one had fixed attributions. The president of the privy council enjoyed all the authority, and sent the business now to one member of the council and now to another, so that no one was specially charged with any department, with the result that I can find no one who has a complete knowledge of any branch of the service.' To the French, the system of justice appeared to contain three principal defects. The nobles and functionaries could only be tried by the Aulic Council of Düsseldorf; there were no commercial courts; and the law, which consisted mainly of provincial statutes and local custom, was unsystematized.

The Diet of the Duchy of Cleves was even more advanced in atrophy and impotence than the representative assembly of Berg, since while the College of Towns was no larger, the extreme exclusiveness of the aristocracy had here reduced the College of Nobles to a congregation of three. This however was of no importance, since the duchy was administered on the intelligent and energetic lines of the Prussian bureaucracy. The French admired the strict order and economy which prevailed everywhere in Cleves. The duchy was divided into two circles and twenty-nine bailiwicks. For each circle there were two resident councillors who supervised and controlled, one in the towns, and the other in the country districts, the execution of all the orders of the government. There was thus no room for the malpractices of subordinate officials.

The French official was bound to confess that he found little trace of public discontent with the existing régime. The grievances which were most generally felt in the Duchy of Berg were the exemption of the nobles from taxation, and the exclusive privilege of the four towns represented in the Diet. There was no serious complaint of the judicial organization in either province, only that litigation was somewhat costly in Berg, and that the Aulic Council was slow[1].

As the Grand-Duke was about to take possession of his new territory, he received a sudden call to Bayonne (February 20, 1808). The lieutenant of the Emperor readily forgot the little German duchy in the excitement of that Spanish drama in which he played so unscrupulous a part, and which lured him from Düsseldorf to Madrid, and then from Madrid to Naples. Beside the prospect of a Spanish throne, Münster and Cleves, the objects of so much negotiation, sank at once into matters of complete indifference.

The Grand-Duke of Berg had paid two flying visits to his principality before he was summoned away to Spain. His theatrical displays of magnificence may have pleased the mild inhabitants of Düsseldorf, who were unaccustomed to splendours, and his martial achievements were followed with pride and interest by the inhabitants of the duchy. 'Your subjects,' said his Minister of Finance, in language which perhaps was not entirely hollow, 'who remember that scarce two years ago you were in Moravia, having subdued the capital of Austria; that not a year ago you stood under the walls of Königsberg after riding through Berlin and Warsaw, are astonished to-day suddenly to learn that you are in the capital of Spain, and are proud to see the name of their sovereign connected with so many brilliant undertakings.' Yet despite these diversions the foundations of a French administrative system were laid down under Murat. 'Our Grand-Duke,' so runs the *Journal Politique de Mannheim* (Aug. 22, 1806), 'occupies himself without relaxation with the administration of his States. The territory of the Duchies of Cleves and Berg is divided into six *arrondissements*. In each *arrondissement* a provincial council will be established. There is a question of constructing a new castle in the town. A plan of a new university is being devised; also a plan of new schools and houses of education[2].'

Three ministers (Justice and Foreign Relations, Interior,

---

[1] *A. F.* iv. 1225; Agar's report.

[2] The proposal before the Council, Aug. 2, 1806, was that a university should be founded in the Convent of Düssel at Duisburg. *Staatsraths-Akten*, Düsseldorf Archives.

Finance), a Council of State, a Privy Council consisting of the ministers and two councillors of State, formed the organs of the central government. An old college friend of Murat's, by name Agar, accepted the portfolio of Finance and the title of Count of Mosburg. Fuschius, a Bavarian judge, was placed in the Ministry of Justice, while another native, the Count of Nesselrode, chief of an old family of diplomats, formerly Grand-Marshal and Director of the commission of the Berg Estates, was entrusted with the portfolio of the Interior. A supreme Court of Appeal for the whole duchy was established at Düsseldorf, and a legal commission assisted by lawyers from each of the provinces of the duchy was appointed to frame a Civil Code[1]. The sale of ecclesiastical lands, and the abolition of tithes and feudal dues, paved the way for the régime of equality, and the Estates of the grand-duchy helped to complete the process by voluntarily surrendering the fiscal immunities of the nobles. By an excellent decree State officials were forbidden to receive contributions in kind from the domains. A Prussian enactment which forbade burghers to acquire noble land in Cleves was abolished, and a common land-tax admitting of no privilege and no exceptions was a most beneficial innovation. As a provisional measure, provincial councillors were appointed to hold the civil registers, to collect statistics, to report upon local finance, roads, and bridges, to inspect churches, hospitals, and schools, to provide for the billeting and provisioning of troops, and to propose encouragements for agriculture and commerce[2]. Everywhere save in the capital, French municipal institutions were introduced. Not a penny was to be spent in the dark. 'The budgets of the municipal councils are to be transmitted to the Provincial Councillor, who will transmit them to the Minister of the Interior. The budgets of the larger towns are

---

[1] The instructions given to this commission in the Council of State at Düsseldorf (April 17, 1807) were (1) that it should follow the order and arrangement of the Code Napoléon, and should only depart from it where it was indispensable for the public interest of the duchy; (2) that the 'jurisconsults should penetrate themselves with the laws and customs of their several provinces,' so as to see how far they might agree with the Code Napoléon. *Staatsraths-Akten,* Düsseldorf Archives.

[2] Cf. Winkopp, *Der rheinische Bund,* i. 118 ff., and *A. F.* iv. 1842.

decreed by us, those of the smaller towns are decreed by the Minister of the Interior.' The Director, the 'Adjoint,' the Commissioner of Police, the Municipal Councillor, were to be nominated in the larger towns by the Grand-Duke, in the smaller towns by the Minister of the Interior. There was no room for autonomy, for variation, for picturesque survival, for miscellaneous dinings at the public expense, for secret municipal jobbery. 'No official employed in municipal administration may have any interest, direct or indirect, in any enterprises whatever which concern the commune.' To the government of Murat must belong the credit of having introduced into Germany the first enlightened and comprehensive municipal ordinance. The decree of October 13, 1807, was for the Duchy of Berg in one sense what the Municipal Corporations Act of 1835 was for England. It provided a clear, rational, and homogeneous plan of government. In another sense, however, it differed from the Liberal ordinance of the Melbourne ministry, for it betrayed certain vices incidental to a military despotism which was jealous of the labouring classes, and anxious to obtain the complete disposal of all local resources for its military ends[1]. Nor are these the only changes which belong to the Murat period. Roads were made, internal custom duties were abolished, a new administration was established for the coal-mines of Werden and Essen, and decrees were issued organizing the management of the forests, the functions of notaries, and the penalties for military desertion [2].

At rare intervals a letter from their absentee ruler would disturb the equanimity and excite the energies of the Council of State. On February 2, 1808, His Highness, 'wishing to give to his State a constitution as conformable as possible with that of the Kingdom of Westphalia,' ordered his Council *immediately* to submit projects for the application of the Code Napoléon,

[1] Thus the municipal officers were required to 'regulate military billets and to order requisitions to be made for the public service.' The commissioner of police was charged 'with the repression of mendicity and vagabondage, with the direction of guilds and corporations of artisans, with measures adapted to prevent unions of working men being formed for the purpose of strikes or raising wages.' *Recueil des Actes du Gouvernement du Grand-duché de Berg*, Düsseldorf, 1808; *A. F.* iv. 1842.

[2] *A. F.* iv. 1842.

for a Judicial Code, for a division of the territory into two or three departments, for a new monetary system, and a new system of weights and measures. The Council, which had not met for ten months, adopted, as was natural, the line of least resistance in dealing with this enormous programme. After a week's interval they decided to recommend that the French Civil Code and Code of Civil Procedure should be adopted on January 1, 1809, that a commission should be appointed to propose 'regulative dispositions' upon points, such as serfage and entails, where there was a conflict between the old and the new law, and that the French monetary system and the French system of weights and measures should be introduced[1]. A project was prepared for the division of the duchy into four departments, and another for the abolition of serfage, and on June 28, 1808, a draft law of mortgage was submitted to the Council[2]. Of the drafts and memoirs so busily and often so ably prepared by the German members of his Council, but few can have received serious attention of the Grand-Duke, whose face was never seen in Düsseldorf after the Prussian war had called him to the front in 1806. A restless cavalry officer on his promotion, he never put his heart into the internal affairs of the duchy, whose size and importance he undervalued and despised. At first he was either struggling to annex new territories or combating the Emperor's claims to Wesel. During the last six months of his rule he was dreaming of the throne of Spain, and having made up his mind that in any case he would never return to Berg, was determined to 'squeeze the orange before it slipped from his hands.' On July 15, 1808, by the Treaty of Bayonne, the Grand-Duke formally ceded his duchy to Napoleon; and the faithful Agar, Minister of Finance, being instructed to sell the domains of the duchy and to anticipate the revenue, left a legacy of needless embarrassment to his successor[3]. The vulgar greed of the Grand-Duke excited the ire of the Emperor himself. 'Your agents,' he remarked, July 30, 1808, 'are packing up every-

---

[1] *Staatsraths-Akten*, Düsseldorf Archives; Mosburg to Bassano, May 1, 1809; *A. F.* iv. 1225.   [2] *A. F.* iv. 1842.

[3] Count Beugnot, while complaining of this conduct in his memoirs, wrote a letter of flowery compliment to the culprit: '*Vous avez fait*

thing and transporting it to the left bank; your studs are going towards the Tyrol. That creates a detestable impression in the country and in Germany. Is it worth while to show avidity for trifles?' So great was the Emperor's indignation that, in defiance of the express terms of the Treaty of Bayonne, he would not permit a penny from the arrears of the grand-ducal revenue to be exported to Naples [1].

On July 31, 1808, Count Beugnot, an experienced administrator who had spent some months as Minister of Finance in the new Kingdom of Westphalia, took over the control of the duchy. The Imperial Commissioner, as he was called, was inducted into the business by the Count of Mosburg, with whom he enjoyed the advantage of a daily conference for a period of three months [2].

Beugnot was vain and jealous, sensitive and intelligent, upright and prolix. He thought Mosburg unscrupulous, and being of a cautious and conservative temperament, he was inclined to moderate the pace of reform. But of his zeal and industry there can be no question. In a notable passage of retrospect he has depicted not only his own sensations upon assuming the office of Imperial Commissioner, but also the spirit which animated the civil servants of the Empire. 'It was then,' he writes, 'a position in Europe to be a Frenchman, and it was a great position to represent the Emperor anywhere; save that I should not have abused my office with impunity, I was in Germany what the proconsuls were in Rome. The same respect, the same obedience on the part of the people, the same obsequiousness on the part of the nobility, the same desire to please or gain my favour. We were at that time under the charm of the Peace of Tilsit, the invincibility of the Emperor had not yet received a wound. I came from Paris,

comme le bon Dieu, vous avez tiré une assez belle machine de chaos.'—Murat, *Lieutenant de roi*, Comte Murat, Avant-propos.

[1] Lecestre, *Lettres inédites*, i. 226, and cf. Murat to Napoleon, Sept. 28, 1808 : '*Il est cruel pour moi d'avoir toujours à me justifier.*'—A. F. iv. 1714 a. Murat wrote to Agar to say that the revenues of the duchy were guaranteed him till Aug. 1. The Emperor, however, refused to allow the outstanding sums to be remitted. Murat to Agar, July 19, 1808 ; Agar to Beugnot, Dec. 28, 1808 ; *Staatsraths-Akten*, Düsseldorf Archives.

[2] A. F. iv. 1225.

where I had passed my life at his Court, that is to say, in the midst of the memorable works and miracles of his reign. In his councils I had admired this genius who dominated human thought; I believed that he was born to chain up fortune, and it seemed to me quite natural that people should be prostrate at his feet. . . . I presented myself in the grand-duchy, under the empire of these ideas; nothing astonished me in the consideration and even the respect of which I was the object; yet I did not allow myself to be lulled to sleep by these flattering deceptions, I worked from morn to night with a singular ardour, and astonished the natives of the country, who did not know that the Emperor exerted upon his servants, however distant, the miracle of the real presence [1].'

If Verres had been controlled as closely as the 'proconsul' of Berg, the world would have lost a famous oration. Count Beugnot was directed to correspond with a minister in Paris, and to submit every week to the home government a detailed account of everything which might interest the Emperor in the grand-duchy, and in those circles of Germany which were covered by the ducal postal system. This was not all. The minister in Paris corresponded directly with all the ministers of the duchy, particularly with Count Nesselrode, Beugnot's most influential colleague and rival. He received reports from all the chiefs of the civil and military service, all the circulars and decrees of the prefects, a monthly report from the director of every part of the revenue, accompanied by statistical tables. Every ten days the receivers of the *arrondissement* sent him a statement of their payments into the Treasury. He kept an alphabetical register of all the notes furnished by the functionaries of the duchy, whether military or civil. The *procureur-général* was instructed to report to him upon the administration of justice, and all the minutes and reports of the Council of State at Düsseldorf were sent to Paris. And we may be sure that all this multifarious information collected by a Gaudin, a Bassano, a Roederer, was carefully digested for the use of the Emperor himself [2].

[1] Beugnot, *Mémoires*, i. 312–3.
[2] *Feuille de travail*, Nov. 15, 1812; *A. F.* iv. 1226, 1843; Roederer, *Œuvres*, iii. 425.

THE GRAND-DUCHY OF BERG

There was now no longer any diplomatic obscurity about the Duchy of Berg. It was virtually owned by Napoleon, who intended that it should be governed as a French province. From July 31, 1808, 'all the administrative acts and judgements of the courts, and the acts of the notaries,' were 'made under the authority and entitled with the name and titles of His Imperial and Royal Majesty [1].' It is the Emperor who drafts the decrees on military organization, who settles the numbers, the equipment, and the movements of the regiment of Berg. It is he who orders the fortifications of Düsseldorf to be destroyed and the town to be embellished. Nor is his interest solely military. He must have the budget for 1808 in receipts and expenditure; he must know what the duchy yielded him for August, what it will yield him per month, in fact he must have a 'perfect knowledge' of the duchy. He must have it divided into departments and districts, furnished with justices of the peace and municipalities; in short, an administration which assimilates it as soon as possible to the institutions of France. A few weeks later he orders that the Prussian officials should be dismissed, and that a scheme for the division of the duchy into departments should be instantly supplied him [2]. The Spanish war diverts his attention to a distant quarter, and to larger issues. If he does not annex the duchy it is because nothing would be gained by annexation, and something might be lost. Had he not formally promised that he would not carry the French frontier beyond the Rhine, and how would the manufacturers of France regard the inclusion within the Empire of formidable competitors? He does not then expressly annex. On the contrary, just before the outbreak of the Austrian war in 1809, when he is sending circular letters to the members of the Rhenish Confederation, he remembers the anomalous situation of the Grand-Duchy of Berg. He has a nephew four and a half years of age, the Prince Napoleon Louis, son of the

---

[1] *Staatsraths-Akten*, Düsseldorf Archives.

[2] *Corr.* xvii. 474, no. 14,280; 507, no. 14,313. The duchy was divided into four departments (Rhin, $190\frac{1}{2}$ square miles, 351,394 population; Sieg, 214 square miles, 138,550 population; Ruhr, 214 square miles, 231,400 population; Ems, 269 square miles, 215,150 population). *Tableau statistique du Grand-duché de Berg jusqu'au* 13 *déc.* 1810; *Affaires étrangères*, Berg, 13.

King of Holland. By a patent of March 3 the boy is made Grand-Duke, while the Emperor reserves to himself and to his successors the right to dispose of the duchy in case of the death of the prince without heirs. Three days later the child's father is curtly informed of the news. Nothing could be more satisfactory. Balm has been administered to diplomatic sensibilities, while the realities of the situation remain unchanged. In Düsseldorf, rule Beugnot and Nesselrode; in Paris, Bassano and Napoleon [1]. An inspired passage in the *Moniteur* reported the Emperor's reception of the child. 'Never forget,' he said, 'that in whatever post you may be placed by my policy and the interests of my Empire, your first duties are to me, your second towards France. All your other duties, even those which you owe to the people whom I may confide to you, only come after these [2].'

On one occasion, in the autumn of 1811, the Emperor himself descended on Düsseldorf, and in a series of notes jotted down on November 2, with a view to a council summoned for the next day, he expounded his ideas of the government appropriate to the country.

'For the general organization one must first have a Council of State. The present Council does not appear to be one. It ought to act as a Court of Cassation, it ought to be the supreme judge in administrative cases, the interpreter of the law, the reviser of budgets and accounts. Whereas it should represent the country, His Majesty sees nothing but foreigners in it. If the country has representations to make, the Council of State should be its organ and possess its confidence. Masters of requests and auditors must be created in connection with it. A list of the most heavily taxed persons should be presented for the composition of the departmental electoral colleges. His Majesty does not wish electoral colleges for the *arrondissements*. If it suits His Majesty to have an assembly of the country it shall be composed of the colleges. The members of the colleges shall be named in the first instance by His

---

[1] Beugnot was first ordered to correspond with Gaudin, Duke of Gaieta. In 1809 Maret, Duke of Bassano, became the minister responsible for the affairs of Berg. He was succeeded by Count Roederer, Sept. 24, 1810.

[2] *Moniteur*, 1810, no. 203.

Majesty; they shall be renewed in conformity with the French constitutions.'

The document goes on to say that the French judicial system must be introduced by January 1, 1812, that a university and a *lycée* should be established at Düsseldorf, that four or five secondary schools teaching French, Latin, and mathematics should be set on foot in the duchy, and that on and after January 1, 1812, all young people of the country should be compelled to quit foreign schools, and to receive the remainder of their education either in the duchy itself or in France. A bishopric and a chapter were to be erected at Düsseldorf, the parishes to be divided and circumscribed, and the principles of the Concordat introduced. A school of theology was to be founded in the university, and no *curé* was to be ordained who had not received his education either there or in France. The ministers and pastors of the Lutheran and Calvinist communities were to be named by His Majesty, and 'the rights of police to be established.' Finally, under the heading of military organization, the Emperor observed that means must be sought to obtain officers for the army from natives of the duchy, since the existing officers were nearly all foreigners, and that lists of young people should be made out, who could receive an education at St. Cyr or at St. Germain. On the next day the Emperor fairly astounded the Council of the duchy by his extraordinary grasp of the ducal finance, and having roundly abused Beugnot for certain liberties which he had presumed to take with the treasury, left the commissioner to carry out as best he could the comprehensive instructions which have been indicated above[1]. To the King of Westphalia he wrote on November 3, 'I have seen the grand-duchy[2].' He had seen it in two days.

[1] *Corr.* xxii. 548, no. 18,229; Beugnot, *Mémoires,* i. 373-96.
[2] *Corr.* xxii. 555, no. 18,239.

CHAPTER X

PROBLEMS OF GOVERNMENT IN BERG

'Les hommes sont impuissants pour assurer l'avenir ; les institutions seules fixent les destinées des nations.'—NAPOLEON.

'THE Grand-Duchy of Berg,' wrote Beugnot on March 14, 1809[1], 'has been made out of provinces formerly possessed by fifteen different sovereigns holding very various ranks in the political system of Germany. Each one of these provinces has preserved up till now its peculiar laws, statutes and customs supplemented by the Roman Law, the Canon Law, the feudal institutions, the doctrine of the universities, and the authority of the commentaries. In the midst of such a chaos, the judges are as confused with judicial reasonings, as are the litigants with the diversity of judgements, and law-suits last centuries because the more they are investigated, the more complicated they become. The courts are by turns powerful and feeble, independent and servile. Sometimes they meddle with the administration and judge the conduct of ministers. Sometimes they have recourse to the ministers to obtain permission to fulfil their most simple duties.' The French observer was struck by the fact that there was no *Ministère public* to prosecute the criminal, or to defend the helpless and the absent. Save in the old Prussian province of Cleves the procedure was entirely written. The prisoner appeared at the bar loaded with chains, and was liable to the horrid tortures of the sixteenth century. The courts were numerous, and the total number of judges exceeded two hundred, but in the districts which had formerly belonged to Bavaria, judicial posts were bought, sold, and bequeathed as so much private property, and the main object of the judge was to replace the capital expended in purchasing his charge at the expense of the litigant upon whose

[1] *A. F.* iv. 1833.

PROBLEMS OF GOVERNMENT IN BERG

fees he was supported. Equality before the law was not recognized, for public functionaries, nobles, and officers of the fisc were incapable of being tried before the inferior tribunals. Nor was there a clear or satisfactory delimitation of judicial competence, for there was no matter so important that it could not be tried in the inferior courts, so long as it did not concern a privileged person. In that case it would have to go before the Aulic Council of Düsseldorf or the Regency of Münster.

The transplantation from one country to another of a code of laws, and of a system of judicial organization, must in all cases be a delicate proceeding, for though the elementary principles of justice are universally appreciated, nation differs from nation in the principles of their application. To an Englishman there is something abhorrent in the secret processes before the *juge d'instruction* in a French court. To a Frenchman nothing can be more revolting than the spectacle of a single judge conducting a criminal trial. Yet both Frenchmen and Englishmen are agreed upon the main principle that justice must be done without fear or favour, and that while every effort should be made to detect crime, the accused person should have the benefit of all the protection which it is in the power of society to bestow. The immediate introduction of the French codes into the Grand-Duchy of Berg seemed to the conservative mind of Count Beugnot to savour of indiscretion. 'Germany,' as he reminded his government, 'had not, like France, been levelled by the legislation of iconoclastic assemblies.' It would require time and instruction before she could properly attune herself to the new melodies of the Code. Nor was there any danger in delay. Divorce was scarcely known even in the communities separated from the Roman Catholic faith, and consequently the clauses in the Code which regulated that institution would be of little practical import. Entails were little known, and, since feudal succession had already been abolished by decree, it was unlikely that a delay in the introduction of the Code would tend to promote inequality of partition. These representations were received and rejected. On November 12, 1809, an imperial decree ordered that the Code Napoléon was to have the force of law in the Grand-Duchy of Berg from January 1, 1810, and at the same time the imperial commission was requested instantly to furnish a draft scheme for judicial organization. Beugnot had no option but to obey, and a scheme upon the French model—a Court of Appeal, ten courts of *arrondissement*, and justices of the peace—was submitted to the consideration of the Duke of Bassano. But at the same time the Imperial Commissioner pleaded for delay. The new courts could not, he argued, well be established until a new method of criminal procedure had been inaugurated; the imperfect education of the local barristers, the difficulty already experienced in making the Code understood, the fact that the Penal Code was not yet sanctioned in France, all pointed to delay, to some transitional arrangement. Why not adjourn all judicial innovation in the Duchy of Berg till the French system is complete, and the German judge can be guided by a copious stream of French precedent? Or if that were impossible, could not the transition be effected gradually? 'I insist,' he wrote, 'upon the need of transitions, and some form of schooling, because, to my regret, I have daily experience of the feebleness of the lawyers of the grand-duchy [1].'

The greater part of two years passed in discussions and projects. Count Nesselrode, the Minister of the Interior for the grand-duchy, pressed for the introduction of the Westphalian Code of Civil Procedure, which had been formed indeed upon the French prototype, but contained certain simplifications. 'It was,' he wrote, 'already well translated into German; in it the forms of procedure were developed with more precision and detail than in the French Code,' and it was finally recommended by the proximity of the kingdom, and by the familiarity of the grand-ducal jurisconsults with the Westphalian legislation [2]. A second question which came up for discussion was the constitution of a Court of Cassation for the grand-duchy. Count Beugnot, who distrusted the vagaries of Teutonic jurists, and actually proposed to prohibit all German commentaries upon the codes, suggested that a single Court of Cassation should be formed for the whole Confederation of the Rhine. 'Such a court, far more useful than the old imperial Court of Wetzlar, though with different attributions,

[1] Beugnot to Bassano, Feb. 7, 1810; *A. F.* iv. 1833.
[2] *A. F.* iv. 1833.

would implant and cultivate in the States of the Confederation the beneficent principles of French legislation, and would preserve Germany from the contagion of commentaries, and the erudition, good and bad, under which the Code Napoléon is stifled.' A legal committee formed in Düsseldorf itself suggested that the Council of State of the grand-duchy should act also as a Court of Cassation, following a precedent which had been set in the kingdom of Westphalia. But in the end, possibly owing to representations as to the feebleness of the local bar and bench, a third course was adopted, and the Court of Cassation in Paris was given jurisdiction in the Grand-Duchy of Berg.

The desirability of establishing commercial courts was another question which occupied the attention of the jurists of Düsseldorf. The institution was unfamiliar to the Germans, and it was open to doubt whether its introduction would be in any way beneficial. When Henry II created the first merchant judges and consuls in France, a large number of laymen had already been able to familiarize themselves with judicial functions, either as '*échevins*' of towns, or as mayors, *prudhommes*, or legal assessors in the ordinary courts. The legal profession had not yet become a highly specialized and technical branch of human activity, and in most of the towns judicial functions were placed in the hands of the inhabitants. But in Germany the legal profession now formed a distinct class, and the verdicts of amateur judges would fail to command confidence or respect. Nor did the motives which had prompted the establishment of merchant judges in France continue to exist even in the interior of the Empire. They had been established in order that commercial matters at least might be freed from the ruinous and interminable prolixity of ordinary procedure, from 'the hydra of chicane,' against which l'Hôpital struggled. But with the new code of procedure this motive disappeared, and 'the interest of commerce in all its severity' could exact no more expedition than was now afforded to it. It was doubtful whether the merchants of Berg would find any real advantage in being submitted to the ruling of temporary amateurs, taken from among themselves. On the contrary, they would probably prefer to plead before permanent magistrates, whose experience and training would give them the required knowledge. It was accordingly proposed that the Courts of First Instance should act as Courts of Commerce, and this modification of the French system was accepted by the authorities in Paris.

In the end, not only were all the French codes published without modification, but the French judicial organization was substantially introduced in its entirety [1]. There was a Court of Appeal at Düsseldorf, an inferior court in each *arrondissement*, and below them the justices of the peace. All the judges were nominated for life by the sovereign, required to submit monthly reports in French upon the work of their courts, while annual reports were submitted to the Court of Appeal of the grand-duchy by the *procureur général* [2].

The introduction of the jury, and the spectacle of a prisoner at the bar with his hands unfettered, afforded some gratification to the natives of Berg. The old local judges tended to become the *juges de paix* in their own neighbourhood, and discharged their functions with competence. In the Prussian provinces which now formed the Department of the Ruhr, and in the States of the Prince of Nassau, part of which formed the Department of Sieg, the bench was distinguished for an excellent tradition of knowledge and integrity. But the Duchy of Berg presented an unfavourable contrast. 'The coarsest ignorance occupied in some places the curule chair, most of the magistrates were of such mediocre intelligence that they did not know how to write correctly even in their mother tongue, and, what is worse, they passed in public opinion for corruptible judges.' No imputations were levelled against the ability of the Court of Appeal at Düsseldorf, but the judges knew nothing of the statutes and customs of the various provinces which composed the duchy, and should have been recruited by representatives from each of the judicial areas of which the State was composed. The *procureur général*, after commenting upon the lacunae in legislation, and upon the laws, 'incoherent and often contradictory,' which ruled the grand-duchy, proposed that a

[1] The Civil Code came into general use Jan. 1, 1810; the judicial system, Jan. 1, 1812.
[2] *A. F.* iv. 1833.

PROBLEMS OF GOVERNMENT IN BERG

committee should be formed of the Council of State, with instructions to choose such of the French laws as should be susceptible of application to the grand-duchy, and it would, he said, be equally desirable that interpretative or supplementary laws, as well as imperial decrees or pronouncements of the Council of State, relative to the five codes, should be declared common to the grand-duchy, and inserted without delay in the Bulletin of Laws, as they passed in France[1].

'A complete system of homogeneous laws' was under the circumstances too much to expect, but the influence of the Court of Cassation in Paris would no doubt tend to adjust the interpretation of the five French codes to the imperial model. A special law of mortgages drafted by Treilhard and Duchatel was sent down from Paris (since it was represented that the arrangements of the Civil Code were not suitable to the needs of the duchy), and formed an important departure from the French civil law[2]. There was, however, a strong desire, both on the part of the authorities in Paris and on the part of the ministers at Düsseldorf, to apply to the grand-duchy all the French legislation which was capable of transplantation. The draft decrees concerted in the Council of State at Düsseldorf (frequently at the request of the minister in Paris) were tested and amended in the capital of the Empire before they were permitted to pass into law. The decrees of the Emperor were executed without delay. There was not a clerk or an usher in the law courts of Berg who did not receive his nomination from Napoleon, and the ambitious lawyer who wished to rise wrote a manual of French civil procedure, and bowed his head to the study of Pothier.

The condition of the agricultural poor previous to the French occupation was no doubt in many places deplorable enough. Serfage was prevalent, feudal dues were numerous and *corvées* heavy. In some places, however, the hard outlines of the law had been softened by custom, by administrative ordinance, or by philanthropic feeling[3]. We are assured by

---

[1] *Rapport sur l'administration de la justice dans le Grand-Duché de Berg pendant l'an* 1812 ; A. F. iv. 1834.

[2] A. F. iv. 1833.

[3] Seeley, *Life and Times of Stein*, i. 110.

the proprietors of Münster that it was easier to find tenants where the tenure was servile, than where the tenure was free. It was true that the serf in Münster could not cut wood for any purpose but firing, save with his lord's leave, that his 'colonate' was subject to mortuary dues and admission dues, but in revenge his tenure was fixed, and he had the right to bequeath it to his lawful descendants born upon the colonate. Serfage in such a case was apt to be less hard upon the individual serf than upon the economic development of the country. It arrested the free circulation of labour and stereotyped agrarian methods [1].

No question excited the interest of the Council of Düsseldorf so much as the proposed abolition of serfage and feudalism. A society of somewhat conservative German lawyers and proprietors found themselves directly menaced, in a most sensitive quarter, by the application of French revolutionary precedents, and the fiscal interests of the domain were enlisted on the side of the landowning class. The problem had already been settled on the lines of compromise by the Westphalian government before it engaged the attention of the Grand-Ducal Council. But even Westphalian moderation was outdone in the scheme which was first presented to the Council by Sethe, the president of the commission appointed to study the question. 'It is a recognized fact,' said that cautious jurist, 'that the heritages possessed at present by serfs originally belonged of full right to those whom we now call lords,' and it followed that nearly all the dues paid or services performed by the peasant were the result of explicit contract and the exchange for value received. It was argued that it would be unjust to abolish without compensation to the landlord, and this, as we shall see, was the principle adopted in Westphalia. But while in Westphalia all heriots and all labour services of an indeterminate or personal character were deemed to have originated in servitude, Sethe held that in the grand-duchy they were the fruit of contract. A commission was sent to Münster, the home of the large proprietor and the serf, to consult with a local committee of lawyers, administrators, and landowners, and the Council at Düsseldorf laid down for its guidance the aims and principles which should

[1] *A. F.* iv. 1837.

be kept in view. These were the abolition of all personal servitude, the consolidation of proprietary rights, and a complete indemnity to the lord for the loss of non-servile dues and services[1]. The centre of interest was now shifted to the exact discrimination between those services which were and those which were not to be abolished without compensation. The Münster commission took a view extremely favourable to the landlord, but the Council was more liberal to the serf, and the imperial decree of December 12, 1808, which was constructed upon the Council's draft, was distinguished by a spirit of impartiality and justice.

The main provisions of this important act of legislation were as follows:—Serfdom and the colonate were declared to be abolished, and with them went four classes of service: forced labour in the lord's house, dues upon manumission, mortuary dues save where they had been paid from colonates, and lastly, all personal *corvées* and transport services. These, being deemed servile, were abolished without compensation. On the other hand, the 'dues resulting from a colonate' were abolished subject to compensation, the scale of which was fixed. The peasant was given power to purchase immunity from seigneurial dues, and the lord was forced to sell, if he was offered a hundred francs capital for four francs revenue. The 'colon' or villein was to own the timber on his land, and whenever there was a complication of rights, as for instance where both lord and peasant had rights in the same wood or pasture, there was to be a division for the triple purpose of simplifying tenure, of emancipating the individual, and of assisting agricultural development. The early ideal of the French Revolution—a free peasant proprietary—had not lost its momentum, but it was now allied with a greater respect for inherited and vested interests, and supplemented by the institution of certain privileged entails or majorats.

The subtle distinction between services founded on contract and services originating in serfdom escaped the notice of the peasant. 'We are free from Hand- and Spanndienst,' they cried, and 'Hand- and Spanndienst' they refused to pay. Some recalcitrant peasants of Mark were sued by their lords, and the

[1] *Staatsraths-Akten,* Düsseldorf Archives.

judgement went for the plaintiffs. Then money was subscribed, and Johann Giesbert Alef of Westerfilde, provided with a petition, travelled to Paris in the spring of 1811 as the peasants' orator. For six months the youth loitered in the streets of the French capital, watching an opportunity to present his paper to the great man. At last, on July 9, the moment came, and as the Emperor and Empress were stepping into their carriage at St. Cloud, Alef sprang forward with his petition. The Emperor read the paper, and then, with Louise for interpreter, began to cross-examine the rustic petitioner, pouring in questions, volley upon volley, for the space of two hours while the horses were champing at their bits. In the end, another interview was appointed for the morning of the eleventh, but when Alef and a bilingual friend arrived at the palace they found that the Court had flitted to Trianon. To Trianon then the two hastened, and were announced to His Imperial Majesty. But the most propitious moment had flown. His Imperial Majesty sent back word that he had not time to master the question (being now deep in the fortifications of Danzig), but that justice should be done to the peasants. The matter was, however, transferred to competent hands. On the very same evening Alef was summoned before Count Merlin, the *procureur général* of the Court of Cassation, and M. Daniels, who translated the Civil Code into German. After much questioning the two lawyers drew up a report which was forwarded to Beugnot, and was made the basis of a decree issued September 13, 1811. How this decree was regarded by the peasants may be seen by the following petition, drawn up by a deputation of peasants from the *arrondissement* of Dortmund on October 23, 1811 :—

'Your Imperial Majesty has deigned in his wisdom and his justice to declare himself by his decree of September 13 the father of the agriculturists, who have been oppressed for several centuries. Our chains are broken; we are made like unto the other subjects of your Majesty, and shall rejoice with them in equal rights. Our hearts are kindled to the most profound gratitude for the Great Man destined by Providence to create a new and better order of things, and we and our most distant descendants will not cease to bless the memory

PROBLEMS OF GOVERNMENT IN BERG

of your Majesty. However great may be our adversaries, however powerful may be their efforts to prevent the entire execution of this beneficent decree, we are persuaded that your Majesty will cause respect to be paid to a decision dictated by wisdom and love for his faithful subjects. May Heaven pour down blessings upon our benefactor and his august dynasty [1].'

The abolition without indemnity of fiefs, feudal succession, and feudal services by the imperial decree of January 11, 1809, and the abolition of seigneurial jurisdiction on December 17, 1811, gave an impulse to the subdivision of property, which is said to have had the most salutary effects upon the agriculture of the duchy. Numerous clearances, improved drainage, and better crops were the result of the French legislation, and of the stimulus imparted to the general life by the consuming energy of Napoleon. And no less important was the decree of March 31, 1809, which permitted the marriage of noble with peasant, and peasant with burgess, sweeping away in one general and comprehensive clause the invidious and caste-like distinctions of the Prussian Code [2].

There are some countries which are by nature pre-eminently designed for a policy of free trade, countries which have a differential advantage in the production of commodities which are in general demand, and depend for their prosperity upon the cheap acquisition of raw materials on the one hand and upon the ready acceptance of their manufactures by foreign consumers on the other. Such a country was the Grand-Duchy of Berg. It was neither economically self-sufficient, nor were its products confined to the home market. On the contrary, it had the reputation of being one of the most active manu-

---

[1] *A. F.* iv. 1837. According to Beugnot's calculation the interpretative decree of Sept. 13, 1811, further defining dues and services of feudal origin, was so favourable to the peasants, that the Crown domains alone would be compelled to restore them 600,000 francs for rents, &c., unlawfully levied since 1808. Beugnot to Roederer, Nov. 8, 1811.

[2] ' *Nous avons d'ailleurs considéré que le code prussien en définissant la basse classe de la bourgeoisie se trouvait dans une opposition absolue avec la nature des choses et nos institutions qui font du service militaire un patrimoine commun d'honneur auquel tous les citoyens sont également appelés.*'—*Staatsraths-Akten*, Düsseldorf Archives.

facturing centres in Germany. It was, so to speak, the Birmingham and Sheffield, the Manchester and Leeds of Germany rolled into one. The excellence of the Remscheid steel was acknowledged throughout the world. In the immense pastures of Buenos Ayres it was with shears 'made in Germany' at Remscheid that the flocks were shorn. Not a vat of wine or brandy but was bound with the steel from the mines of the County of Mark; not a vessel braved the ocean without a Remscheid girding. It was a merchant of Remscheid who set up the first forge in North America; a detachment of Remscheid men started the iron works of Silesia and South Prussia, and it was to Remscheid that Catherine II addressed herself for skilled pioneers to exploit the resources of her Russian mines. The wire, the needles, the ploughshares of the grand-duchy were exported chiefly to Spain and Portugal, but also to other European markets. Silesian and Spanish wool fed a prosperous cloth manufacture, and some hundred thousand families were supported by the industries of iron and steel, cloth and wool, cotton and silk. Before the war began it was calculated that an export trade was done in these articles to the extent of 60,000,000 francs, a small figure enough now, but at that time equal to one-fifth of the total export trade of France [1].

All this prosperity was absolutely ruined by the continental blockade, and by the fiscal system of the French Empire. The ironmasters were unable to send consignments to their dépôts at New York and Charlestown, and the trade with Spain and Portugal utterly ceased. The export trade, which stood at 55,000,000 francs in 1807, declined to 30,000,000 in 1808, to 18,000,000 in 1811, to 11,000,000 in 1812. It might have been thought that provinces compelled to lose all their seaborne trade, owing to the imperial wars, would at any rate have been partially compensated by the fiscal hospitality of France herself. But the Grand-Duchy of Berg was treated by France with as much jealousy and aversion as if she had been an enemy. Her cottons were forced to pay a heavy duty at the French frontier, on the pretext that otherwise they would under-

---

[1] *Mémoire sur les fabriques et manufactures du Grand-Duché de Berg*, par J. G. Diederichs, maire de Remscheid; *A. F.* iv. 1839.

sell the French article, and that they laboured under the disadvantage of resembling too closely the cotton goods of Oldham or Manchester. It had been hoped, among the coal-owners of the Ruhr department, that the coal mines of the duchy would profit by the prohibition of English imports into Holland, but a decree of January 6, 1811, imposed prohibitive import duties upon the Dutch frontier. 'Every new extension of France brought desolation to the heart of the inhabitants of the grand-duchy.' There was a general desire among the manufacturers to be annexed to the French Empire. '*Hors la réunion*,' they wrote, '*nous avons peu d'espoir.*' Death or emigration were the alternatives. If the annexation were not permitted, most of the captains of industry had resolved to migrate to the left bank, so as to obtain free access to the French consumers. 'Two-thirds of our manufacturers,' ran the petition, 'will go to France, the rest to Russia and Austria[1].' Nor did the serious calamity which had befallen the industry of the duchy escape the notice of the government. A report of November 15, 1812, stated that the grand-duchy had lost by emigration, in the current year, twelve or fifteen manufacturers of cotton stuffs or hardware, and five or six thousand workmen of different trades[2]. 'Your Excellency,' wrote Beugnot to Roederer on November 20, 1812, 'knows as well as I do the financial conditions of the grand-duchy. It is clear that all the taxes upon general property fall in value day by day. Experience has betrayed almost all the hopes of the budget of 1812. I predict nothing less sad for 1813 if the Rhine, the Elbe, and the Weser remain closed to the exportations of the grand-duchy. I even predict its approaching ruin, if it is insensibly led to produce nothing and to manufacture nothing save for its own consumption[3].'

Yet these uncomfortable facts were not allowed to influence the course of policy. 'There is no languor,' said the Emperor (January 1, 1813), wilfully shutting his eyes to the truth; 'the

---

[1] In 1811 an influential deputation of commercial men went to Paris to petition for the incorporation of the grand-duchy in the French Empire, as the only means of rescuing their fatherland from its precarious position. Goecke, *Das Grossherzogthum Berg*, 77.

[2] *A. F.* iv. 1226.   [3] *A. F.* iv. 1839.

Berg people made a considerable sale at the Leipzig fair last year[1].' On May 8, 1813, an imperial decree was issued commanding the confiscation of all the colonial goods which were to be found in the Grand-Duchy of Berg. It was represented that the total amount of these goods did not exceed the value of 800,000 francs, that they had all been bought in France and had already paid heavy duty. 'The execution of the decree would,' said Beugnot, 'reduce seven or eight thousand workmen to emigrate and beg, ruin the cotton and lace manufactures, and discourage all future importations of colonial raw material from France.' This prognosis was correct. On May 14, 1813, Count Nesselrode was able to report to Roederer upon the effects of the execution of the decree. 'Only last week,' he wrote, 'three houses of Elberfeld closed, and a fourth, which employed more than 200 workmen, did the same the day before yesterday. Two others have announced to their workmen that they will wind up at the end of the week. Such is the report which the commissioner of police at Elberfeld made me yesterday—a sensible man, who assures me that in less than ten days all the houses which make cotton must necessarily follow that example[2].' Sudden commercial ruin generally leads to crime and disorder, and in the manufacturing cantons of the grand-duchy thefts and burglaries increased to an alarming extent during the year 1813. 'It is to be remarked,' wrote the Minister of the Interior, 'in the reports of the mayors of rural cantons such as Remscheid, Kronenberg, &c., that the native workmen are taking to presenting themselves at the end of the week before the houses of manufacturers who live in isolation to ask for succour. It is true that they behave with decency, and express the most affectionate gratitude when aid is afforded them. But these visits are made in bands of ten individuals or more, and assistance is demanded with so firm a countenance that no manufacturer has yet had the courage to refuse it[3].'

It is needless to accumulate further evidence of the ruinous effects of the French connection upon the commerce and manufacture of Berg.

In the complacent retrospect of Count Beugnot the unpleasant

[1] *A. F.* iv. 1839.   [2] *A. F.* iv. 1854.
[3] Nesselrode to Roederer, June 25, 1813; *A. F.* iv. 1854.

facts, upon which he so honourably insisted at the time, are completely effaced. We learn how the manufactures of the duchy progressed, being favoured by the opening of the Italian market and by some privileges procured by the Emperor for the merchants of Berg at the fair of Leipzig. The discovery of coal at Ottweiler and Oberdries in 1809 is regarded as a happy compensation for the losses occasioned by the great floods which signalized that year. Yet the broad fact remains that France ruined the manufacture and commerce of this little State. Instead of encouraging the importation of raw material by low duties and drawbacks, she discouraged it by high tariffs and confiscations. While the mill-owner was liable to have his raw cotton seized in Berg, and his manufactured cotton seized at Leghorn, the old exit by way of Amsterdam was closed, partly by the maritime war and partly by the Dutch custom lines. An open market in France was denied, and yet this was the only satisfactory compensation which France could have offered. The policy was wilfully persisted in, against the light, against the reiterated reports, recommendations, and draft decrees of the men in power at Düsseldorf. And for all this industrial and commercial loss the French could offer no recompense. The mining engineers of the grand-duchy had received their training either in the celebrated school of Berlin or in the mines of Silesia, and the French specialists had nothing but admiration for the order, the skill, and the economy with which the mines were worked [1]. Nor was there any department of manufacture which was assisted to improve its technical processes by the French occupation.

The visit of the Emperor had stirred a great problem of educational statesmanship. It was, perhaps, a natural assumption that the Germans, who were so behindhand in the arts of administration, would be equally inferior to the French in educational methods. The dream of a new university founded in a German city by French statesmen, managed upon superior French models, and attracting to its service all the talents of Germany, was grateful to the pride of the Emperor and his

[1] *Rapport général sur les mines, usines et salines du Grand-duché de Berg par l'ingénieur en chef des mines et usines de l'Empire Français*; A. F. iv. 1225.

servants. A connected system of State education, penetrating, tolerant, and secular, and the general diffusion of instruction in the French language, promised to satisfy equally the twin French tastes for civilization and ascendency. Yet Beugnot upon further examination was bound to admit that the primary schools in the grand-duchy were upon a better footing than they were in France, that 'a more considerable mass of illumination was spread among the inhabitants of the country,' and that there was not a parish which, if it had to communicate directly with the Imperial Commissioner, could not find some farmer to speak or write with tolerable fluency in Latin[1]. It is possible that the secondary education was not equally good, and that the establishment of three *lycées* at Düsseldorf, Dortmund, and Dillenburg, represented a distinct gain to the grand-duchy. But the University of Düsseldorf was never destined to be more than a fabric of paper. The budgets of the grand-duchy, overcharged with military expenditure, could not spare more than the most paltry sums to education, and a contribution of so small an amount as 30,000 francs from the public treasury to the endowment of the new university was too heavy an addition to the educational charges to be risked. The amiable Beugnot would have wished to organize the University of Düsseldorf 'after the principles generally admitted in Germany,' adding, however, an Academy of Fine Arts to correct the austerity of the Teutonic curriculum. But the order came from Paris that the French model must be strictly adhered to, and a decree was concerted between Nesselrode and Roederer to give effect to this injunction. There were to be five faculties—Theology, Law, Medicine, Mathematical and Physical Science, and Letters. There were to be two Professors of Theology, one Catholic and one Protestant, and three Professors of Letters. The endowment of the university from all sources was to amount to 114,000 francs. The professors

---

[1] Beugnot to Roederer, Jan. 17, 1813; *A. F.* iv. 1838. '*Je doute*,' he concludes, '*qu'un administrateur allemand, transporté sur quelque point de la France que ce soit, trouvât matière à une telle remarque.*' In the Department of the Ems there were 230 primary schools, one for every 300 inhabitants. *Notices statistiques sur le département de l'Ems* ; *Affaires étrangères, Corr. pol. : Berg*, 14.

were to be named by the Emperor upon the designation of the Minister of the Interior, and every year one or two deans or professors of the university were to be designated by the minister to visit all the schools of the duchy. It was a penurious, provisional, unpromising scheme. A German critic remarked that the university, if so constituted, would only be a university of the third rank. While the professors were too few, the curriculum was too narrow. The science of Political Economy, for instance, though ardently pursued at all the chief German universities, was banished under the Napoleonic *régime* as a dangerous heresy. It was pointed out that there was no provision for the teaching of speculative and transcendental philosophy, a branch of inquiry peculiarly congenial to the German temperament and intellect. Chairs of Forestry and of Administrative Law were now recognized appendages of a German university system, but they were absent here, nor could the whole field of Theology, dogmatic and historical, be covered adequately by two professors. '*En Allemagne*,' remarked Nesselrode to Napoleon, '*il faut payer les savants en poids d'or*.' It was not only the gold which was wanting to this paper university, but, what was far more essential than gold, a comprehensive view of human needs in the field of education [1].

The religious policy of the administration was formed upon the broad principles of tolerant Erastianism which were characteristic of the Napoleonic system. The concordat was introduced, and the ecclesiastical corporations were suppressed, with due regard to existing interests. By a decree of November 12, 1808, all property belonging to religious communities other than those devoted to educational and charitable purposes was henceforth to be administered by the *Régie*, a department of the domains, and more than one otiose but harmless chapter of aristocratic ladies was forced to wind up its charming and fastidious existence [2]. The Catholics of Berg, the Lutherans

---

[1] The criticisms of Professor Sartorius of Göttingen (Oct. 23, 1812) are to be found in *A. F.* iv. 1838. The comments of Count Nesselrode might have been written by Napoleon himself. They breathe an insolent contempt for physiocrats, metaphysicians, and ecclesiastics.

[2] The Chapter of Elten, the revenue of which exceeded 44,000 francs, was only open to such princesses and countesses of the Empire as could

of Mark, and the Calvinists of Nassau-Siegen were put on an equal footing, and the minority in any parish was expressly relieved from the obligation of paying Church dues to the confession of the majority, on the ground that 'everything must be averted which can give to one or other confession the appearance of a governing Church[1]. It had been the usage in Berg for controversial sermons to be preached at certain high festivals, and as these discourses were said to abound in indecent invective against the Protestant faith, they were forbidden by the government. A similar bridle was placed upon the zeal or intolerance of the other side, and at the request of the Catholic clergy the eightieth article, denouncing the mass, was ordered to be omitted from a forthcoming edition of the greater Heidelberg Catechism[2].

While the *Règlements Organiques* secured the subservience of the Catholic clergy to the State, the bonds which bound the Protestant communities were no less strict. Organization, doctrine, ritual, discipline, patronage, were all shaped and controlled by the Head of the State. A Calvinist synod could not assemble without government authority, or execute a synodal decision which had not received government approval. The Protestant festivals were regulated by decree, and the Emperor might have the satisfaction of reflecting that on the first Sunday of October every Lutheran or Calvinist pastor in the Grand-Duchy of Berg was thanking a bountiful Creator for a copious or a niggardly harvest. It was intended to refuse ordination to any Protestant applicant who had not undergone a determinate course of study in the University of Düsseldorf, and seminaries were to be instructed to train up a Catholic clergy in the Christian and imperial religion. A decree of January 1, 1812, ordered all young citizens of the grand-duchy, who were receiving their education abroad, to quit their schools and universities, and to obtain the remainder of their education

---

show seventy-four quarterings. The ladies were not bound to celibacy, nor were they compelled to reside there for more than three months during their lives. A. F. iv. 1865.

[1] *Cultus*, Düsseldorf Archives.

[2] A. F. iv. 1838 ; *Neue Intelligenz-Nachrichten für das Sieg-Departement*, Feb. 29, 1812.

PROBLEMS OF GOVERNMENT IN BERG 213

either in the grand-duchy or in France. The strictness of this rule was so far relaxed on January 7, 1813, that young ecclesiastics of Berg were permitted to study at the seminary of Cologne, but a regulation which prevented a German youth from attending the classes of Halle and Göttingen, in order that he might imbibe knowledge in Düsseldorf or Paris, was not framed in the true interests of education[1].

In course of time the grand-duchy assumed the air of a French province. The administration was, after the French manner, divided into seven principal sections—customs, registration and stamps, posts, waters, forests and mines, direct contributions, indirect contributions, domains. A Council of State of ten members, three ministers, and the Imperial Commissioner, formed the central government. The French coinage and the French tariffs were introduced, and the French forms of administration were, says Beugnot, 'as well understood as in their native country and better respected.'

'Nowhere, perhaps,' proceeds the same authority, 'was the control of expenditure better or more surely established. We aimed at making a model administration, and we hoped that we might be permitted to publish its history. I had already occupied myself with the statistics of the grand-duchy. M. Roederer had undertaken the development of the theory, and the third part would have been filled by tables indicating the best methods of execution. Time failed us, but some special subjects furnished matter for reports which may still be consulted with advantage. Among others, I mention works on the origin of the colonates or villein tenures in the portions of Germany which border on the Rhine, on the mortgage system, on coinage, and on lotteries.'

The memoirs of Beugnot, despite their prevailing tone of complacency, do not fail to indicate the weak points of the situation. It is clear that considerable uneasiness was caused by the decree which, conferring the duchy upon the Prince-Royal of Holland, seemed to indicate an annexation at some future time to that heavily indebted kingdom[2]. Again, during

---

[1] *A. F.* iv. 1838.

[2] A bulletin of March 1809 says that the appointment of Prince Louis Napoleon was popular, but too much credit should not be attached to this. *A. F.* iv. 1225.

the Austrian war and the German troubles of 1809, the gravest apprehension was felt by the French Commissioner, who was aware that Major Schill had intelligences in the old County of Mark, and that many of the nobles of the duchy, among them the sons of Count Nesselrode, his colleague, were serving in the Austrian army. So critical seemed the situation, that Count Beugnot actually took upon himself to falsify the bulletin announcing the battle of Essling, a piece of foolish impudence and a vain precaution. As a matter of fact, it may be doubted whether the danger was ever great in 1809. In the spring there had been a tiny agitation in the County of Mark. The president and the syndic wished to summon the Estates, but when the Imperial Commissioner gave out that if that body met, it would be dispersed as an unlawful assembly and its members arrested, the agitation withered under the threat, and all relapsed into quiet [1]. Nevertheless it was remarked that there were many desertions in the country, and an official report opines that it would be imprudent to employ the troops of the Duchy of Berg in Germany, at least for their first campaigns [2]. But although the Austrian sympathies of Mark and Münster were unconcealed, there was to be no rash heroism in Berg. How many peasant revolts, national risings, and deep conspiracies and hopeless causes have not been led by priests, fanatics, and men of religion! In Scotland, in Ireland, in Spain, in the Tyrol, in Arabia, prophetic and priestly agencies have often played a decisive part in the crisis of a great emotion. But in the Duchy of Berg, the Churches were not cast in the spirit of the Scotch Covenanters or the Spanish priests. The German religious temperament, naturally tranquil, introspective, and resigned, was framed by history to long habits of submission to the powers of the earth. The clergy of Berg were no exception to this rule, and in the pulpits both of town and country no occasion was lost of preaching obedience to the government of Napoleon [3].

As a member of the Confederation of the Rhine, the Grand-Duchy of Berg was bound to furnish a military contingent. This was at first fixed at 5,000 men, or one-tenth of the population,

[1] *A. F.* iv. 1225.   [2] Ibid.
[3] *Bulletin de police*, March 2, 1809; *A. F.* iv. 1226.

but with the territorial acquisitions of the duchy, and the growing military appetite of Napoleon, the blood-tax was steadily increased. A decree of May 13, 1807, introduced conscription, and since the population of the duchy had been increased by more than 3,000,000 by the union of Münster and Mark, the contingent was raised to 7,000. In the budget of 1808 we find that 4,459 men were paid for by the State. By August 29, 1808, the number had risen to 7,200. On June 25, 1811, it stands at 8,180. On October 12, 1811, the Emperor orders two new regiments of Lancers, or 1,200 men. Then comes the Russian disaster, and the last great rally of imperial France and her German allies. To this also Berg must contribute [1]. A brigade of cavalry 2,500 strong, an infantry regiment 1,680 strong, a company of horse artillery and eight field-pieces are demanded instantaneously. It may easily be imagined that the conscription which provides these victims to perish by hundreds on the parching sierras of Spain, the snow-swept plains of Russia, or in the great butcheries of Central Germany, is regarded with growing aversion by this quiet home-loving people. 'A father who has six or seven boys bitterly deplores the departure of one of them. The mother cannot tear herself from them, and every departure of conscripts is marked by scenes of great and unaffected violence, but just as every virtue pushed to excess is very near to a vice, these tender fathers and mothers have the barbarous cowardice to induce their children to mutilate themselves, and even help them to do so. Indeed the number of *pollice truncati* is so considerable that one is, so to speak, obliged to avert one's eyes.' This is from an official report of March 1809 [2]. Another report of the same date, while noting that the conscription is already established in the rural districts, alludes to the 'invincible repugnance' with which it was regarded by the industrial classes in the towns [3]. But when

[1] *Mémoire historique sur la conscription dans le Grand-duché de Berg*; A. F. iv. 1873. The *Feuille de travail* of Nov. 15, 1812, states that 5,870 men and fourteen guns were with the Grand Army in Russia, while 800 were in Catalonia. The total effective of the Berg forces was reckoned, Oct. 1, 1812, at 8,048. *Feuille de travail*, Nov. 11, 1812; A. F. iv. 1226.

[2] A. F. iv. 1225.

[3] *Bulletin de police*, March 2, 1809; A. F. iv. 1225.

once the recruiting machine had been started, it went on rolling over family feeling and love of home with a momentum to which it seemed idle to offer resistance. In 1810 there appears to be no difficulty in raising the men. In 1811 the country is reported 'submissive and quiet, the conscription easy.' The annual quota of 1,850 men goes with the rest to bleed or starve in Russia in 1812. But in the next year patience had reached its term. There were loud murmurs, there was resistance. An English dragoon who was in Düsseldorf at the time describes how the order came down to that city, that the Grand Army must be supplied with a reinforcement of 5,000 infantry and 500 cavalry. The names of all the male inhabitants of the duchy were already in the keeping of the authorities. Lots were drawn, and the dragoons sallied out in every direction to secure their prizes. 'It was shocking,' writes George Farmer, 'to see the poor wretches brought in, twenty or thirty in a string, tied round the neck with one cord, the end of which was fastened to a mounted policeman's saddle.' To attempt escape was hazardous, if not futile. The 'conscriptable matter,' as Napoleon had come to term it, was confined in a barrack, and strictly guarded by tried veterans. If a conscript managed to break the barrier, the authorities did not even care to look for him. A party of soldiers was quartered upon the house of his parents, or else the father was seized, thrown into prison, and kept there till his son had rejoined the standard. The method was found effectual. Within the knowledge of George Farmer there was not a single runaway who was not by this method recovered for the army [1].

This was not all. Convenient high-roads traversed the Grand-Duchy of Berg, leading either to Hanover, or to Magdeburg, or to Cassel. French armies passed through the country on their way to the German and Russian wars; French soldiery was quartered on the people. The food, the lodging, the hospital accommodation, the fodder for the horses, the

[1] *The Memoirs of George Farmer*, 11*th Light Dragoons*, ed. G. R. Gleig, i. 285 ff.; and cf. *Instruction sur l'emploi des garnisaires*, A. F. iv. 1873. The prefect cannot, without special authorization, place more than four 'garnisaires' with one individual, or quarter them upon one house for more than one month.

PROBLEMS OF GOVERNMENT IN BERG 217

wine for the officers and men came from the purses of the inhabitants. 'I am informed,' writes Beugnot, February 23, 1810, 'that 12,000 men are to occupy the duchy. I am to prepare hospital accommodation for 1,200. I read in the instructions of the *intendant général* the positive instruction to nourish the troops imposed on the inhabitants, and I see but a small hope of reimbursement.' The food of a common soldier came to two francs a day, that of an officer to six or seven francs or even more [1]. 'It is evident,' wrote the prefect of the Ems department, August 11, 1810, ' that in a poor country like this few inhabitants can sustain this charge for long [2]. Indeed, a little arithmetic shows us that if the force were to remain for a year, the charge would exceed the total annual revenue of the duchy [3].'

Before the French occupation the taxation had been light, and the aims of government modest and restricted in Berg and Cleves. 'Prince Joachim,' wrote Agar, May 1, 1806, 'can only expect a revenue of 1,700,000 francs.' 'I send you our budget,' wrote the Prince to the Emperor, March 28, 1806; 'your Majesty will see it leaves me nothing [4].' In 1808, as we know, Mark, Münster, and Tecklenburg were added to the duchy. Here, too, the taxation had been light. Daru reckoned the net revenue of the new provinces at 1,219,441 francs 46 centimes, but they had been occupied and drained by a French military occupation, and they were ceded subject to conditions which impaired their immediate value. The French Emperor claimed arrears of revenue, half the domains, and a war contribution. It was eventually settled that the arrears and war contribution together were to amount to 1,523,527 francs 89 centimes. The imperial share of the domains was estimated at 250,000 francs a year. It follows from this, that if the fiscal system were unchanged, all the receipts of the first year,

---

[1] *A. F.* iv. 1225, and cf. Beugnot to Roederer, June 14, 1810, *A. F.* iv. 1873.

[2] Pick, *Monatsschrift für rheinisch-westfälische Geschichtsforschung und Alterthumskunde*, 1877, 105 ff.

[3] The general receipts of the duchy were 7,840,733 francs in 1811 ; *A. F.* iv. 1226.

[4] *A. F.* iv. 1225.

and some of the receipts of the second year would be consumed in liquidating the debt to the Emperor, while there would be a permanent annual deduction of revenue equal to about a fifth of the whole amount[1].

The receipts were not unchanged. In the old provinces and in the new, the French fiscal system was introduced—a tax on land and movables, a stamp tax, a patent tax, the *centimes additionnels* for local government. There were stringent custom duties; the municipal excise duties, which were variable, were exchanged for a subvention which was fixed, and fixed, some said, unduly high. The figures in the budget mount up ambitiously. We might expect some 3,000,000 francs. But in 1808 the public charges stand at 6,910,000, exclusive of the expense of keeping up the princely palace and paying the princely revenue. The receipts mount sympathetically; in 1808 the general receipts stand at 7,840,733 francs, the budget of the Prince at 4,050,000. In 1813 the general receipts alone mount to 992,257,173. In short, the revenue is more than tripled.

Of this swollen budget something between one-third and one-half was spent upon war. In 1808, 37,000 francs were devoted to public instruction, and more than 2,500,000 to the army. In 1813 the department of the Minister of the Interior received 1,559,000 francs, while the Minister of War swallowed 4,334,000, or nearly three times as much[2]. With such a military charge imposed upon it, what hope was there that the State chest would be able adequately to meet the claims of public instruction, which (so far as its higher branches went) was, according to the Count of Mosburg, 'in an afflicting state of decadence,' or those of justice, which demanded something better than a mere living wage for the occupants of the judicial bench? Then too, even assuming that the revenue of the old régime had been unduly light, was it wise for a new administration, would it be wise for any administration to triple its budget in five years? We know how delicate are the problems of incidence, how difficult it is equitably to diffuse any sudden addition to the volume of taxation. It is not then surprising if, in the reports of the prefects of the grand-duchy, we overhear

[1] *A. F.* iv. 1225.
[2] *A. F.* iv. 1842, 1863 A and B.

the murmurs of the taxpayer. The direct contribution is too high, the subvention in lieu of municipal excise is too high, the increased import duty on salt is a hardship, the customs are vexatious, and the French custom-house officers insolent [1]. In 1811 there were more than 600 complaints lodged against the incidence of taxation by the Department of the Rhine alone [2]. The grievance of the customs was very real. One prefect, after alluding in general terms to the vexations of the *douaniers*, speaks of 'sudden and unexpected seizures of merchandise, made in a tumultuous manner without any of the forms which the French laws have introduced to guarantee the rights of peaceable citizens.' Another mentions that the *douanes* have occasioned a great diminution in the cattle and transit trade. Against the *douaniers*, who are frequently assisted by the soldiery, it is next to impossible to obtain justice. A circular was sent round to the law courts explaining that, according to French law, an employé of the customs cannot be sued for acts committed in discharge of his functions, except in virtue of an authorization given by the Director-General of the Customs [3]. The merchant whose consignment of goods from Hamburg has been seized upon the frontier must first seek this permission, and then, if he is lucky enough to get it, lodge his complaint before the Council of Prizes, which sits at Paris, 150 leagues away, a court whose laws and procedure are utterly unknown to him. Rather than face the risk and expense he will sit at home, brooding over the wrong that is done him. And so, in 1813, when the storm ultimately bursts, the custom-house men have to fly for their lives.

Yet it must not be imagined that the government was insensible or remiss. Beugnot and his colleagues were responsible neither for the army, nor for the customs line, nor for the sequestration of half the domains for the payment of pensions to the relatives and generals of the Emperor, nor for the war contribution. They were forced to discover new

---

[1] Report of the Prefect of the Sieg, Nov. 20, 1810; Pick, *Monatsschrift*, 1877.

[2] *Feuille de travail*, Nov. 15, 1812; *A. F.* iv. 1226.

[3] Beugnot to Nesselrode, Nov. 18, 1810; *Staatsraths-Akten*, Düsseldorf Archives.

fiscal resources, and they took pains that the extra burdens should fall equitably upon the taxpayers[1]. The ugly symptoms were reported to Paris, mollified perhaps by the spirit of deference or optimism, but nevertheless patently ugly. It was on the whole an honest, industrious, and deserving administration, zealous in the cause of law, of administrative order, of scientific and sanitary progress, anxious yet without bustle or iconoclasm to make of the grand-duchy a pattern State; and if it failed to content the inhabitants, the cause of this failure lay quite outside its own sphere of action and motive.

There were murmurs in 1810, but the country was quiet and submissive. Trade was dying, taxes were rising, the regiment of Berg was being decimated in Spain, but the country did not stir. In 1811, when Napoleon came to Düsseldorf, it was noticed that his reception would have been cold had it not been for the plaudits of his suite and of the French residents. Only for a lad of genius, Heinrich Heine, was the old glamour still untarnished. 'The nobles,' writes Beugnot, 'have the *esprit prussien*; they are "free-thinkers" indifferent in morals and in politics, "anti-Gallican" in fact[2].' A year later there are deeds as well as murmurs; a large emigration of workmen, then a sensible diminution of the transit trade; then an opposition to the French municipal régime[3]. The Emperor determined to apply the tobacco monopoly to the grand-duchy. It was in vain that Beugnot protested, showing by official figures that the smuggling was so great that the tax was not worth the trouble to collect. 'It is not,' replied the Emperor, 'a question of your duchy but of France. I know well that you will gain nothing by it; it is possible that you may lose, and what matter if France obtain a profit[4]?' To enforce this unpopular monopoly, to burn English wares, and to screw every penny out of the country in order to assist the shattered finances of France, a new set of administrators was

---

[1] In 1812 the complaints of unfair incidence are greatly diminished in number. *Feuille de travail*, Nov. 15, 1812; *A. F.* iv. 1226.

[2] *Aperçu général de la situation du Grand-duché*, 1 août 1811; *A. F.* iv. 1226.

[3] *Feuille de travail*, Nov. 15, 1812; *A. F.* iv. 1226.

[4] Ibid.

sent into the country. The populace rose in revolt. The tobacco was detestable; the Germans swore they would never smoke it, burnt the tobacco shops, thrashed the employés, and formed bands to resist this new form of tyranny. On January 22 and 23, 1813, there were seditious meetings of workmen at Ronsdorf and Solingen, with cries of 'Hurrah for Alexander and the Cossacks!' In February formidable riots broke out in the Department of the Sieg, which had to be quelled by soldiery. Plague, military commissions, the burden of retreating and advancing armies, contributed still further to disturb the last four months of the duchy's precarious existence. Crimes of violence sensibly increased[1]. The magistrates and the juries refused to condemn even in the teeth of the plainest evidence[2]. 'There was a coalition,' wrote Beugnot, 'which extended from the heads of the government to the commissioners of police,' against France, the conscription, and the blockade[3]. On November 2 the Cossacks appeared at Lippstadt and Dillenburg, and the Imperial Commissioner was forced to 'give his departure the colour of a momentary absence[4].' And so, on November 8, Beugnot left Düsseldorf, and the Grand-Duchy of Berg had come to an end, leaving in its train much misery and few regrets.

When, on September 24, 1810, Roederer was appointed to the post of Minister and Secretary of State to the Grand-Duchy of Berg, Napoleon told him that his administration should be the training-school of the States of the Confederation of the Rhine[5]. There is certainly much to admire alike in what was achieved as in what was proposed by the governors

---

[1] *Rapport mensuel, juillet* 1813 : '*Plus de* 70 *vols, dans* 17 *avec effraction, ont été commis dans les trois départements du Grand-duché dans le courant du mois de juin*'; *A. F.* iv. 1886 A.

[2] *Rapport sur la situation du Grand-duché*, Nov. 4, 1813, *A. F.* iv. 1226 ; and cf. *Rapport sur la situation administrative du Grand-duché pour le second trimestre de* 1813 (April 1, 1813), complaining of the 'inconceivable indulgence of the Assize Courts.' 'In the last session of the Department of the Ruhr a homicide, an infanticide, and a dangerous thief were acquitted.'

[3] Beugnot to Roederer, Nov. 15, 1813 ; *A. F.* iv. 1865.

[4] Ibid.

[5] Roederer, *Œuvres*, iii. 425.

of this small principality. They achieved the abolition of caste, they introduced a substantial improvement in the lot of the peasantry, and under their rule all the trammels were removed which impeded the free transfer of land and the free entrance into trades and handicrafts. So broken was the power of the Ritterschaft, so active were the sales and acquisitions of property as the result of the French legislation, that in 1815 it was exceptional to find an estate of over 300 acres [1]. Feudal institutions were gone, never to return, despite the interested efforts of a class to revive them. But it was not merely by their laws that the French left a permanent mark upon the duchy. Their administration was a pattern and a precedent. The Prussians, indeed, had done good bureaucratic work in Mark and in Münster before the French occupation, but it was the French who first adequately expounded the arts of finance and administration to the whole region. To the slovenly government of the Bavarians in Berg, the French methods, combining as they did strict control with prompt, orderly, and intelligent action, and distinguished always for their clear definition and distribution of functions, were related as the railway train is related to the stage coach. And combined with greater despatch there was a finer taste and a more alert perception of the thing to be done, so that in the bridges and quays, in the delicious gardens and pleasant avenues of Düsseldorf, the visitor may still enjoy the permanent memorials of French rule [2].

The vice of the government was that it was tyrannical, and afforded no scope for the political education of its subjects. The Estates were never summoned a second time, and the Council of State, which possessed no powers of initiative, and was forbidden to correspond with the prefects, was often not even consulted upon important measures [3]. Since the news-

---

[1] Treitschke, *Deutsche Geschichte*, ii. 274.

[2] Immediately after the Emperor's visit a decree was issued for the embellishment of Düsseldorf, for the construction of quays and bridges, and for the completion of the new port; *A. F.* iv. 1837.

[3] Roederer to Beugnot, Aug. 31, 1811. 'Dans toutes les occasions où il n'y a pas lieu d'appréhender de mauvaises difficultés de la part du conseil d'état ou d'une commission du conseil d'état, il est bon de prendre son avis. Cela donne plus de sécurité à l'Empereur. S. M. m'a plusieurs

PROBLEMS OF GOVERNMENT IN BERG 223

papers were censured and restrained from publishing any political news which had not already appeared in the French official organs, nothing more trivial or contemptible can be conceived than the journalism of the duchy[1]. While the vicious system of administrative law protected the agents of the administration from the normal action of the law courts, commerce and industry were paralysed by a system which sacrificed the interests of the duchy not only to the plan of campaign against England, but to the self-interested jealousy of the mercantile community in France. Great was the havoc of the conscription. Yet if many things were suffered, much also was learnt, and many hindrances to larger knowledge were removed. So swift a destruction of mediaeval detritus, so rapid an initiation into modern ideas, could scarcely have been carried out by a force less powerful than the Empire of Napoleon.

fois demandé, en signant des lois générales, si le conseil d'état approuvait cela ? toutefois sans y insister.' Cf. also Beugnot's Instructions to the President of the Council, *Staatsraths-Akten*, Düsseldorf Archives.

[1] These local newspapers have consequently been seldom preserved. For instance, there are only eleven known extant copies of the *Echo der Berge*, which enjoyed a tolerable circulation (400 regular subscribers) at the time, and these would have perished but that they fell into the hands of a man who was interested in the advertisements of horse sales. The paper is an entirely worthless rag, as I can testify, having seen the surviving numbers in the Düsseldorf Archives.

CHIEF AUTHORITIES: Beugnot, *Mémoires*; Roederer, *Œuvres*, vol. iii; Lumbroso, *Lettres de Murat*; Goecke, *Das Grossherzogthum Berg*; Pick, *Monatsschrift für rheinisch-westfälische Geschichtsforschung*, 1877; *Recueil des Actes du Gouvernement du Grand-duché*, 1808; *Sammlung der Gesetze und Verordnungen, welche in den ehemaligen Herzogthümern Jülich, Cleve und Berg und im vormaligen Grossherzogthum Berg ergangen sind*, ed. Scotti, 1821–2; Bormann und Daniels, *Handbuch der f. die königl. preuss. Rheinprovinzen verkündigten Gesetze, Verordnungen und Regierungsbeschlüsse aus der Zeit der Fremdherrschaft*, vii. 1–349, 1834; A. Winkopp, *Der rheinische Bund*.

To these printed sources must be added the unpublished correspondence of Beugnot, Nesselrode, Bassano, and Roederer; the police reports; the reports of prefects, commissions, judges, &c.; the memoranda and petitions of merchants and public bodies, lying in the *Archives Nationales* in Paris and in the *Staatsarchiv* at Düsseldorf.

CHAPTER XI

THE ESTABLISHMENT OF THE WESTPHALIAN KINGDOM

'Les États ne se fondent que par la politique.'—NAPOLEON.

AMONG the political creations of Napoleon in Germany the most curious and important was the Kingdom of Westphalia, which for six years exhibited to the world the spectacle of a licentious Court and a good constitution, of beneficent reforms sacrificed to an insane policy, of Latin enlightenment transfusing Teutonic darkness, and of Teutonic industry honestly enlisted in the cause of a Latin government. Formed in 1807, after the downfall of Prussia, the kingdom was mainly composed of the confiscated States of the Duke of Brunswick, of the Elector of Hesse-Cassel, and of the Prussian King. To these territories were added the County of Stolberg, a Prussian fief, the County of Rietberg, a fief of Hesse-Cassel, the territories of Göttingen, Grubenhagen, and Osnabrück taken from Hanover, and the Abbey of Corvey taken from the Prince of Orange. On November 15, 1807, the Hessian part of the County of Henneberg and the Principality of Corvey were attached to the kingdom, the area of which was calculated at something over nineteen hundred square leagues. The net revenue on October 1, 1807, was estimated at nineteen million francs, and the population at two million souls, and a glance at the map will reveal how arbitrary was the construction and how unnatural were the boundaries of this modest State.

Yet, although comparatively small, the Kingdom of Westphalia covered some of the most historic ground in Germany. It was in the forests of the Department of the Weser that Arminius met and defeated the Roman legions, and it was mainly within the limits of this kingdom that Charles the Great fought out his long struggle with the Saxon race[1]. The

---

[1] Some attempt was made to exploit these memories in the interests of

abbeys of Hersfeld and Fulda were founded in the first age of the conversion of Germany to Christianity, richly endowed by the monarchs of the Carolingian House, and famous as centres of learning and piety. In the mountains of the Harz, renowned for their mines of silver, the ancient city of Goslar, once the capital of the Saxon Emperors, still shows the Kaiserhaus of Henry III. Although Hildesheim, in the Department of the Ocker, cannot boast such memories as these, the traveller may still admire in this, one of the most beautiful of mediaeval German cities, an ancient fountain of Roland the paladin of Charles the Great, and the house of Leibnitz, perhaps the most accomplished mind in the history of Germany. Not far from Hildesheim is the city of Brunswick, which, owing to the genius and energy of Henry the Lion, became in the twelfth century a centre of civilization in Northern Germany. That great prince who raised five cathedrals, all extant at the present day, has left an abiding impress upon his capital, and the old ducal castle, built, so it is said, in rivalry of the Emperor's house at Goslar, the plan of which it closely follows, recalls the most famous feud of German mediaeval history. A few miles south of their capital, the Dukes of Brunswick could show in the park of the castle of Wolfenbüttel a library which, founded in the middle of the seventeenth century by Duke Ernest Augustus, became one of the richest collections north of the Alps. The catalogue of the library, written in the small neat hand of the founder, serves to remind the visitor of how, amid the dreary horrors of the Thirty Years' War, it was possible for a fine nature to preserve and cultivate a taste for letters. An eminent writer upon chess, a zealous and efficient governor, the prince-librarian left to his descendants a persistent tradition of culture, and though few people would now care to read the tedious scandals of Duke Ulric's *Octavia*, the fact that both Leibnitz and Lessing were librarians at

the new kingdom, cf. *Archiv für die Geschichte, Geographie, Topographie und Statistik des Kön. Westphalen*, J. P. Rosenmeyer, Cassel, 1808, where Westphalia is termed 'the classic soil of German courage and Roman defeats,' or again, the 'red soil of the Holy Vehm.' From these tumid memories the laborious editor descends to chronicle the prosperous fortunes of the chicory business.

Wolfenbüttel is familiar to many who have never heard of the Aquitanian Register or of the smoke-blackened Icelandic codex of Egil's Saga which form part of its treasures.

At the extreme south-east of the kingdom stood the town of Halle, whose university was only second in reputation to that of Göttingen. Here Wolf elaborated his famous theory of the Homeric poems, and here Gellert composed his meek pastoral literature to the delight of eighteenth-century readers. But the largest and most important town in the kingdom was unquestionably Magdeburg, which, standing in a bend of the Elbe, commands the avenue into Prussia. It is recorded that during the negotiations at Tilsit, Queen Louise implored Napoleon to spare her this, the principal fortress of her kingdom; but the Emperor was inexorable, and this ancient city, established by Otto I as the seat of an archbishopric, and a centre whence Christian influence might spread through the Slavonic plains to the east, was now after eight centuries severed from the March of Brandenburg and given to Westphalia.

Among the rolling pine-clad hills, threaded by the delightful waters of the Lahn and the Fulda, dwelt the Hessians, a tough, hard-featured race proudly reckoning its descent from the Chatti, the warlike and formidable opponents of the Roman legions. Ever since the day when Luther and Zwingli held dispute over the Sacrament in the picturesque schloss at Marburg, Hesse had been the great north-western bulwark of the Protestant cause. In all the wars of religion the Hessians had poured their blood freely on behalf of the Gospel. They had fought against Charles V and Ferdinand II, against Philip II and Louis XIV. Even in the eighteenth century, when their rulers were base and venal, the Hessian sword had always been hired out to a Protestant bidder, and in the Highlands of Scotland, in the plains of the Netherlands, and in the American colonies the Hessian infantry battled stoutly in the British cause. In temper, sympathy, and historic tradition no German stock was more alien to France.

An acute observer, commenting upon the governments which had previously held sway in the Kingdom of Westphalia, says that the rule of Brunswick was the mildest, and that of Prussia the sharpest, that of Hesse-Cassel the most oppressive, and that of Hanover the most sleepy. It seems, indeed, almost impossible to exaggerate the misgovernment and backwardness of Hesse, which in geographical extent and importance was the principal factor in the new kingdom. The Hessians, says de Villers, were 'the least instructed of all the Protestant peoples,' and under the last Elector they had been the worst governed. That jealous and miserly despot had drained the wealth, impoverished the spirit, and stunted the intelligence of his subjects. So grotesque were his suspicions that he forbade foreign travel and prohibited applause at the theatre for fear of encouraging the spirit of popular criticism. That he speculated in corn and in soldiers, raising the price of wheat to fill his own coffers, and levying a tax of eight Reichsthalers on the marriage of persons liable to military service, is a proof of his signal avarice. And no better tribute can be paid to the completeness of his authority, than the fact that for two years he succeeded in keeping his people ignorant of the course of the French revolution. Redeeming the wicked profusion of his predecessors by a parsimony no less extravagant, William banished the most trivial as well as the more expensive luxuries from his Court. The effects of this unparalleled meanness were more especially felt in his capital. The castle of Cassel fell into disrepair; the stock-in-trade of the shops was reduced, and the town became poorer and poorer every day. 'There is not even a bit of ribbon to be found here,' said the Queen of Westphalia, 'and when one asks why, the answer is that the ex-Elector could not suffer, and did not suffer, any luxury at the Court[1].'

Aristocratic exclusiveness mingled with a rude and primitive simplicity were the salient features of this province. At Marburg, where the professors received part of their salaries in wheat, barley, and hay, no plebeian was permitted to matriculate without special licence. Delicate travellers from

[1] Villers, *Coup d'œil sur les universités et le mode d'instruction publique de l'Allemagne protestante*, Cassel, 1808; Winkopp, *Der rheinische Bund*, vi. 126 ff., 144 ff.; Fulda und Hoffmeister, *Hessische Zeiten und Persönlichkeiten*, 22–45; Schlossberger, *Briefwechsel der Königin Katharina und des Königs Jerome von Westphalen*, i. 99, 111, 211; Zinserling, *Westphälische Denkwürdigkeiten*, 6, 7; Bignon to Talleyrand, Nov. 30, xii; *Affaires étrangères, Correspondance Politique: Hesse-Cassel*, 18.

France shuddered at the coarse and hideous appearance of the Hessian peasantry, at the long matted hair of the men, at the short petticoats, the curious coifs, and the wrinkled faces of the women, without reflecting that this debased appearance was partially connected with exhausting *corvées* and burdensome dues. In the neighbourhood of the capital alone there were signs of civilized grandeur. The huge and hideous fabric of Wilhelmshöhe, built, like the Pyramids, by the forced labour of a servile population, loomed from its beautiful woods upon the russet city, while beneath the favourite promenade of the Cassel burghers, the skilful hand of Lenôtre had planned the glades and avenues, the fish-ponds and the bowling-green which were demanded by the taste of the cultured Frenchman [1].

On the day of the signature of the Peace of Tilsit, July 7, 1807, Napoleon made his choice of a Westphalian king. 'My brother,' he wrote to Prince Jerome, 'I have just concluded peace with Russia and Prussia. You have been recognized as King of Westphalia. Your kingdom comprises all the States named in the enclosed list. . . . You must procure a secretary who is very well acquainted with German, and you must begin at once to think of some distinguished Alsatians, whom you can propose to me as likely to assist you in your administration. I intend to give you a regular constitution which effaces all vain and ridiculous social distinctions.'

The youngest brother of the Emperor, while endowed with no small social charm and natural facility, was uncultivated, lazy, and voluptuous. From his early youth he had shown a propensity to extravagance which Napoleon had hoped to correct by the stern discipline of the sea. Jerome, however, was not of the stuff of which sailors are made, and was more intent upon cards, dinners, and flirtations, than upon the capture of British cruisers or the acquisition of maritime knowledge. As an ensign he borrowed money from his admiral, as a lieutenant he ignored the orders of his superiors, as a captain he took upon himself to confer promotions. Escaping once from the tedium of ship-life among the Antilles, he found his way to Baltimore, where he conquered the heart

---

[1] *Précis de l'université de Marbourg*, Marburg Archives ; L. de Grainberg, *Lettres sur la Westphalie* (Carlsruhe, 1807).

THE KINGDOM OF WESTPHALIA

and the hand of Miss Pattison, the beautiful daughter of an American merchant. Though Jerome was fully aware that a marriage contracted during minority without the consent of relations was legally invalid in France, he trusted that he would be able to overcome all obstacles. Napoleon, however, had other designs for his favourite brother, and absolutely declined to sanction the match; and with a flagrant lack of chivalry, Jerome consented to barter his wife and unborn child for ambition. Fortified by this act of prudential baseness, the prodigal youth received rapid advancement. In 1807 he was put in command of the contingent of the Confederation of the Rhine, and charged with the double duty of reducing the Prussian garrisons in Silesia and of forwarding supplies to the main army. With Hédouville as chief of his staff, and Vandamme and Montbrun to assist him, the Prince made a successful opening, and though his own conduct was marked by incompetence, luxury, and sloth, eight strong fortresses fell before the German troops under his command. Shortly after the end of the campaign, August 23, 1807, the Prince was married to Catharine of Würtemberg, a fair young woman of twenty-four. She was kindly, steadfast, and simple, well educated after the German manner, a Protestant in religion. It is to her credit that though she stood out for a year against her marriage, and went to it as to a sacrifice, she never wavered in her fidelity to Jerome, finding as she tells us 'the purest and most constant happiness' in her union with him. She has left memoirs which betray a sweet and submissive disposition, a childish mind, and a total absence of any sense of public responsibility.

An influential deputation from the various provinces of the new kingdom was summoned to Paris to give advice upon the situation, and to do homage to their sovereign. On the morning of August 16, 1807, the emissaries were presented to the Emperor in the Tuileries. 'Religion,' said Napoleon, curvetting before the dazzled Germans on the high far-striding steed of principle, 'is an affair of conscience, not of the State. Small States are no good. You will have a great kingdom reaching perhaps to Hamburg. The soldiers are to protect, not to quell you. The nobility is not to count. He who distinguishes himself and shows merit is to be promoted. Kings are not for themselves, but for the happiness of their people.' His eye then rested upon the ecclesiastical accoutrements of Abbot Henke, professor of evangelical theology in the University of Helmstadt. 'What, are you a Protestant?' Then seizing the golden cross which hung upon the abbot's breast, 'What does that bring you in?' he asked. 'Two hundred thalers,' said the abbot. 'It is well worth while. Keep your religion. In every religion one can be a good man.' A deputy breathed a hope that the war contribution might be remitted. The Emperor stabbed him with a look and passed on. Then another ventured an assurance of loyalty. 'We will do our best,' he said, 'to serve your Majesty.' 'That's right,' said Napoleon quickly. 'The Germans are instructed, learned, patient men. There are no traitors among them. If they give their word, that is enough. In a few days you shall have your constitution. You shall make your remarks on it.'

On the next day the deputies dined with the King, and on August 22 they chose a committee to comment upon the draft constitution which had been submitted to them. Five days later their criticisms and their wishes were submitted to Jerome. They petitioned for the exclusive use of the German language in all the acts of the government. They desired an assurance that all places should be filled as far as possible by natives. They commended the employés and pensioners of the old government to the consideration of the new King. Remarking upon the 'sensible loss' which would result to the kingdom from the intended annexation of half the domains from the Emperor, they petitioned to be released from the arrears of the war contributions which had been levied on them during the last year. As the city of Magdeburg had suffered greatly in the war, it was their prayer that it might be occupied by as small a garrison as possible. Then turning to the internal reforms specified in the constitution, and first of all to the proposed abolition of serfage, they drew the attention of the King to the distinction between true personal serfage and territorial charges, arguing that there was no 'odious serfage' in Westphalia, and that if services due to Westphalian lords were to be abolished, a full and entire compensation should be paid to the expropriated owners. Finally, they petitioned that all existing entails and family settlements should be preserved, that a uniform system of taxation should not be introduced until a careful estimate of land values had been made, that the Civil Code should not be put into force for three years, and that the language of the law courts should be German.

These observations were too far-reaching to please either the Emperor or the King. If the population of Paris stared on 'the German pedants' as 'beasts from a menagerie,' King Jerome treated them as little better than schoolboys. With a few vague and breezy assurances they were sent back to their homes. 'All that is good,' said the King, giving a final audience at St. Cloud on August 30, 'shall remain. I will alter nothing. I am not changeable. My subjects are Westphalians, not Frenchmen. In a few years I shall speak and write German. I will appoint only natives [1].'

The expected constitution was promulgated on November 15, 1807, and may be considered either in the light of a treaty or in that of a decree [2]. It stipulated the conditions under which the Emperor was willing to renounce his 'right of conquest,' and to present to Westphalia a certain degree of independence. As a member of the Confederation of the Rhine, the new kingdom was bound to furnish a contingent of 25,000 men to the French Empire. Of this number exactly half was for the present to be furnished by France, though it was to be paid, clothed, and kept by the King of Westphalia. Provisionally the French contingent was to garrison Magdeburg, which was to be at once a royal town and an imperial fortress. By the second article the Emperor reserved one-half of the allodial domains of the expropriated princes to be employed as a recompense to the French officers who had rendered most service during the late war. The Kingdom of Westphalia was declared to be hereditary in the direct lawful line of King Jerome, and it was to devolve to the Emperor or his heirs and descendants, natural and legitimate or adoptive, in case the natural and

---

[1] *Neue Fakkeln*, xii. 179 ff. ; *Verhandlungen der Deputirten des Königreichs Westphalen zu Paris*, Kiel, 1852 ; *Zeitschrift des Historischen Vereins für Niedersachsen*, 1886, 148 ff.

[2] *Corr.* xvi. 167, no. 13,362.

legitimate descent from Jerome should fail. The King of Westphalia was to remain a French prince, and together with his family to be subject to the dispositions of the pact of the Imperial Family, and in the case of a minority the Regent of the kingdom was to be selected from among the princes of the Royal Family by the head of the French Empire. The Civil List was fixed at 5,000,000 francs. The Code Napoléon was to form the civil law of the Kingdom of Westphalia from January 1, 1808. Procedure was to be public, and trial by jury to be introduced in criminal cases from July 1, 1808, while conscription was declared to be a fundamental law of the kingdom. The French monetary system and the French system of weights and measures were also introduced. All previously existing estates and corporations were abolished. Serfage and individual privilege were suppressed, and the nobility were no longer to be allowed to claim the exclusive right to any employment, function, or dignity, or exemption from any public charge. It was decreed that the system of taxation should be uniform throughout the kingdom, and that the land-tax should not exceed one-fifth of the revenue.

These provisions secured the predominance of the French Emperor, and the prevalence of the most valuable principles of French civilization. The King was to be aided by four ministers. There was to be a Minister of State, a Minister of Interior and Justice, a War Minister, and a Minister for Finance, Commerce, and the Treasury. The ministers were to be assisted by the Council of State and the Estates of the kingdom. The members of the Council were named by the King, and the appointment of a councillor was revocable at will. This body drafted laws, assisted the administration with advice, and acted also as a Court of Cassation, and as a High Court for administrative cases. The many doubtful points both of private and of constitutional law which arose during the first few years of the kingdom were discussed and decided in the Council of State, which performed the same kind of office towards the Westphalian Constitution which the English Privy Council has performed towards the Canada Act, and the Federal Court towards the American Constitution. The Estates of the realm were to be composed of a hundred members named by the depart-

THE KINGDOM OF WESTPHALIA

mental colleges. Of these members seventy were to be chosen among proprietors, fifteen among merchants and manufacturers, and fifteen among savants and other persons who had deserved well of the State. One-third of the assembly was to retire by rotation every year, but was subject to re-election. The Estates were denied the right of initiative or open discussion. They were only permitted to discuss bills drafted by the Council of State, and submitted to them by order of the King, upon finance, upon alterations in the monetary system, or upon the civil and military code. Further, no bill was submitted immediately to the whole assembly. The Council of State was divided into three sections, and the Estates into three corresponding commissions. Every bill was discussed at a joint meeting of a section and a commission, and then two orators, one representing each body, reported the discussion to the legislature. The legislature listened in silence, and voted by secret ballot.

The Estates may have been fairly representative of the kingdom, but the constitutional purist would not be satisfied by the method of their election. In every department there was an electoral college, the members of which were chosen for life by the King from the wealthiest landowners, merchants, and manufacturers, or from the most distinguished artists and savants of the district. This college named the members of the Estates, and also presented candidates for the departmental, district, and municipal councils, and for the places of justices of the peace.

The territory of the kingdom was divided into departments, the departments into districts, the districts into cantons, the cantons into municipalities. The department was administered by a prefect, the district by a sub-prefect, the municipality by a mayor. In each canton there was to be a justice of the peace elected for four years, in each district a civil court of first instance, in each department a criminal court, and for the whole kingdom a court of appeal. The judges were named by the King, and if during the first five years of office their conduct was satisfactory, their patents were made out for life. The justices of the peace were indeed removable, but since they were nominated by the electoral college, there was some guarantee that they would not be dismissed with caprice.

If the constitution was far from perfect, for the Hessians

who formed the majority of the population it meant the exchange of darkness for light. The old aristocratic Landstände of Hesse, of Brunswick, of Prussia, and of the bishoprics were not to be compared even to this dumb legislature, which reposed upon a basis of equality not privilege, which enlisted the energies of the middle class, and was capable with enlightened direction of becoming a powerful instrument of progress.

Napoleon was fully alive to the value of the principle of social equality. 'Take care,' he wrote to Jerome, 'that the majority of your council be composed of non-nobles, but so that no one may perceive this, mind that you maintain the third estate in a majority in all the posts. I except some places at Court, to which you must summon the greatest names. But in your ministries, your councils, if possible in your law courts and court of appeal, and in your administration, let the greater part of the persons employed be non-nobles. This will go to the heart of Germany, and perhaps annoy the other class. Do not mind that. The declared principle is to choose talents wherever they can be found [1].'

A Council of Regency nominated by Napoleon was sent to Cassel to take over the civil administration from General Lagrange, and to prepare the way for the new monarch. Beugnot, Siméon, and Jollivet were admirably qualified for the task of organizing the new kingdom. Of Siméon, indeed, it seems difficult to speak too highly. He was an urbane and dignified old jurist, of great tact and discernment, and thoroughly penetrated with the best French administrative spirit. As a Councillor of State he had helped in the formation of the Civil Code, and was highly qualified to superintend its introduction into Westphalia, and his circulars to the prefects, printed in the Westphalian *Moniteur*, form a kind of lucid manual upon the principles of French administration. But for a total ignorance of German, and a courteous pliancy of character which prevented him from asserting his convictions in the face of opposition, he would have been an almost ideal public servant. As it was, Reinhard, the intelligent French minister at Cassel, regretted that he was not placed at the head of *all* the branches of administration. Jollivet, who under the Consulate had liquidated

[1] *Corr.* xvi. 174, no. 13,363.

THE KINGDOM OF WESTPHALIA

the debt of the four Rhenish departments, brought to his task an observant if somewhat malicious mind, and a ripe experience of finance, while to Beugnot there was but one serious objection, that he suffered from the *maladie du pays* which was so common to Frenchmen and so fatal to the expansion of France. While General Lagrange remained at the War Office, Napoleon succeeded in seducing Johann von Müller, the famous historian of Switzerland, to assume the portfolio of Secretary of State. Loud were the laments of Perthes the publisher, and of the friends of German liberty, at the unexpected apostasy of a revered leader. A conversation with the Emperor at Berlin, in 1806, had converted the ardent Gallophobe into the admirer of the Corsican's genius, and the rest was contrived at Paris. It was a fine advertisement for the new kingdom to have enlisted the services of the 'Tacitus of Germany.'

It was a misfortune that the Emperor who had chosen the Council of Regency did not also choose the Court. Jerome was not the kind of young man to consort with the wise and the good; nor would the attractions of Cassel have been sufficient to entice the distinguished. A few personal friends of his early youth, Meyronnet, Duchambon, Lecamus, Rewbell, La Flèche, Salha; some officers from the Silesian campaign, such as Morio, d'Albignac, and the Prince of Hesse-Philippstadt; a dull poet, Bruguière, an *émigré* who had sold tooth-picks at Hamburg, a few nonentities, and, most important of all, the Count of Truchsess-Waldburg, Minister of the Court of Würtemberg at Paris, who came to escape from his debts,— such was the composition of the new Versailles. More than one quite obscure person declined to accept Jerome's advances.

The royal entry into Cassel, made on December 7, 1807, was attended with a show of popular enthusiasm. The castle of Wilhelmshöhe was rechristened Napoleonshöhe, and as the furniture was not to the French taste, a large order was sent to the upholsterers of Paris. On the day of his arrival the King pronounced the Regency at an end, appointed its members to be provisional ministers, and required them to swear an oath to 'exercise faithfully and loyally the functions conferred upon them by His Majesty of Westphalia.' In an allocution to the Council of State, Jerome declared that he could not permit the ex-members of the Regency to exercise in Westphalia an authority independent of his own. He was determined to let the world know that he was autocrat and master in his own home. Eight days afterwards there followed a ministerial revolution. The capable Lagrange was summarily dismissed, and the portfolio of War passed into the hands of a young aide-de-camp, Colonel Morio. Von Müller was invited to relinquish the State secretariat and given the more congenial post of Minister of Education. To the vacant office was attached the Ministry of Foreign Affairs, a post which Napoleon had expressly declined to create that he might keep the diplomatic relations of the kingdom under his own control, and this fifth portfolio was given to an ignorant but honest young Creole, who had accompanied Jerome in his American voyages, and was now an indispensable element in his life. It was fortunate that Westphalia had no foreign policy, seeing that it would have fallen to Lecamus, Count of Fürstenstein, to direct it. Jollivet, writing soon afterwards to the French Court, refers to one of the functions discharged by this highly endowed personage. 'A *comédienne* of Breslau, whom the King had known during his Silesian campaign, seems to have been drawn to Cassel by the agency of M. Lecamus and the order of his master [1].' As if this were not enough, Jerome petitioned for the army contractor Hainguerlot as Minister of Finance, in place of Jollivet whom he disliked, and whose retirement he foresaw.

This cool proposal put the coping-stone to Napoleon's ire. On January 4 he wrote three boiling letters to the youth. 'I have received your letter relative to the speech which you have pronounced at your Council of State. I have found this speech ridiculous. No Frenchman will swear the oath which you demand, save the Frenchmen to whom I shall accord the permission to pass into your service. Neither my Councillors of State nor my officers can swear this oath to you. If Beugnot and Siméon wish to remain with you, they can do as they wish. If they have sworn the oath which you have exacted, I will strike them from the list of my Councillors of State. . . . As to Hainguerlot, I can only be astonished at your levity. He is a man prosecuted for fraud, on criminal charges such that he

---

[1] *Revue Historique*, xv. 391; *Mémoires du roi Jérôme*, iv. 240.

is the horror of France. Ask Siméon, Beugnot, Jollivet, what they think of him. . . . I have your letter of December 15, relative to General Lagrange. I disapprove your conduct. General Lagrange is not your subject; he is not responsible to you for what he has done in his administration; you have not then the right to dishonour him. . . . What pleasure can you take in dishonouring the military uniform? . . . You must clearly grasp the fact that you have no jurisdiction over the Frenchmen whom I send you, and that you ought only to inform me of what they do. I reserve my right of adopting a course suitable to my interests and my experience. If this conduct does not suit you, send me back the Frenchmen you have, and go on with Germans. I have your letter of December 28, where I see that you intend to give the property of Fürstenstein, worth 40,000 a year, to Sieur Lecamus. I know nothing more insensate than this step, equally contrary to your interests, fatal to the State and especially to yourself. What has Sieur Lecamus done? He has rendered no service to the country, only to your person. . . . If you have done this you must go back upon it, or Sieur Lecamus must renounce his character of French citizen, in which case he loses all rights of inheritance in France. . . . What sort of finance can you expect to have with the conduct you keep? You have devoured 3,000,000 in two months at Paris; you will devour 30,000,000 without rhyme or reason in less time than that. You must not think the Kingdom of Westphalia is an estate [1].'

In these short and stinging phrases the Emperor indicated the subordinate position of the Westphalian kingdom.

The supply of ability at the disposal of the King, though not overwhelming, was adequate to the needs of the State. On the departure of Beugnot in March 1808, the portfolio of Finance was given to a young and vigorous German. Baron von Bülow, a cousin of the famous Prussian minister von Hardenberg, had distinguished himself by saving the funds of the treasury of Magdeburg from the clutches of the French during the Jena campaign. Having served Prussia with fidelity, he now transferred his loyalty to the Westphalian government. But though his ability as a financier was unquestioned, and

---

[1] *Corr.* xvi. 229–32, nos. 13,433, 4, 5.

though his integrity was applauded by Reinhard, he lived in a thick cloud of suspicion. Opening his doors once a week to all who had a request to prefer, he seemed to the French to be aiming at more popularity than was either convenient or safe. It was certainly his object to further German interests and to dispense with the services of French subordinates; it may be that he was kept acquainted with the secret movements of German nationalism. At any rate, the French plotted his overthrow. One said that he was a Prussian traitor, another that he belonged to the Tugendbund, a third that he had robbed the departmental chests to please the King. On October 3, 1809, Madame von Bülow found a police spy sitting at her husband's desks and examining his papers. It was a premature act on the part of the police, and it caused a great scandal. The King was reported to have said that his Minister of Finance was an imperturbable liar, and the Minister of the Interior held that the King had set the police upon his colleague. Supported, however, by the upright Siméon, and partly also by his own merits—for he was really indispensable and paid the King's Civil List punctually—von Bülow managed to tide over the incident. But during a political visit to Paris his influence was undermined, and, accused of intrigues with Prussia and of plotting the financial ruin of the kingdom, he was arrested, deposed, and pensioned off (April 9, 1811). In him the kingdom lost an honest and able servant, who detested Napoleon. The vice of Bülow was not treachery but complaisance. General Eblé said that he and Bülow had once agreed to make a joint remonstrance to the King upon the subject of Court extravagance, but that Bülow drew back at the decisive moment [1].

Far worse things are insinuated against his successor, Karl August Malchus. He is said to have carved his way to fortune by treachery, and to have stopped at nothing so long as he could retain the royal favour. His arrogant speeches disgusted the Estates, and he was probably the most unpopular man in

---

[1] Bülow undoubtedly tried to evade the strict execution of Napoleon's decrees against smuggling. He ordered an *auto da fé* of worthless wares to save the pockets of the Osnabrück merchants. Fulda and Hoffmeister, *Hessische Zeiten und Persönlichkeiten*, 163.

THE KINGDOM OF WESTPHALIA

the kingdom. But to contrive resources for Jerome was a rôle which would fritter away the most amiable of reputations, and there is every reason to believe that Malchus brought a certain dogged ability to the task. He was the Thomas Cromwell of Westphalia, a pliant servant, harsh, brutal, egoistic, but an authority on finance, and more influenced by French administrative ideas than von Bülow. Honours rained down upon his hard head. He was made a Baron, a Commander of the Order of the Westphalian Crown, and afterwards Count of Marienrode. Finally he became Minister of the Interior,— '*homme sans conceptions et sans entrailles*,' says Reinhard, who tells us how the tithes of the district of Hildesheim were corruptly sold for the benefit of the minister's relations [1].

The department of the Interior was more fortunate. Among the ministers of Charles Ferdinand, Duke of Brunswick, few were more loyal and devoted than the Baron de Wolffradt. When the Duke, blinded in both eyes and shattered by bullets, was about to be carried out of his country, Wolffradt with tears in his eyes entreated that he might be permitted to share his exile. The Duke took his hand, held it for some minutes in silence, and then implored him to stand by the duchy whatever might happen. Having promised that he would never desert the subjects of his old master, Wolffradt became their patron and protector at the Westphalian Home Office. A great respecter of ancient German forms, caring little for French methods and knowing little of the French language, Wolffradt stood as barrier against ill-considered change. A rough man, but honest and intelligent, appreciating and employing ability, whether French or German, he thoroughly earned the confidence of his colleagues and of the public.

While these two important offices went to Germans, the portfolio of War was always given to a Frenchman. Morio, the successor of Lagrange, who had better military capacities than

---

[1] After the crash Malchus became the scapegoat of the old order. For some vigorous abuse, cf. Fulda and Hoffmeister, 136-8; *Neue Fakkeln*, iii. 94; *Le royaume de Westphalie* (Paris, 1820), 156-7; *Der Volkwitz der Deutschen über den gestürzten Bonaparte*, i. 23 ff. The charge of corrupt sales of the public domain is probably false. Cf. *Notes concernant le Comte Malchus de Marienrode*, Pancoucke.

Napoleon's description of him, '*une espèce de fou*,' would imply, was one day (August 1808) ill-advised enough to style himself captain of the guard, and to drill the household troops on his own authority. For this ebullition the favourite was deprived of his office, which was given to the excellent General Eblé, the best type of French soldier, at once brave and able, honest and public-spirited. But the Westphalian service was regarded with dislike by distinguished Frenchmen, and in 1811 Eblé petitioned for leave to return to France. His successors at the War Office were General d'Albignac and Salha, the companion of Jerome's early odyssey, a sailor turned landsman and ennobled under the title of Count von Hone.

There were, too, several able and industrious men in the Council of State, such as Leist, Professor of Law at the University of Göttingen, who had a principal share in the official translation of the Civil Code; Martens, the famous international lawyer; von Dohm, a well-known Prussian statesman and publicist, and a voluminous author, who deserves to go down to posterity if only for his noble treatise on the improvement of the civil status of the Jews; and the caustic and witty Hanoverian Baron von Berlepsch, whose *Beiträge* are a sufficient evidence of his interest in the economic condition of his country. In the King's private library at Wilhelmshöhe a studious young man was deeply immersed in the ancient monuments of German and Scandinavian literature. This was the great Jacob Grimm, royal librarian and auditor of the Council of State, who was destined to lay the foundations of Teutonic philology, and to reveal in all its poetry, pathos, and humour, the folklore, the custom, and the myth of Teutonic antiquity.

Nor were the elections to the Estates otherwise than reassuring. 'Nobles,' says Häusser, 'were chiefly chosen to represent the landed proprietors. In the Elbe department we find the names of Alvensleben, Blumenthal, Schulenberg; in the Fulda department, Berlepsch, Mengersen, Pirbeck, Münchhausen, Schlieffen; in the Ocker department a Count Brabeck, two Herren von Münchhausen, a Baron Pless, and a Sievedorf; from the Saale, amongst others, the hereditary Counts of Stolberg-Wernigerode; from the Werra department two Freiherren von Baumbach and a Dörnberg; from the Weser the names of Borries, Hamerstein, Münster.' It is indeed hardly an exaggeration to say that all the talents of the country rallied round the new monarchy [1].

'Be a constitutional king,' wrote Napoleon to his brother. 'The benefits of the Code Napoléon, the publicity of procedure, the establishment of juries, will be so many distinctive characteristics of your monarchy. And if I may tell you all my thought, I count more upon them for the extension and consolidation of your kingdom than on the result of the greatest victories. It is necessary that your people should enjoy a liberty, an equality, and a degree of well-being unknown to the people of Germany. This method of government will be a more powerful barrier to separate you from Prussia than the Elbe or fortresses or French protection. What people would wish to revert to Prussian despotism, when it has once tasted the benefits of a wise and liberal government [2]?' Inspired by these monitions, Jerome baptized his reign with a shower of edicts and honourable professions. The unfamiliar experiment of a constitutional government excited the interest and riveted the attention of Westphalia, and when the Reichstag was solemnly opened in the Orangerie at Cassel (July 2, 1808) its future was regarded with curiosity and hope. Yet the initial ceremonial was overstrained and grotesque. Warned by a salvo of twenty-one cannon, the president and eight deputies went out to meet the royal cavalcade. Clothed in white silk, with a mantle of purple flowing from his shoulders and a plumed toque glistening with diamonds on his head, Jerome was escorted to a pavilion where it was ordained that he should repose after the fatigues of a drive. Then, as the gaudy procession passed into the hall, the ushers with staves and daggers, the pages in uniforms of gold, the assembly rose up with cries of '*Vive le Roi*!' and when the incoming group had posed itself picturesquely on the dais, the deputies were severally presented to the monarch in the murderous Provençal accent of Siméon. After

---

[1] Häusser, iii. 241–2; Thimme, ii. 90. Even the proudest men petitioned to serve as prefects; cf. Hardenberg to the Minister of Finance, Jan. 3, 1808, in the Marburg Archives. There were, however, a few notable exceptions. Bülau, *Geheime Geschichte*, v. 480.

[2] *Corr.* xvi. 166, no. 13,361.

the oath of allegiance had been taken both in German and in French, Jerome addressed his first parliament. 'Brave and good Westphalians,' he concluded, 'on this solemn occasion when you exercise for the first time your constitutional rights, you will prove your attachment to my person in seconding my views for the welfare of my kingdom, that welfare which we should all cherish. We will work in concert, I as King and father, you as faithful and affectionate subjects.' 'A light ironical smile,' says an eyewitness, 'played on the lips of the deputies,' as the father of the Westphalian people, aged twenty-three, descended from the throne. At four in the afternoon the members of the Reichstag were invited into the great hall of the palace to 'assist at' the dinner of their Majesties. Baron de Wendt, Bishop *in partibus* and Prior of Hildesheim, the star of the Prussian Eagle on his breast, preceded the royal pair to the table, chanting a Latin grace from a sumptuous prayer-book, and as the King reached his hand to drink, the act was saluted by a salvo of cannon. The starving legislators, who had misapprehended the nature of the occasion, were mortified to discover the vicarious character of the feast, nor was their chagrin entirely expunged by the costly illuminations of the night[1].

There is every reason to believe that parliamentary government would have succeeded in Westphalia if it had been given a fair trial. Though the letter of the constitution was clearly designed to check free and open discussion, Westphalian practice was better than French theory. When a bill had been drafted by the Council of State—and we are told that the deliberations of this body were earnest, thorough, and animated—it was handed over to one of the standing committees of the parliament. But the members of this committee, so far from keeping the measure to themselves, invited the criticisms of their fellow deputies. Every evening an informal gathering was held at the president's house, which was attended by most of the members of the Chamber, and to this meeting the printed draft of the Council was submitted. Illumined by the instructive and unpretentious criticisms of their abler colleagues, the committee then went into conference with the section of the

[1] Strombeck, *Darstellungen aus meinem Leben*, ii. 14–26.

THE KINGDOM OF WESTPHALIA

Council of State which was in charge of the bill, and 'the keenest desire was shown on both sides to bring the law to the highest pitch of perfection.' The amendments were then printed and circulated among the members, so that every member came prepared to the decisive session, at which the orators of the Council and of the Estates developed the motives of the law. 'Their orations,' says a Westphalian legislator, 'were often masterpieces of logical arrangement and statesmanlike sagacity. One has only to recall the names of Wolffradt, Leist, Johann von Müller, names which it would be difficult to match in more recent times. What would have been the use of further discussion? Every one had had full opportunity of communicating his views by letter to the committee, and the affair had been frequently debated at the gatherings at the president's house[1].'

Nevertheless the session was marked by one storm, which revealed the weak spot in the constitution. A bill for a land-tax was presented to the Estates, and thrown out by sixty-one votes to twenty-four. A patriotic deputy from the Weser department, Hofbauer, who was chosen as the 'reporter' of the Estates, moved the rejection in a vehement speech. Among Court circles he was stigmatized as a traitor. Was the King to go without his revenue? There was nothing for it, then, but that the Estates should be dissolved, and the land-tax passed as a decree. But the wise Siméon was not so autocratic. 'These gentlemen,' he said, 'would like some more amendments; would they kindly tell us what? If their amendments are acceptable, we will alter the bill and bring it in again.' It was ascertained that objection was chiefly taken to the forty-ninth article, which dealt with the taxation of houses, and that the bill had been rejected *en bloc*, because the chamber was not entitled to improve it in detail. Divested of its objectionable features the bill was submitted anew, and passed on August 18 by eighty-three votes to seven. Four days later, after a session which had lasted fifty-one days, the first Westphalian parliament was dissolved. On the whole, it had shown more zeal than might have been expected, and more independence than was relished by the Court. But its temper was neither revolutionary nor

---

[1] Strombeck, *Darstellungen aus meinem Leben*, ii. 45–7.

obstructive, and it might have been safely trusted to co-operate with the government in its formidable task [1].

The populace of the Kingdom of Westphalia was variously affected towards the new government. Not many weeks had elapsed since the King's arrival in Cassel, when Jollivet gave a lugubrious report of the state of opinion in the capital.

'All the world is sad. The King does not receive many marks of respect. He rides often in the streets, but is rarely saluted. He has lost in public opinion. Some affairs of gallantry have already hurt him. It is generally known that one of the Queen's ladies has been dismissed because of him. The first Chamberlain (Lecamus) has nevertheless found means of retaining this woman in Paris, to crown his deserts. . . . The mothers of Cassel who have pretty daughters fear to let them go to Court balls and festivals. The Queen is liked [2].' The quiet little German town was alternately interested, excited, and shocked by the whirl of gaiety and dissipation in which it had become suddenly involved. The gross immorality of the Court, the utter lack of dignity and self-respect in the King, the arrogance of the French courtiers and minor officials, the interference of the new police, were all calculated to engender irritation. Reinhard, the French minister, writing home on June 15, 1809, says, with a good deal of penetration, 'In this sudden creation there are no interests or habits which have not received a shock, no employé who has not lost either a part of his salary or emoluments, no individual who has not made painful efforts either to learn or to unlearn. This state of things, independently of clandestine manœuvres of an inflammatory tendency the existence of which is unquestioned, necessarily produces an irritation which will calm down or increase according to events. It requires upon the part of the government a firm and consequent bearing, tempered by much wisdom [3].' The same observer notes that the attachment to the new order of things made most progress in the provinces which

---

[1] The reluctance of the Stände to abolish guilds and corporations was overcome by the statement that the abolition had already been decreed in the constitution. Thimme, ii. 435.

[2] *Revue Historique*, xv. 390.

[3] *Mémoires du roi Jérôme*, iii. 206.

had already changed rulers, or in those which, like the Duchy of Brunswick, had enjoyed the benefits of a liberal administration, and had become familiarized with political change. In Hesse, on the other hand, or in the old Prussian provinces, the spirit of discontent was deeply seated, because the population was ignorant and passionately attached to its ancient ways. Indeed, it is one of the most curious facts in Westphalian history that the Hessian peasantry, which had most to gain from the principles of French government, should have resented the rule of Jerome most keenly; but the cottage almost always is sentimental, and in these rude men of the cottage the sentiment of loyalty to an ancient though hard dynasty outweighed the abolition of labour services and feudal dues.

Nevertheless the new administration rapidly made friends. Even German patriots, like Ch. Rommel, acknowledged the excellence of the reforms which were introduced so speedily and comprehensively by their French rulers. The inclusion of a number of honoured names in the Ministry and the Council of State diffused confidence, while the creation of departmental and electoral councils put into welcome activity many slumbering energies. Many of the nobles must have keenly resented the abolition of feudal dues and *corvées*, by which they lost considerably, but, on the other hand, there were substantial compensations for these losses—places at Court, prefectships, commissions in the army, decorations and pensions, membership of the Legislative Assembly [1]. Some narrow Catholics, Lutherans, and Calvinists disliked the favour which was accorded to the Jews; no doubt many Westphalian Catholics disliked the strict application of the *Règlements organiques*. The capitation-tax was an obnoxious novelty, the presence of French troops a reminder of subjection, the levity of the Court a matter of heart-searching to the serious. Still, the people were steadily rallying to the monarchy, some filling the bureaux, some the law courts, others the army. To the peasant mind could anything be more exciting to ambition than the uniform of the mayor—white trousers, a dark-blue coat with silver

---

[1] The employés of the Westphalian government were paid on a scale higher than that which prevailed in France. *Histoire de l'esprit public à l'égard de la France* ; *Affaires étrangères, Corr. Pol.: Westphalie*, 1.

buttons, a light-blue scarf with a white fringe, a French cocked hat, and a sword dangling at his side? Or if that splendour was too transcendent, was there not the milder dignity of a seat on the municipal council, the '*unnütze Prahlrath*,' as the joke went? There was some life in the quiet country-side now, what with the movement of troops, and the gatherings of district and departmental councils, and the new justices of the peace, and the new prefects and sub-prefects, and the royal progresses with fireworks and triumphal arches and ornamental speeches; and every now and again a villager returning from Cassel with strange tales of masked balls and brilliant doings, of the castle lit up by night with fairy lanterns, and of the fine uniforms of the French gentlemen as they swaggered down the old streets and ogled the girls. By 1809 the monarchy had, most luckily for itself, enlisted upon its side the greater mass of Westphalian opinion.

Two years before, there was a well-grounded fear that French ascendency would mean the proscription of all things German, beginning with the language. Of the four members of the Council of Regency who governed the country in 1807, not one knew a word of German, nor was the acquisition of the German language regarded by them as necessary or practicable. On the contrary, Beugnot calmly asserted that it was the duty of the Germans to learn French. 'Our literatures,' he said, writing to a German professor, 'would approach each other with equal success, if there did not exist between them a barrier difficult to cross—our ignorance of your tongue, the extreme difficulty of learning it, and the almost complete impossibility of speaking it. I have there touched the true point of the difficulty, your language, which isolates you from Europe, and retards you. But you will be forced to speak the French language, and I regard this obligation as a great means of advancement for science and letters in Germany[1].'

In August 1807, as we have seen, a Westphalian deputation requested that German should be the official language of the Kingdom of Westphalia, and that all places should be given to natives. But, though Jerome promised to learn German himself, no pledge was given that the language was to be official,

[1] Bülau, *Geheime Geschichte*, v. 489.

and the matter was left in convenient obscurity. Reinhard confesses that he could never find out what the official language was. Since the King never arrived at any comprehension of the German tongue, reports and memoranda addressed to him were written in French, and the same rule applied to communications which passed between ministers, and to the debates in the Council of State over which the King frequently presided. 'We Germans,' writes Wolffradt, 'had much against us, being for the most part unaccustomed to address so important an assembly in a foreign and unfamiliar tongue, in the presence of French ministers who not only had a command of the language and the subject, but who by their talent and eloquence had shone in the French legislative assemblies and shone here also. But the King listened to us gladly, asked us when he did not quite understand to make our meaning clearer, and very often we won a victory [1].' The decrees published in the official bulletin were in French, but accompanied by a German translation. If the prefects corresponded upon cults, hospitals, charitable institutions, sanitation, public instruction, statistics and arts, they were required to write in French. On the other hand, the communications which passed between the ministers and the Estates, and much of the official correspondence of the departments, were in German.

In the army the same dualism was apparent, for the word of command was given in French in the guard and the *corps d'élite*, and in German for the troops of the line. On the whole, the language difficulty was not so great a grievance as might have been expected, and it tended steadily to diminish with lapse of time. German was the language of the law courts and the legislature, and the German text of the Civil Code was the official Code of the kingdom. As the Minister of the Interior, the Minister of Finance, and the Minister of Education were all Germans, the greater portion of the administration was carried on in that language. The *Moniteur Westphalien* was bilingual, and both languages were to be taught in the *lycée* and burgher schools at Cassel. On the other hand, the Court spoke French, the choice of administrators and public servants was restricted, at any rate in the higher branches, to those who

[2] *Denkwürdigkeiten eines ehemaligen braunschw. Ministers, Deutsche Rundschau*, xlvi. 65.

wrote and spoke both languages, and in four departments, Justice, War, Police, Foreign Affairs, the business was largely if not entirely conducted in the language known to the heads of the departments.

The fear that all the high places would be given to Frenchmen proved to be illusory. The Frenchman does not willingly emigrate, even to Germany. For the first few months, a miscellaneous crowd of French adventurers gathered together in Cassel in the hope of making a fortune out of the new kingdom. But they were bitterly disappointed. Westphalia was not an El Dorado, nor was Cassel a city of delights. 'Things,' wrote Jollivet, 'are not going as was expected. The French who had repaired to Westphalia are retiring in numbers and entirely discontented. They are bored in the town, they are displeased with the Court, where, say they, there is neither money nor pleasure[1].' Even the men who had high posts, like Beugnot or Eblé, longed to be rid of them and to quit this provincial arena for a more brilliant stage. Nor was there any desire among promising and talented young Frenchmen to enter the Westphalian service. It was, as we have seen, with a certain difficulty that Jerome recruited his Court, and when once he had departed with his suite of fifty mediocrities the flow from Paris to Cassel ceased. When a capital devours a country, as Paris had devoured France, young men of distinction do not value proconsulates. So, in default of Frenchmen, the administration of Westphalia came to be managed almost entirely by Germans. The Prussian, Baron von Bülow, is Minister of Finance; the Brunswicker, Baron von Wolffradt, is at the Ministry of the Interior; the Prussian, Count von Schulenberg, is President of the War section of the Council of State; von Müller and Leist hold successively the portfolio of Education. All the prefects, judges, and local officials are German. Even the Court becomes increasingly German, and a Würtemberger, the Count of Truchsess-Waldburg, receives the high office of Grand Chamberlain. In the army the French influence was more predominant. The Minister of War, the three divisional generals, and about one-fourth of the officers were either French or Poles. On the other hand, the brigadiers were all Germans,

[1] *Revue Historique*, xxi. 391.

and some two-thirds of the officers were recruited from the nobility of Hesse and Brunswick. The rank and file, with the exception of 1,100 Dutchmen, were entirely recruited from the kingdom itself. Considering that the Westphalian army was a new creation, that its fidelity was at first a matter of speculation, that under treaty obligations it would be bound to co-operate in any future war with French troops, and that France was admittedly the first school of war in Europe, the French element in the Westphalian army was perhaps not excessive.

Hardly had the kingdom settled down when it was disturbed by a series of unexpected incursions and abortive risings. This is not the place to describe the great events of 1809: the Austrian declaration of war, the severe check administered to the French arms at Aspern and Essling, the hard-contested fight at Wagram, and the humiliating Peace of Vienna imposed by Napoleon on his vanquished foe. But though the fate of Germany was decided in the valley of the Danube, ripples from the great wave of Teutonic resistance passed into the Kingdom of Westphalia, and threatened to sap its newly-laid foundations. On five separate occasions the Westphalian population was provided with a signal for revolt, and the failure of five conspiracies and incursions seems to demonstrate that the State was more firmly established than might have been imagined.

The first of these occasions was the expedition of Lieutenant Friedrich Wilhelm von Katte, of the twenty-seventh regiment of Prussian foot. It was the design of this young officer to surprise the fortress of Magdeburg, to hoist the Prussian flag, and to appeal to the Prussian provinces incorporated in the Kingdom of Westphalia to return to their old allegiance. On the night of April 2-3 Katte, who had enrolled some old Prussian soldiers, arrived at Stendal, a small town north of Magdeburg, obliged the gendarmes to give up their horses and arms, and then, dispersing through the villages placards which announced that a general insurrection was about to take place over the whole Confederation of the Rhine, marched upon Magdeburg. The attempt ended in a miserable failure; a detachment sent by General Michaud easily dispersed the insurgents; the Minister of Prussia gave satisfactory assurances; and the Elbe department resumed its tranquillity. Of the eleven prisoners captured in the only skirmish, four were executed.

The second occasion was more serious. The Baron von Dörnberg, a man of fifty-one years of age, quiet, reserved, with black shining eyes, reminding an admirer of William the Silent, who had served successively in the Hessian and Prussian armies and followed Blücher from the field of Jena to the last struggle at Lübeck, became upon the French conquest a member of the Tugendbund, an association which had for its object the awakening of a German spirit of nationality. To propagate this spirit among the Hessians, his fellow countrymen, Dörnberg returned to live upon his own estates. Being a distinguished soldier he was offered a commission in the new Westphalian army, and with a singular lack of honour accepted the pay and the uniform of the prince whom it was his object to betray. At once a landed proprietor, a colonel, and a royal chamberlain, Dörnberg was able to enlist in the conspiracy a certain number of people from all classes of the community. Of the Hessian peasantry, so conservative and so loyal, he had little fear. A justice of the peace, named Martin, obtained some recruits among the middle classes, and Dörnberg was able to count on a few highly placed courtiers and officials, on a considerable number of the lesser Hessian nobility, and upon a sprinkling of officers and soldiers from the Westphalian army. The grievances and ideals of this motley aggregation of men were by no means identical. The lesser nobility resented the loss of their privileges and the contempt of the alien Court; the peasantry wished simply for the old ruler, the old taxes, the old ways; of the educated men some were patriotic Hessians, some dreamt of a Pan-Germanic union, some had received insults from Frenchmen, others had not received their salaries. Old Hessian officers, who could not get commissions in the new army, joined because they were idle and chagrined, and then there were all the broken men common to an impoverished country which has been vanquished in war. The King saw that there was a general spirit of unrest, due, as he thought, to the material misery of the kingdom, to the poverty of the government, and the weight of the taxes, and the same fact was commented on in the despatches of Reinhard. Yet the notorious unease and fermentation does not seem to have stimulated the activities of the government.

It was arranged that on the evening of April 22 the insurgents were to collect in the villages round Cassel, and march in eight converging columns on the capital. Meanwhile Dörnberg and his friends within the town were to seize Jerome and the French generals, and imprison them in the castle. Help from over the border, from Major Schill, from the Duke of Brunswick-Oels, from the Austrians, was counted upon to complete the conquest. As to the future settlement there was no clear understanding, and had the movement succeeded it would certainly have disclosed queer divergences of opinion between the different sections of the conspiracy.

Three days, however, were sufficient to disclose and crush the insurrection. The peasant levies collected prematurely, and Dörnberg, seeing that the secret was abroad, rode out of Cassel to join his friends. The main force, starting from Homberg some 5,000 strong, was met by General Rewbell, who had only 200 foot, 25 horse, and two guns, and scattered at the second volley. The columns of the north were confronted with some Polish lancers of the Guard at Wolfshagen, made no resistance, and were taken prisoners. Three other columns dispersed without firing a shot. On the whole, Jerome had every reason to congratulate himself on the demeanour of the country. The army remained faithful, though there were a few desertions; many of the villages requested help against the insurgents, and the prefects and sub-prefects all did their duty. Great as had been the alarm, the insurgents were remarkably ill-equipped for their task. They were ill-armed, ill-disciplined and drunken, and their numbers were, all things considered, surprisingly small. Yet it must be remembered that if a few regiments of the Westphalian army had been detached from their allegiance, immediate failure might have been converted into temporary success.

Among the conspirators of April there were two men who had not been summoned in time to participate in the movement. These were Colonel Emmerich, an old Hessian officer (aged seventy-five) who lived on an English pension in Marburg, chewing the cud of anti-Gallicanism, and a certain medical professor of the Marburg University, by name Dr. Sternberg.

In the month of June the auguries seemed to these two gentlemen favourable for a revolt. The Archduke Charles of Austria had urged the Elector of Hesse to raise the standard in his old dominions; the Elector of Hesse was in correspondence with Sternberg. In the south of Westphalia there were but few troops, and the nearest important French force was far away at Hanau. Why, they reflected, should not Marburg be stirred up to rise against the tyrant? South Hesse too would rise, and Austria, fresh from her victory at Aspern, would fly to the assistance of the tough veterans of the American war. But success, as Sternberg saw, really depended upon the ability of Austria to afford assistance, and accordingly he counselled delay until the Austrian troops were on the frontier. Unexpectedly an attack of typhoid laid him low, and the conspiracy was deprived of its brain. The old colonel babbled in the taprooms, was cross-examined by the prefect, and then, losing his head, determined to precipitate the catastrophe. On the night of June 23–4 he entered Marburg at the head of forty or fifty peasants, disarmed a piquet of veterans, and rang the tocsin furiously. But Marburg remained impassive, offering closed shutters instead of open arms, and the insurgents were easily driven from the town by the Westphalian general in command. Not a single Westphalian official gave countenance to this abortive revolt [1].

Meanwhile a more serious danger menaced the eastern province of the kingdom. Major Schill, a famous Prussian partisan, who on his own initiative had carried on a brilliant warfare in the later stages of the Franco-Prussian war (1806–7), left Berlin on April 28, 1809, on the pretext that he was going to exercise his troop of hussars. Under this innocent pretence Schill was meditating one of the most audacious exploits in history, nothing less in fact than the overthrow of the French dominion in North Germany. As he marched to Potsdam he halted, harangued his soldiers, and, amidst enthusiastic acclamations, told them that they were now entering into a war to

---

[1] I follow here the account given by W. Varges in the *Tägliche Rundschau*, 1889, nos. 258–9. In some material respects it differs from the story as told by Lynckner, *Die Insurrectionen*, being based upon additional material obtained from the Marburg Archives.

THE KINGDOM OF WESTPHALIA 253

the death against an alien tyranny. On May 2 he entered the capital of the Duke of Anhalt-Dessau, publishing abroad that he had come to overthrow the French domination, that he was followed by an army of 13,000 men under Blücher, that Prussia had declared war upon France, and that a Prussian army would shortly invade the territory of Westphalia. The news came to Jerome, and Cassel was for many days in a state of the wildest alarm. The major was at Halle, then at Halberstadt, soon it was expected that he would march upon Cassel itself. If his force was the vanguard of a Prussian army, would not all the Prussian provinces rise? Already it was reported that recruits were freely joining him.

Everything, however, turned out unfortunately for Schill. He had calculated on an Austrian victory on the Danube, on Prussian support, on the assistance of the Hessian rebels, but now he learnt that the Austrians were beaten, that the timid Prussian government had declared him guilty of high treason, confiscated his property and put a price upon his head, that the Hessian revolt was crushed, and that overwhelming forces were converging upon him. There was nothing for it but to turn northwards and recross the Elbe. A few miles south of Magdeburg the invaders met a detachment of General Michaud's garrison, and in a lively skirmish lost seventy men and twelve or thirteen officers. All hopes of taking the great fortress of Magdeburg were shattered by this repulse, and the band of invaders left Westphalia to escape into Mecklenburg.

Hardly had the excitement caused by these events subsided, when the kingdom was threatened by a more serious peril. The heir to the Duchy of Brunswick was the Duke of Brunswick-Oels, fourth son of the famous Charles William Ferdinand. An intrepid and resolute soldier, Brunswick was determined to recover his ancestral domains, and collected round him a band of fighting men, some 1,700 strong, to aid the design. The Black Legion, or *army of vengeance*, was composed of patriots and adventurers drawn from every source, companions of Katte, Dörnberg, and Schill, Prussian deserters, *franc-tireurs* of the Pomeranian and Silesian campaigns, and Gallophobes from every State of the Rheinbund. Reinforced by an Austrian army and by the troops which had followed the Elector of Hesse-Cassel into his Bohemian exile, Brunswick entered Saxony at the head of 10,000 men. The opening stage of the adventure was brilliantly successful. Dresden and Leipzig fell into the hands of the invaders, and the Electorate lay prostrate at their feet. But then the wheel of fortune was reversed. Jerome beat the Austrians at Waldheim on June 27, recovered Dresden on July 1, and the armistice of Znaim, which followed immediately on the battle of Wagram, withdrew from the Duke the co-operation of his Austrian allies. A prudent man would have submitted to fate, and packed up the black uniforms and lugubrious shakos for use upon another occasion. It was clear that Austria was on the brink of peace with Napoleon, and though there were rumours of an English descent at Cuxhaven, there was no certainty of co-operation in the west. Brunswick, however, was not prepared for so tame a finale. While Jerome was in Dresden, he determined to make a dart on Westphalia and to call upon the subjects of his father to rally round the House of Guelph. The officers and men of the Black Legion were apprised of his intentions, and 1,300 foot, 650 horse, and 80 artillerymen elected to follow their leader on his desperate raid against the French Empire. With this small force the Duke crossed the Westphalian frontier, and entered Halle, where he was warmly received. His great hope was that the English might be in time to assist, and that the Westphalians, who had responded so feebly to the call of a Hessian colonel or a Prussian major, would rise at the invitation of a reigning duke, a member of the ancient House of Guelph. But a series of foiled revolts had bred caution in the people and steeled the temper of the soldiery. At Halberstadt on the night of July 29–30, the Black Legion was confronted by the fifth Westphalian regiment of the line, and, after a night of desperate but victorious street fighting, lost 400 men killed and wounded, of whom eighteen were officers. On July 31 the Duke entered his capital, and met with a reception of mingled distrust, fear, and cordiality. It was in vain that he won a small success against Rewbell on August 1, a few miles outside Brunswick. On the next day the defeated general effected a junction with Generals Gratien and Thielmann, and the odds against the Duke became overwhelming. Neither an English army nor a *levée en masse* of Brunswickers was at hand to redress the balance, and there was no course left but flight. Aided by a friendly peasantry the Black Legion gained the mouth of the Weser, and sailed away in safety upon an English fleet.

If these movements had been simultaneous, if no one of them had been divulged until the Austrian declaration of war, the Kingdom of Westphalia might have gone down with a crash. As it was, each movement in itself was so ill-designed and so feeble that it enlisted very little active support. The imaginations of men are naturally feeble, and it is difficult to stir them with ideals when the actual is not wholly intolerable. It was not until the evils of the Napoleonic régime had stamped themselves deeply upon the common life, that the minds of these patient Germans caught fire; not till they found their trade throttled by the blockade, their purses emptied by the fisc, their homes burdened by military billeting, their sons carried away to the wars never to return, that they began to feel that the yoke was more than they could bear. But in 1809 the government of the French had not displayed its harshest features; on the contrary it had created careers, abolished abuses, conciliated interests, healed differences, excited hopes. The Westphalians were on the whole prepared, albeit perplexed by misgivings, regrets, and loyal memories, to give the experiment a fair trial. Perhaps they were over slow to read the signals of the Spanish revolt; perhaps the habit of brute obedience was too strongly rooted in the Hessian soldier to permit the growth of a discriminating patriotism; perhaps the shopmen of Cassel valued too much the custom of a luxurious Court, and the burgess was too habitually deferential to comfort and to authority. In any case, in the short span of six months the pinchbeck Kingdom of Westphalia had known and survived seven leaders of revolts [1].

---

[1] That there was a good deal of sympathy for the rebels even in Cassel is clear from the account of F. Müller, *Kassel seit* 70 *Jahren*, who tells us that the picture of the Duke of Brunswick-Oels was in every house, and that even in the booksellers' shops you could see pictures of Schill, Brunswick-Oels, Höfer, and Pius VII. A song on the death of Schill was openly sung in the streets.

CHAPTER XII

WESTPHALIAN PROBLEMS

'Si l'Angleterre a la nation pour elle, ayons pour nous la législation.'—
NAPOLEON.

IF, as Napoleon said, experience is everything in administration, faith also goes for something. The French administrators in Westphalia were not only experienced, but they had faith in their own value. It is only necessary to read the letters of Beugnot or the speeches and circulars of Siméon to see how saturated men can become with the belief in the superiority of the language and civilization of their own country. They speak kindly, considerately, condescendingly, to the poor Westphalians, explaining everything in the lucid French manner as a master might expound a beautiful text to a class of stupid and backward boys, now calling attention to a grace of phrase, now to its inner logical coherence, now to its bearing on life. The official letters and documents of this time have all the air of being written by men who regarded themselves as missionaries of civilization, and who wish to impart the mysteries of their creed. '*Nous avons l'intention,*' wrote the Minister of Justice when announcing a legal appointment, '*de vous appeler ici comme un missionnaire digne d'y fonder le culte nouveau de la justice!*' 'To found the new cult of Justice,' could any call be more inspiring?

One of the first articles of the new creed was the abolition of feudalism. In France this had been effected hurriedly, and in the turmoil of the Revolution all attempt to discriminate between services which were the product of mediaeval servitude and services which were the product of free contract had to be abandoned. But in Westphalia, where the Crown was a large landowner and the government by no means indifferent to the support of the local nobility, legislation was less trenchant, and the thirteenth clause of the constitution, which declared the unconditional abolition of serfage, passed through the crucible of successive legal refinements. By a decree of January 23, 1808, all labour services were preserved which were defined either by deed or by recognizance in the rolls of the manor. Similarly the fine or right of entry (*Weinkauf*) due from the peasant when he took up his copyhold was still to be acquitted in cases where it was fixed either in deed or roll. The old communal, municipal, and public *corvées* (*Communal-Fröhnden, Burgvesten,* and *Landfröhnden*) were maintained, but all such services were capable of being redeemed by money payments; indeterminate services, the obligation of performing domestic service in the master's house, personal *corvées*, heriots, and marriage-dues were abolished, and the lord lost his control over the education and the career of the peasant. With the same idea of satisfying legitimate expectations, it was provided that although entails were abolished, the heir in tail, born before January 1, 1808, might receive the inheritance for himself alone and with the free right of disposition. Some proprietors complained of these proceedings as too revolutionary. The government replied with justice that, according to the liberal principles of the Code Napoléon and of the act constituting the Kingdom of Westphalia, all rights of serfage and feudalism might have been suppressed, even the 'territorial rights mingled with feudalism'; that the suppression had been general in Genoa, Parma, Piacenza, and Tuscany; but that the Westphalian government had preferred an equitable temperament between the rigour of the laws and the respect due to long possession. They had kept everything which they could keep without violating principle [1].

These changes, conservative though they were, could not fail to cause a good deal of disturbance in the rural districts. Peasants refused to work upon the land, and their masters appealed to the law. Further decrees were accordingly issued to interpret the decree of January 23, 1808, which abolished serfdom. It was laid down that no *corvée* was to be considered indeterminate (*ungemessen*) which was fixed either by reference to the number of work-days or by reference to the size of the

[1] *Moniteur Westphalien*, May 10, 1808.

area upon which work was to be done. All hunting services, fixed or unfixed, were abolished save those which had for their purpose the destruction of noxious beasts. Proprietors were prohibited from buying or selling *corvées*, or demanding a different kind of service from that originally designed. Nor were any new *corvées* to be created. In doubtful cases the burden of proof lay upon the peasant, and the service was to be provisionally performed until the court had pronounced upon the case.

A decree issued August 18, 1809, laid down a tariff for the redemption of Church tithes and of those agricultural services which were retained, but owing partly to the ignorance of the peasant, partly to the lack of specie, and partly to the difficulty of obtaining the requisite statistics as to the average prices of corn and hay during the last thirty years, little was done to redeem either the services or the tithes. In truth, the Westphalian government failed to deal satisfactorily with a difficult problem. Its piecemeal legislation was too favourable to the landlord, and was not only productive of disturbance and unrest, but also brought less substantial benefit to the peasantry than might have been fairly expected. The redemption of tithes and labour services was an idle flourish, so long as the peasants were unable to borrow money upon easy terms, and it was not until the formation of the Hessian rural bank in 1832 that the work of redemption really began [1].

Agrarian individualism, agrarian mobility, and agrarian subdivision was the note of the Civil Code. The prefects were instructed to stimulate the abolition of rights of pasturage on communal lands according to Article 815, which provided that nobody could be constrained to remain in community (*dans l'indivision*) and that partition could always be demanded. The 'right of detraction' which penalized the acquisition of property in new provinces was done away with. Fiefs were converted into allods, and 'Erbverträge' or compacts to determine the succession were abolished. But the King reserved to himself

---

[1] *Bulletin des lois du royaume de Westphalie*, i. 334; ii. 190; iv. 108, 174; Sugenheim, *Geschichte der Aufhebung der Leibeigenschaft*, 411 ff.; Hildebrand, *Jahrbücher für Nationalökonomie und Statistik*, i. 412 ff.

the right to create hereditary titles and to authorize the recipients to entail their lands to male descendants in the direct line. Thus while the normal operation of the Code promoted subdivision, a special class of property was created in the 'Majorat,' which, being inalienable and incapable of being mortgaged, was designed to consolidate the position of the princes, barons, and knights of Westphalia. Nor was it thought advisable to give an unrestricted application to the rules of inheritance as laid down by the Civil Code. The peasant properties in Osnabrück, for instance, were so small as to be incapable of subdivision consistently with the performance of the services due from them, and the government, to protect its own proprietary interests, was willing to preserve in certain localities the old condition of things, such as the restriction on alienation without the consent of the lord, and the customary rules of inheritance.

Hand in hand with the liberation of agriculture came the liberation of commerce. The 'jurandes' and 'maîtrises' were abolished, and their property passed to the Crown. Henceforth any one might practise any trade upon taking out a patent at a trifling cost.

The new system of justice was an even greater boon. An official translation of the Code was prepared [1], and the professors of Halle and Göttingen eagerly set themselves to lecture upon its contents. The French law of procedure, both civil and criminal, was also introduced with some modifications suggested by common sense or German tradition. The benefits of uniformity, speed, and publicity recommended these new codes. The Hanoverian litigant was no longer obliged to pay for mountains of documents drawn up by grasping advocates; the inhabitants of the Prussian provinces were no longer placed at the mercy of the *juge d'instruction*. The triple principle that all criminal cases were to be heard in public; that nobody was to be condemned save by the verdict of a jury; and that there was to be no appeal from the decision of a criminal court, was both new and welcome. The abolition of seigneurial jurisdic-

---

[1] The official translation contained the German and French text, accompanied by the Latin translation which had been made for the Kingdom of Italy.

tion must have meant the removal of many ignorant and oppressive sentences.

Lord Halifax wrote in a famous tract, 'The Character of a Trimmer,' that 'the laws depend as much upon the pipes through which they are to pass as upon the fountain from whence they flow.' In Westphalia, if the fountain of law was French, the pipes were German, and it might perhaps have been expected that the clear fluid would have been darkened or obstructed in its transmission to the litigant by the ignorance, by the learning, or by the ill-will of native judges. Yet all witnesses concur in testifying that the French system, though administered by German judges, worked from the first with singular smoothness. 'M. Siméon,' wrote Reinhard to Champagny on August 10, 1809[1], 'by the liberality and width of his mind has succeeded in completely regenerating the judicial system, and in conciliating all suffrages. On no side does one hear that his administration is embarrassed, although no department of government has undergone so great a change both in form and substance. The credit must partly be attributed to the manner in which he is seconded, the Kingdom of Westphalia in its five universities and in its ancient dicasteries containing a great number of jurists, who are familiar with all the new ideas, and who have made a specially profound study of the Code Napoléon and the French forms. M. Siméon has been zealously seconded, and even the mass of the nation has recognized the excellence of the new institutions.' Three years later the same observer wrote that the judicial system was working so well that one might have believed that the Code Napoléon had been introduced for ten years.

We have an even more valuable piece of evidence in the memoirs of Friedrich Karl von Strombeck, a lively and honest writer, who reports upon the legal revolution from a German standpoint. Von Strombeck at the time of the French occupation of Brunswick was Chancellor (*Abtei-Rath*) of the Abbey of Gandersheim, then governed by the Princess Augusta Dorothea of Brunswick, a sister of the reigning duke. With some pretensions to classical scholarship—he accomplished a metrical translation of the elegies of Propertius—with

[1] *Mémoires du roi Jérôme*, iv. 290–1.

a taste for travel, a competent knowledge of French, and the zeal for new things common to so many Germans of his generation, von Strombeck was just the kind of man to act as an intermediator between the two civilizations. As a youth he had been familiar with the polished little circle of *émigrés* who had settled in Brunswick, and had practised his French upon an archbishop, a pair of bishops, a marshal of France, and a president of Parliament. A minor poet of the sentimental order was almost compelled to sympathize with the early enthusiasms of the French Revolution, and a visit to Paris in 1805 converted Strombeck into a warm admirer of the Emperor, and effected his introduction to the Civil Code. The Prussian war came upon him like a thunder-clap. His mistress the abbess fled to Rostock, his master the Duke died of his wounds at Altona. The circumstances were difficult, and von Strombeck behaved in a manner neither discreditable nor heroic. He accompanied his mistress to Rostock, visited his dying master, and then returned to administer the revenues of Gandersheim. But however much he might regret the calamity which had befallen the progeny of Henry the Lion, he was not long in finding consolations. The French soldiers enlivened the city of Brunswick with a ceaseless round of balls and entertainments, and the young German ladies soon discarded patriotic scruples, to share the fashionable pleasures of their polite conquerors. Strombeck was not behindhand. He entertained one French officer at 'a small festivity,' while another visited him almost every day, accompanied him in his rides on his excursions to the Harz and the Brocken, and received an invitation to stay at his country place. Despatched to Cassel as one of the deputies of the Duchy of Brunswick to congratulate the King on his accession, von Strombeck was flattered by the amiability of the royal pair. He was offered the prefectship of the Department of the Ocker, but reflecting that the work of the office would be too heavy to permit the discharge of his duties to the abbess, he petitioned for a judicial post, and was made President of the Civil Tribunal of Eimbeck, a new court whose jurisdiction extended over Gandersheim and that portion of the Leine department which lay between the Weser and the Harz.

Here he experienced one of the purest of human pleasures, the joy of creation. At first everything was to seek. There were not enough copies of the Code to go round, the officials did not know their business, the court was stowed away in an inconvenient room in the Rathhaus, and until the new procedure was introduced shift had to be made with the old. Yet good will and a certain practical skill can do much, and 'at the beginning of May our court was in so good a condition, that several cases which had waited several years for decision in the Hanoverian courts were terminated.' Strombeck was, in fact, fortunately situated. He had studied the Civil Code through and through at a time 'when to many other lawyers in the land the existence of the book was hardly known'; he could correspond at length with Siméon, the Minister of Justice, who knew no German, and he was singularly free from legal pedantry. Further, he had the advantage of being fully impressed by the superiority of French law and French legal procedure. So when the new procedure came into force on March 1, 1809, he wrote some instructions and forms for the justices, clerks, and ushers of his own district. These were afterwards expanded and printed in a book entitled *Formulare und Anmerkungen zu der Processordnung des Königreichs Westphalen*, which became the leading textbook on procedure in the kingdom. Strombeck, in fact, set himself to be the Westphalian oracle on the Codes. His library of French legal literature was the largest in the kingdom; his manual on Procedure in Correctional Cases had a wide sale; and, incited by him, his brother Frederick Henry, a judge at Helmstadt, composed two treatises, one upon the organization of French public trials, and the other a handbook of Westphalian civil procedure.

When Hanover was annexed in 1810, Strombeck received an invitation from Siméon to sit as President in the new Court of Appeal about to be established at Celle. The new court was composed almost entirely of members of the former High Court of Appeal of Hanover, but a new spirit was infused into its proceedings[1]. In the first year of its

---

[1] Strombeck prints decisions of the court of Celle in his *Rechtswissenschaft des Gesetzbuchs Napoleons*, Braunschweig, 1812.

installation the court gave 4,492 decisions. Such promptitude had hitherto been unknown. The interminable pleadings were cut short, and cases determined on the spot after hearing the advocates on both sides. Litigation was a matter of months, not years. Strombeck is a warm advocate of the merits of orality, although it seldom happened that a really able or eloquent barrister pleaded before him. He says that he found it easier to attend, that he obtained a keener insight into the heart of the matter when he had heard the actual voice of the barrister than was possible under the old system, when the judge had to sift masses of dry documents stuffed out with the common Chancery forms. Orality was especially valuable in small criminal cases, which at Eimbeck could be so disposed of at the rate of half a dozen at a sitting. In the larger criminal cases it was, he thought, equally important that the accused should be brought face to face with his judge. Innocent men are often condemned on the other system. On the other hand, he is willing to admit that in civil cases the old written methods may be more congenial, where the judges are no longer in the bloom of youth, and have acquired habits of leisurely and quiet consideration—the case of the majority of German lawyers [1].

Yet there was a dark side to the history of the law courts during the period of the Westphalian kingdom. The penal laws which had prevailed in this part of Germany before the French occupation were characterized by their mildness, and there was little crime. But the introduction of conscription brought in its train a new category of penal offences, the commission of which was condoned by public sentiment, and sharply punished by the law. It is no uncommon thing to read in the Westphalian *Moniteur* of a father being sentenced to a heavy fine or a year's imprisonment for having given shelter to his son who had fled from the conscription or deserted the

---

[1] It would appear that Siméon submitted a memoir to the Emperor in which objections were urged against the jury, objections probably prompted by the King or some of his German advisers. Napoleon replied (June 24, 1808) that the jury of judgement must be established in Germany both because enlightened people desired it, and for political reasons. *Corr.* xvii. 328, no. 14,127.

colours. Edict after edict was passed to intensify the penalties meted out to this luckless part of the population. On April 10, 1813, the penalty of death was declared against any one 'who by money or by intoxicating liquors shall procure, solicit, or favour desertion.' The penalty of desertion was death, and by an edict of March 8, 1813, every conscript who did not join within the required time was liable to be sentenced to three years' hard labour by a Military Council. These penalties, it is true, were subsequently repealed and were exceptionally severe.

The principle of religious toleration was part of the common stock of revolutionary ideas, and it was applied in the Kingdom of Westphalia. Indeed, with a Protestant queen and a Catholic king, toleration had every chance of thriving. The Protestants and Catholics, however, were so distributed in Germany after the settlement of Westphalia that there were not many Catholics in the Protestant, or Protestants in the Catholic districts. The last musket in the war of religion had been fired off before Charles I lost his head, and the work did not need to be done over again. Fulda remained Catholic, Hesse was 'Reformed,' the Lutherans held sway in Hanover. The exercise of religious rites was not prohibited to the cults which were in a minority, but Lutherans and Catholics were excluded almost entirely from offices of State in Hesse, while in the greater part of the Hanoverian territory a Catholic or a Calvinist would not have been admitted to public employment. But the religious temperature was low, and the territorial maxim 'Cuius regio, eius religio,' though illogical and indefensible in theory, had proved to be a workable and satisfactory compromise. There was, however, one section of the community, powerful by reason of its wealth, and yet both in the Catholic and Protestant districts treated as a pariah class. These were the Jews. Their disabilities, save in the Duchy of Brunswick, where under the enlightened rule of the late Duke they had been treated with marked liberality, were numerous and degrading. They were subjected to a special tax, confined to special towns, excluded from the schools, universities, and armies, and from all share in political power. All these burdens and disabilities were removed by the decree of January 27, 1808. By a later ordinance

(March 31, 1808), a consistory was established for the supervision of the Hebrew cult, and one of the duties enjoined upon this body was to see that 'the rabbis and schoolmasters profess under all circumstances obedience to the laws, and specially to those which are relative to the defence of the country; that they should teach that military service is a sacred duty, during which the law dispenses from those religious observances which should not be compatible with it; and that prayers should be recited in all the synagogues for the King and his family.' The Jewish community was profuse in its thanks, and their spokesman, the eminent and liberal Jacobson, observed that 'the songs of Zion would now freely resound upon the mountains of Westphalia.' The State gained some devoted soldiers who spent their lives upon distant battlefields, and the penurious King made frequent drafts upon the long purses of his Hebrew financiers.

The Kingdom of Westphalia, like many other parts of Germany, was full of well-endowed cathedral chapters, abbeys, and monasteries, admission to which was confined to persons of noble blood. The statutes of these bodies were now revised in a democratic direction, and it was stipulated that a tithe of the revenues of all prebends, chapters, abbeys, convents, and priories situated in the kingdom should be paid to the State. But the indigent government was unable for long to content itself with so modest a share of these inviting endowments. On May 13, 1809, six nunneries were confiscated, and it is fair to add that the ejected nuns were properly provided for. A year later a general edict of confiscation swept all the abbeys, priories, and chapters of the kingdom into the treasury net, exception only being made in favour of the foundation of Wallenstein at Homberg, and such institutions as could be proved to exist for public instruction. It would seem that no great harm was done to the cause of piety, learning, or charitable endeavour, and that the money now available for masquerades had formerly been devoted to the support of indolence.

That the Church should be subordinate to the State was a cardinal maxim of the Napoleonic policy. The candidates for ordination had to be submitted to the King's approval, and the clergy were required to keep the civil registers, to pray for the King, to read royal decrees on the conscription and the blockade, and to celebrate the royal and imperial birthdays and the victories of the French arms. A circular of the Minister of the Interior to the bishops lays it down that 'one of the first duties of the clergy is to preach obedience to the sovereign, without which there is no public tranquillity or individual security.' Yet although the Westphalian State regulated the constitution of the Protestant synods and consistories, and nominated the Catholic bishops, it had not a complete control of the Catholic organization. The Westphalian metropolitan was the Prince-Primate, a dignified and independent member of the Confederation of the Rhine, and while this was so, there could be no independent Church in Westphalia, in the sense in which such an institution existed in France. In the autumn of 1812, King Jerome stirred this question of an independent national Church for Westphalia. It was a very delicate question, one of those questions which alarm susceptibilities rather than affect interests. But King Jerome stirred it. He proposed that the Bishop of Corvey should be made Archbishop of Westphalia, that the church of St. Martin at Cassel should be converted into a Westphalian cathedral, and that the pensioned canons of Paderborn and Hildesheim should form the new chapter. But the Emperor would hear nothing of it. The Duke of Bassano was instructed to write that in the condition of things it was inopportune to convert the chief Protestant church in Cassel into a Catholic cathedral; that even in ordinary times such measures would require ripe consideration; that it was always very dangerous to meddle with religion; that attempts of the kind embittered people; that one did not know how far things might go; and that since Cassel was Protestant, it was well to leave the Protestants in peace. The King was distinctly told that if he persisted in the project he would meet with the displeasure of his brother, and finding little support in his own council, dropped the plan.

If the Church in Westphalia was controlled, it was not enriched by its French master. The salaries of the lower clergy, already small enough, were reduced, and were also paid with great irregularity. Many of the clergy were very hardly hit by the State bankruptcy in 1812, and the Church property of several communes was through this and other causes reduced to about a third of its previous amount. It should be remembered also that the Church was now subject to taxation from which it had been previously exempt. And these material evils were accompanied, it would seem, by a certain lack of social prestige. In every village the *Landprediger* had now a rival, if not a superior, in the mayor. New authorities, new areas, a new spirit broke down his old, and perhaps unhealthy, monopoly of village power. Before his own rustic congregation he would be exposed to many humiliations. The mayor would requisition his horse, the tax-collector would distrain his cow, the mayor's secretary would quarter two French officers and their servants on his parsonage. He would be forced to send his gardener to work on the fortifications of some garrison town, and the village would know it, and feel that the old authority was gone, never to return [1]. The French occupation is also credited with having produced a decline in church-going, and a large increase in the number of illegitimate births. It is probable too that the clergy, especially in Hesse, suffered in consideration from the homage it was compelled to pay to the new dynasty, for though it is true that several preachers refused to read the royal decrees or to give out the prayers for the King, on the whole the churches accepted the situation in Westphalia as they accepted it elsewhere. It was not from the pulpit that the cry of liberation proceeded [2].

The problems of poor-relief and the principles of charitable administration had occupied serious attention in many German towns ever since the beginning of the sixteenth century, and they were perhaps more adequately understood in the Protestant part of Germany than in the regions dominated by the Roman

---

[1] *Blicke eines Landpredigers auf die vergangene Zeit*; *Neue Fakkeln*, vii. 73.

[2] Pastor Gehrens admits that he preached several political sermons to which the government might have taken exception. But this was in Hesse (Gehrens, *Dreimalige Verhaftung*, 63). In the Prussian provinces the clergy would seem to have been more docile. A writer in *Neue Fakkeln* (v. 34 ff.) knew *one* priest 'who even before the Peace of Tilsit prayed aloud in the pulpit for Frederick William and Alexander.'

Church. It is evident, however, that the administrators of Westphalia found much to condemn in the arrangements which had hitherto prevailed for the administration of charity. There were a large number of institutions and endowments, but they were neither correlated one to another nor guided by common principles. The mobility of labour was not understood in the Middle Ages, and the mobility of pauperism would have been regarded as a crime against municipal self-sufficiency. A strict law of settlement is the natural product of close industrial oligarchies, of guarded vested interests, and of urban autonomy; and it is only when local ties are loosened, when large markets take the place of small ones, and industry and commerce are liberated from their fetters, that the principle of a free settlement becomes a necessity of poor-law organization.

By a decree of March 24, 1809, every commune was made responsible for the poor who had resided a year in it. The poor who had not obtained a settlement by a year's residence were charged to the parish in which they were born, or to that in which they had last obtained a settlement. Every applicant for relief was instructed to apply to the mayor, who, after satisfying himself that the pauper could not obtain support from his own family, could take one of three steps. If the applicant were old or infirm he would be sent to a hospital; if able-bodied, he was put to work; if a child, he might be sent either to a workshop or to a school. The support, so far as possible, was to be paid in kind. If the commune were too poor to bear the charge, the mayor was to appeal to the sub-prefect, and the sub-prefect to the prefect. The prefects were reminded that 'every charitable institution which did not tend to the extinction of mendicity departed from the principles of good government.' A central bureau of charity was established at Cassel, with instructions not only to secure a better employment of charitable funds, but 'to destroy and diminish causes of indigence by giving to the poor the habit and taste for work, and by teaching the children a trade.' It was to report progress every three months to the Minister of Justice and Interior. By establishing an easy law of settlement, as well as by laying down uniform and sober principles of charitable administration, the Westphalian government conferred a lasting benefit on the country. Unfortunately the times were exceptionally difficult, and a severe strain was put upon a new and not entirely perfect system. The internal disturbances caused by the abolition of the feudal system, by the anti-Napoleonic propaganda and by conscription, the decline of trade and commerce which resulted from the continental system and the requisitions of the troops, produced a large amount of destitution and vagabondage, and severe edicts were issued against able-bodied beggars. The commune proved, as in England, to be too small a unit for effective administration, and there was a general disinclination among the villages to submit to a new and burdensome imposition. The stipulation that the assistance given to the poor was, if possible, to be rendered in kind was intended to discourage pauperism, but in reality it discouraged the ratepayer by rendering the rate an irritating and recurrent drain upon his resources. Over large tracts of Westphalia there were then no regular villages, and the isolated householder was required to cart a weekly contribution of bread or vegetables over many miles of bad road to feed some pauper who had become charged to his commune, and for whose existence and well-being he regarded himself as in no wise responsible. The grumblings of ratepayers are perennial, and may generally be disregarded, but there is some reason for thinking that the Westphalian machinery, though a great improvement on anything which had hitherto existed, was incapable of meeting all the problems created by a system which uprooted so many men from industry and agriculture, and then, after five years of barrack life, returned them with loosened lives to their country.

The French had long lost the feeling for local autonomy, and the efforts to decentralize the government of the Ancien Régime had not had time to fructify, before the revolution supervened. That catastrophe eliminated the aristocracy, sowed hate and jealousy in every village, and prevented any further development of the constitution on the lines laid down by Turgot and Necker. A centralized bureaucracy was a necessity for France, being, as it were, not only a kind of anaesthetic or healing drug, but also the elementary condition for the preservation of all that was precious in the revolutionary movement. Among the lethargic inhabitants of Westphalia the mission of the bureaucracy was not to calm but to excite, not to preserve but to communicate. There were tenacious and irrational customs to be eradicated, bad and confused methods of administration to be reformed, innumerable local differences to be transcended. It was necessary that the inhabitants should be shaken out of that lazy acquiescence in the legacies of the past which had become habitual to them. The whole country required an education in business habits. It was time that questions of practical administration should be decided by the light of reason and convenience rather than by laborious reference to ancient records. The new administration did all this. It was worked very largely by Prussian officials who had already acquired the rudiments of the governing art. It was instructed by the circulars of the sage Siméon, and there is very good evidence for the statement that the prefects and sub-prefects were capable and honest men. On the other hand, it was to a certain extent vitiated by the fact that the prefects were permitted to make a profit out of their allowance for official expenses—a plan which encouraged the employment of cheap and corrupt clerks in the lower rungs of the administration.

In after years wholesale charges of corruption were brought against the Westphalian bureaucracy, and some special indictments are too pointed and circumstantial to be mere figments of the enemy[1]. Some corruption then we must assume, but, on the other hand, there was abundant display of honourable activity. It was a happy thought of C. D. Bode to collect the 222 circulars and ordinances issued by the prefect of the Department of the Werra during the course of a single year (1810). A substantial volume is filled with these documents, which present a lively picture of the various cares of a Westphalian prefect[2]. Now he is issuing a manifesto in favour of clover; now he prescribes the operations of the woodman; now he is putting pressure upon the reluctant communes to defray the expense of their registers of the Civil State; now he amalgamates

[1] *Das Königreich Westphalen und die Franzosen*, W. Wagener, 1813 (a violent diatribe), and *Neue Fakkeln* (Deutschland, 1814), i. 31; iii. 1–12.

[2] *Verhandlungen der königlichen Präfectur des Werradepartements*, C. D. Bode, 1812.

the charitable funds of Marburg. We may well believe with a satirical writer that the Boeotian mind was fairly confused with orders so novel, so frequent, and so copious. A picture has been drawn for us of the Westphalian village under the new dispensation. Twice a week the canton messenger came with a packet of official despatches. The village schoolmaster must copy them in his presence, while the school-children take holiday. Then the mayor was summoned and the municipal council, and there was deliberation. It was in vain that the parish priest represented that the school was being neglected, for the schoolmaster was now the mayor's secretary, and could snap his fingers at the consistory. As the mayor was often an illiterate, and the council was a knot of rustics drawn from the plough, the business proceeded slowly and suspiciously. 'What the others wish, that I wish too, only I will not be the first to sign': such was the common refrain. Nor was the interpretation of the documents a thornless path. A village municipal council had to send into a town a mile distant for an explanation of the word *adjourniren*, for the new government had its own terminology. And meanwhile the school-children remained untaught. The old-fashioned folk looked on all these busy doings with great disdain, and there must have been many a knowing and unfriendly nod when commune after commune declared a deficit. There was, indeed, some ground for the contention that the whole machinery was too expensive, both in time and money, for rural needs. If so, the French committed a grave error, for it is the catastrophe of political idealism that slow men dislike quick ways, and that there is nothing which easy-going people resent more keenly than a government which is too good for them [1].

---

[1] In the Archives of Marburg there is a collection of communal budgets which forms an unfavourable commentary on the system. Thus every one of the nine communes of the Canton of Friedewald (district Hersfeld, department Werra) shows a large deficit in 1811. The village of Friedewald (population 995) is typical. Its total income amounts to 126 fr. 80 c., its expenditure to 638 fr. 13 c. The main items of expenditure are : Salary of mayor, 310 fr. 80 c. ; office expenses of mayoralty, 75 fr. ; communal tax-collector, 18 fr. ; subscription to the Bulletin of Laws, 12 fr. ; subscription to the Departmental Bulletin, 8 fr. 9 c.

Perhaps also it may seem to us that the principle of political centralization was carried too far in this government. Let us suppose that a master has to be appointed to a primary school. There must first be an examination held by the pastor or the consistory. If the candidate be declared fit, then the patron or the commune recommend him for election, and the mayor or the sub-prefect present his name and qualifications to the prefect. The prefect reports to the Director-General of Public Instruction. If there should be no division of opinion, the Director-General, who is a member of the royal council, is competent to decide by himself. But if the competence of the candidate should be disputed, then he would be bound to refer it to the ministry, and the whole question would be thrashed out by the highest dignitaries of the State[1]. Or, again, let us suppose that a piece of communal land has to be acquired or alienated, or let out on lease. There must be (1) a valuation by experts; (2) a recommendation of the municipal council; (3) a reasoned recommendation of the mayor of the commune and the canton; (4) a memoir of the sub-prefect; (5) a memoir of the prefect; (6) a report of the Minister of the Interior; (7) a debate in the Council of State; and (8) the consent of the King. Our first impulse is to condemn in a most unhesitating fashion so complex a piece of mechanism. In a land of expensive men and women, accustomed to high standards of government, and to all the material facilities, the citizen moves the government, not the government the citizen. The vigorous man of the town settles down on some drowsy country-side, and at once the air is filled with complaints of the posts, the roads, the drains, and the beggars. He insists upon improvements, he worries officials, and by degrees he reconstitutes the administrative environment to suit his brisk and various appetite. But in Westphalia there were no expensive men and women, no private self-appointed missionaries of the material facilities. The missionary of the higher and the more expensive civilization was the government. From the very necessities of the case, the government was forced to be didactic. It was like a schoolmaster who has to teach a new lesson to an ignorant class, of whose characters, attainments, and

[1] Von Müller to the Minister of the Interior, Jan. 17, 1809 (Marburg Archives).

dispositions he is imperfectly informed. An unceasing vigilance, a luxury of precautions, a great central storage of driving power, were necessities. Every appointment had to be scrutinized where the candidates were ill-known and might possibly be disaffected. Every act of the most subordinate official had to be carefully prescribed. As the State was putting an unwonted strain upon local revenues and local authorities, as it was insisting upon administrative luxuries and expensive standards, while at the same time it was abridging the resources of the towns by the abolition of guilds and municipal excise duties, it was natural that it should be concerned for the careful management of communal revenues. In a small kingdom like Westphalia, such a measure of centralization does not involve insuperable difficulties. A short journey would bring every prefect face to face with his minister. Indeed, the central government was really an office for transacting local affairs. The most important department, that of the Interior, was, as we have seen, governed by a German and manned by German clerks, and it was currently said to err upon the side of sympathetic conservatism. The system was not, then, wholly lacking in elasticity. On the contrary, it was often intelligently adjusted to local needs. A salient example of this is afforded by the story of the *centimes additionnels*. The *centimes additionnels* were taxes levied for local purposes in the form of so many centimes to every franc of national taxation paid into the central government. Financiers still dispute the expediency of raising local revenue in this way. It may be urged in favour of it, that it is simple, that it involves only one assessment instead of at least two, and that the persons who pay most to the imperial exchequer are those who are fitted to make the heaviest contribution to local purposes. On the other hand, if there be any inequality in the incidence of imperial taxation, the *centimes additionnels* exaggerate instead of correcting it. Again, local needs vary, but the *centimes additionnels* provide a uniform contribution, and it may well happen that a district which contains few rich men is just the one which requires the largest amount of local expenditure. But whatever be the arguments for and against it, the system had been adopted in France, and it was copied in Westphalia. It provoked a general outcry. It was said that the local charges were too new, too high, and too unevenly distributed. The government had no doubt at first attempted to heap too many charges on the departmental account. The official expenses of the prefect, sub-prefect, the hospitals and prisons, the churches and schools, the *gendarmerie*, and the courts were all to be paid out of local taxes. This was all very French, but it was seen to be unwise. First the local charges were strictly limited and defined, but even so they exceeded 2,000,000 francs. Then in 1810 the *centimes additionnels* were abolished, and the departmental and cantonal costs were taken over by the public treasury; while finally, in 1812, a compromise was arrived at, and part of the local expenditure, amounting to about 500,000 francs, was retransferred to the departments, and met by the imposition of five additional centimes to the franc. But no fiscal triumphs were possible in Westphalia. The extravagance of the Court and the military requisitions forbade them. It was calculated that in 1813 alone 50,000,000 francs were expended in the kingdom on the French troops, largely in the shape of requisitions, a burden that fell exclusively upon the communes. It is no wonder that the sum of local indebtedness mounted up rapidly, and that every centime demanded by the central government was grudgingly paid. This is the simple reason why so many excellent schemes for public works remained in the sphere of pure literature.

Amidst much that is disappointing, one characteristic victory may be noted. By February 1810, 30,000 reluctant and suspicious Westphalians had been vaccinated by their French conquerors. A central committee was established for the propagation of this new prophylactic, and vaccination was made compulsory for entry into universities, public schools, and workshops. The annual tables submitted to the government attest a solid success for sanitary science, which may perhaps be partially reduced in our estimation when we recollect that the institution of military conscription provided a constant supply of patient victims to the doctor's lancet.

So far as the internal administration went there was but one serious blot: the high police, placed under the separate control of a so-called *Secrétaire des Commandements*, who had all the attributions of a Minister of Police. The institution was in itself repugnant to the German character, and it was worked in Westphalia with a singular amount of unnecessary friction. Neither M. de Bercagny, the first chief of the police, a gentleman who had been in turn a soldier, a monk, a general, a vicar, and an army contractor, nor M. de Bongars his successor, knew a word of German, and many of their subordinates were in the same position. But if their information was generally either deficient or ludicrously mistaken, their interference and espionage were harassing and persistent. Siméon told Reinhard, in 1809, that complaints were raining in on all sides against Bercagny, and that every one accused him of exercising his office with a view to making a fortune in two days. The opening of private letters by the police was carried so far that no one dared trust to the post. There was scarcely a prominent man in the kingdom who was not 'shadowed,' and, as under the later Roman Empire, an odious tribe of informers battened on the system. A hare could not be brought into the market of Cassel unless provided with a 'certificate of origin'; every blind violin-player had to pay four sous a day. A bear-leader or an ape-leader was compelled to buy a patent. The police were ordered to confiscate every work that ran counter to 'the principles of the constitution, to the respect due to the ruler, to public tranquillity, or to the different religions.' By such harassing and trivial regulations the French name was made odious. 'The high police,' wrote Reinhard, 'is at war with all the ministries save that of Foreign Relations, and with all the departmental administrations; it renders irremediable the schism between the French and the Germans by exalting the fears and suspicions of the one, and inspiring in the other either indignation or terror [1].'

The Universities of Germany occupied a place in the national

[1] German writers are never tired of expatiating on the venality and oppression of the Westphalian police; cf. *Neue Fakkeln*; Wagener, *Le Royaume de Westphalie*. Perhaps, however, the most instructive passages are to be found in the correspondence of Reinhard (*Revue Historique*, xx. 347-8). 'General Bongars issues a circular (May 17, 1811) to all the mayors of the kingdom ordering the immediate arrest of all suspected persons. ... M. Savagner ... was arrested last Thursday night in his bed, and his papers visited. The next day he was informed of his dismissal and banishment from Westphalia.'

life very difficult for the Frenchmen of the Napoleonic age to understand. Though poorly endowed and often strictly dependent on the State, they exerted an influence over German opinion which was made all the greater by the unattractiveness of political employment, by the emptiness of the public press, and by the natural tendency of the educated Teutonic mind to abstract speculation and abstruse research. A series of secular changes had transformed a number of narrow theological and legal seminaries into places of deep liberal and independent learning. While in the Catholic south the abolition of the Jesuit order had placed the machinery of education in the hands of the State, in the north the Protestant consistories had been obliged to concede their control to the lay authority. The substitution of the State for the consistory in the Protestant universities of the north, and for the Jesuits in the Catholic universities of the south, was indeed attended by some disadvantages. The professors, who were both appointed and dismissed by the State, were forced to submit their programmes half-yearly to the government together with a list of their auditors. They were rebuked or praised by a Minister of Education according as they were supposed to have evinced idleness or zeal, and rescripts were issued by the government, directing the number, the subject-matter, and sometimes even the tone of their lectures. But the substitution of State for sectarian control was, nevertheless, a step on the road to liberty. The governments of the eighteenth century were, for the most part, more tolerant and more enlightened than the religious bodies, and their influence was exerted towards freeing the universities from the pedantry and obscurantism which had hitherto checked the progress of science. The accession of Frederick II in 1740 brought with it the honourable recall of the philosopher Christian von Wolff to the University of Halle, from which he had been expelled in 1723 on the charge of rationalism, and from that moment Halle, though closely controlled by a niggardly government, though destitute of university buildings, and less richly endowed than the poorest of modern Oxford colleges, stood forward as the champion of free inquiry. While the connection with the State brought an increasing measure of liberty, the titles of *Hofrath* and *Geheimrath* awarded to the most distinguished savants served to give a prestige to the teaching profession out of all proportion to its miserable endowments. An attempt was made to bring university studies into relation with national needs, and while the old Latin disputations were discarded in favour of lectures given in the German tongue (a cardinal reform inaugurated by Halle and followed by Göttingen), the university course was lengthened to a period of three years (1804) for Prussian subjects who wished to enter the government service. In this, as in many other educational reforms, Prussia set an example speedily followed by other States.

These were in the main reforms of machinery, but all through the pre-revolutionary and revolutionary period a new spirit was breathing itself into the intellectual life of Germany which did far more to transform the ideal of culture than all the princes and bureaucracies. This spirit was not French or Latin; it was Greek. The renascence of Hellenism which we associate with the names of Winckelmann and Heyne and F. A. Wolf was not merely an affair of learned scholarship; it provided ideals for art and life, a new set of canons for literary criticism, and a new view of the scope and possibilities of education. Together with this Hellenistic movement another intellectual tendency, equally profound, was beginning to assert itself in Germany. The earlier philosophers of the century had been mainly nurtured upon mathematics and natural sciences; and physics, mathematics, and cosmology formed an essential part of a course of lectures delivered by a professor of philosophy. The influence of this juxtaposition upon the character of metaphysical and moral speculation was very marked. The mind regarded as a fixed product of nature was analysed with a view to the discovery of the postulates of thinking, while the analysis of character as a fixed product was expected to yield the postulates of morality. Neither Wolff nor Kant cared for history, nor were their modes of thought influenced by it. The genesis of moral ideas, the development of psychological processes in time, the revelation of Nature in events, were subjects to which they did not turn their attention. The new thinkers, however, Fichte, Hegel, and Schelling, had received a literary education, and were essentially historical in their treatment of philosophical problems. Striking with the wand of history the hard and stoical rock which Kant had planted on the ground, they made it to flow with streams of obscure but comforting eloquence. They found everywhere spirit, reason, order, and looked upon the history of the world as upon a kind of Divine drama, in which every act and every scene has its place and significance. While the doctrine of the Trinity was shown to have a deep philosophical import, humanity was assured that it was inevitably destined to realize a large and larger measure of the Divine Spirit. The writings of these thinkers definitely mark the triumph of the historical method.

Meanwhile increased attention was being devoted to the problem of pedagogy. As the learning of the learned became more deep and vital, they began to realize how cheap and miserable was the mechanism which went under the guise of school teaching. There were in Germany in the middle of the eighteenth century three kinds of public school: the village school, the Latin school in the towns, and 'the learned school,' *Gelehrte Schule*. The village school was generally kept by the clerk of the parish, and did not aim at providing more than the most elementary instruction. In most of the small towns the Latin school, which had not advanced beyond the standard fixed in the sixteenth century, was the only public school available. It would generally be held in an old broken-down monastery of the sixteenth century, and the impecunious schoolmaster would eke out his miserable pittance by conducting his flock to help in the choral services at marriages and burials. The methods of punishment were drastic and Orbilian; the curriculum and the textbooks two centuries behind the age; the informing spirit ecclesiasticism cut and dried.

The condition of the *Gelehrte Schule*, which aimed at providing a liberal education for boys who wished to enter the learned professions, was in some instances more satisfactory. It had been improved by the action of the State in Brunswick, in Electoral Saxony, in Prussia, and in Brunswick-Lüneburg. But, for the most part, these schools remained till the last decade of the eighteenth century in a state of great inefficiency. The nobles and the wealthier burghers had long ceased to send their boys to school, and preferred to employ private tutors. The schoolmaster was miserably paid, and his profession despised.

The curriculum was narrow and stifling, and no attention was paid to the idiosyncrasies of the boys or to the development of real intellectual interests in the school. It is a standing disgrace to the Germany of Frederick the Great that it did so little for popular education.

It is not the least of the services of French naturalism that it directed attention to the problem of pedagogy. To restore the family to its natural and wholesome state, to reassert the legitimate influence of the parent over the child, and to sweeten and enliven the life of the young, became an object of general concern in an age which believed that man was naturally good, and that the restoration of domesticity was the best antidote to social artifice. To these aspirations the *Emilius* of Rousseau gave a dazzling embodiment. That famous treatise contains much that is both unwise and unpractical, but it gives expression to some very important truths. That the influence of character is more important than that of precept, that education begins with the family, that the mind of the child should be drawn on gently and not compelled to another's will with harshness, that instruction is better conveyed through visible symbols or actual experiences than through mere words—these truths are mingled with a shallow psychology which sees nothing in a child but self-love, and nothing in the principle of authority which can give tone to character. The seed scattered with so fantastic a gesture produced in Germany a flowering crop of educational theory. Almost all the deepest minds, Herder and Goethe, Jean Paul Richter and von Basedow, Heyne and Wolf, concerned themselves with the problem, either in its theoretical or in its practical aspect. It became one of the objects of the universities to provide skilled teachers for the public schools. At Göttingen Gesner founded a *seminarium philologicum* for the purpose of training teachers, and the influence of this distinguished scholar was imprinted in the school ordinance for Hesse-Cassel issued in 1775. A similar institution was founded in 1779 at Helmstadt, and its members trained not only in polite learning but also in the theory of teaching. In the famous *Philanthropinum* at Dessau, founded in 1779, Basedow carried into practice his theory of undenominational education, and of the teaching of dead and living languages through the medium of conversation.

The gymnasium at Weimar was revolutionized by no less a person than Herder, who widened the programme of studies by the introduction of history, geography, and statistics, abolished or limited the use of the rod, and encouraged the development of special aptitudes. The educational reformers aimed in the main at three objects: to substitute a real and quickening education for the mechanical drill of learning grammar and catechism by heart; to train a supply of cultured teachers; and to humanize school discipline. In the course of the campaign it was realized that the training of boys destined for commerce and retail trade should be different from that given to boys who were intending to enter one or other of the learned professions. The spectacle of an intending shopkeeper loading his memory with the *Thesaurus* of Gruterus or Gronovius, while his mind was untinged with mathematics, geography, or elementary science, was familiar and afflicting, but it was not until the middle of the century that anything was done towards remedying the evil. In 1747 Hecker founded at Berlin the first *Realschule*, or modern school, in Germany, for the purpose of instructing boys not destined for the learned professions. A *Realschule* was founded at Brunswick in 1754, and at Helmstadt in 1755, and an active educationalist, E. Trapp, professor of pedagogy at Halle from 1779 to 1783, and then in the Ministry of Education at Brunswick from 1786 to 1790, threw himself into the movement, decrying the acquisition of languages as a medium of education.

The starting of these modern schools was not only a benefit to the class which frequented them, but it was a necessary condition for the advance of the public classical schools. In whatever town there was a *Realschule*, there the *Gelehrte Schule* was only frequented by boys for whom a good classical education was a real necessity. The growth of these modern schools was, however, slow, and the educational dualism which now obtains so completely in Germany was far from being fully developed by the end of the eighteenth century. All that can be said is that the main lines were sketched out.

The enlarged conception of classical studies acted, of course, most directly upon the classical schools. In 1736 Ernesti had passed a severe condemnation upon the system of teaching the dead languages which then prevailed, when the ancient languages were studied as providing a museum of elegant phrases and flowers of speech, and it was more important to chatter about Salmasius and Casaubon than to realize the beauties of Homer and Virgil. The *Thesaurus* had taken the place of the text, and to the *Thesaurus* was added the commentary. It was a revelation when Gesner, in 1737, laid down the thesis that the value of the ancient authors was that they trained taste and literary insight, and that the object of a classical education was not linguistic mimicry, but a good general knowledge of antiquity, of its poetry and art, its eloquence and pathos, its thoughts and manners. The great classical scholars of a later generation diffused this liberal spirit not merely through the universities, but also through many of the schools in the region which surrounded them. They trained the masters, they wrote the textbooks and commentaries, they were consulted by town councils as to the choice of teachers, in many cases they were invited to superintend or reorganize particular schools. The land-school at Ilfeld and the gymnasium at Göttingen were chiefly controlled by Heyne himself, and the correspondence of the greatest of European scholars is full of solicitude about the smallest details of scholastic administration [1].

It may be asked whether under the circumstances Germany in general or the Kingdom of Westphalia in particular had anything to gain educationally from the French conquest. The two great *desiderata* of the universities were liberation from State control and more ample endowments. The Napoleonic régime was favourable neither to the one nor to the other of these requirements. If the governments of Hanover and Hesse chastised their professors with whips, it might be expected that the government of Napoleon would chastise them with scorpions. What educational liberty, or *Lehrfreiheit*, had been left to the University of France? What chance was there that the liberty accorded to Germany would be more extensive? In everything which pertained to the substance and method of university education, Germany was now far superior to France. In France the revolution which paralysed education had been

---

[1] Paulsen, *Geschichte des gelehrten Unterrichts auf den deutschen Schulen und Universitäten.*

succeeded by the Empire which paralysed thought. In Germany a new literature, a new philosophy, a new humanism, a new pedagogy had been the product of a generation. In France there was no divinity, no philosophy, no Greek, no political science. There was only Chateaubriand, Barante, and the *Moniteur*. In Germany there were all the kings of European scholarship and thought.

It must, however, be admitted that while the intellectual atmosphere of Germany was charged with novelty, the political conditions were unfavourable to any very rapid or concerted improvement. A vigorous university like Göttingen, which had become the greatest school in Europe, not only for classical antiquity but for legal, political, and economical studies, was a bright centre of light, but its rays did not penetrate everywhere. The public schools were controlled by the municipal authorities, and municipal authorities are often impervious to the higher culture. In the south of Germany little progress had as yet been made in scholastic reform, and, as happens in a country broken up into small political units, there was not only the greatest inequality in educational advance, but also an excessive number of old and unflourishing institutions. The most, therefore, that might be expected from the French, was that with their genius for administration and their sense of symmetry, they might level inequalities, concentrate endowments, and introduce some uniform scheme both of popular and of technical education. So might the dislocation caused by war and conquest have been balanced by some tangible good.

The Kingdom of Westphalia contained no fewer than five universities, Göttingen, Halle, Marburg, Helmstadt, and Rinteln; the first two famous, the third respectable, while the fourth and fifth were small and unimportant. Of these learned bodies, Halle had invited the wrath of Napoleon during the Prussian war of 1806, and had seen its lecture-halls closed and its students dispersed. Specially designed as it was for the training of Prussian civil servants, the University suffered severely in popularity by its incorporation in the Westphalian kingdom; and when its activity was renewed by permission of the Emperor in May, 1808, it was found that the attendance of students had shrunk to a fourth of its accustomed figure[1].

[1] Steffens, *Was ich erlebte*.

The King was inclined to manifest an interest in bodies which reflected so much distinction on his State. He visited Göttingen five times, gave 200,000 francs to the observatory, and presented the University with some astronomical instruments which had been of service to him during his cruises at sea, and which he naïvely assumed would be of equal value to the pupils of Gauss and of Mayer. The servile *Moniteur* remarks upon the occasion of the first visit that the young King carefully questioned the professors as to the course of their studies; but a less trammelled observer informs us that his curiosity was limited to a bread-tree, and his admiration to an equestrian performance in the riding-school. It was, however, a good augury for Westphalian education that the first Minister of Public Instruction should have been Johann von Müller, one of the best-known and best-liked men among the *savants* of Germany. Nobody could have been better fitted from his accurate acquaintance with the university system, his high ideal of knowledge, and his zeal for education, to superintend the work of his department. His successor—for he died in 1809—Baron von Leist, was less distinguished but highly competent, having done brilliantly as a youth at Göttingen, in which university he had been promoted to a chair of law. But his character was marked by two grave defects: servility to those in power, and a lively appetite for the adulation of his inferiors.

In a letter to Goethe the French minister describes von Müller as occupied in 'protecting his universities as the hen does her chicks, while the greedy falcon of finance swims in the air.' It was, indeed, from the first inevitable that the falcon would make a swoop upon a prey which was at once helpless and inviting. On March 28, 1809, von Müller received a letter from the King announcing his intention to suppress the Universities of Marburg, Rinteln, and Helmstadt, together with several schools. The minister pleaded hard for the condemned institutions. They brought money into the country; their suppression would scarcely add 600,000 francs to the treasury, a sum less than the cost of furnishing a palace; they had been famous in the past, they were useful in the present, and Marburg was not only the sole university of the Reformed Church in Westphalia, but upon the advent of the King had obtained a formal promise that its foundation should be respected [1]. The shock of the unequal controversy is said to have cost von Müller his life, but his worst fears were not realized, for owing to the intervention of Baron von Berlepsch, the prefect of the department, the *Philippina* of Marburg was rescued from destruction. By a decree of December 10, 1809, the Universities of Helmstadt and Rinteln, and the schools of Klosterbergen and Riddagshausen, were abolished and their revenues transferred to the Universities of Göttingen, Marburg, and Halle. Though the complaints of the antiquaries filled the air, there was much to be said for the concentration of endowments. The revenues of the Westphalian universities had never been large or evenly distributed, and they were now greatly diminished by the confiscation of half the domains of the kingdom to the Napoleonic dotations [2]. It was better that three universities should flourish than that five should starve, and the determination of the government, arrived at in 1810, to pay the professors from the State chest, and to subsidize the university institutions from an educational fund (*Studienfonds*) formed from the endowments of Marburg, Helmstadt, Rinteln, Klosterbergen, and Ilfeld, was a step in the right direction. But the gains accruing from the concentration of endowments, the absorption of monastic libraries, and the more exact adjustment of revenue to needs, were outweighed by serious financial losses. Half the revenue of Göttingen had been derived from lands which were now appropriated by Napoleon. It became increasingly difficult for the government to collect the revenues which supplied the *Studienfonds*, and the remittances of the State to professors and institutions were apt to be tardy, irregular, and insufficient. In 1813 the financial credit of the University of Göttingen was such, that the bakers refused to supply bread and the butchers refused to supply meat to the hospital. There was the same tale of destitution in Halle, where the students, being almost entirely composed of poor country folk, could pay no fees, and the professors were

---

[1] *Mémoires du roi Jérôme*, iii. 334-8.

[2] It is worth noting that Marburg with under 200 students was richer than Göttingen with 700 (Müller, *Aus sturmvoller Zeit*, 168).

remunerated in government paper which no tradesman would accept[1].

Placed under the authority of the prefect of the department, the universities were required to submit their programmes to the Minister of Instruction, and it was expected that in these documents laudations of the King should hold a place. The university jurisdiction was summarily abolished, and the aged Heyne, the *doyen* of Göttingen, watched with anguish the uncorrected youth swaggering off with rapiers at their sides to the five duelling-grounds, under the very eyes of the impotent beadles and professors. The students of the University were forbidden to wear moustaches, as well as caps of a certain shape and colour, which were regarded as emblems of their clubs or societies. They avenged themselves by wearing women's bonnets and straw hats, and by sending their shorn moustaches to the pro-rector. 'It is said,' writes Reinhard, who reports these circumstances, 'that 400 students from other countries have sworn to leave Göttingen at the end of the next term, and to go to Heidelberg[2].'

Heyne, whose correspondence with von Müller throws a curious light upon the history of his University, says that the zeal for theology and philosophy was declining, because it was felt that these studies were no longer of practical use. Every year the dreadful conscription days levied their toll of victims and emptied the lecture-halls. The new police pried into everything, censured the lecture-lists and the *Gelehrte Anzeigen*, the learned organ of the Georgia Augusta University. The mayor said that nothing could be printed without the consent of the *Oberpolizei-Inspector*, and meanwhile the government had actually made a monopoly of the printing and sale of the official German translation of the Code Napoléon. 'If the schools are to be dependent on the prefects, then I give up all hope that anything will come of it.' It was not, however, the

---

[1] A petition of the pro-rectors and professors of Göttingen (April 29, 1808) states that 130,000 francs, or half the university revenue, was derived from ten bailiwicks of monastic or conventual land now annexed by the State (*Affaires étrangères, Corr. Pol.: Westphalie*, 2). Thimme (ii. 298 ff.) depicts the financial anxieties of Göttingen, and Steffens (*Was ich erlebte*) the sorrows of Halle.

[2] *Revue Historique*, xvii. 340, 5.

prefect who was the foe of university education in Westphalia, but crippled finances and the blighting political suspicion which suppressed all liberty of association and all freedom of speech. 'I will burn the town of Halle,' cried Jerome, in 1809, after the episode of Schill. 'I don't want savants; I want ignoramuses and soldiers[1].'

There was no general reorganization of the Westphalian schools, but there were several draft schemes. A single high school for each department, an educational council of laymen and ecclesiastics in each departmental capital—these projects were ventilated and laid aside, probably because they were found to involve expense. There was a plan for the organization of mathematical instruction in the higher schools, and for a mathematical seminary at Göttingen. Something also was accomplished. The whole educational system was placed under the immediate control of the sub-prefects and prefects, and under the ultimate control of the Director-General of Education, and a new mode was devised for the appointment of elementary teachers. A *lycée* and a burgher school were established at Cassel, and it must be remembered to the credit of the administration that no undue attempt was made to force French down the throats of the people[2]. One prefect was foolish enough to think that the French codes would extinguish legal studies, and that the liberated energies of Germany should be devoted to agriculture, mining, and commercial education. On the whole, the French bias was in favour of practical and technical studies. Since the cavalry must have sound horses, lectures on the veterinary art were introduced into the curriculum at Göttingen. The revenues of the Harz Mountains were meagre, but they might be increased by skill, and a course on mining was added to the university programmes. A theoretical and practical school of forestry was decreed in 1811, but never came into existence. A new faculty for French

---

[1] The correspondence of Hövel, the prefect of Göttingen, with von Müller, throws a favourable light on the zeal and intelligence of the local official (Thimme, ii. 296). The remark of Jerome has been reported by Reinhard. *Affaires étrangères, Corr. Pol.: Westphalie*, 3.

[2] Two hours a day were allotted to French in the State schools, a fair but not tyrannical allowance (F. Müller, *Kassel seit 70 Jahren*, i. 42).

literature was founded at Göttingen. In the matter of the fine arts, music excepted, the French were superior to the Germans, and the light comedies which were the joy of Jerome may have refined, though they could not elevate, the public taste of the playgoers at Cassel [1].

But there was unconscious humour in the suggestion that an Academy of Arts should be founded in the Westphalian capital, seeing that it had been robbed of all its masterpieces of painting and statuary by the French, and that its museum was converted into a chamber of deputies. Of the 299 pictures which were taken from the Electoral picture-galleries to adorn the walls of the Louvre or Malmaison, 244 were recovered at the Second Restoration, but there were some irreparable losses, and the 'Caritas' of Leonardo da Vinci, which had been the jewel of the *Fredericianum*, has never been seen since it was stolen by Denon in 1807 [2].

[1] It is to Jerome's credit that he attempted to allure Beethoven from Vienna to Cassel (Thayer, *Beethoven*, iii. 67).

[2] Volkel's *Erinnerungen* (*Zeitschrift des Vereins für Hessische Geschichte und Landeskunde*, Neue Folge, ix. 249 ff.).

CHAPTER XIII

THE RUIN OF WESTPHALIA

' En m'apprenant que votre administration est mauvaise, vous ne m'apprenez rien de nouveau.'—NAPOLEON TO JEROME, Dec. 10, 1811.

THE commerce of the region now known as the Kingdom of Westphalia had been stifled by innumerable tolls and customs barriers, and by 'an immense catalogue of enormous contradictory and arbitrary duties upon almost all the products of nature and art.' While the law was various, antiquated, and dilatory, the fiscal resources of the vanished governments were limited by noble and ecclesiastical exemptions, by financial ignorance and fraud. In the old Prussian provinces so complicated was the tariff, and so prevalent was dishonesty, that only one-tenth of the estimated revenue was realized upon the principal items. While the excise was administered on four separate systems in the Prussian provinces, each of these systems was totally different from that which was adopted in Hanover[1]. Every little fraction had, in fact, its own fiscal system, and all systems were bad, being characterized by three great vices—the exemption of the rich, impediments to transit, and a large number of irritating duties upon commodities. All the governments had been forced, partly owing to the exemptions of the nobles, and partly owing to the action of the provincial Estates, to eschew taxation, and the revenue was mainly raised from taxes upon commodities and from the yield of the domains. But though the fiscal system was confused and vicious, there is no reason to think that it was oppressive. It was acknowledged by the ministers of the new monarchy that the government of Brunswick had been wise, moderate, and economical, that the rule in Hanover was mild

[1] Circulaire du Ministre des Finances à MM. les Préfets, *Moniteur Westphalien*, ii. 317.

and paternal, albeit somewhat improvident, and that the strictest economy had been practised in the Electorate of Hesse.

There is no reason to suppose that there was any active discontent with the form of government in any of the small provinces and principalities which were welded together into the Kingdom of Westphalia. But if government was not an irritant, it was an incubus. Industry was undeveloped, transport slow and costly, and there was a general lack of accumulated capital and of commercial activity. A Dutch observer, General Dedem de Gelder, remarked that in Hesse nobody worked. The great men were idlers living on pensions, the people privileged beggars. There was no instruction, no art, no trade, and the primary necessities of life, not to speak of the luxuries, were imported from abroad. There was, no doubt, more stir in the Departments of the Ocker, the Elbe, and the Saale, provinces which had been to a certain extent affected by the enlightenment which proceeded from Brunswick and Berlin, but it was symptomatic of the whole area that no less than one-eighth of its total revenue was paid away in small pensions to persons who regarded a pension as a dispensation from activity. In his opening address to the Estates (July 2, 1808), King Jerome professed that 'his efforts would constantly tend to divert the spirit of the nation from its tendency to live upon prebends and salaries [1].'

The government of Jerome displayed for the first time in Germany the leading principles of enlightened finance. A few light taxes were imposed upon articles of general consumption, such as meat, corn, beer, brandy, and tobacco, and all taxes upon luxuries, which were both expensive to collect and unprofitable when collected, disappeared from the budget [2]. Internal communications were freed from the burden of toll and duty. Some 10,000,000 francs were raised from a land-tax, which was not an inequitable sum, considering that the chief wealth of the kingdom lay in agriculture. A patent tax

---

[1] *Moniteur Westphalien,* i. 341.

[2] There were no less than 1,682 articles on the Prussian excise tariff of 1804. On the Westphalian tariff of 1808 there were ten articles; on that of 1810, twelve articles; cf. Hassel und Murhard, *Westfalen unter Hieronymus Napoleon.*

upon industries, light, easy of control, and far from inquisitorial, involved the principle that every man was free to enter any industry or trade. Drawbacks upon the re-exportation of alien articles taxed upon the frontier, and upon the exportation of home-made beer and brandy, encouraged alike native industries and foreign importation. Raw materials and all articles which paid internal consumption duties were admitted into the kingdom free, while foreign manufactured articles were liable to a duty of six per cent., an amount which may safely be described as having been dictated by fiscal rather than by protective aims. Indeed, save in the case of iron and copper, which were safeguarded by especially heavy duties, there seems no indication of a desire upon the part of the Westphalian financiers to protect home industries at the expense of home consumption. The import of salt—a government monopoly—and of English wines was prohibited, the latter prohibition in pursuance of Napoleon's command, but otherwise import and export were left entirely free from those barbarous restrictions which had defaced the earlier tariffs. The introduction of personal taxes into a country which has no experience of them is always attended with difficulty, and the Westphalian financiers were somewhat unfortunate in their experiments in this direction. In 1808 they proposed to raise 4,000,000 francs by a tax assessed upon the household, and varying from fifty francs to sixty centimes according to the ascertained size and assumed prosperity of that unit. But great complaints were made that the tax bore too lightly upon the wealthier classes, and substantial deficits in 1808 and 1809 attested the difficulty of collecting it. Accordingly in the autumn of 1809 a commission was appointed to investigate, and a short time afterwards it submitted a plan for a new tax to the financial committee of the Estates. There were long debates, and the resistance was so stubborn that the ministers were forced to withdraw their plan, and to enact it by decree on March 15, 1810. A graduated poll-tax and a two per cent. income-tax upon incomes over 1,000 francs was now introduced, only to meet with the same criticism as its predecessor. It is probable enough that the system of classification adopted (for the purposes of graduation the population of the kingdom was divided into ten classes) showed, as was alleged, great local ignorance, and that both poll-tax and income-tax bore too heavily on the poor. But in its principle and design the tax was reasonable enough, and the mistake of the Westphalian financiers was not that they contemplated the taxation of personalty, but that they approached the tax with insufficient knowledge of detail. The result was felt to be unsatisfactory, and on January 12, 1811, the income-tax was abolished while the poll-tax was increased. The profits from the mines, the domains, the forests, and the salt works, a State lottery, a somewhat burdensome stamp-tax, a tithe of the revenues of prebends, abbeys, convents, and priories, formed other items of the Westphalian budget. It was provided that a sum of 4,500,000 francs annually should be devoted to the service of the debt, and the strictest arrangements were enforced for the collection, the expenditure, and the audit of the revenue. 'A single central administration,' wrote von Bülow in 1808, 'sets all forces in motion, a single hierarchical order is everywhere introduced, principles congenial to the constitution serve as the basis of all rules, clear instructions suitable to the localities define every detail of the service, and it only requires a short period of rest and peace to bring this administration, emulous of its great prototype, to a height from which it would have no cause to shun comparison.'

We do not contend that the system was perfect. The expenses of collecting the consumption taxes came to $13\frac{3}{4}$ per cent. of the total, 10 per cent. too much. The salt monopoly encouraged smuggling, the million gained by the stamp-tax was not worth the trouble which it cost to collect, the charges assigned to the departmental and communal exchequers were probably too high; there were widely distributed complaints as to the assessment of the personal tax. But, compared with the previous financial systems which had maintained in these parts of Germany, a Westphalian budget was a model of wise and lucid statesmanship. There were no exemptions, no privileges; there was no obscurity or complexity, no sinister respect for vested interests. The rubble of feudalism, of local tradition, had been swept away, and a new building equipped with all the modern appliances for bright lighting rose from the ground.

With a good system of finance, a zealous and well-directed

administrative class, and a sound though somewhat autocratic constitution, the Kingdom of Westphalia possessed many elements of success. But it was confronted by two deadly enemies, Jerome its king, and Napoleon its creator. The selection of Jerome to rule Westphalia is one of the many instances in which Napoleon's family pride and affection overpowered his political judgement. No one was more thoroughly aware of that young man's foibles than the elder brother, who instructed Ganteaume to keep a tight hand upon him at sea, and Fouché to dog his movements on land. But he reflected that responsibility might harden a character as yet fluid and unformed, and, with a distrust as genuine as his affection, arranged for a supply of secret information as to the doings and sayings of the King. During the first few months Jerome appeared to justify the favourable expectations of the Emperor. Everybody, Grimm, Strombeck, Wolffradt, was charmed by the young man's obvious amiability. The ministers and Councillors of State reported that his apprehension was quick, and that he had a peculiar capacity for summarizing discussions, and as he toured through the country to make the acquaintance of his new subjects, his frank and popular bearing was warmly appreciated. But power developed rather than repressed the weaker elements of his character. 'Counsels,' said d'Albignac in 1809, 'the King receives from no one; he is the most absolute man of my acquaintance [1].' Siméon and Eblé agreed that though his desires often changed, they were always the desires of a despot. 'The Emperor likes one to have character,' he would say, and 'character' for him was equivalent to self-will. Thus his decisions at the Council of State, instead of being based upon the opinions submitted to him, were the result of 'chance inspiration [2].' To these disqualifications of self-will and impetuosity he added that of a prodigal taste for display and dissipation. We need not believe all the stories which are told in the *Secret History of Westphalia* and in other scandalous chronicles. To Jerome's credit be it said that he managed to retain to the end the affections of his shy but amiable wife. But that the Court was both licentious and wildly extravagant is one of the best-attested facts in history. The Civil List was

[1] *Revue Historique*, xvii. 331.   [2] Ibid. 335.

THE RUIN OF WESTPHALIA

fixed at 5,000,000 francs, a huge sum in comparison with the total Westphalian revenue, but the King regularly exceeded it by at least 2,000,000. Parties, suppers, masked balls, illuminations, royal progresses, equestrian statues, costly private theatricals account for much. Huge sums were sunk in building and in the purchase of estates. The gardens of Napoleonshöhe were transformed, the castle restored and refurnished, while the amenities of the park were increased by aqueducts and temples, pavilions and pagodas, fountains and grottoes. The Queen on her birthday received a house and garden at the gate of Cassel, with silver plate, and 50,000 francs for the furniture. A new hall was built to house the Estates, since the Orangerie was deemed inadequate. Nor did Jerome take the slightest pains to get value for the money so lavishly expended. 'The King, having lately breakfasted with a banker named Jordis, said to the gardener, as he went out, "This house belongs to me." The bargain was concluded for 30,000 thalers. It had cost M. Jordis 3,000; the improvements are estimated at 5,000 [1].' Public functions, private theatricals, and fancy-dress balls in constant succession swelled the account. The costumes must come from Paris, and as it was the King's chief pleasure to emulate the feats of the quick-change artist—to appear, for instance, in the course of one evening ' as a draper, a sailor, an elegant chimney-sweep, and a Savoyard '—the bills of the tailor and the milliner were a serious item in the budget [2]. Add to this the royal gifts, for as the King once explained to his ministers, he saw nothing in royalty save the pleasure of giving; to the favourite ladies diamonds and pearls, to the favourite men titles and estates, to the generals horses, to the chamberlains carriages, to all and every one who might come his way twenty-five Jeromes [3]. As if this munificence were not enough, he created the Order of the Crown of Westphalia at the annual cost of 300,000 francs, charged on the Abbey of Quedlinburg. So fast did the gold fly that by 1809 he had not only pillaged the public treasury of 2,000,000 francs in defiance of the constitution, but he had run up a debt on his own account which probably exceeded 10,000,000. No wonder

---

[1] *Revue Historique*, xvii. 339.
[2] Fulda und Hoffmeister, *Hessische Zeiten und Persönlichkeiten*, 139.
[3] *Mémoires du roi Jérôme*, v. 189-94.

that his ministers were in despair. One of the Councillors of State told the French ambassador that if by doubling the Civil List one could establish the certainty that the expenditure would be perfectly regular, and the King interested in the finances of the State, it would be a most advantageous bargain for Westphalia.

Profligate expenditure and autocratic ways do not accord with constitutional government, and after its first meeting the Reichstag was only once again summoned in January 1810. But though the pomp of the earlier assembly was increased, there was an air of unreality about the proceedings. The deputies were summoned for January 7, but it was Carnival, and business must be postponed till the round of balls and festivals had been completed, and though every member drew twenty francs a day during attendance, the opening was actually deferred for three weeks, a gratuitous waste of over 16,000 francs. The interest of the occasion in reality centred round the new hall and the new costume of the legislators, a blue coat embroidered with orange silk, a white silk scarf, a blue silk mantle lined with white, and a black samite toque adorned with ostrich feathers. 'The Reichstag is only a comedy,' said the Minister of Finance with brutal frankness to a member, and the remark was confirmed by the fact that its decisions had been for the most part anticipated by the convenient method of provisional decree. Of the many measures submitted by the government during a session of seven weeks, one only—a bill for a stamp-tax—was rejected, and that by the narrow majority of six voices. All the hopes of 1808 had vanished; there was a general feeling that the kingdom was doomed, and that annexation to France was at hand[1].

For this general depression Napoleon was even more responsible than his brother. No one indeed saw with greater penetration the needs of these German provinces or the benefits which French rule could bestow upon them. From the Emperor's letters to Jerome it would be possible to compose

---

[1] Hassel und Murhard, *Westfalen unter Hieronymus Napoleon*; *Minerva*, ii. 55; Strombeck, *Darstellungen*, ii. 74 ff. The government with some dexterity threw its driest bones to the legislature—the five last books of the Code of Civil Procedure, which had already been enacted by provisional decree.

a *florilegium* of excellent advice suitable for the consumption of a young man called upon to rule a small State. He must be strictly economical; he must not try to emulate the pomp of wealthy rulers; he must surround himself with the best talents; he must cultivate the middle classes, and adapt himself to the simple manners of a simple people; he must not give rewards which are disproportionate to merits; he must acquire a knowledge of military tactics, and of judicial and financial administration, and when war breaks out he must serve 'like a young soldier who has need of glory and reputation.' In a single sentence written December 10, 1811, Napoleon expressed the final criticism on his brother's policy: 'The King raises too many troops, spends too much, and too often changes his principles of administration.' Nor has any more complete judgement been passed upon Jerome's character than the following: 'You have many pretensions, some wits, some good qualities, but spoilt by fatuity, by an extreme presumption, and you have no knowledge of things [1].'

Yet in spite of all this penetration Napoleon ruined Westphalia, treating the kingdom as a mere financial and military asset in his great game of politics. On April 22, 1808, a treaty was signed at Berlin by Malchus on behalf of the Westphalian, and by Daru on behalf of the imperial government, for the purpose of adjusting the financial claims of the French Empire and its German satellite. It was essentially one of those occasions on which generosity is the highest wisdom. These provinces were poor, and their resources had been drained by a military occupation extending over a year; they were now to be governed by a French prince, upon French principles, and in alliance with the French Empire. If the new connection was to be made acceptable to the inhabitants, it was of primary necessity that taxation should be light, and that the injuries to historic sentiment should be healed, so far as such injuries ever can be healed, by an increase in material affluence. This, however, was not the policy of Napoleon, or the spirit of the Treaty of Berlin. By that arrangement every penny was wrung from the Kingdom of Westphalia which the French Empire could claim upon any pretext, good or indifferent; the greater

[1] Lecestre, *Lettres inédites*, 217-8, 282, 307, 327-8.

portion of the debts of the ex-Elector of Hesse, amounting to a credit of some 20,000,000 or 30,000,000 francs; domains to the value of 7,000,000 francs, or, in other words, half of the domainial revenue of the kingdom; and a war contribution fixed at 26,000,000 francs, to be paid in eighteen months dating from May 1, 1808. Lastly, the Emperor refused to be responsible for the charges, amounting to 8,000,000 francs, which had been incurred during the military occupation of 1807. Nor do these provisions exhaust the full significance of the transaction, for the reserved domains were exempted from public burdens, and, being cultivated for the benefit of absentee French landlords, were often administered in a slovenly and corrupt manner [1].

Turn where they might, the financiers of the new kingdom could not make the deficit on the first year less than 40,000,000 francs. The Empire required Westphalia to maintain a French force of 12,500, and a Westphalian force of equal number. The estimated expenditure, therefore, was not lower than 35,000,000, and to this must be added the arrears of 1807 (8,000,000), and the first instalment of the war contribution, 20,000,000. In other words, a debt of 60,000,000 or 70,000,000 francs, a revenue of 20,000,000 or 30,000,000. From the very beginning, therefore, the government was driven to resort to all manner of expedients. The Jews of Cassel lent 1,800,000 francs; a forced loan of 20,000,000 was issued, but only half covered, despite flatteries and menaces, and all the influence which the government could bring to bear. It was in vain that Jerome appealed to the Emperor, that he represented the misery of the population, and the utter ruin which faced the country, if the Treaty of Berlin were to continue in force [2]. Napoleon replied with flouts and jeers. 'I was for two years in France without

---

[1] On the calculation of Malchus the reserved domains, after the incorporation of Hanover, involved an annual loss to the State of two millions in addition to their annual value (F. von Specht, *Das Königreich Westphalen*, 27). The maladministration of the reserved domains is depicted in *Neue Fakkeln*, iii. 35 ff.

[2] '*L'audience que le roi a donnée à M. le Fèvre avant son départ avait pour objet de le charger de me dire et même de déclarer à Votre Majesté . . . qu'il étoit impossible que le royaume de Westphalie pût aller encore plus de deux mois et demi.*'—Champagny to Napoleon, Aug. 19, 1809; *A. F.* iv. 1706 b. Cf. *Revue Historique*, xvii. 346.

finances. The King of Naples is hardly beginning to regularize his. In Italy I was so for six years.' Or else he rebuked Jerome for his luxury—a theme which Jerome's conduct pressingly invited, and to which the Emperor returned again and again.

Yet in the end the resistance of the impoverished debtor led to a relaxation of the monstrous Treaty of Berlin. By the treaty of January 14, 1810, which ceded Hanover to Westphalia, the war contribution was reduced to 16,000,000 francs, to be paid in ten annual instalments. But although this was a great alleviation, the gift of Hanover was accompanied by conditions which rendered it an additional burden to the recipient. Napoleon reserved to himself a revenue of 4,559,000 francs, free of taxes, for ten years from the domains of Hanover. Six of the dotations instituted by the Emperor in the Kingdom of Westphalia, and representing a revenue of 145,000 francs, had been retained by Jerome. The French donees were now to be placed in possession. The Hanoverian debt was to be taken over by Westphalia. The contingent of the Kingdom of Westphalia was fixed at 26,000 men, of whom 4,000 were to be cavalry and 2,000 artillery, and until the end of the maritime war Westphalia pledged herself to keep up 6,000 French troops over and above the 12,500 which she had promised to maintain by Article 5 of the constitution. Of these 18,500 men 6,000 were to be cavalry.

It was calculated that the Emperor, by reserving to himself practically all the Hanoverian domains, would leave the kingdom an annual deficit of 2,000,000 francs on the Hanoverian account. This deficit, indeed, could perhaps in time of peace have been made good by improved administration, but the burden of maintaining 18,500 Frenchmen in addition to the Westphalian army was quite crushing. Reinhard says that it was calculated that Hanover would cost 10,000,000 francs more than it would bring in [1]. As it was, the cost of the 12,500 French troops, which amounted to 10,000,000 francs, had never been met by any regular financial expedients. The item did not occur in the

---

[1] According to Malchus, what with the reserved domains, the Civil List, and the army, there would be left 1,500,000 francs wherewith to defray the expenses of Hanoverian administration and to meet the service of the debt; cf. von Specht, 29.

budget. It was met by hand to mouth expedients; by the sale of national goods and the secularization of ecclesiastical lands; by loans contracted at usurious rates; by the suspension of payments due to State creditors. It was now proposed to increase the item already covered with such difficulty and ignominy by a half. No wonder that when the terms of the treaty reached Cassel they aroused grave disappointment. It was only by desperate measures that the French troops received their pay as it was, and in August complaints reached the Emperor that the pay was in arrears. His letters during September 1810 are full of complaints: the King was wasting money recklessly over a camp at Cassel; he was disturbing Europe by his preparations for war; his administration was conniving at the importation of English wares; he was making himself ridiculous by awarding grand titles to his friends. Jerome, on the other hand, complained that his country was treated more severely than a hostile State; that French troops were moved about; that requisitions were levied by the sole order of the Prince of Eckmuhl; in fact, that he was no longer ruler of his own kingdom.

Meanwhile, negotiators were disputing as to the terms of the formal deed of cession. It was not till March 11, 1811, that the deed was signed, and then the Emperor refused to ratify, and in the correspondence which followed the King raised again the two main questions of the troops and the domains. An additional degree of acrimony was imported into the negotiations by an event which occurred in December 1810. The Court of Westphalia suddenly learnt that the northern part of Hanover, and almost the whole of the Department of the Weser, had been incorporated in the French Empire. Jerome was told that he had not executed the stipulations of the treaty relative to the cession of Hanover, and that the Emperor was consequently free to discard it. This was a mere pretext. The spoliation of Westphalia was part of the policy of the continental blockade, as Champagny in a letter to Reinhard (December 14, 1810) clearly showed, writing thus: 'The annexation of the Hanseatic towns necessitates the union of those parts of Hanover and Westphalia which may contribute to render the territory of those towns contiguous to the Empire.' The King was forced to acquiesce in a decree which deprived him

THE RUIN OF WESTPHALIA 299

not only of half his recent acquisitions, but of the richest department of his original kingdom. It was in vain that he pleaded for territorial compensations in the direction of the Rhine. The imperial authorities held that Hanover had never belonged to Westphalia, and consequently that in offering Jerome the southern part of the Electorate, they were giving him compensation for the loss of the Weser department. In the treaty of May 10, 1811, it was stated that the King of Westphalia *ceded* to France that part of the Department of the Weser which had been already annexed by the *Senatusconsult* of December 13, while a portion of Hanover, situated south of a line determined in that document, was to be incorporated in the kingdom. The French troops at the charge of the Westphalian exchequer were reduced to their old number, and the Emperor renounced his claim for arrears due from the districts of Hanover which Jerome was forced to disgorge.

On the whole the Hanoverian incident, though humiliating enough, brought some relief to Westphalian finance, for in the end the military burden was not increased, while the debt to France was reduced by 10,000,000 francs. But that Napoleon had any sympathy with the embarrassments of the exchequer at Cassel is negatived by all that we know of these transactions. He thought Westphalia a fair prey, and he was determined to exact the uttermost farthing. It was only the farthings he could not exact that he consented openly to remit.

It must be avowed that Jerome was not morally in a position to plead for favours. The Emperor naturally enough retorted to his extravagant brother that the remedy was in his own hands, and that kings who outstep a liberal Civil List have no claim to consideration. What indeed was the use of a Westphalian minister at St. Petersburg with a salary of 80,000 francs, and a Westphalian minister at Paris with a salary of 100,000 francs, when from the nature of the case Westphalia could have no foreign policy? Why create an expensive knightly order, when even the officials of the State did not receive their pay regularly? Why these buildings and balls, these lavish gifts to favourites, and extravagant costumes? There was no possible apology forthcoming. An economical Court might have lived upon 3,000,000 francs a year, which would have represented a sum less by 24,000,000 to 30,000,000 than that expended on King Jerome's frivolities.

But the main item in the Westphalian expenditure was not the Court but the army. The contingent of the kingdom, as we have seen, had been fixed in the first instance at 25,000 men, half of whom were to be provisionally composed of French troops. Conscription was declared to be a fundamental law, and it was made illegal to hire substitutes. In itself the size of the army was not abnormal for these regions, for in the Electorate of Hesse alone, which was only a part of the Westphalian kingdom, there used to be a standing army of 33,000 men. This army, however, so far from being a burden upon the exchequer, was a considerable financial asset, for it was hired out to foreign powers at a remunerative rate. Further, when the Hessian soldier returned from the wars in which he had contributed to swell the pecuniary receipts of his monarch, he was not kept in expensive barracks, or collected into expensive camps, or made to take part in expensive manœuvres; he quietly reverted to his plough and his family. Thus, from the financial point of view, the military demands of Napoleon constituted an innovation. The Westphalian contingent would, in any case, be far more expensive than all the added military establishments of Hesse and of Hanover, of the Prussian provinces and of Brunswick. It might, therefore, have been expected that the military forces at the charges of the State would have been strictly limited to its treaty obligations. This, however, was not the case. If Jerome could be said to entertain a respectable passion, it was to win military glory, and to see something of '*la grande guerre*.' All through the Silesian campaign he kept complaining to his brother that he was removed from the theatre of great events, and his first thought upon obtaining a kingdom was to raise as large an army as he could. His contract to France only required him to raise 12,500 men: the figure eventually was almost tripled. If he had insisted that for every additional Westphalian over and above the stipulated number a French soldier should leave the country, or that some portion of the war tribute should be remitted, there would have been a justification for thus swelling the numbers of the Westphalian army. But Jerome actually took pride in outstepping his strict obligations, and pressure from Napoleon coincided with his ambitions [1]. 'Instead of the 20,000 men,' wrote the Emperor, January 30, 1808, 'have 40,000; you can manage it.' A year later (January 15, 1809) a demand equally urgent, though less exorbitant, comes from Valladolid: 'Your contingent ought to be 25,000 men; it is very important to complete it. You know that if the war were carried into your territory, and you suffered a reverse, the consequences would be serious to your kingdom.' On February 7, Jerome is advised to diminish his luxury, to economize part of his Civil List, so as to increase his military establishment. Writing from Paris a month later the Emperor says: 'Reinforce your troops as much as possible, that you may be able to maintain order at home, to repress an insurrection in Hanover, and even, if you have a respectable corps, to go where circumstances may demand. If you can form a corps of 10,000 men and of 1,500 horse with twelve pieces of artillery, you may make yourself talked about all the more gloriously, from the fact that you will be acting with your own troops. But you must not raise too many corps, for I do not know how far one can trust your soldiers. . . . Send me every five days a report on your troops made in the subjoined form. Take care to put the number of companies and battalions per regiment;' and again, on April 9: 'You ought to have 14,000 men of your own troops, and to reinforce your army as much as possible.' In the army bulletin of 1809, the fact is recognized that the Westphalian contingent amounts to 15,000 [2].

So far the Emperor had persistently encouraged the increase of the Westphalian contingent, while urging that it should be formed slowly. But in September 1810 he takes up another tone. There was peace in Germany, and yet it was announced to Napoleon that the pay of the French troops was three months in arrear. At the same time the negotiations with regard to the incorporation of Hanover were causing friction between the two brothers. Napoleon wrote with some irritation: 'I have recommended you to form your contingent gradually

---

[1] *Mémoires du roi Jérôme*, v. 110.
[2] *Corr.* xvi. 297, no. 13,512; xviii. 228, no. 14,718; 256, no. 14,764; 349, no. 14,865; 455, no. 15,042.

and by degrees as your monarchy organizes itself. Of all the allied troops yours are those whom I am bound to distrust most. . . . If I were to count on the 30,000 men you may have as being 30,000, I should be much deceived. . . . My system would be in great peril if I regarded the Westphalians as sure soldiers. You ought not to aim at having a large number of troops, but a small number of good troops which you must form progressively [1].' Notwithstanding, when the Russian war was imminent, the Emperor was glad enough to avail himself of the additional forces which Jerome had raised, and the details of whose organization must have been regularly submitted to him. 'I see with pleasure,' he writes, 'that you can have two divisions forming 20,000 men, of whom 2,500 are cavalry. Do you include the 4,000 men you have at Danzig [2]?' Then after demanding fifty-four guns and four companies of sappers, with all the necessary equipment, he concludes with just the kind of suggestion to appeal to Jerome: 'If you collect the *personnel* which I have just indicated, I shall not see any difficulty in bringing up your army corps to 30,000 men, with the help of small contingents of the Confederation, so as to form three fine divisions [3].'

That was indeed the paramount ambition of Jerome, to command a whole army corps of his own troops, to see '*la grande guerre*,' to rival Davoût and Massena and Soult, to make his weight felt in the wars and the treaties of the Empire. Some vague expectations of more substantial advantages may indeed have flitted across his mind. The size of the Westphalian army would be a pledge of loyalty which might evoke some act of generosity in response, such as enlargement of territory, a diminution of the war contribution, a reduction of the French garrison. However much Napoleon might ventilate his distrust of Westphalian fidelity, Jerome knew well enough that when the next war came the Emperor would be only too glad of every conscript who could carry a musket. Then the young man was nervous and took alarm. He was conscious that if a sudden fate seized Napoleon, he would be called upon to fight for his throne.

[1] *Corr.* xxi. 102, no. 16,894.
[2] *Corr.* xxii. 109, no. 17,654.
[3] Reinhard reports that the number on the effective list (including 1,100 men serving in Spain) was 28,258. *Mémoires du roi Jérôme*, v. 119.

Prussia was his mortal enemy, and so long as Prussia lasted he felt insecure. 'If I am not to reign in Berlin,' he said in 1808, 'the King of Prussia will drive me out, and my kingdom will end with the life of the Emperor.' And the Emperor played on these fears, writing, ' I doubt whether you will get much out of your troops against Prussia some years hence,' as if a Prussian war were an inevitable thing. Then there were the events of 1809, the insurrection of the peasants, the escapade of Schill and of the Duke of Brunswick-Oels, the English descent on Walcheren, the movements of the Austrians in Northern Germany. Even after the defeat of Wagram had crushed Austria, and Schill had fallen in the square of Stralsund, the young man was uncomfortable at times, and Napoleon had to remind him that all things were well. Mere idle love of pomp was mingled with ambition and uneasy fears, and an expensive body of household troops—a pure luxury condemned by Napoleon—was in itself a bitter criticism on Jerome's military policy.

The burden imposed by these armaments was such as to arrest all civil progress. On two several occasions, from 1807 to 1808 and from 1812 to 1813, the army had to be equipped anew with everything, arms and clothing, transport and artillery, horses and all their appurtenances. In the space of four years the foundries were called upon to produce no less than eighty pieces of ordnance. The uniforms were various and ridiculously splendid. And yet all the expense of the Westphalian army, great as it was, might have been met, had not the French army of occupation remained undiminished in spite of a distinct and written understanding that it was only to occupy Magdeburg, while the native forces were below the stipulated strength [1].

Disastrous though it was to the finances, the Westphalian army may be considered as a solidifying and unifying influence in the kingdom. Catholics from Paderborn, Lutherans from Cassel, Calvinists from Marburg, Prussians and Hessians, Hanoverians and Brunswickers, were through it bound together in a common profession under a common master. The men were paid at a higher rate than had obtained under the old régime,

---

[1] Von Specht, *Das Königreich Westphalen*, 30 ; *Recueil des planches représentant les troupes à différentes armes et grades de l'armée royale westphalienne*, 4° (in the Landesbibliothek at Cassel).

and the degrading penalty of flogging was abolished. It was the only German army in which the common soldier was not liable to the knout, or in which Jews were permitted to hold commissions. It was the only German army in which promotion was strictly regulated by merit, in which the private could rise to be a general. Nor was there any difficulty in recruiting the regiments. The whole agricultural population of Hesse had been accustomed to the profession of arms, and found their pinched village existence dull and unexciting. The gentry were not sorry to learn the profession of arms in the most brilliant school of war which Europe had seen since the days of Condé and Turenne. Regrets indeed there were for the old rulers and the old fashions, but the young men did not believe that they could ever return, and never had a profession been opened out to them where the chances of early distinction were so great and dazzling. It was to Jerome's credit that he was attentive to the needs of his soldiers. He frequently visited the barracks, chatted with the privates, tasted their food, and entered into all the details of regimental life. 'It would be difficult to find an army,' says von Borcke, 'where there is more internal order and more care for the soldiers.' 'Nothing finer could be seen,' says another officer, speaking of the royal guard. 'One detail only shocked me: these essentially German troops manœuvred to foreign words of command[1].' It is a remarkable fact that the army grew not only by conscription but also by voluntary enlistment, and that the men were eager for the taste of war. In September 1808 Jerome offered the Emperor a regiment of light horse for the Spanish war. 'When,' he wrote, 'to tranquillize them, I told them that it was not certain that they were going to Spain, they answered that it was a misfortune for them, since it was the only place where there was fighting.' Of fighting, indeed, the Westphalian army was destined to have its fill. The division which started for Spain 5,800 strong, and was subsequently raised to a strength of 8,000, struggled home a miserable war-worn remnant of 800 men. Of the 16,000 men who marched into Russia, who poured out their blood at Smolensk and Valentina, at Borodino and the Beresina, scarce

[1] Von Borcke, *Kriegerleben*; *D'Jéna à Moscou: Fragments de ma vie*, de Sackow, tr. Veling, 103.

THE RUIN OF WESTPHALIA

2,000 lived to tell the tale. At the battle of Borodino alone 186 Westphalian officers were returned as killed or wounded. Nevertheless after this unparalleled disaster a new army was called for and a new army was made, and in the summer of 1813 nearly 30,000 Westphalian conscripts were ready to take the field. In all, during these six years, more than 600,000 men out of a population of 2,000,000 had become 'conscriptable matter,' and of these about 38,000 had been slain or had fallen in foreign lands [1].

To these evils must be added a general and growing uncertainty as to the ultimate destiny of the country, an uncertainty which paralysed the will and sapped the energies of the servants of the State. The appearance of French custom-house officers in Westphalia itself (August 1809), the annexation of Holland and of the Hanseatic towns, the offer and subsequent withdrawal of Hanover, the annexation of the Department of the Weser (May 10, 1811) to the French Empire, showed how little respect Napoleon entertained for the boundaries of his dependent States. After the last exhibition of the Emperor's restlessness, all kinds of wild rumours were in the air: Swedish Pomerania and Naples were to be annexed; Murat was to have Poland; Prussia was to be swallowed by Westphalia. There seemed to be no end to the humiliations in reserve for Jerome and his luckless kingdom. The hard hand of Marshal Davoût weighed heavily on the north. On May 13, 1811, Jerome complained that an agent of the Prince of Eckmühl was residing in Cassel for the purpose of supervising his actions, and that this agent had gone to the Minister of War, and threatened on behalf of his master to seize the town and territory of Magdeburg unless the King of Westphalia forthwith repaired its fortifications and provisioned its magazines. The personal conduct of the Prince was still more irritating to Jerome's *amour propre*. He treated Westphalia as if it were his own property, stopping where he pleased, punishing whom he pleased, 'announcing loudly,' says Jerome, 'that his plan of conduct was to press the button on my subjects to make them

[1] Specht calculates that the total strength of the Westphalian army (including the *gendarmerie* and without the veterans) was 29,046 men in 1813 (*Das Königreich Westphalen*, 77–8).

desire union with France.' Meanwhile French troops were steadily poured into the exhausted and indebted country. On November 17, 1811, instead of 12,500 foot and 1,500 horse, there were 25,000 foot and 10,000 horse quartered in Westphalia.

France was now fast drifting into war with Russia, and the Kingdom of Westphalia was merely a pawn in the game. As the Westphalian towns were being filled up with French troops, some friction between French and German was to be anticipated. Napoleon declared that all offences against French officers must be judged by the French military tribunals, that the *Grande Armée* was constituted, and that martial law was to be proclaimed in Magdeburg. The various contingents of the Grand Army marched eastward over Westphalian roads, and plunged the country in misery. 'In Hanover, in Magdeburg, and in the principal towns of my kingdom,' wrote Jerome, December 5, 1811, 'the proprietors abandon their houses and try to get rid of them at prices however low. Everywhere misery besieges families; capital is exhausted, and the noble, the bourgeois, and the peasant, overwhelmed with debts and needs, seem to expect no other aid than vengeance, which they call for with all their desires, to which they direct all their wishes.' On the first six months of 1812 the deficit amounted to 30,000,000 francs, while the debt was estimated at anything between 140,000,000 and 200,000,000. Credit there was none, nor was there any chance of a diminution of expenditure. After February 1, the *Grande Armée* was constituted, and henceforward all the troops cantoned on Westphalian territory were at the charge of the government. Catharine, who upon Jerome's departure for Russia was made Regent of the kingdom, wrote to her husband in despair. Three of her advisers agreed that if the war lasted over next year 'the kingdom would go to pieces of itself, like a machine which stops work because the wheels are broken [1].' The financial expedients of the government sufficiently indicate the character of the situation. The land-tax, which was to be levied monthly, was fixed at twenty-five per cent. of the net revenue; the King decreed a forced loan of 5,000,000 francs; two-thirds of the debt taken over by the Westphalian kingdom from the governments which preceded it were repudiated. The arrears

[1] *Mémoires du roi Jérôme*, v. 494.

THE RUIN OF WESTPHALIA

of 1808–11 were to be met by 3,000,000 of paper hypothecated on the State domains. The expenses of local government were to be assured by *centimes additionnels* amounting to one-twentieth of the land-tax. The stamp-tax and the beer-duty were raised, and the arrears of interest on the debt capitalized. Reinhard, in reporting these steps to the Duke of Bassano, said that the servants of His Majesty sorrowfully agreed that all these measures, violent though they were, would not effect a radical cure, and that the proportion between receipts and expenses would not be made up [1].

The Russian catastrophe made a final end of this miserable kingdom. Ever since 1809 the feeling against the French had been steadily growing. The most optimistic observer described it as a 'general *malaise*,' but it was in reality smothered indignation. The Queen was in constant fear that her husband would be assassinated. The Prussian envoy in Cassel wrote in December 1811, that the King at any moment expected to be driven from his capital, and that he had three horses ready saddled and bridled every night for himself, six horses for his wife's carriage, and an escort, in case a sudden flight should be necessary. So great was the hatred of the French, that when the poor inhabitants of the Weser heard that they were to be annexed to France, they offered a whole year's contributions to the King of Westphalia, in order that the French might find nothing when they occupied the country [2]. The officials on the northern frontier represented in the most harrowing terms the lot of these 'new Frenchmen,' who, incorporated in the 'greatest empire of the world,' were driven to desperation by taxes, customs, conscription, and police. No destiny appeared to be so pitiable as absorption into France, and yet it was the general opinion among Westphalians that this was to be their lot [3]. Here and there, as at Brunswick, a fracas broke out between the French and the Westphalian troops, but it was soon put down. The power of Napoleon was too great, and no one seriously dreamed of resisting it.

---

[1] *Mémoires du roi Jérôme*, v. 497–8; Decrees of May 31, June 12, June 28, 1812. [2] Ibid., v. 17.
[3] *Histoire de l'esprit public à l'égard de la France*; *Affaires étrangères, Corr. Pol.: Westphalie*, i.

When in 1813, by unspeakable efforts, a new army was created and equipped to replace the thousands who had left their bones among the snows of Russia, the Kingdom of Westphalia was utterly ruined. The property-tax alone swallowed one-fourth of the income, and peasants left their lands untilled rather than pay so crushing a tribute. So desperate was the situation that a decree was actually passed to transfer these waste lands free of all seigneurial charges to the communes, provided they made themselves responsible for the payment of the land-tax. Nor was it only the landed proprietor who suffered. A man in the lowest class of life, without a square inch of real property, had to pay eight francs thirty centimes to the State; a poor family of four members was charged thirty francs sixty centimes. Meanwhile the total debt stood at 200,000 francs, and though two-thirds of it had been repudiated, it was calculated that the payment of interest alone upon the remaining third would absorb almost one-fifth of the normal revenue [1].

No one can seriously contend that Jerome was a good king, nor that he was deficient in attractive qualities. He was good-natured, affable, and clement, alive to the sufferings of his people and capable of describing them with obvious sincerity. He would have been delighted to play the rôle of a benevolent despot and to encourage art and learning, though he had none of the first and little of the second [2]. The clemency which he showed to the rebels of 1809 is both remarkable and highly creditable to his heart and to his judgement. On one occasion in that critical year, 1809, he showed a glimpse of higher qualities still, of a touch of that intrepid flame of genius which blazed out so often from the heart of his famous brother. It was on April 22, when the peasants were known to be marching on the capital, and the allegiance of the army was suspected to be doubtful. Lecamus and Reinhard advised flight, but Jerome was for brave counsels. Summoning his German officers, he

[1] Malchus, *Ueber die Verwaltung der Finanzen des Königreichs Westphalen.*

[2] He is recorded to have taken one book out of the *Fredericianum* during his rule—*Le précis historique de la vie de Madame la Comtesse de Barry, avec son portrait.* He did not return it. *Zeitschrift des Vereins für Hessische Geschichte und Landeskunde,* Neue Folge, ix. 286.

addressed them as follows : ' I know the heart of soldiers, I do not know that of traitors. Nevertheless, a man whom I have loaded with benefits has basely betrayed me. If any one of you repents of being bound, I give him back his word. In two hours' time you will return to swear me a new oath. Those who hesitate are free, and may range themselves with my foes. I give my royal word that they can do so in all safety. I would rather fight enemies than suspect traitors round me.' All swore the oath, and the situation was saved. But although capable, like Richard II and Edward IV of England, of occasional bursts of effective action, he was despotic, irregular in mood, and incurably selfish. No public interest was allowed to stand in the way of his personal dissipations and ambitions. The scale of his expenditure, personal and political, was criminally extravagant; the immorality of his Court has almost passed into a proverb. Although there were good and able heads in the Westphalian administration, and plenty of honest and excellent advice near at hand, Jerome went his own base, vulgar ways, scattering money on lacqueys and uniforms, like a *parvenu* in a comedy, ' dancing in the costume of Figaro to the sound of castanets,' while his servants were unpaid and his exchequer empty. The shy and placid Queen could offer him no sound advice, nor would he have received it if she had. She, too, was fond of luxury, and dazzled by Napoleon. 'The ministers,' she wrote on July 1, 1812, ' see in you only the vassal of a small State which has need of great economy ; but you must consider yourself also as the brother of the Emperor, as a French prince whose lot is linked to his.' There was no danger of Jerome falling into such an error. Even when he had returned in disgrace from the Moscow campaign, and the last vestiges of public confidence in him had been irretrievably shaken [1], the old megalomania reasserted itself. A second class of Knights of the Crown of Westphalia was created, 500 in number, with a pension of 120 francs apiece, and a long edict was issued regulating the attributions of the Grand Chancellor and Treasurer-General of the Order of the Crown. By this time he had thrown all scruples to the wind. The concern

[1] A police edict enforcing silence upon Russian affairs only deepened the general impression that Jerome had been disgraced, and that he would be removed from Westphalia when Napoleon returned from Russia.

was ruined and bankrupt; with the remaining assets the debtor might enjoy a last carnival.

It is doubtful whether even a Turgot could have made the people happy and contented. The continental blockade crippled the merchants; the war loan and imperial exactions made bankruptcy probable; the French army of occupation was a heavy burden upon the overtaxed populace. To all these even a Turgot would have had to submit, for they were part of the imperial policy which shaped and controlled the destinies of the kingdom. It would have been difficult even for the most upright ruler to maintain his self-respect, and what was still more important, his administrative religion, in the face of the blighting and restless interference of Napoleon. 'It is by the *Moniteur*,' said Jerome, bitterly, to the French ambassador, 'that I learn that I lose a fourth of my territory and a third of my revenues. . . . One does not cede men as one cedes a flock of sheep, or at least one does not tell them so.' On several occasions he threatened to resign, so intolerable seemed the position to a king with any pretensions to honour. He knew that Jollivet and Reinhard reported all his actions to Paris, that he was closely watched, and might at any moment be called upon to share the degradation and exile of his brother Louis. He knew that obedience to the will of Napoleon would serve him better than a careful study of the interests of his subjects. Alternately protesting and servile, he grew more and more reckless as the hand of his master tightened on the kingdom. By 1812 he had ceased to govern[1]. A more conscientious man would have resigned, and a strong man would have broken loose.

[1] *Revue Historique*, xx. 356.

CHIEF AUTHORITIES: *Administration des finances du royaume de Westphalie*, 1810; Berlepsch, *Ueber Grundsteuer in Deutschland*; Bode, *Verhandlungen der königlichen Präfectur des Werradepartements*; Bülau, *Geheime Geschichte*; Bülow, G. P. von, *Rückblicke auf mein Leben*, and *Beiträge zur neueren braunschweigischen Geschichte*; *Bulletin des lois du royaume de Westphalie*; Ducasse, *Les rois frères*; id., *Mémoires du roi Jérôme*; id., *Napoléon et le roi Jérôme* (in the *Revue Historique*, xvi–xxii); Gehrens, *Unter der vormaligen westphälischen Regierung erlittene dreimalige Verhaftung und Exportation*; *Geheime Geschichte des ehemaligen westphälischen Hofes*; Goecke, *Das Königreich Westphalen*; Grimm, *Kleinere Schriften*; Hassel und Murhard, *Westfalen unter Hieronymus Napoleon*;

Heyne, *Briefe*; Kleinschmidt, *Geschichte des Königreichs Westphalen*; Lynckner, *Geschichte der Insurrectionen unter dem westphälischen Regiment*; Malchus, *Ueber die Verwaltung der Finanzen des Königreichs Westphalen*; Masson, *Napoléon et sa famille*; *Mémoires du Général Dedem de Gelder*; F. Müller, *Kassel seit siebzig Jahren*; id., *Aus sturmvoller Zeit*; J. von Müller, *Briefe*; *Minerva*, July, 1826, Dec. 1840; Mazade, *Correspondance de Davoût*; *Le Moniteur Westphalien*; *Neue Fakkeln*, 1814; Rambaud, *L'Allemagne sous Napoléon I*; *Le Royaume de Westphalie*, 1820; Strombeck, *Darstellungen aus meinem Leben*; Specht, *Das Königreich Westphalen im Jahre* 1813; Thimme, *Die inneren Zustände des Kurfürstenthums Hannover unter der französisch-westphälischen Herrschaft*; Voss, *Die Zeiten*; Zinserling, *Westfälische Denkwürdigkeiten*; *Zeitschrift des Hist. Vereins für Niedersachsen*, 1886-91.

CHAPTER XIV

THE GRAND-DUCHY OF FRANKFORT

'Tout prêtre qui se mêle des affaires politiques ne mérite pas les égards qui sont dûs à son caractère.'—NAPOLEON.

WE know Freiherr Carl Theodor Anton Maria von Dalberg, Prince-Primate of the Rhenish Confederation, Archbishop of Ratisbon, temporal sovereign of Frankfort and Aschaffenburg and some thirty square miles in the centre of Germany. No German had been more pliant or more useful to the Emperor of the French, giving as he did the shelter of a pious and respectable reputation to acts which, however rapid, dazzling, and forcible, were signally lacking in the quality of unction.

The territory of the Prince-Primate, as modified in 1806, though small and disjointed, contained within its limits two famous cities, Ratisbon and Frankfort, the first the ancient seat of the imperial Diet, and the second the crowning place of the Emperors and the most important commercial town in Southern Germany. Together with these he retained in the Principality of Aschaffenburg a portion of the ancient Electorate of Mainz, and the summer residence of the Prince-Electors.

It was now fourteen years since the free city of Frankfort had been inducted into the methods and principles of French democracy. In 1792, General Custine proclaimed within its walls the rights of man, and proceeded to levy a heavy contribution upon his last and most opulent disciple. In the wars which ensued, the burghers of Frankfort encountered many experiences sufficient to trouble the dreams of an enthusiast. Prussians and Hessians, Austrians and Walloons, were in turns quartered upon them. The city was bombarded and partially burnt in 1796, and silver and shoe-buckles were melted down to meet the demands of a French general. If there was a fortune to be made out of the business of war commissariat, this did not compensate for other losses—for the decline in the value of Austrian securities, for the interruption of the English trade,

THE GRAND-DUCHY OF FRANKFORT 313

and for the French customs line which shut off the Transrhenane market. Further the city incurred the special displeasure of Napoleon as being a great *entrepôt* of English wares [1]. Accordingly, in 1806, General Augereau was ordered to levy a war-contribution of 4,000,000 francs upon the Frankforters, and the town was deprived of its ancient freedom and incorporated in the States of the Prince-Primate [2].

We need not here enter into the details of the constitution of Frankfort. The Senate was extremely aristocratic, and so exclusive, and jealous of its privileges, that no Roman Catholic or Calvinist could obtain civic office. The finance was controlled by a small committee of the Senate, and the utmost secrecy prevailed as to the management of the municipal funds. Nothing is so difficult to dislodge as a prosperous oligarchy, especially when it is supported by historic sentiment, and since it must be admitted that French military government was but an indifferent commendation of democratic blessings, it is not surprising if the burghers of Frankfort obstinately declined to deviate from their dim, narrow, and comfortable ways.

There was, however, one community in the city which had every reason to salute the advent of the Prince-Primate with enthusiasm and hope. The Jews of Frankfort numbered five hundred families, and were reputed to enjoy great wealth. But they laboured under heavy disabilities, dating from the second decade of the seventeenth century. They were confined to a particular quarter of the town; they were prevented from frequenting the public promenades, from owning landed property, or from engaging in agricultural and manual pursuits. Commerce, indeed, was open to them, but even in commerce the Frankfort Jews were debarred from certain profitable undertakings. The trade in arms, in spices, in corn and wine, the retail trade in cloth and silk, were reserved to Christians.

On January 2, 1807, solemn homage was done in Frankfort

---

[1] Erdmannsdörffer, v. 164. The Emperor spoke of Frankfort in 1805 as a '*foyer de conspiration et de contrebande anglaise.*'

[2] Augereau was personally popular, but the volume of business done per week was diminished by some 500,000 francs, and the burgesses were pawning their clothes to supply French soldiers with food. *Rapport de G. Rapp,* 14 *avril* 1806; *A. F.* iv. 1594.

to the new Prince. 'His bearing,' writes an observer, 'his gracious behaviour won the sympathy of the Frankforters. He is in the highest degree gracious, humane, civil. Gradually and with the greatest caution he has undertaken the most necessary alterations in the constitution of the town. The ruling burgomasters have been appointed for life; he has named the first syndic a member of his first Privy Council; the others are now Councillors of the High Court of Appeal; the best of the noblemen have been made his chamberlains; the consistory has been allowed to stand intact, only it has received an additional member for educational affairs in the shape of Professor Vogt, his librarian. Everybody is pleased that he is at the head here. At his entry into the town, the numerous Jews gathered fresh courage, hoping to be released from their slavery, and sought all means to salute the Prince. The poor Jews were puffed up with pride, owing to the kind behaviour of the Prince (in comparison with the former inhumanity of the town magistrates), and his promise to lighten their yoke. If they appeared in court and did not immediately get justice, they would behave with great licence to the magistrate. "Good Herr Burgomaster," they would say, "do I get right or do I not get right? No? But I know where Albini lives. I know where the Primate lives." When the Emperor Napoleon drove through the town, they ran from one gate to another with raging cries of "Our Messiah," and returned drunk with victory. . . . Then the Sachsenhauser [1], to whom all this was utterly repulsive, spread ropes across the streets to trip them up as they hurried home. As you can imagine, this led to beatings and lawsuits. The temper of the populace, Christian and Jew, became hotter and hotter. Hitherto the Jews had been forbidden to be seen on the promenades. Now they tried to walk in them. Christian burghers beat them and cast them out. The Jews complained to the Prince, and he at once permitted what had hitherto been so shamefully forbidden. But soon the Christian judges found that the Jews had no legal right to frequent these promenades, because several years before they had refused to contribute to them. The Prince would not contravene any legal right, and took back his permission, but caused part of the very narrow

---

[1] Sachsenhausen is a suburb of Frankfort.

THE GRAND-DUCHY OF FRANKFORT

and stiff promenade to be changed into an English garden, and gave every one free right of entry [1].'

The cheerful auguries of Jews, liberals, artisans, and Calvinists, were not entirely disappointed. The *Reformierten* were allowed to have church clocks and towers, to set up their own schools, to enter into all guilds and trades, and to fill all public offices [2]. Primary assemblies in the fourteen different quarters of the town were invited to elect two deputies apiece to a council which should deliberate upon fiscal measures. The Prince-Primate himself was present at each of the fourteen primary assemblies, as also at the assembly of twenty-eight. Such a revolution of affairs had never been known at Frankfort. A body of shopmen and artisans, of professional men and clergymen, was invited to decide whether the town should endure more indirect taxation [3], and not unnaturally they made an end of such time-honoured patrician finance.

The question of the Jewish disabilities was one of considerable difficulty, and the benevolent intentions of the Prince were viewed with the keenest dislike by the Senate and burghers of Frankfort. The permission given to the Jews in 1806, to walk in the public promenades and to frequent the coffee-houses, was regarded with extreme disfavour, and a letter from the Prince-Primate to a French Jew named Singer, who had been turned out of a coffee-house on the ground of his Hebrew extraction, created a widespread feeling of unrest. The Senate, which was still, despite the Dalbergian reforms, saturated with the old patrician sentiment, led the anti-Semite movement. Owing to the burning of a portion of the Jewish quarter in 1796, during the bombardment of Kleber, some of the Jews had been received into the Christian portions of the town. These it was now the desire of the Senate to confine again within the limits of the Ghetto. The merchants and traders of Frankfort had constructed their oppressive code with a view to the enjoyment of industrial monopoly, and the protectionist will be inconsistent

---

[1] *Carl Ritter: ein Lebensbild*, von D. G. Kramer.

[2] The text of this decree (Dec. 25, 1806) can be read in Winkopp, *Der rheinische Bund*, ii. 304–5.

[3] *Bulletin de Francfort*, May 8, 1807; *Affaires étrangères, Corr. Pol.: Allemagne*, 733.

if he blames them for defending their pecuniary interests against the dangerous competition of an astute and laborious race. They represented to the Prince that any enlargement of the rights of the Jews would spell the complete ruin of the wholesale and retail trade of the city.

Influenced by these representations, Dalberg and his Council prepared an ordinance (November 30, 1807), the provisions of which fall far short of the enlightened ideas which he shared with his own councillors, and with the best Germans of his time. The Jews were again to be restricted to a special quarter of the town; they were still to be treated as foreigners, whose rights were both strictly defined and only conceded upon payment of a considerable yearly tribute. Numerous branches of trade were still closed to them, but they were permitted to acquire land, to hold mortgages, and to sublet to Christians within the quarter assigned to them. Jewish apprentices could be received by master-workmen, and brought up to a trade. Jew children could attend the Frankfort gymnasium. The Jew could be employed as a farm labourer, though he was not permitted to acquire agricultural land, and consent was given to the establishment of Jewish factories and workshops, provided that none but Hebrew labour was employed in them.

On the other hand, the State took upon itself to exercise the strictest and most jealous supervision over the Hebrew community. The appointment of the Chief Rabbi and the two sub-Rabbis was to be controlled by the Prince; the Hebrew prayer and hymn books were to be censured, and no Hebrew marriage could take place without the sanction of the Prince's commissioner. The consistory of the Augustan Confession (representing the religious views of the Frankfort patricians) was to have jurisdiction over all Hebrew matrimonial disputes. Jewish schools were to be under State supervision, the instruction was to be given in German, nor could a private tutor be employed without special leave of the government [1].

This ordinance produced a bitter feeling of disappointment among the Jews, and it is said that some of the rich Jewish houses thought of migrating from the town. The proposal

[1] *Neue Stättigkeit und Schutzordnung der Judenschaft zu Frankfurt am Main*, Paris, Nov. 30, 1807; Winkopp, iv. 303-21.

THE GRAND-DUCHY OF FRANKFORT 317

that the Ghetto should be built up again was regarded with peculiar repulsion, not shared however by Goethe, who was a Frankfort burgher, and regarded the ordinance with marked approval [1].

The complexity of the task which he had undertaken gradually entered the mind of the elderly prelate. He was confronted with a strong patrician opposition in Frankfort which he had not the requisite force to overcome. French troops were quartered upon him, and loud were the complaints of their excesses and lack of discipline. The representatives of the French Empire in Frankfort, General Hédouville and M. Bacher, were continually urging him to a root and branch reform of his State, but save in Aschaffenburg and in Wetzlar reform was opposed. Dalberg knew that Bavaria was pleading for Ratisbon, and he felt that her plea would be successful. In an access of discouragement he wrote to Napoleon to ask him to organize, the primatial State. It was the Emperor's property, '*sa propriété*.' When once an order was established, the Primate's zeal would, he believed, be sufficient to maintain it. 'But,' concluded the letter with naïveté and truth, 'Heaven has not given me that energetic genius which creates a new and better order of things [2].'

Notwithstanding this appeal no constitution came from Paris. In October the Emperor passed through the town 'with the greatest celerity,' speaking a few words with the Prince at the post-house [3]. His thoughts were doubtless of Erfurt and Spain, and with such problems in the air the organization of the primatial State might well be left to a moment of greater leisure.

But in the spring of 1810 the internal affairs of Germany again engaged the attention of Napoleon. Austria had been beaten at Wagram in 1809, and was compelled to accept a humiliating peace. There was no immediate prospect that she would again disturb the peace of Europe. The allied, or rather the subject, kings of the Rhenish Confederation were entitled to receive some territorial benefits and rectifications of frontier,

[1] Darmstaedter, *Das Grossherzogthum Frankfurt*, 256.
[2] Dalberg to Napoleon, June 24, 1808 ; *Affaires étrangères, Corr. Pol.: Allemagne*, 734.
[3] Bacher to Champagny, Oct. 15, 1808 ; ibid.

and as Champagny reminded his master, 455,000 German souls and 13,939 square miles of German soil remained at the disposal of the French government [1]. As the Court of Bavaria clamoured for Ratisbon, some compensation would have to be found for the Prince-Primate. In a treaty signed February 16, 1810, at Paris, between Dalberg and the French Empire, the former was compensated for the loss of Ratisbon by the Principalities of Hanau and Fulda, and his dominion so formed was in future to be styled the Grand-Duchy of Frankfort. The new grand-duchy contained about 100 square miles and some 300,000 inhabitants. Save for the enclave of Wetzlar, it was geographically continuous, but so curiously shaped that the main roads connecting Hanau with Fulda and Aschaffenburg respectively necessarily passed through the dominions of other sovereigns. The populations, swept so suddenly into a common political net, differed widely in temperament and tradition. Fulda was Catholic and of a rigid antique type. The men of Hanau were 'reformed.' The proud burghers of Frankfort looked down with disdain upon the ignorant Catholic peasantry of Aschaffenburg. The divergences, the hostilities, the distrusts, the suspicions, were curiously strong. Yet the woodsmen of the Spessart, the market-gardeners of the Main valley, the ploughmen and herdsmen of the Rhone, would all meet at times in the market-square at Frankfort, and chaffer their wares under the shadow of the Römer, the symbol of a dim and vanished unity.

In the mere matter of acres the Prince-Primate was a gainer by the recent changes. But there were certain harsh and unpleasant features in the bargain to which he had affixed his signature. He had to provide an endowment for the Dukes of Eckmühl and Wagram from his share of the Rhenish tolls, and 4,200 men for the army of the Confederation ; the Emperor reserved for his own use domains in Fulda and Hanau to the value of 600,000 francs, while the remainder of the domainial rents in these principalities were to go to the creditors of the Rhenish tolls. Again, France took the opportunity of shifting on to the shoulders of the Grand-Duke of Frankfort her share of the debts of the Electorate of Mainz, while finally it was provided that upon the decease of the reigning Grand-Duke, his princi-

[1] *Affaires étrangères, Corr. Pol. : Allemagne,* 738.

THE GRAND-DUCHY OF FRANKFORT 319

pality was to lapse to the King's stepson, Eugène Beauharnais, Viceroy of Italy. An additional article stipulated that the Code Napoléon and the organic laws of the French administrative régime should be instantly put into operation in the grand-duchy.

The nomination of Prince Eugène to the succession of the grand-duchy was doubtless an unpleasant surprise to the city of Frankfort. It will be remembered that four years before, Dalberg in an access of prudence and servility had nominated the Emperor's uncle, Cardinal Fesch, as his coadjutor and political successor. But although the prospect of a Fesch' domination in Frankfort might have been acceptable to Napoleon in 1806, it was far otherwise in 1810. In the quarrel which had arisen between Napoleon and the Papacy, Fesch had espoused the cause of the Church, and the Emperor, having already annexed the Papal States, discovered a conviction that the temporal rule of spiritual persons was inconsistent with the spirit of the times. While he punished the ingratitude and independence of his uncle, Napoleon determined to reward the loyalty of his stepson. If the Emperor's marriage with Marie Louise was productive of an heir, it might be well that the boy should be entitled King of Rome, and that the whole of the Italian peninsula should be entrusted to his rule. In such a case it would be necessary to provide a solace for Eugène, and the Grand-Duchy of Frankfort would give to the husband of a Bavarian princess a commanding position in Germany. In any case, it would be gratifying to the Court of Vienna to feel that the Beauharnais dynasty was not destined to reign permanently in Milan.

It may, perhaps, be conjectured that Napoleon was dissatisfied with the conduct and bearing of the burghers of Frankfort. The main object of the Emperor's care in 1810 was the vigorous enforcement of the continental blockade. Not a yard of English cloth or a bale of English wool was to find a market on the continent. The city of Frankfort, though for four years it had been subject to Dalberg, still preserved the lineaments of its ancient constitution, and its burghers were guilty of the unpardonable sin. They bought and were suspected of buying English wares. The prevention or detection of so heinous an offence could most easily be effected in a Gallicized province.

In this miniature State nothing was suggestive of permanence. It was to be governed by an elderly prelate; it was to go upon his death to a stranger; its finances were crippled in order that Frenchmen might be spared taxation; it was subjected to specified military burdens as a member of the Confederation of the Rhine; it was made up of a concourse of the most heterogeneous parts, two imperial towns, a lay principality, two spiritual territories, and several counties and knightly possessions; and it was devoid of a natural frontier. Finally, it was not even under the complete control of its nominal ruler, for the director of the imperial domains, Gentili, exercised an *imperium in imperio*, and exasperated the manager of the grand-ducal finance by his exorbitant pretensions.

Six months after the formation of the grand-duchy, the Prince-Primate offered to make the French resident at Frankfort his principal minister, with a right of inspecting all the branches of the administration. If Bacher was instructed to decline, it was because France was already completely mistress of the situation. 'The Grand-Duke,' wrote Hédouville to Champagny on December 15, 1810, 'has kindly permitted that henceforth all the acts of his government shall be communicated to me before being published, so that I may transmit them to your Excellency before you are informed of them by the Gazettes.' While the French resident controlled the policy of the Prince-Primate, the French army awed his subjects. In October and November 1810, a military commission sat in Frankfort for the purpose of detecting and burning English and colonial merchandise. The Grand-Duke wrote personally to several of the most distinguished merchants to urge them to comply with the imperial decree [1], and goods to the value of 865,000 francs were publicly burnt in the streets of Frankfort. 'The domiciliary visits,' says a French witness, 'were conducted with the greatest rigour, not only among traders and merchants, but also in private houses [2],' and, to add to the indignity, the bonfires

---

[1] *A. F.* iv. 1654.

[2] Bacher to Champagny, Nov. 1, 1810; *Affaires étrangères, Corr. Pol.: Allemagne*, 738.

THE GRAND-DUCHY OF FRANKFORT

were lit to the strains of the military band. The same scenes of wanton destruction were enacted all over the duchy. General Molitor's researches in Fulda extended even to the country villages, and resulted in seizures valued at 440,000 francs; and if General Friant's holocaust of colonial wares at Hanau only amounted to half this sum, it was none the less viewed with the greatest repugnance [1].

Meanwhile the army head quarters at Frankfort was costing the citizens 30,000 francs daily, without counting the expenses of the great train of artillery which was voyaging through the duchy from Magdeburg [2]. 'The merchants of this city,' wrote Hédouville, 'are sufficiently prudent to allow us to hear groans rather than murmurs [3].' It was, then, to the accompaniment of audible groans and suppressed murmurs, that the new civil machinery of the grand-duchy was to be set working.

By the wish of the Prince-Primate, the constitution was drawn up upon the model provided by Westphalia. The separate provincial and municipal constitutions were abolished, and the duchy received with some delays and much dislike the boon of legal, administrative, and fiscal unity [4]. The privileges of the nobility suffered the same fate as the municipal independence of the capital, and it was proclaimed that all men should be equal before the law. But the liberty of the subject was not equally assured, for although toleration was extended to the recognized forms of worship, there was no guarantee for the freedom of the press, for the freedom of public meeting, or for freedom of speech. On October 10, 1810, the Prince-Primate, at the desire of Napoleon, ordered the cessation of all the political newspapers in the grand-duchy. In future there was to be but one official organ, the editor of which was

---

[1] *A. F.* iv. 1654.

[2] Beust to Feltre, Aug. 22, 1810; *A. F.* iv. 1653.

[3] Hédouville to Champagny, Nov. 18, 1810; *Affaires étrangères, Corr. Pol.: Allemagne*, 741.

[4] It was not till March 1811 that a central Bureau of Finance was established at Frankfort. Until then separate financial systems existed for Aschaffenburg, Hanau, Frankfort, and Fulda. 'It is evident,' writes Bacher, Jan. 17, 1811, 'that the dethroned aristocracy seeks to perpetuate itself under the veil of mystery with which all the operations of finance were formerly enveloped.' *Affaires étrangères, Corr. Pol.: Allemagne*, 741.

to be named by the Minister of Police[1]. The precaution was superfluous, for. the servile and arid journalism of the duchy had been for the last four years steadily losing its readers under the petrifying censure of the French resident. It is needless to add that conscription was part of the fundamental law of the new State, but though this might have been anticipated, a Primatial decree making the obligation retroactive came as an unpleasant surprise[2]. The new fiscal system of the duchy was strictly drawn up on the French model by M. de Bilderbeck, 'the director of the domains in the service of France,' and the stamp and registration tax were unpopular novelties. 'In general,' says Hédouville, 'men have great difficulty in renouncing their ancient privileges to subject themselves to the French régime[3].'

Under these circumstances nothing is more surprising than the readiness with which Germans accepted posts in a government avowedly formed upon the French model, and in the interests of a French neighbour. Dalberg was able to command the best abilities and the most respectable names of the grand-duchy, and the new machinery supplied a stimulant to the torpid wits of an incurious population. The debates of the Council of State which sat in the Electoral chamber of the Römer often resolved themselves into a lively conflict between the conservative councillors of Frankfort and Hanau, and the more enlightened bureaucrats from the old Electorate of Mainz. 'The great battles of the time,' says Darmstaedter, 'the opposition between industrial compulsion and industrial freedom, between French and German law, between bureaucratic regulation and self-government, were here fought out in detail in the quiet chamber of the old Rathaus[4].' The Primate and the ministers, however, assisted by the powerful argument supplied by the French garrison, were able to prevail against the forces of reaction. The trade-guilds were abolished, the duchy divided into four departments, and the leading principles of

---

[1] Salomon, *Geschichte des deutschen Zeitungswesens*, 111 ff.

[2] Fénelon to Champagny, Feb. 26, 1811; *Affaires étrangères, Corr. Pol.: Allemagne*, 742.

[3] Schwebel to Champagny, Feb. 27, 1811; *Affaires étrangères, Corr. Pol.: Allemagne*, 742. Hédouville to Champagny, April 2 and May 17, 1811; ibid. 743. [4] Darmstaedter, 98.

THE GRAND-DUCHY OF FRANKFORT

French administration—the division of the executive and judicial powers, and the concentration of executive power in the hands of a single person—were adopted, to the great expedition of affairs [1].

In the matter of legislation the Westphalian precedent was followed, and it was arranged in the constitution that a representative assembly was to be summoned, to consider projects of laws submitted by the Council of State, to receive the yearly budget, and to consent to taxation [2]. The electors to this body were to be named by the sovereign for life. In every department these electors would form an electoral college, composed, two-thirds of wealthy proprietors, one-sixth of the richest merchants and manufacturers, and one-sixth of men distinguished in science and art. Each of the four electoral colleges so constituted was required to choose three proprietors, one merchant or manufacturer, and one savant to represent it in the Assembly. On October 8, 1810, the members of the colleges met in the capitals of their respective departments. Their work was done with despatch, and on October 15 the first and only parliament of the grand-duchy was opened in Hanau, which had been selected for the purpose on account of its central position.

To the genial despot of Frankfort the meeting of the States afforded the harmless luxury of a liberal demonstration. Three projects of law were submitted, discussed in committee, and passed without a single black ball. On October 26 the Assembly dispersed, after a session which had lasted eleven days. Nor was it ever again collected together.

The introduction of the French system of local government was attended with some benefits. While the prefects of Hanau, Fulda, and Aschaffenburg were men who had already distinguished themselves in the government of those provinces, the important prefecture of Frankfort was confided to an enlightened aristocrat, Max von Günderode, who had held administrative posts in several small principalities, and was now

---

[1] The frontiers of the four departments follow the irregular lines of the older territories, as is shown in the map.

[2] The drafting of the *Organisationspatent*, Aug. 16, 1810, is defective. It merely states that no poll-tax can be levied without consent of the Assembly.

prepared to address himself with zeal to the many problems of municipal government in Frankfort. It is true that the departmental councils were in the first instance nominated by the Prince-Primate, but they were none the less capable of performing a useful rôle by ventilating local grievances and suggesting local remedies. 'The memoirs of the three departmental councils of Aschaffenburg, Fulda, and Hanau,' says M. Darmstaedter, 'remind the reader of the *cahiers* of 1789.' The council of Aschaffenburg petitions for the abolition of labour services, the subdivision of the Almend, and freedom for the corn trade. The men of Hanau and Fulda wish that more waste land might be reclaimed, more fallow brought under cultivation, that some system of insurance against hailstorm and cattle disease might be started, that measures might be taken against Hebrew usury. Fulda is very Catholic. It prays for moral legislation against brandy, dancing, gambling in foreign lotteries. The Aschaffenburgers wish for the equalization of the land-tax, the men of Fulda for the abolition of the property-tax; the men of Hanau complained, as well they might, of military burdens. But on the whole, in these three departments it is the local, the agrarian questions which interest. For high politics the councils have little taste[1].

A bolder spirit, however, animated the council of Frankfort. With narrow municipal jealousy they complained that so many places had been given to 'foreigners.' Being men of substance themselves, they desired to substitute indirect taxes for the property-tax, seeing that the indirect taxes would fall upon the poor. They complained that the police was too numerous, the project of school reform too costly, and that a unversity (which had been proposed) would not be suitable in a city of commerce. They denounced the harshness of the conscription, and the unequal incidence of the burden of billeting. It was remarked, not without irony, that in spite of the express terms of the constitution, laws were frequently published in the government organ without the consent of the Estates, and finally, a wish was expressed that this body might be convoked, and that no new laws or burdens might be imposed upon the duchy without its consent. These frank and selfish criticisms

[1] Darmstaedter, 113.

THE GRAND-DUCHY OF FRANKFORT 325

nettled the philanthropic autocrat of the grand-duchy, and the prefect and two councillors were summoned to receive a rebuke from his lips [1]. The departmental council of Frankfort had said its say, nor was it ever again summoned, and though the councils of Hanau and Aschaffenburg once met in 1813, it was only to distribute military burdens. And so the government of the grand-duchy became an undiluted bureaucracy.

In the villages we suspect that the change was of the slightest. Institutions are unlike machines. They depend very much upon the men who work them. Now the men who worked the new French institutions in the villages of the grand-duchy were the same solid, phlegmatic Teutons who had worked the old German institutions, the quaint archaic products from which Jacob Grimm has distilled poetry. A grand-ducal ordinance of November 19, 1810, pronounced that in all the rural communities and smaller towns, the old officials should continue to act. The *Stadtrath* and *Dorfgericht* became the municipal council; the burgomasters and *Schultheissen* were christened mayors, and were permitted to walk about in red and white scarves. It was the old caste in a new play—a play which none of the actors understood, and few were zealous to learn. The performance was slovenly and listless; there were long pauses for the prompter, and when the curtain fell, little had been acted and less learnt, and all that the players remembered was that the gestures were puzzling, and the piece too stimulating for their taste.

In the realm of law there was a revolution. On September 15, 1809, the Grand-Duke announced that the Civil Code would be introduced on May 1, 1810. The family council and the justices of the peace were recommended as beneficial institutions 'to secure the property of families, and to lessen the noxious quality of litigation by reasonable arbitration.' The grand-duchy had neither justices of the peace nor notaries, ushers nor proctors. It had, on the contrary, fiefs and entails. An ordinance of July 25, 1810, therefore determined that the French Civil Code should be regarded as the common civic law book from January 1, 1811, though local custom and precedent

[1] They were, however, subsequently invited to lunch. Darmstaedter, 116.

was still to be respected wherever the French law shed no certain light.

Civil marriage was introduced, and the keeping of the civic registers entrusted to lay persons. Marriages, however, were not to be concluded before a competent priest or pastor had testified that no ecclesiastical obstacle stood in the way; nor could a divorce be pronounced save with the testimony of an authorized ecclesiastic. In this way Dalberg harmonized his duties as a priest of the Roman Church, his sensibility as an enlightened reformer, and his timidity as a member of the Rhenish Confederation.

Von Mulzer, one of the Frankfort councillors, defended the introduction of this foreign law, saying that in truth it was less foreign than the Corpus Juris, and contained within it many German formulae. His contention was probably correct. In any case, the emendations which the councillors of the grand-duchy thought fit to propose are not very numerous or important, and the Civil Code found general acceptance.

The improvement of the penal law was yet more important, for the country was still governed by the barbarous *Carolina*, although it had ceased to put its worst provisions into practice. The consequence of having a penal law which is too severe for the times is that the administration of the law is not severe enough, and it was to meet this need that the French Penal Code was adopted in the grand-duchy[1].

In the first four years of the Prince-Primate's rule (1806–10), great improvements were introduced into the judicial organization of Frankfort. The substitution of one system for many systems, the severance of justice from administration, a stricter definition of the competence of the courts and of the course of appeals, were acknowledged benefits. Litigation was made more expeditious and less costly, and we are told that cases which in former times would have lasted a year were now settled in the course of a few weeks. But there was still privilege; there was still an aristocratic organization. The nobles must be judged by noble *Schöffen*, and the Houses of Frauenstein and Limburg had the perpetual right to two places on the judicial bench which tried civil cases in the second instance, and

[1] Feb. 19, 1812.

THE GRAND-DUCHY OF FRANKFORT 327

sat as a court of first instance over privileged persons and criminals.

When the grand-duchy was established in 1810 further changes were introduced. A Ministry of Justice was created, and the Council of State assumed the additional duties of a court of cassation. It was not, however, till January 1, 1813, that the system of judicial organization was reformed in all its branches, and adjusted to the French model. Then all privilege was swept away, and, save for the spiritual jurisdiction of the Catholic Church, the status of persons was no longer permitted to affect the composition of the law courts. While two courts of appeal were established at Frankfort and Aschaffenburg respectively, each consisting of a president and six judges, in the four departmental capitals and in Wetzlar the existing courts were continued as courts of first instance. By a wise economy the functions of the justice of the peace were combined with those of the district mayor. But some judicial powers still remained to the aristocracy, for a clause in the act of the Rhenish Confederation preserved to the lords '*basse et moyenne jurisdiction en matières civiles et criminelles*,' and this was exercised in two degrees, roughly corresponding to the petty and quarter sessions of our justices of the peace.

A battle arose over procedure. While Seeger, a typical Roman jurist of the German Reichsstadt, wished to import only so much of the French procedure as was necessitated by the terms of the Civil Code, the Grand-Duke, more expansive and receptive, pleaded for the orality and publicity of the new French law. 'Publicity,' he said, 'is the palladium of truth and justice. The English, who are of German origin, are still true to this principle.' But though the lineage of written procedure was Roman rather than Teutonic, Dalberg, failing to convince his Council, was compelled to assent to a compromise. The procedure of the grand-ducal law court remained for the most part written, secret, inquisitorial; but in criminal cases there was (1) a public examination (*Vernehmung*) of the accused after the instruction, and (2) a second public examination in which the accused, his counsel, and the prosecution were heard, but no witnesses. The Grand-Duke pleaded for the jury, reminding his Council of the old German *scabini*; but here again he was defeated by the stubborn conservatism of the Frankfort jurists.

Nevertheless, there were some marked improvements. Torture was abolished; the courts were instructed to form a free judgement upon the total moral impression left upon their minds by the evidence; and by the prohibition of the practice of referring points of law to university faculties, a greater sense of responsibility was given to the bench, and a vast economy effected in time and trouble [1].

Unity, swiftness, definition, equality before the law, improved procedure, the elimination of archaic barbarism, these were the advantages of the new system. The peasant might complain that he had to walk further to get his justice, but the justice was better when he got it. Nevertheless, in the capital, where the Roman jurists had so firm a footing, these new ways were from the first suspect, and the Civil Code, the Penal Code, and the Code of Procedure were abolished in 1814, as soon as the power of Napoleon was broken. But the organization of the courts was left practically unchanged.

It would appear that the educational policy of the Grand-Duke was marked by a considerable measure of zeal, moderation, and enlightenment. A general curator of public instruction was appointed to supervise all the educational institutions of the duchy. In each department the prefect was assisted by a committee of inspectors, partly clerical and drawn from all the confessions, and partly lay. This committee recommended schoolmasters to the curator, examined candidates for the post of teacher, saw that the programmes were properly carried out, and administered the funds allocated to educational purposes. The delicate question of denominational instruction was solved by a compromise. While the primary schools remained, as they had always been, denominational, their course of studies was prescribed and their teaching controlled by the State. The religious instruction given in these schools was placed under the supervision of the parish priest, but he was bound to report twice a year to the educational committee. For the secular

---

[1] Schröder (*Lehrbuch der deutschen Rechtsgeschichte*, 812) describes the '*Aktenversendung*,' a useful practice when courts were weak and ignorant, and only abolished in the smaller German States in 1879.

THE GRAND-DUCHY OF FRANKFORT

instruction the mayor of the district or commune was primarily responsible. On the other hand, the secondary schools were entirely divested of a denominational character, and it was arranged that religious instruction should be given simultaneously to members of all the confessions.

The communes were compelled to keep their schools in repair, for which purpose they were permitted to raise a school rate, and empowered to receive a grant in aid charged upon the stamp-tax. Private schools could only be started with the permission of the government, and were placed under government supervision. The Prince-Primate, however, was not exempt from one of the dominant foibles of his German contemporaries, and, having a little State of his own, attempted to stuff it at once with all the educational apparatus. So a law-school was established at Wetzlar for the purpose of instructing the grandduchy in the French codes and their German offshoots, and all intending judges were warned that they must take the Wetzlar degree. So, too, a school of medicine must be started at Frankfort, a school of forestry at Aschaffenburg, while a university containing some seventy students was allowed to linger on at the last-named town—the remnants of the old High School of Mainz. The system was half French, half German. The special schools for law, medicine, and forestry were French; so, too, was the curator and the State control. But the schools were not barracks, the scholars were not boarders, and there was a place still left for ecclesiastical supervision.

When the grand-duchy was established in 1810 a strong current had set in for the removal of Jewish disabilities. In the Kingdom of Westphalia the Jews, as we have seen, were put upon a footing of complete equality with the Christians in 1808, and both in Baden and in Bavaria they were admitted to civic rights in the course of 1808 and 1809. It is true that certain restrictions upon trade and settlement were imposed upon the Jews by French legislation in 1808, owing to the growing evil of Hebrew usury in the agricultural districts; and there was some ground for the advice given to the Prince-Primate by one of his councillors, Eberstein, that in view of the backwardness of the rural Jews in Fulda, complete and universal equality should not be insisted on. But the Westphalian example weighed more heavily with the Prince-Primate than the counsels of Eberstein, which might seem not only ungenerous but lacking in deference to the imperial will; and in the constitution of 1810 it was laid down that all inhabitants of the duchy, whatever their creed, were to enjoy equal rights. The Council of State, despite the opposition of the town of Frankfort, decided that under the terms of this document the Jews were no longer foreigners, but citizens of the grand-duchy.

The epilogue to this story is curiously dishonourable. There was great embarrassment in the treasury, mainly owing to the financial and military requirements of the Protector of the Rhenish League, and Dalberg saw the glitter of hope in the Hebrew pocket. Although his constitution and his Council had proclaimed the Jews to be already citizens, he determined to make them buy their civic rights. It had been the custom for the Jews of Frankfort to pay an annual sum in return for the protection of the city. At twenty years' purchase this sum would amount to 440,000 gulden, and it was intimated to the Jews that this was to be the price of their freedom. After a year's haggling the bill was paid, and on December 28, 1811, the government Gazette announced that the Frankfort Jews were now entitled to the same civic rights as the Christian burghers [1].

If the members of the grand-duchy had been asked in 1814 to summarize their experiences of the Napoleonic period, we can hardly doubt but that it would have been described both as an uncomfortable and a discomforting age. The lawyers of the *Kammergericht* of Wetzlar would have complained of an occupation gone, of a complicated and gainful science rendered suddenly obsolete. The city of Frankfort would have regretted the revolution which first deprived it of its special privilege as the coronation place of emperors, and then of its jealously guarded autonomy. Serfdom indeed had been abolished, but in the south-western States of Germany serfdom amounted to little more than a restriction upon mobility, which could almost always be removed by the payment of the manumission fee; and though the peasants were freed from feudal dues and *corvées*,

---

[1] The Jews in the Fulda department paid 60,000 gulden, those in the Aschaffenburg department 36,000 gulden for their civic rights.

THE GRAND-DUCHY OF FRANKFORT 331

they had been made liable to a new slavery in the shape of military conscription. The memory of domiciliary visits in search of colonial wares, of wanton conflagrations, of a crushing burden of taxation, of bankruptcy only avoided by forced loans and the timely assistance of the House of Rothschild, would have been printed indelibly on our imaginary catalogue. No merchant of Frankfort would be likely to forget how the 4 per cent. bonds, which in 1804 stood at 99, sank to 54 in 1812. No taxpayer forgot the stamp and registration tax. The pensioners and salaried officials of Hanau and Fulda had good cause to remember the last three years of the grand-duchy, for they did not receive a penny of their pensions or salaries, since the administrator of the reserved domains appropriated to the use of the Emperor the fund from which those pensions or salaries should have been paid. For the men of the Frankfort regiment—and in all nearly 7,000 were raised for the wars—there was the glory and excitement of the camp, and the release from some sordid cares. Fired with great hopes, the officers of the second battalion marched off to the Russian war, dreaming of the conquest of Turkey and Greece, and saying to themselves, as one has written in his journal, that 'they would plant the eagle of Napoleon on the limits of the world.' But of that force, 1,700 strong, only 77 men returned to the familiar waters of the Main, and the two battalions contributed to the Peninsular war were decimated at Vittoria and at the Bidassoa[1]. The sound and stir of armed men, the forced billeting, the requisitions and miscellaneous plundering of armies were a familiar, nay, they were a constant feature of these times. The villages on the great high-road from Frankfort to Fulda, especially those which were regular halting-places, would have cause to remember the great passing of troops before and after the Russian campaign, and the shattered multitude which streamed back from the field of Leipzig. Upon many a homely calendar these years must have been inscribed in symbols of confusion and woe. The Emperor with his keen instinct knew the feeling, and his passages through the grand-duchy were swift and furious. His last visit has

---

[1] Sansey, *Les Allemands sous les aigles françaises: le régiment de Francfort*, 72 ff. In all, the grand-duchy furnished 6,679 men.

been described to us by an eye-witness. He arrived in the afternoon of October 31, 1813, after Leipzig had been lost, and the Bavarians under Wrede had gone over to the allies; and the Prince-Primate, having discovered that 'to sustain the system of the concordat at this juncture' his presence was necessary at Constance, had bolted from the sinking ship. Staying in the house of the Bethmanns, who were leading merchants in the city, Napoleon spoke some kind words to a trembling deputation. 'Be wiser than Wrede. The town has nothing to fear. The cannonading' (which was audible) 'is a trifle.' The next morning, about midday, the carriage drove up to take him away. As he descended the steps he saw a lady in the crowd, with her hand behind her back. A sudden spasm of fear caught him, and he cried out sharply, 'Show your hand!' Then his carriage blotted him from sight, and thundered away towards France [1].

[1] Eilers, *Meine Wanderung durch's Leben*, 229; Hédouville to Champagny, July 21, 1813; *Affaires étrangères, Corr. Pol.: Allemagne*, 731.

CHIEF AUTHORITY : Paul Darmstaedter, *Das Grossherzogthum Frankfurt* (a very complete and careful monograph, which has been taken as the basis of this chapter). Wherever I have utilized an authority not mentioned in Darmstaedter's bibliography, I have given a reference in a footnote.

CHAPTER XV

THE HANSEATIC TOWNS

' C'est par l'argent qu'il faut tenir les hommes à argent.'
' Il y a en général une présomption défavorable contre ceux qui manient de l'argent.'—NAPOLEON.

THE position of the Hanseatic towns after the breach of the Treaty of Amiens may well excite commiseration. If commerce can have a memory, a sentiment, or a conscience, these cities might have expected favourable treatment from France. They had been excellent customers for French wine and sugar, and in the winter of 1794-5 several provinces of France had been saved from starvation by immense consignments of corn from Hamburg and Bremen. They had opened their hospitality to a large number of French emigrants, and in the struggle between France and England they both professed and observed a strict neutrality. Yet their situation and resources were such that they were doomed to suffer by the war. On the one hand the Elbe and the Weser were blockaded by the English, on the other hand the cities were forced to lend money upon disadvantageous terms to the French. While British men-of-war ruined the maritime trade, French consuls inspected the passports of travellers, and supervised the policy and movements of the municipal senates [1].

Many motives combined to urge Napoleon to the control of the Hanseatic cities. They were wealthy, and could therefore feed, clothe, and support the conscripts of the Empire. They harboured a maritime population, and could therefore contribute sailors to his fleet. There was a considerable English and French royalist colony in Hamburg, and the *Hamburg Correspondent*, with its circulation of forty thousand copies a week, was the oracle of most of the coffee-houses in North Germany.

---

[1] Some useful information as to the effect of the English blockade upon the commerce of Hamburg has been collected by Hitzigrath (*Hamburg und die Continentalsperre*, 1900). It was the cause of 193 bankruptcies.

Add to this the fact that Hamburg was the chief distributor of English goods on the continent, that Hamburg and Bremen commanded respectively the mouths of the Elbe and the Weser, and that the advance of a French army into the heart of Germany would be threatened if these cities, so accessible to England, were left unsecured upon the flank, and the action of Napoleon is fully accounted for. In 1805 he was at war with England and he had designs upon Germany, and seeing in the control of the Hanseatic cities a means of throttling British commerce, of muzzling the German press, and of fortifying his own military position, he sent his secretary Bourrienne to Hamburg as minister plenipotentiary to the Circle of Lower Saxony. There he was to observe the policy of the Northern Courts, to censure the press, and to secure the expulsion of Englishmen and *émigrés* from the Hanseatic territories. From that time forward the 'free cities' were placed under the close inspection of the French police [1].

After the battle of Austerlitz the French appetite grew, and on February 25 a new set of instructions was issued to Bourrienne. He was commanded to persuade the magistrates of the three towns that they had everything to fear from Prussia, and everything to gain from France. 'You will induce them,' the document continued, 'to offer that which it would not be proper for France to demand. The intention of His Majesty the Emperor is that the Hanseatic towns should first furnish a lump sum of 6,000,000 francs, and every year during the wars which France will have to sustain, a sum of 2,000,000 payable by quarters every three months. When the offers which shall be made to you, but which it is your duty adroitly and artistically to provoke, shall answer to the intentions of His Majesty, you will transmit them to your government as propositions new to it, but such as in your opinion should be favourably received. You will cause them to hope that such will be the case, and you will even go so far as to promise that it shall be so [2].'

Bourrienne had many conferences with the magistrates of Hamburg, in the hopes of convincing them that the protection

---

[1] Bourrienne, *Mémoires*, vi. 307, 346.

[2] These instructions (*Affaires étrangères, Corr. Pol.: Hamburg*, 119) are not quite accurately represented in Bourrienne's *Mémoires*, vii. 138-9.

of the Emperor was well worth the sum demanded. The magistrates urged that the sum was too high, that the town was less rich since the war, and finally it was politely intimated by the Senate that circumstances did not permit them to accept the *generous* proposition of the Emperor.

As Napoleon was anxious that the three cities should acknowledge his protection, so Prussia was desirous of incorporating them in a Federation of Northern States which should serve to counterbalance the Rhenish Confederacy. The advances of the Prussian agent, the Baron de Grote, were received as coldly as the insidious proposition of Bonaparte. The Hanseatic towns let it be clearly understood that their main interest lay in preserving the neutrality which had been guaranteed to them in 1803, and in preventing any belligerent powers from entering into their respective territories [1].

This word had hardly been spoken when war broke out between France and Prussia. Without warning, without apology, without explanation, French troops occupied the three cities. 'My brother,' wrote Napoleon from Berlin to Louis, King of Holland (November 4, 1806), 'Marshal Mortier ranges himself under your command in Hanover and in the Hanseatic towns. . . . My intention is that you divide your army into two corps; that you give to Marshal Mortier the command of the eighth corps of the Grand Army; that you form it so that it amounts at least to 12,000 men, with as much cavalry as possible, and twenty-four pieces of artillery. With this corps Marshal Mortier will go to Hamburg, will take possession of the town, as also of Bremen and Lübeck [2].' It is rarely given to belligerents to preserve an attitude of entire correctness, and if the occupation of these towns had been merely a precaution to prevent their falling into the hands of English, Prussians, or Swedes, the action of Bonaparte might be condoned. General Blücher, fleeing from the field of Jena, had made his last stand under the walls of Lübeck, and that city had experienced to the full the cruelty and the licence of victorious soldiery. A temporary military occupation until the conclusion of the war, an occupation which respected the property

[1] Cf. Abel's memorandum of July 8, 1806; *Affaires étrangères, Corr. Pol.: Hamburg*, 119.   [2] *Corr.* xiii. 475-6, no. 11,171.

of these neutral republics, and was studious to soothe their wounded feelings of honour, would have had much to recommend it. This, however, was far from being the spirit of Napoleon's instructions to Mortier. That officer was commanded to disarm the inhabitants of Hamburg, to occupy Cuxhaven, to seal the river hermetically so as to prevent any Englishman escaping, to assure himself of the houses of the English bankers, to put seals on the bank of Hamburg, to seize all English merchandise, to arrest the English and Prussian consuls, and to prevent all communication with England. 'You will send a regiment,' Napoleon continues, 'to do the same thing at Bremen. . . . Provisionally you will interdict the navigation of the Elbe and the Weser to all nations. You will get hold of everything which belongs to Prussia and England. There is a good deal of building-wood which belongs to Prussia. I need not tell you that the principal point is to begin by disarming and arresting all native Englishmen, even English bankers established in the country for twenty years; they must answer to me for French travellers arrested on the sea. You will send them all to France. Your command will extend to Lübeck, where you will perform the same operation [1].'

Marshal Mortier, a clement and popular soldier, refrained from carrying out to the letter these barbarous instructions. The bank of Hamburg, the main pillar of Hanseatic credit, was spared in deference to the entreaties of the burghers. No English banker was deported, for the excellent reason that no English banker, indeed no Englishman, save the five members of the English factory, was left in the town. It is true that the French ordered the dissolution of the English factory, whose charter dated from 1611, and that its surviving members were under sentence of deportation to Verdun. But the sentence, partly through the good offices of Bourrienne, was never carried into effect, and by naturalizing themselves as burghers of Hamburg, and appropriating the funds of an ancient institution, the last of the English merchant-adventurers obtained security and affluence [2].

[1] *Corr.* xiii. 542, no. 11,267.
[2] Bourrienne, vii. 176–8; *Corr.* xiv. 17, no. 11,356; Hamburg Complaints: Parliamentary Papers, 1835.

THE HANSEATIC TOWNS

In all three cities strenuous efforts were made to conjure the wrath of the Emperor, and while Lübeck, which had been commended by Bernadotte, sent a suppliant deputation, and Bremen accepted the inevitable with grumbles, Hamburg assured His Majesty that her submission to the Berlin decrees was and should be entire. Nevertheless, no Prussian or English cities could have been more harshly treated. The military occupation was accompanied by embezzlement, by insolence, by financial exactions, and it had come to stay. The excesses of the illiterate Clement at Bremen, the rapacity of General Gratian and his Dutch troops at Lübeck, and the profligate reign—happily a brief one—of General Dupas at Hamburg, when the French General's scullions drank champagne in the kitchen, and the head quarter's mess-bill exceeded 80,000 francs a month, these were memories not easily effaced. Shoes and clothes, caps and corn, wood to the amount of 140,000 francs, were freely requisitioned, and, while the Dutch staff-officers ate and drank 5,000 francs a day at Bremen, a fraudulent inspector of reviews made a fortune out of Lübeck. The Savings Bank at Hamburg, one of the most useful institutions for encouraging thrift among the needy, was seized under the pretext that it was a deposit of foreign money. The famous Hamburg Poor-House, probably the best foundation of the kind then existing in Europe, was converted into a military barrack, and the whole establishment turned adrift without a penny of compensation. The Eimbecksche Haus, a municipal wine-cellar, dating from the fourteenth century, and one of the most popular resorts of the town, was seized by the French soldiers, who sold or swallowed the priceless vintages. All kinds of extortions were practised on the pretext that desirable objects were of English manufacture. There was a perfect plague of passports, and three bottles of wine could not be transferred from house to house without an official permit. Some of the generals, notably Bernadotte, were honourably distinguished for true French courtesy and probity, but these were exceptions, and as the troops were, for the most part, raw conscripts, and the officers men of low birth, acts of gross insolence were not uncommon. Everywhere English goods were confiscated, and their owners compelled to repurchase them from the French government [1]. On this pretext 16,000,000 francs were extracted from Hamburg, and about 3,000,000 from Lübeck and Bremen. In vain did Bourrienne attempt to secure a respite for the unfortunate towns. The Emperor insisted that the money should be paid on the nail [2]. Nor was this the end. These towns which provide pay, food, lodging, hospitals for the French troops, are required in 1808 to contribute 3,000 sailors to the French navy. The quota was excessive in a population of 200,000, and the Emperor in the end had to be content with one-sixth of the original figure. But, meanwhile, not a whaler was allowed to quit the Elbe and the Weser, and the maritime population was kept, so to speak, under seal, in order that so precious a material might not evaporate.

In the winter of 1808-9 there was a general cry of misery. The Burgomaster and Senate of Hamburg represented (January 25, 1809) that out of a population of ·100,000 there were scarcely 2,000 capable of contributing, while in Lübeck 1,050 families, constituting one-fourth of the population, were obliged to have recourse to public charity. The price of food was constantly rising; all credit was lost, and it was doubtful whether the cities would ever recover their old markets [3]. So profound was the discouragement that many rich inhabitants of Hamburg sold their shares in business to buy land in Holstein and Mecklenburg [4]. There was only one source of hope, and that was contraband. Some thirty miles from the mouth of the Weser lies the island of Heligoland, a thin strip of grassy down a little over two miles in circumference, rising out of the German Ocean. Politically attached to the Kingdom of Denmark, it was inhabited by a population of pilots and fishermen whose prosperity had been injured, and whose sustenance even had been endangered, by the maritime war. On September 5, 1807, after England had broken with the Danes, the *Majestic*, with

[1] *A Journal of the Defence of Hamburg*, 284-5; Bourrienne, vii. 179, 247-8, 292, 327; viii. 15, 56, 64. As a subsequent decree forbade the sale of the repurchased goods in Germany, they rotted away in their warehouses.

[2] *Corr.* xii. 67, no. 13,217.

[3] Overbeck to Champagny, Feb. 20, 1809; *Affaires étrangères, Corr. Pol.: Hamburg*, 120.

[4] *Quelques réflexions sur la position actuelle des villes anséatiques*, ibid.

THE HANSEATIC TOWNS

Admiral Russell in command, sailed into the tiny harbour, landed a party of marines, and hoisted the Union Jack. The Frisian fishermen—there were 400 houses on the island—stared and submitted, little divining the curious revolution which was to be effected in this solitary station of birds. A miscellaneous crowd of merchants, clerks, and smugglers, rapidly poured into the island of sea-gulls, and the applications for passports became so numerous that, in May 1808, Canning was obliged to restrict their issue. The English merchants on the island, who formed a Chamber of Commerce, reported that from August 9 to November 20, 1808, upwards of 120 vessels fully laden had discharged their wares on the island, and that the annual value of goods transhipped and imported would amount to 8,000,000 pounds sterling. Such was the influx, that what with kegs, cases, and human beings, there was hardly place to stand, and by May 1810 all the building-room in the lower town was exhausted. Though the food consisted of hung meat and stewed prunes, though the prices were exorbitant and the huts stifling, there was a fine quality of excitement in the life. When the French government prohibited refined sugar, the traders of Heligoland deluged the continent with the raw article. When the raw article was forbidden, they shipped rivers of *eau sucrée*. When the *douanier* refused *eau sucrée*, they put their hands into their pockets and coolly bribed him. Coffee passed as horse-beans, sugar as starch, the aliases of pepper were legion. Along the whole North German coast the smugglers of Heligoland found an accomplice population. Bourrienne reckons that in Hamburg alone the number of smugglers amounted to 6,000. The citizens would walk across the Danish border to Altona, and return with coffee, indigo, and sugar concealed about their persons. Mock funerals would be organized in which consignments of colonial goods played the rôle of corpse. Not a trick was left untried. By 1809 the blockade had practically broken down. The Heligoland traders reported that between June 12 and 30 in that year, sixty-six loaded vessels and seventy boats, charged with British merchandise to the value of several hundred thousand pounds, had safely landed their cargoes on the mainland. Indeed, the real obstacle to active intercourse with the continent did not come from the French side, but from the English Orders in Council. The

French *douanier* could, unlike the Dane, always be corrupted, but a more plenteous supply of British licences was needed to satisfy the vigorous appetite of the merchants of Heligoland [1].

Immediately after the battle of Wagram, Napoleon turned his mind to the question of the Hanseatic towns. Their conduct had been irreproachable during the disturbances created by the exploit of Schill, but their political situation had not 'issued from the provisional stage.' On September 26, 1809, he wrote from Vienna to Champagny to say that he had determined after reflection 'to leave these towns imperial towns.' It would be equally prejudicial to their interests to unite them to the Kingdom of Holland or the Kingdom of Westphalia. 'I shall be much more the master of these towns when I have them under my immediate authority.' Accordingly Reinhard, the French minister at Cassel, was to go to Hamburg to concert with Bourrienne the project of a constitution. The towns were to be under the French Protectorate; they were to have a minister at Paris; they were to maintain an armed force, the superior grades of which were to be filled by the Emperor of the French. 'In fine,' wrote Napoleon, 'I desire to have the authority, whether it be over the police and direction of these towns or in any other manner which may be judged suitable. I already have the posts [2]. I desire also a homage of sovereignty, such, for instance, as the nomination of the burgomaster on a triple list formed by the States, or something else of the same nature.... If a little increase in territory is indispensable to these towns, I will not refuse to grant it. They must also furnish a contingent to the Confederation. It is necessary that soon after the peace the whole

---

[1] Colonial Office Papers, Heligoland, 1, 2, 3; Foreign Office Papers, Heligoland, 1; *The Year of Liberation; A Journal of the Defence of Hamburgh against the French Army under Marshal Davoût in* 1813; *An Account of the interesting Island of Heligoland*, London, 1811; Bourrienne, *Mémoires*, vii. 193–4; *Bulletin d'Oldenbourg*, March 30, 1811; *Affaires étrangères, Corr. Pol.: Allemagne*, 743.

[2] In 1806 the Post Office was transferred from the Count of Thurn and Taxis to the officials of the Grand-Duchy of Berg. Mr. Nicholas, the British consul at Altona, made a secret arrangement with these officials for the forwarding of English letters. Norway, *History of the Post Office Packet Service*, 162.

of Germany should be organized, and that the provisional régime should cease. It seems to me that this is the affair which demands most preparation. As Protector I wish also to have the right of giving *exequatur* to foreign consuls, so as to be able to get rid of them if necessary. I wish also to be able to send away from the towns foreigners who shall be suspected of plotting things contrary to my interests[1].'

The detailed instructions were prepared by Champagny in Paris. Everything was to be managed with the greatest possible dissimulation. The minister of Cassel must spend a fortnight in Hamburg, talk with the leading citizens, and suggest certain views informally as if they proceeded from himself. Would it not be well that the towns should enter into the Rhenish Confederation, that they should style themselves imperial towns, take the arms of the French Empire, and concede to their Protector a 'regular legal and tutelary influence' over foreign relations, the press, and foreign intrigues? Meanwhile Reinhard and Bourrienne were secretly to reduce the three municipal constitutions into 'a code which His Majesty can sanction[2].'

The inhabitants of the three cities were too much concerned with their own misfortunes to embrace with alertness the prospect which was opened out to them. Reinhard was forced to admire 'the cosmopolitan and patriotic spirit' of Hamburg, which constantly 'assimilated heterogeneous elements while preserving ancient institutions, and knew how to follow the progress of modern civilization, and to animate with the love of country men who appear to be animated by nothing better than the love of money.' Nowhere save in England was so much important public work done for nothing, and it may account for the high feeling of municipal patriotism in Hamburg that it was one of the few German cities uncontaminated by aristocratic privilege[3]. Reinhard did full justice to these considerations. He ordered the constitutions of the three

[1] *Corr.* xix. 517-8, no. 15,862.
[2] Instructions to Reinhard and Bourrienne, *Affaires étrangères, Corr. Pol.: Hamburg*, 120.
[3] This is forcibly stated in the *Histoire de la ville de Hambourg, de sa religion, de son gouvernement et de son commerce* (Paris, 1809), ii. 548.

cities to be reduced into a code, but recommended that the changes should be as few as possible. At the same time he drafted a federal constitution which should prescribe the relations of the towns to one another, and also the relations which they were to bear towards the Protector. Further, in the joint memoir upon the situation which was sent in to the French government by Reinhard and Bourrienne, full expression was given to the feelings and desires of the Hanseatic burghers. A moving picture was drawn of the common misery. The public debt of Hamburg had increased from 20,000,000 francs to 50,000,000; the expenditure of Lübeck from 50,000 marks to more than 1,000,000; the capitation-tax was raised twenty-five times a year to meet the demands of the military occupation; morality was undermined by the customs, 'a pest the ravages of which will be felt in future generations'; the sugar refinery of Hamburg, the only important branch of industry which could establish itself in that city, was fast disappearing. The burghers wished to retain the flag and the arms of their respective cities, and the common title Hanseatic. The French control over their commerce and external relations was already so complete that it was hardly worth while to struggle against the substantive claims of the French Emperor [1].

Napoleon read the memoir of Reinhard and Bourrienne, and ordered a treaty to be made with the Hanseatic deputies upon the lines suggested by those envoys. The '*villes unies*' were to enter as a single State into the Confederation of the Rhine, and to furnish six guns and 2,646 men to the Grand Army. Champagny submitted a draft according to which the ideas of the burghers were to be reconciled with those of the Emperor. The towns were to be styled imperial and Hanseatic; they were to adopt the flag and arms of the French Empire without relinquishing their own civic ensigns. They were to engage to execute all measures required in the name of the Emperor relative to the continental system, the press, and foreigners. Their commercial conventions and constitutions were to be codified; the French law, the French monetary system, were to be introduced, and the internal affairs of the '*villes unies*' were to be settled by an annual congress of twelve senators, four

---

[1] *Affaires étrangères, Corr. Pol.*: *Hamburg*, 120-1.

THE HANSEATIC TOWNS

from each town, who were to sit for fifteen days at most in each of the three towns in turn. The chiefs of the contingent were to be named by the French Emperor [1].

All this elaborate constitution-making came to nothing. Another year elapsed of military rule and nominal independence, of sharpened commercial edicts and systematic smuggling, of growing impoverishment on the one hand and undiminished exigence on the other.

It was in this year that Marshal Davoût, that stern but upright man of discipline, first laid his heavy hand on Northern Germany as commander of the thirty-second military division. He was one of those men who, like Champagny the Foreign Minister, live to develop and execute the ideas of a master. He, too, was a fervent believer in the continental blockade, blind to economic and reckless of spiritual forces, standing out for all time as the honest fanatic of Napoleonic statesmanship in its decadence. Finding the French name hated throughout North Germany, a population ragged, half-desperate, openly disaffected, trade ruined, agriculture ruined, a general spirit of ill-ease ominous of impending calamity, he stiffened his bull-dog neck and military back, and determined to break the restive beast. A valiant man of war, entirely incorruptible, devoted as a favourite hound, a good strict ruler of the camp, utterly intolerant of pillage, he has earned his place among the great soldiers in the Arch of Triumph. But he was a bad statesman and a worse counsellor, and from his ceaseless and devouring suspicions Napoleon could only learn how to misread the political signals [2].

Yet, further east in the city of Danzig, there was a man who gave brave and wise counsel, if Davoût and his master would listen. Of all the French generals of this time, there was no one so fearless and honest as the Alsatian Rapp.

---

[1] *Corr.* xx. 87, no. 16,085; Champagny to Napoleon, Jan. 13, 1810; *Affaires étrangères, Corr. Pol.: Hamburg*, 121. The drafts of Bourrienne and Reinhard may be found in *Archives Nationales, A. F.* iv. 1706 b.

[2] Davoût's correspondence, containing many interesting enclosures, is in *A. F.* iv. 1654-7. Many of the Marshal's letters have been printed by de Mazade; cf. also Vigier, *Vie le Davoût*. The ungenerous remarks made by Napoleon at St. Helena (Gourgaud, July 14, 1817) should be discounted.

Cherishing no illusions, Rapp was brave and loyal enough to speak unpleasant truths. When the French imposed an export duty of sixty francs on the ton, Rapp wrote to the Duke of Feltre as follows: 'These measures are absolutely against the interests of the Emperor. One has only to take the map to be convinced at once. Danzig is killed, and Königsberg, Elbing, and Memel will enrich themselves with its remains [1].' While Davoût was urging stricter press censure and domiciliary visits, Rapp was forwarding through him to the government in Paris a diagnosis of the situation in Danzig, so searching, so luminous, so damning to the political wisdom of the commercial decrees, that an intelligent and unbiased ruler must have reconsidered the whole situation. Here was a clear case of a city absolutely ruined by the cessation of commerce. This cessation of commerce was due to four causes, each of which was the direct result of the action of the French government—a heavy export duty upon grain and wood, a decree that no Danzig trade should be carried by other than Danzig bottoms, a decree that all return cargoes must come from France, and an annual charge of 800,000 francs for the maintenance of a French garrison. The whole series of transactions was shown to be absurd, of no profit to France, and of infinite harm to Danzig [2]. Yet in April a fresh burden of over 6,000,000 francs was laid upon the city. 'Know, Monsieur le Maréchal,' wrote Rapp, 'that I have never passed for an alarmist, but I cannot but be disquieted when I see that no attention has ever been paid to the reports which I have sent in [3].'

Neither Davoût nor Napoleon gave heed. In the distance there loomed the possibility of a Russian war, pointing, they thought, to a stricter enforcement of the continental blockade, and a more rigorous control of Germany—the ante-room to the steppes. In December 1810 Holland was annexed, and then the Hanseatic towns, the Duchy of Oldenburg, and other fragments of Germany between the Baltic and the Dutch border. To a deputation of the burghers collected in Paris, the

---

[1] Rapp to Feltre, Aug. 24, 1810; *A. F.* iv. 1653.

[2] *Considérations sur l'état actuel de Danzig*, written by Chef de Bataillon Goll and forwarded by Davoût, Jan. 29, 1811; *A. F.* iv. 1654.

[3] Rapp to Davoût, April 4, 1811; *A. F.* iv. 1654.

THE HANSEATIC TOWNS 345

Emperor explained his ostensible motives. 'Your union to the Empire,' he said, 'is a necessary consequence of the British laws of 1806 and 1807, and not the effect of an ambitious calculation. You will find in my civil laws a protection which in your maritime position you can no longer find in political laws. Maritime commerce, which has made your prosperity, can now only recover with the help of my maritime power. We must reconquer at the same time the law of nations, the liberty of the seas, and general peace. When I shall have more than a hundred vessels of the line, I will vanquish England in a few campaigns. The sailors of your coasts and the materials which arrive in the mouths of your rivers are necessary to me. France in its ancient limits could not construct a navy in time of war. While its coasts were blocked, it was reduced to receive the law. To-day, with the increase which my Empire has received in the last six years, I can construct, equip, and arm twenty-five vessels of the line a year [1].'

It was hardly of less importance that the new acquisitions would facilitate canal communication between the Rhine and the Baltic. In four or five years it was hoped that a new canal might join the Elbe to the Weser and the Weser to the Ems, while the canal already existing between Hamburg and Lübeck might be repaired and widened [2].

An intermediate commission, consisting of three members, the Count de Chaban, Marshal Davoût, and M. Faure, was appointed to introduce the French system, and sat from February 9 to December 31, 1811. The Hanseatic senates were abolished, and a uniform provisional municipal system upon French lines was substituted for them. The territory was divided into three departments: Ems Supérieur, Bouches de Wéser, Bouches de l'Elbe, each of which was subdivided in the French manner into *arrondissements*, cantons, and communes. In February and March the commission organized the administration of justice. An official translation of the French codes was commanded. An imperial

---

[1] *Corr.* xxi. 485, no. 17,482.
[2] *Corr.* xxi. 310, no. 17,197 ; xxii. 15, no. 17,553. Champagny told the Consul-General at Hamburg that the Rhenish-Baltic canal was the principal object of the annexation. Champagny to Leroy, Dec. 14, 1810 ; *Affaires étrangères, Corr. Pol. : Hamburg,* 121.

court was established at Hamburg, consisting of four chambers, two civil, one criminal, and one for the decision of points of constitutional law. Justices of the peace were appointed in each canton, and there was a court of first instance in each *arrondissement*. German was to be employed concurrently with French in the courts and in all public and private acts. Acts drawn up in French and requiring registration were to be accompanied by a German translation. A strict decree was issued to punish offences and thefts committed in the imperial forests. The number of Hamburg newspapers was reduced from fifteen to six, and the usual official bulletin in French and German was commanded. The imperial lottery was now so important an ingredient in French rule, that all competing institutions were prohibited. A special commissioner was sent into each of the departments for the purpose of superintending the naval conscription, and the imperial decree of March 24, 1810, establishing practical schools of marine, was made applicable to these newly incorporated provinces of the Empire [1].

While the agents of the free towns accredited to foreign Courts were naturally recalled, the salaries of the Hanseatic functionaries were reduced to the French level. Commissioners were sent into each department to collect statistics and personal information, and conferences were held with the former members of Hanseatic senates upon points as to which the intermediate commission desired information.

The French were, on the whole, satisfied with the public temper, for while it was admitted that the three towns regretted their independence, not a day passed without some member of the Hanseatic senates coming to solicit a post in the government [2]. In the country districts there was said to be some show of enthusiasm to greet the new prefects [3]. The unfortunate inhabitants had suffered so much during the last

---

[1] *Collection des procès-verbaux de la Commission du Gouvernement établi à Hambourg du 9 févr. au 31 déc.* 1811 ; A. F. iv. 1706 c.

[2] Chaban to Montalivet, Jan. 21, 1811 ; F^{ie} 50.

[3] *Rapport sur le voyage de M. Keversberg, préfet de l'Ems Supérieur, à travers son département,* F^{ie} 56. ' *M. le Préfet n'a vu sur sa route que l'effusion la plus franche des sentiments d'admiration et d'amour que ces peuples ont voué à leur nouveau souverain.*'

THE HANSEATIC TOWNS 347

few years, that any political change might seem to portend an alleviation in their lot, and the union with France was naturally represented by French authorities as the most unmingled blessing which Providence could confer upon man [1].

It was one of the established maxims of the imperial government to ascertain, though not necessarily to execute, the wishes of its new subjects. A deputation from the three Hanseatic departments was accordingly summoned to Paris to advise the Minister of the Interior upon the needs of those localities, and twenty-eight sittings were held (May 16—July 25, 1812) under the presidency of that official. The deputation recommended a reduction in the scale of the land-tax, on the ground that the population was poor, and the soil for the most part light and sandy. They petitioned for the abolition of the customs line which separated them from the French Empire; for a higher scale of pensions and salaries, owing to the dearness of provisions and the necessity under which all officials lay of knowing both languages; and they requested that all judicial posts should be given to natives of the three departments. A commission was recommended for the purpose of reclaiming marsh land, and measures were suggested for the better organization of charity and for prison administration. It was represented that the greater part of the inhabitants of these provinces could read and write, that reading habits were generally diffused, and that the schools were excellent; but since there was no provincial university, it was suggested that one might eventually be developed out of the Academy of Bremen.

The deputation proceeded to point out that, by the annexation of Holland and the Hanseatic departments, France was becoming a great Protestant power [2]. They suggested that a Protestant, if possible a Protestant Councillor of State, might be appointed to assist the Minister of Cults in all matters pertaining to his religion, and that a central consistory might be formed under his presidency. The French government was urged to preserve the existing Church tithes and endowments,

[1] Cf. Davoût's proclamation, *A. F.* iv. 1706 c.
[2] The religious census in the Hanseatic departments was: Lutherans, 889,730; Catholics, 193,598; Calvinists, 51,302; Portuguese Jews, 182; Memnonites and Anabaptists, 162; Quakers, 20.

to create three Lutheran consistories at Hamburg, Bremen, and Osnabrück respectively, to permit Lutheran dogma to be taught in schools, and to establish a chair of German Calvinistic Dogma for the instruction of intending ministers, who would otherwise continue to be compelled to obtain their theological training in Geneva.

Mingled with these positive recommendations there were many grievances. It was pointed out that the exportation of cattle, one of the greatest resources of the inhabitants of Oldenburg, had been forbidden since the union, that the wine-trade of Hamburg and Bremen suffered from 'a thousand small vexations,' that the contract under which part of the conscribed sailor's pay was to be sent to his family had been inadequately fulfilled, and that merchants and travellers suffered many odious annoyances at the hands of the French customs officers on the frontier [1].

To Marshal Davoût nothing could be more revolting than the thought that plaintiff Germans should be permitted to ventilate their opinions in the French capital. 'The residence of the deputies in Paris,' he wrote, 'is very harmful to the service of your Majesty. Their return will dissipate the chimerical hopes which these people try to foster for their relations [2].' There was, however, no fear that the government of the later Empire, now embarked upon the Russian war, would show undue leniency to its new subjects. The full unmitigated weight of the French fiscal system, with its heavy property tax, its door and window tax, its patent tax, its personal and movable tax, its tax upon registration, and its *droits réunis* or duties upon wine and brandy, tobacco and salt, was laid remorselessly upon this exhausted and penurious province. The heavy import-duties into France and Holland raised the price of linen by 20 per cent., and completely closed the Dutch market against it, and though the customs line between France and Holland was removed on August 23, 1812, the line existing between Holland and the Hanseatic departments was still maintained. In other words, the only

---

[1] *Compte-rendu des opérations de la Commission des Députés au Corps Législatif des départements anséatiques*, F^{ie} 57–60.

[2] Davoût to Napoleon, April 20, 1811; *A. F.* iv. 1706 c.

THE HANSEATIC TOWNS 349

possible material compensation which could have been easily offered to the 'new Frenchman' for added fiscal burdens and vanished political independence, that is to say, free access to the French and Dutch markets, was by an almost inconceivable spirit of jealousy denied to them.

Spiritual consolations were sketched in outline, but obliterated by the rude hand of war. All kinds of reports were invited and composed upon the state of the sciences and the arts, of the theatre and of medicine in the new departments of France. Two eminent men, Cuvier and Noël, were sent to reconnoitre the educational institutions of the country, which France was to induct into the full blaze of her shining culture. The peasants were here, as elsewhere, declared free from the more degrading services, and the monasteries and nunneries—homes of ease and ignorance—received a short shrift. It would be possible, indeed, to form a selection of administrative documents in which one would read of nothing but the solicitude of the imperial government for the illumination and development of a backward province.

But an historical portrait painted from such material would have been disowned by every German inhabitant. For them the French rule meant still what it had meant from the beginning—an army of spies and custom-house officers, of insolent soldiers and corrupt officials, of extortion, repression, and despotism.

CHAPTER XVI

THE RHINE DEPARTMENTS

'Halt fest am Reich, du kölnischer Bauer, mag es fallen süss oder sauer.'—OLD PROVERB.

AT the outbreak of the great war in 1792 there was a long strip of territory upon the left bank of the Rhine, extending from Cleves to Deuxponts and Saarbrück, which formed part of the German Empire, and was inhabited by a German-speaking people. Few districts of equal area, even in Germany, were so various in their political, social, and economic characteristics. Nine bishoprics or archbishoprics, seven abbeys, two religious military orders, seventy-six princes or counts, four imperial towns, and a vast number of imperial knights exercised sovereign authority in this westernmost rim of Germany, and succeeded in giving a distinctive colour to their several dominions. Nor were political subdivisions the sole cause or type of difference. There was great variety of climate and soil, of occupation and temperament. The contrast was great between the pleasure-loving, wine-growing Franconian of the south, of Worms and Speier, of Kreuznach and Zweibrücken, and the thrifty, enduring Low German who drove his plough on the Hundsrück, or gathered his sparse harvest of hay on the cold heights of the Eiffel. Great, too, was the contrast between the population of the Rhine valley, between Bingen and Bonn, and the dwellers in the wide plains of the lower river. Here a narrow strip of sunny vineyard bred a joyous, careless, excitable tempera-ment. Peasants lived from hand to mouth, hoping for a good vintage ; and when the fine year came and the vats were full, they would drink and frolic with their casual fortune. The poor swarmed into the cities, and lived on the alms so bountifully distributed by their priestly rulers, for Mainz, Coblentz, and Bonn shone in the favour of a princely Court [1]. But as soon as the northern plain begins, life becomes hard and sober, even solemn. The men are more steady and trustworthy ; they sow

[1] Thayer's *Beethoven*, i. 88.

corn and drive oxen, and in their substantial farmsteads gather plenty.

A distinctive feature of the Rhineland was the political preponderance of the ecclesiastical principalities. If we except the King of Prussia, who owned Cleves, the Elector-Palatine, and the Prince of Hesse-Darmstadt, far the most important sovereigns in this region were the ecclesiastical Electors of Cologne, Mainz, and Treves. The government of these princes was neither barbarous nor pious, neither oppressive nor unpopular. Some of them even showed a zeal for the welfare of their subjects, and improved the schools or diminished the holidays in their dominions. The burden of military service was small, the taxes were comparatively light, and an easy-going population were well content to live under the crosier. But of all forms of temporal government there is none so enervating as the government of priests. The Courts of Cologne, Mainz, and Treves were remarkable for petty intrigue and idle splendour, and a total absence of any serious political interests. Society was divided into rigid castes, each consumed with the shabby ambition of keeping itself unsullied by contact with the caste below it. The old nobility despised the new nobility, and the new nobility despised the burghers. There was a Prussian party and an Austrian party, there were Papalists and anti-Papalists, there were the personal adherents of the archiepiscopal mistress and there was the legion of her foes, there were the obscurantists who regretted the Middle Ages, and there were the fine gentlemen and ladies who fingered their Voltaire and Helvetius. But however numerous the sections into which Rhenish society was split, one feature was common to the whole mass—a strange detachment from all the deeper elements of German life. For these cathedral cities and these archiepiscopal Courts, each so envious of the splendour of Versailles, so careless of the beauties of their own splendid monuments of Gothic, the new literature of Germany, the works of Kant and Lessing, of Goethe and Schiller, might almost as well not have been written. The idea of the intellectual achievements, of the intellectual possibilities of Germany, was entirely foreign to the students of the Catholic universities of Mainz or Cologne. A hard, narrow scholasticism, the husks of a once living but long extinct ardour of life and thought, paralysed the intellect and narrowed the sympathies. The superstitions of Romanism survived without its poetry, and the city of Albertus Magnus had forgotten to think.

In the evening of October 5, 1792, a man was seen shyly wearing the tricolour in the streets of Mainz. It was in vain that the Elector, Carl Joseph von Erthal, had prohibited all reference to Paris news, attempting to delete the Revolution as a censor might draw his pen through an obnoxious passage in a newspaper. The new creed spread eastwards, and found its adherents in the Rhenish cities. Some were caught by the new gospel of equality, others were fascinated by the notion of a Cisrhenane republic; to others the insolence and futility of the French emigrant nobility commended the furies of democracy. The old governments made an ignominious flight before the advancing French armies, packing up their gold and jewels and abandoning the land to their foes. How could men feel any respect or allegiance for rulers of so base a metal? And when Prussian and Austrian armies restored those rulers for a brief period, it was clear that adversity had taught them no lesson which was worth the learning. The old Church coach lumbered along in the old ruts, until in 1794 there was a second dispersion of ecclesiastical gentlemen at the point of the French bayonet. Then for the next twenty years the tricolour waved over the cities of the Rhine.

If in the first flush of enthusiasm some Germans of literary temperament had welcomed the liberating legions of France, this illusion was soon dissipated. The French government was detestable, and the country was the theatre of continuous war. For five years formidable armies inundated these provinces; towns and villages were pillaged, devastated, or burnt; cottages were abandoned, fields remained untilled, industry and commerce perished. Exorbitant contributions amounting to 150,000,000 francs were raised. 'In the time of terror,' say two petitioners (April 2, 1800) to the First Consul, 'the principle was actually laid down that France ought to surround herself with deserts, and "commissioners of evacuation" were sent for this purpose. We were then inundated with a horde of immoral men who came only with the intention of spoil. . . . In our courts sit men who are as completely ignorant of the

THE RHINE DEPARTMENTS

language and laws of the country, as they are ignorant of the rights of the republic, and who defile the sublime ministry with which they are invested. The majority of administrative posts, especially in finance, are occupied by stupid and immoral men, and every resistance to these scandals involves an accusation of terrorism.' Another highly qualified observer paints an equally depressing picture of the situation of the Rhenish provinces at the time of the *coup d'état* of Brumaire. 'Everybody,' he says, 'hides his wealth in order to escape the requisitions of the tax-collector. Most of the municipal and communal authorities imitate the soldiers in demanding unauthorized requisitions, and live by plunder, and the public debt amounts to more than 90,000,000 francs.' The report proceeds to describe how almost all the hospitals and houses of refuge were so indebted or pillaged that they could offer no shelter to the poor; how there were few or no good roads; how all the bridges were crumbling away, and the dykes were 'ready to cede to the force of impetuous torrents.' It depicts the widespread destruction of the castles and country houses which formed the ornament of the country, and the devastation of entire communes, by fire or by 'commissions of evacuation.' The same authority says that the priests were everywhere against the French, that the workshops were idle, and the forests ruined by devastation or neglect [1].

No war can be carried on without havoc, and a large part of these evils may be reckoned among the inevitable consequences of a state of war. But much was also due to the vacillation, the immorality, and the political incompetence of the French government and their agents. The scheme of administration went through several phases. First there was a Central Administration at Aix-la-Chapelle (November 14, 1792), then another Central Administration was established at Treves (January 27, 1795), and then the two were united in the single administration of Aix (March 10, 1795). A year later another plan was tried, and two General Directions

---

[1] *Situation de l'administration civile dans les quatre nouveaux départements sur la rive gauche du Rhin à l'époque du premier Brumaire, an* 8, par le citoyen Shee, F[ie] 43. A similar impression may be gathered from the correspondence of the British minister at Cassel (*F. O. Germany*, 20), and from Metternich's *Mémoires*, i. 258.

(capitals Aix-la-Chapelle and Coblentz) were established, but they too were short-lived. On February 4, 1797, the Directorate charged Hoche, general-in-chief of the army of Sambre-et-Meuse, to reorganize the conquered country, and an Intermediate Commission composed of five members was established by that general at Bonn, which lived on for a few months, during which time it did good work. Requisitions and contributions of war were forbidden; all the French officials were deprived of office, and their acts submitted to scrutiny; an order was issued that the functionaries of the deposed governments should resume their official work. But Hoche died, and Augereau, his successor, imported more of the revolutionary ardour into the government. He protected the patriotic or revolutionary clubs, required the officials of the old régime to swear an oath of hatred to monarchy and anarchy, and pushed forward the sale and division of Church lands. But at last these miserable provinces passed finally out of military control. On November 4, 1797, an Alsatian, by name Rudler, was made government Commissioner for all the land between the Rhine and Moselle. Rudler was, it appears, an honest man, though his enemies accused him of nepotism. He kept out of factions, refused to listen to the clamours of the 'patriots' of Mainz, and his first choice of public functionaries was tolerably good. But so great was the fear of reaction among the party which had saluted the French occupation that not a single rich proprietor or former magistrate was selected to fill any office.

It is, however, to Rudler that the Rhenish districts owe their organization as French provinces. He divided them into four departments (1, Roer, capital Aix-la-Chapelle; 2, Rhin-et-Moselle, capital Coblentz; 3, Mont-Tonnerre, capital Mainz; 4, Sarre, capital Treves), and introduced the laws and institutions of revolutionary France, abolishing the *corvée* and tithes, seigneurial justice and entails, and in fine all the exemptions and privileges of the nobility, as well as publishing laws to regulate civil and criminal procedure, successions, the notariat, and the civil state[1]. The four departments were

---

[1] For Rudler's work, cf. F^ie 42 : *Recueil des règlemens et arrêtés émanés du Commissaire du Gouvernement dans les quatre nouveaux départements de la rive gauche du Rhin*, Strasbourg, an vii–viii.

introduced to the benefits of the French legal system, public procedure, the jury, and the mild and humane Criminal Code of 1795, but the use of the French tongue in the law courts was enjoined, and this, taken in connection with the nefarious character of the public prosecutor Keil, who is described to us in a highly coloured passage as being 'more ambitious than Robespierre, and more ferocious than Fouquier-Tinville,' must have raised doubts as to the excellence of the new civilization [1]. Further, a stable administration was rendered impossible by the jealousies of various French factions which were contending for power in the new departments, and by the weakness of the Directorate in Paris. The true course would have been to select a strong and honest governor, free from patriotic cant, and uncontaminated by revolutionary excesses, and then to support him through thick and thin. But the home government had neither the courage, nor the knowledge, nor the strength to pursue such a policy. Hardly was a governor appointed, but he incurred unpopularity by dismissing one official or by appointing another, and was in consequence recalled. The capable Rudler made way for the cipher Marquis. The cipher Marquis was succeeded by the terrorist Lakanal, whose detestable government aroused a universal outcry. After Lakanal came Dubois-Dubais, and after Dubois-Dubais, General Shee, an honest man with some local knowledge but incapacitated alike by old age and bad health. Five governors in two years would have been too large an allowance under any circumstances: in a new unorganized province racked with war and every form of physical distress, it meant sheer chaos. There were indeed fifteen octavo volumes of regulations, decrees, and instructions of the General Commissioner, to which an apologist might point as a sign that whatever might have been the vices of the French revolutionary government, idleness was not among them. But though the French system was introduced on paper, there was little to commend it to the German mind, so long as the agents of the government were corrupt, extortionate, and tyrannical [2].

---

[1] *Tableau des quatre nouveaux départements depuis leur organisation jusqu'à ce jour, présenté le 21 Vend. au citoyen Jollivet*, F^{ie} 43.

[2] It may interest the legal student to note that among the laws published by the revolutionary government in the four departments

No justification can be pleaded by the French on the score of opposition in the provinces. The Rhinelanders bent their necks to the yoke with the passive apathy of tired cattle. There were no conspiracies, there was no feeling for the old governments; the taxes were paid to an Augereau or a Lakanal with the same docility as they had been paid to the Elector of Mainz or the Duke of Deux-Ponts. Yet, if we except the small knot of professional agitators in the towns, the inhabitants were ground between the lower and the upper millstone. Some of them hated the old order of things: all of them were driven to desperation by the new. Their leaders had preached a millennium, and they were experiencing a hell. Such republican enthusiasm as formerly existed had utterly died away under the pressure of French customs, French passports, French taxes, and French prisons. The 'fêtes décadaires' had resolved themselves into 'some speeches recited precipitately in a low voice,' before a handful of officials. 'There is hardly a commune,' so goes a report, 'in which one can find some privileged souls animated by the spark of the sacred fire,' and the difficulty of discovering men to replenish the official hierarchy steadily increased. 'A great number of cantons,' wrote Shee, April 11, 1800, 'are not only without a commissioner, but still devoid of any administrative action. Aix-la-Chapelle and Coblentz have not even a municipality, Treves and Mainz have very bad ones, and as in several other communes there is no one willing to discharge a public office, our enemies rejoice at the general relaxation of government[1].' The only remedy which seemed possible under the circumstances was thorough incorporation with France. The old governments could not be recalled, the present system of ruling the country like a pashalik was intolerable, and as there was no administrative class sufficiently skilled, upright, and powerful to govern a Cisrhenane republic, independence was out of the question. If it were once recognized that these departments were French, there was some hope that they might be treated with greater consideration, that the officials would be more impartial, and

there were many which belonged to the ancient Monarchy, as the *Ordonnance sur le fait de la Justice* of 1539, and the great *Ordonnance Civile* of 1667.   [1] Fie 43.

that local hates would have a smaller influence on public affairs. The prospect was not one which could be viewed altogether with a sanguine heart, with the old enthusiasm of '92, but it was a way out of a difficulty, and while the *coup d'état* of Brumaire was being prepared, three delegates from the Rhine provinces were travelling to Paris to plead that this course might be adopted.

One of these men, J. G. Görres of Coblentz, though only twenty-three years of age, was already a striking figure, and destined to play a distinguished if somewhat ineffectual rôle in German politics. His Italian strain, for his mother was of that race, gave him a vivacity and quickness of temperament which are rarely found among Teutons of the pure blood. He was a fine popular orator, a brilliant journalist, and afterwards a sympathetic, versatile, and ingenious scholar. He had courage, energy, dash, curiosity, and all the qualities of the spirited temperament. But he was deficient in judgement and measure, and an ill-natured critic might discover in his earlier life the failings of the demagogue, and in his middle age the weakness of the sciolist. At the beginning of the French Revolution he had thrown himself vigorously into the democratic current, and such was his simplicity at the age of twenty that he sent the Directorate, the most warlike of governments, a project for a perpetual peace, which breathes the most fervid enthusiasm for the new Republic. In his journal, *Das rothe Blatt*, he caricatured the prince-bishops and confederate kings without sparing the errors of the French functionaries, and an article directed against the Landgrave of Hesse, then at peace with France, led to the suppression of the paper. A Cisrhenane republic, organized on democratic lines, and protected by France against the assaults of the expelled despots, seemed to him in those days the best means of reconciling the spirit of the age with German patriotism. But with the death of Hoche and the advent of Rudler he came to modify his aspirations. It was clear that France now meant to annex the departments, and that the dream of a Cisrhenane independence was vain. Görres argued, as so many have argued both before and since, that civilization is higher than nationality, and that the true interests of a people are served by giving them the best institutions available, even at the expense of local spirit. By 1799 his conversion to the tricolour had become complete, and there was no more enthusiastic champion of the French union than Görres.

The deputation was received by the First Consul, who assured them that the inhabitants of the four departments could count unreservedly upon the justice of the French government, and that he would never lose sight of their happiness; and after the Treaty of Lunéville had ratified the cession of the left bank of the Rhine, a consular proclamation addressed to the Rhineland recapitulated the advantages of the French connection in the following impressive terms [1]:—

'A solemn treaty concluded between the Republic, the chief of the Empire, and the Germanic Body, and ratified at Paris 25 Ventose, has definitely united your destiny to that of France. The interests and rights of the Republic have become yours; your interests and your rights have become hers. In adopting you she has vowed to you, as to all her children, good will and solicitude; she calls upon you as she calls upon them to promise fidelity to her. Let this promise impose upon all a forgetfulness of the ties from which the treaty has disengaged you, and a respect for those ties which now attach you to the Republic. Let it put a term to the vain apprehensions which prevent some persons from enjoying the advantages of union, and to the mad hopes which induce some others to disguise or pervert them.

'These advantages, what reasonable spirit could fail to recognize them? Odious privileges no longer enchain the industry of the working classes; game no longer ravages the fields of the cultivator, or devours the fruits of his work; degrading *corvées* have ceased for all; for all has ceased the degradation of feudal services.

'The tithe is abolished; contributions of all kinds have been softened down; taxation is equally distributed between the lands of the lord and the ecclesiastic, which were formerly exempt from charges, and those of the individual who used alone to bear them. The internal custom-duties which obstructed the transit from one country to another, or prevented people from going

[1] Corr. vii. 198, no. 5,641.

THE RHINE DEPARTMENTS 359

up the rivers, are suppressed; commerce is free with France—the most advantageous market of the world—and will no longer encounter the obstacles which the old frontiers opposed to it.

'An impartial justice and regular administrations are substituted for' the arbitrary authority of the bailiffs. Such are the advantages which union assures to liberty and property. It does no less for the security and tranquillity of the country. Instead of being covered by opposed and constantly conflicting interests, it will be sheltered by an interest common to 30,000,000 citizens. Instead of being submitted to a multitude of small governments too feeble to defend, but strong enough to oppress, it will be protected by a power which will always know how to make its territory respected. The union of the four departments to France is for them a pledge of prosperity, and their promise of fidelity to the Republic will be an expression of actual affection for her, no less than a recognition of the acts which have brought about the union.'

A year later van Alpen, a worthy pastor of Stolberg (near Aix-la-Chapelle), published a history of the Rhineland, which is curious as illustrating a combination of genuine local patriotism with enthusiasm for the French Republic. A passage taken from the introduction to the second volume may serve to illustrate the attitude of an honest Rhenish antiquary to the government of the French Revolution and the Consulate [1].

'Wild and stormy advanced the new constitution into view: threatening and in bloody garment began Anarchy; with the most awful devastations did she raise her sceptre and terrible throne on the laughing meadows and golden hills of the Rhine; mild and wise had been the last rulers of the left bank of the Rhine, the Kings of Prussia, the Electors of the Palatinate, of Cologne, of Treves, of Mainz. By dint of their great statesmanship smiled the morning glow of reason, truth, and virtue; humanity and love fought many a fortunate fight, won many a decisive victory, overthrew many demons of darkness; by means of their good administration the lovely Rhine-bank bloomed. Then came the hour of devastation; then came the destructive Angel of Dread; then raged the bloody sword; then most hideous war swung its blade over the good, tranquil, industrious,

[1] We make no attempt to refine the author's phraseology.

and towards-perfection-ripening inhabitants. But how all that has altered! How fled the shadows of death, how vanished the darkness of night in the morning of the 18th Brumaire! How fled the demon of devastation before the rescuer Bonaparte!

'The military government of the left Rhine-bank was soon brought to an end by the General Commissioners. This alteration was already popular. Unforgettable remain for us the services of a Shee, a Rudler, a Jollivet, towards the organization of the four departments. Immortal gratitude the last of these commissioners, Jean Bon St. André, won for himself. His memory will live on in the wonderful road to Mainz and Cologne, in the Antonine Church which he gave to the Protestants in Cologne, and in the St. Anne Church which he gave to the Protestants in Aix; in his efforts to further tolerance, unity, industry, trade, arts, knowledge, and well-being.

'At last a decree of the government orders that with 1 Vend. XI, the French constitution shall avail for the four new Rhine departments, and that Jean Bon St. André shall continue his functions as prefect in the Department of Mont-Tonnerre. So we are now united, we make a part of the great Republic and of the most enlightened people of the world, we enjoy all advantages and the protection of the government, just as much as the French nation: we are French. Our four new Rhine departments make the twenty-sixth military division, which will receive new brilliance from the Legion of Honour and the camp of Veterans. Senatorships will be established here. Each department has its prefect, its *arrondissement*, its special court; each *arrondissement* its sub-prefect, its court of justice; each commune one or more justices of the peace, one or more notaries, its mayor. All four departments have their court of appeal at Treves; all will see one of their number elevated to be a member of the legislature. Compare our present constitution with that which preceded it, and you will be content with our position. Trust in the government, hope for the future [1].'

The intelligent Görres was not so sanguine. Being in Paris shortly after Brumaire, he had correctly divined the political situation, and in a pamphlet addressed to his fellow countrymen

[1] Van Alpen, *Geschichte des frankischen Rheinufers: was es war und was es itzt ist*, Cologne, 1802.

THE RHINE DEPARTMENTS

gave vent to his bitter disappointment. Where he had hoped for a republic he found a despotism. 'He had received,' so he wrote, 'a wound which could not heal. The great images which had grown with him were broken.' The only brilliant publicist of the Rhineland retired from politics to become a professor. In a short time all public life ceased. The clubs were closed, the newspapers were censured, and the voice of criticism was completely stilled. It was the price which the Rhineland had to pay for union with 'the most enlightened people of the world.'

When on September 22, 1802, the four Rhine departments, Roer, Rhin-et-Moselle, Sarre, and Mont-Tonnerre, were finally assimilated to the departments in the interior of France[1], the office of General Commissioner was abolished, and the new institutions which the Consulate was creating for France were simultaneously communicated to these provinces. The work of destruction had already been accomplished, and ten years of revolutionary turmoil stood between the Rhinelanders and the days when Worms and Speier were free imperial cities, and the inhabitants of Bonn and Coblentz studied the caprices and enjoyed the festivals of their luxurious princes. Nobody dreamt that the old order could ever return. Those ancient days seemed already fantastic and distant. There was a longing for quiet and stable administration, for honest governors, and steady material development. If France could give these things, the Rhine provinces were willing to accept her, if not with enthusiasm, at any rate with indifference. There was, indeed, no alternative power which could claim their allegiance.

The administration of Napoleon healed the wounds and smoothed the wrinkles. The reign of violence was over, and the reign of order began. The concordat restored and regulated the outward machinery of religion. Free public worship was permitted; bishoprics were founded in Aix, Mainz, and Treves, and seminaries provided by the State undertook the religious instruction of the clergy. The political power and

---

[1] Rhin-et-Moselle contained a population of 203,290; Ruhr, one of 516,287; Sarre, one of 219,049; Mont-Tonnerre, one of 342,316. The largest towns were Cologne (about 38,000), Aix (about 23,000), and Mainz (about 21,000). Bonn had about 18,000 and Coblentz 10,000. *Moniteur*, an X, no. 352, Supplement.

territorial influence of the hierarchy were indeed gone, and gone for ever, but nevertheless the greater part of the Catholic clergy accepted the change without a murmur. At the first approach of the French armies in 1792, the rich abbots and canons had fled with their coffers, leaving their poorer brethren behind them, men who, having never tasted the sweets of wealth or power, had little to regret or to forgive. The Church was now felt to be a democratic institution. There were no splendid sinecures to attract the nobility, no canonical stalls jealously reserved for the men of many quarterings; and the high places being open to all, the peasant sent one of his sons to the seminary, where he learnt the Napoleonic catechism and a few Latin prayers, and was thus trained for the congenial task of preaching to a rustic congregation the duty of fidelity to its French master.

Yet it must not be supposed that the Napoleonic régime was generous towards the clergy. The Catholic Church saw its monasteries abolished, its bishops put on niggardly salaries, the control of education transferred to other hands, divorce and the civil marriage sanctioned by law. The State incomes of the Lutheran clergy were hardly sufficient to keep the wolf from the door, even with the addition of the house and garden provided at the expense of the commune. Yet the Lutheran pastors were as loyal and as ignorant as their Catholic brethren. Possessing little of theology and nothing of Greek, for the luxuries of knowledge were beyond an income of 500 francs, they gave themselves with zeal to the culture of the grape, and it is said that the clear vintages of the Rhine and the Moselle owe something to the well-directed labours of impecunious divines [1].

The continued existence of religious corporations was inconsistent with the levelling policy of Napoleon. Yet some exceptions and alleviations softened the rigour of the decree of dissolution [2]. All establishments whose sole object was education or the relief of the sick were exempted from the general sentence of death. Pensions which, small though they might be, were not smaller than the incomes of the parish priests, were allotted to the expropriated, and six of the largest convents, together with four of the largest monasteries, were

---

[1] Eilers, ii. 141 ff.   [2] July 2, 1802; Daniels, iv. 391.

THE RHINE DEPARTMENTS

reserved for the use of those among the nuns and the more elderly monks who might desire to continue the common life. While the regular clergy were thus deprived of their legal status, the autonomy of the seculars was pierced at a thousand points by the all-pervading energy of the State. The care of the church fabric was entrusted to a council of notables, of which the *curé* and the mayor were ex-officio members, and any application for public funds came under the scrutiny of the municipal council and the prefect, of the bishop, and, in case of disagreement between the two last authorities, of the Minister of Cults at Paris [1].

A form of government conceived in the same jealousy of clericalism was accorded to the churches of the Augsburg Confession. Five consistorial churches were to form the *arrondissement* of an 'inspection,' and each 'inspection' was to be composed of the minister, and of an elder or notable from every church in the *arrondissement*. The body so constituted could only assemble with the authorization of the government, and in the presence of the prefect and sub-prefect, nor could it enforce its decisions until they had obtained the approval of the State. The main duty of the general council of inspection was, however, not to legislate, but to nominate a committee of three persons, two of whom were to be laymen, to supervise the churches and ministers in the *arrondissement*. A function so slight might, one would have supposed, have been safely committed to the Lutheran churchmen to discharge, but Napoleon would tolerate no autonomy, and the names of the nominees had to be submitted for his approval. Above the 'inspections' the First Consul created three general consistories, which were to meet respectively at Strasburg, Mainz, and Cologne. These assemblies again were partially composed of laymen, and could only meet with government permission, and in the presence of prefect and sub-prefect. Since their sessions were limited to six days, and since no topic could be entertained or discussed without due notice given to the Minister of Cults, it is probable that the deliberations of the Lutheran fathers were neither free, animated, nor important [2].

---

[1] Dec. 30, 1809; Daniels, v. 431.
[2] April 8, 1802; Daniels, iv. 292 ff.

The French Revolution, in itself so didactic, had left public education in the utmost confusion. Schools, primary and secondary, had been decreed on a comprehensive scale, but such schools as were created suffered from penury and neglect. The law of XI Floréal X (May 1, 1802) laid the burden of primary and secondary schools upon the communes, except in so far as they were assisted by voluntary effort, and submitted both these classes of school to the strict control of prefect and sub-prefect. At the same time the State undertook the support of the *lycées*, which gave instruction in ancient languages, logic, morals, physics, and mathematics, and of the special schools of law, medicine, and the like. The schoolboys of the Mainz *lycée* long remembered the day when Napoleon himself walked into the class-room and examined the upper forms in Latin and mathematics [1]. For the *lycée*, like every other detail in the Napoleonic system, was made to serve the purposes of its creator. It was modelled upon military principles, and the drill, the uniform, and the discipline of these stringent institutions were intended to acclimatize the student to barrack life, and to produce intelligent and serviceable tools to the hand of a despot.

But more important than the creation of the *lycée* was the decree of March 17, 1808, which constituted the University of France. The educational institutions of the Rhine provinces were now fitted into a comprehensive system directed from Paris, and this incidentally served to promote the design of detaching the four departments from the intellectual influences of Germany. Such a project had been cherished under the Directory, openly declared under the Consulate, and was now steadily pursued under the Empire [2]. The famous German Universities were forbidden, as the seed-plots of all that was imaginative, turbulent, and perilous to the State. An imperial decree enacted that the text-books in the *lycées* should be French, that the teaching should be given in French, and that a third

---

[1] Lerebours, *Napoléon et les Mayençais*, 8.

[2] *Moniteur*, 1802, no. 211 : ' *Les peuples réunis à la France qui parlent une langue différente, et accoutumés à des institutions étrangères, ont besoin de renoncer à d'anciennes habitudes et de se former sur leur sol les moyens nécessaires pour donner à leurs fils l'instruction, les mœurs, les caractères qui doivent les confondre avec les Français.*'

THE RHINE DEPARTMENTS 365

of every hour should be devoted to French grammar and literature. As a knowledge of the French language was an indispensable condition of government employment, the study of German, though never forbidden, tended to take a subordinate place, and even disappeared from the curriculum of the *lycée* of Bonn. Yet it is questionable whether any sense of resentment was engendered by this feature in the educational policy of the Empire. These provinces had kept themselves so curiously isolated from the main stream of German thought and feeling that it was no special privation for the Rhinelander to be cut off from the lectures of Göttingen or Leipzig. Nor was the campaign against the German language waged in a resolute or persecuting spirit. Though French was the language of the government and the laws, the prefect of Mont-Tonnerre exhorted the members of the Society of Science and Arts at Mainz not to neglect 'their original and primitive' tongue, and spoke of the 'happy alliance' which should be made to exist between the two languages. The importation of German newspapers and books was purposely rendered difficult by official regulations, but nevertheless they penetrated into the departments. Though French made considerable progress, German was never eliminated from the primary schools, and the number of bilingual Rhinelanders was sufficient to fill the lower ranks of the official hierarchy. 'The great instrument, language, is wanting to us,' said a French prefect, speaking of the peasants in 1812; 'we must work to make it popular [1].'

It was natural to expect that the popularization of the French language would be effected through the primary schools, but in the distribution of public expenditure and public functions these institutions were abandoned to the communes. Of all the defects in Napoleon's educational statemanship there was perhaps none greater than the devolution of the responsibility for primary education upon a body so ill-prepared and apathetic as the commune [2]. It was idle to expect that the pressure of the prefect from above could atone for the massive apathy of the

---

[1] Lévy-Schneider, *La Révolution française*, March 1902, 235.

[2] The principle was inherited from the preceding government; cf. *Loi qui détermine le mode administratif des recettes et dépenses départementales, municipales et communales*, Dec. 1, 1798.

rural and urban population below. In the Rhineland at least, neither the individual parent nor the collective village cared for education, and as there was no legal compulsion upon the parents to send their children to school, the results were deplorable[1]. An official report in 1814 states that at least one-third of the communes were devoid of schools, and that three-fifths of the children between six and fourteen years of age had escaped any form of State instruction. Even where education was provided, the quality was indifferent. Though an imperial decree ordered the formation of training colleges for elementary teachers, no such college was founded at the public expense in the four departments. And if the teacher was untrained, the inspection was incompetent to discover his defects, for it generally happened that the village Orbilius, chosen by an illiterate mayor whose nomination was mechanically confirmed by a distant academical rector, was supervised by a French inspector who could not understand a word of the language in which the lessons were given[2].

The introduction of the French codes was a welcome innovation, for perhaps in no quarter of Europe had there been a greater confusion in the domain of private law. The numerous small principalities which had existed in the Rhineland before the French conquest had their own several laws, customs, and ordinances, and to these the commissaries of the French government had added a large and incoherent mass of decrees and regulations. The codes thus introduced certainty instead of uncertainty, unity instead of multiplicity, light instead of darkness. It may be thought that Catholic and ecclesiastically-minded communities would willingly have been left in the discomforts of legal chaos, rather than endure the civil marriage and divorce. But it must be remembered that the Revolution had already impressed its idea of the secular egalitarian State upon the departments of the Rhine, and that the Civil Code

[1] ' Public instruction,' says a writer in 1808, ' is almost totally neglected in the rural communes.'—Bodmann, *Annuaire statistique du département de Mont-Tonnerre pour l'an* 1808.

[2] Neigebaur, 117 ff. ; Eilers, ii. 24 ff. ; Heppe, *Geschichte des deutschen Volksschulwesens*, ii. 106 ; Treitschke, *Deutsche Geschichte*, ii. 227, who points with pride to the ripe fruits of the Prussian principle of compulsory education.

THE RHINE DEPARTMENTS

softened rather than deepened the harsh but necessary outlines of French secularism.

The ideal of the best French administrators of this period was that of a soft paternal government which should educate its subjects in the art and method of attaining material prosperity. For all that the Rhine provinces had undergone, for the forcible dissolution of ancient ties, for the horrors of war and of the Terror, they were now to receive material compensations. The abolition of tithes and feudal dues accomplished in the previous period, the high price of corn, the mobility of capital, the strict order and discipline which prevailed in the land, the enthusiasm of the prefects for agrarian development, and the rigorous and intelligent control of local expenditure quickened the prosperity of the villages. Whereas under the old régime two-thirds of the soil in the ecclesiastical principalities belonged either to the Church or to the nobles, now the land was free and the peasant was given opportunities of purchase. On November 25, 1802, the French law relating to the sale of the rural property of the State was published in the Rhine departments, and from this time forward the sales increased in number. In the Rhine and Moselle department alone, domains were sold to the value of four and a half million francs from May 16, 1803, to December 1, 1806. Nor was it the government alone who brought land into the market. Companies of capitalists bought up the estates of nobles and clergy at auctions and sold them again in small lots, and a large and thriving peasant proprietary was thus rapidly formed in the new departments. Indeed, the subdivision of land was carried so far that by 1815 a property of fifty acres was considered a large estate [1].

There are two notable occasions upon which Napoleon directly intervened to safeguard the interests of the Rhenish peasantry. As we have already had abundant occasion to notice, there was no problem of this time more encompassed with difficulty, than the attempt to discriminate between the feudal services or dues which were to be abolished, and the non-feudal services or dues which were not to be abolished without compensation. The decrees of the General Commissioners upon this subject had been confusing and contradictory, being influenced in turn by the

[1] Perthes, i. 269; Treitschke, *Deutsche Geschichte*, ii. 273.

dictates of philanthropy and the interests of the fisc. In the prevailing ambiguity it was to the advantage of all parties that the questions at issue should once and for all be clearly determined. What was the precise state of the existing law? What was the kind of proof of non-feudality which the courts should require? What dues could be safely described as non-feudal? A satisfactory answer to the last of these questions would, of course, imply minute local knowledge. Accordingly, when Napoleon came to Mainz in 1804, finding this among other problems awaiting his solution, he referred it to a commission composed partly of the directors of domains, and partly of the best lawyers of the four departments. The president of this assembly was Bigot de Préameneau, then a member of the Council of State, and afterwards Minister of Cults. A lucid survey of the previous course of legislation from the pen of Bigot was submitted to the First Consul and printed in the *Moniteur*, and a decree was issued upon the recommendations of the commission enumerating the dues and services which were to be presumed 'purely territorial,' and therefore not to be abolished without an indemnity to the owner. No fairer settlement could probably have been arrived at, and since facilities were subsequently given by the government for further emancipation by purchase, the tension between peasant and proprietor was sensibly relieved [1].

The problem of usury, always pressing in a society of small cultivators, was rendered specially acute in Alsace and the four departments by the presence of a large Hebrew element in the Rhenish towns. Napoleon's attention was drawn to this evil in 1806, and it is characteristic of his mental grasp that, advertised of a purely local grievance, he at once addressed himself to the consideration of the whole position of the Hebrew race in the State. The principles upon which he decided to act were at once honourable and sagacious. His object was, in his own words, to 'reanimate the sentiments of civic morality' in a race which was deadened by long degradation, and to 'recall it to the exercise

---

[1] *Moniteur*, no. 19, xix Vend. XIII ; *Décret relatif aux redevances foncières et féodales dans les quatre départements de la rive gauche du Rhin*, 10 oct. 1804 ; Daniels, iv. 554 ; *Décret concernant le rachat des redevances connues sous la dénomination 'Leibgewinn,'* 24 juin 1808 et 6 mars 1810 ; id. v. 368, 484.

THE RHINE DEPARTMENTS

of the arts and the useful professions.' Not only must the cultivator be protected from the Jew, but the Jew must be protected against himself. He must serve in the army, and be debarred from purchasing substitutes; he must be prevented from practising usury; his worship must be controlled by the State. Accordingly, in 1806, a decree was issued to stay the payment of debts owed by the cultivators of the soil to the Jews, pending the promulgation of a well-considered law upon usury; and after the lapse of two years a provisional settlement was made. The decree concerning the Jews of March 17, 1808, annulled all contracts made between Jews on the one hand, and minors, women, and soldiers on the other, unless the agreement was ratified by some person in authority, as for instance the husband in the case of a woman, or the commanding officer in the case of a soldier. If the interest upon any loan exceeded ten per cent., the debt was to be cancelled; if it exceeded five per cent., the rate was to be reduced. No Jew in future was permitted to open business without a patent from the prefect, based upon a certificate from the municipal council on the one hand, and the consistory of the synagogue on the other. Nor could any Jew not actually domiciled be admitted henceforward into the departments of the Upper and Lower Rhine. This decree, framed with the double object of protecting the Rhenish peasant from usury and of weaning the Jew from illicit and debasing forms of commerce, was only to remain in force for ten years. That it partially restored Hebrew disabilities, and certainly violated the abstract principles of equality and freedom, will not be denied. But it must be judged as a disciplinary and remedial measure, devised to arrest a grave evil, and certainly adapted to promote the prosperity of the most deserving class in the community [1].

The efforts of Napoleon to win the loyalty of the rural population of the Rhineland were admirably seconded by vigorous prefects, who encouraged the exportation of grain, provided for the gradual extinction of the communal debt, and, letting out communal property at remunerative rates, applied the rents to local purposes. The zeal of Count Adrien de Lézay-Marnesia,

---

[1] Decrees of May 30, 1806, March 17, 1808 (Daniel, v. 80, 336); and cf. Law on the rate of interest, Sept. 3, 1807 (id. v. 282).

prefect from 1806 to 1810, was long remembered in the Department of the Rhin-et-Moselle. He lined the roads with fruit-trees, founded at his own expense a normal school for the training of village teachers, where lessons were given in the art of grafting, in the preparation of wine and cider, and in the elements of agriculture and forestry. Under his intelligent rule the backward and neglected populations of the Eiffel and the Hundsrück were brought into connection with the great artery of the Rhine by a system of good lateral roads. The garden of the castle of Coblentz was converted into a nursery garden for the department; and though the attempt to acclimatize the Spanish merino led to no great results, the breed of cattle and horses was improved, new crops were introduced, and a general stimulus was given to agricultural improvements [1]. In the neighbouring Department of Mont-Tonnerre, the elderly but vigorous Jean Bon St. André, who had once administered the marine of France, restored the mulberry plantations and the communal forests, drained marshes, reclaimed waste land, and put a bridle upon the inundations of the Rhine. At the end of the Napoleonic period there were even complaints that the peasant had become over-prosperous, that he sat in the taproom playing for gold stakes, and that no wine would content him but the best [2].

The towns benefited in a lesser degree by the policy of Napoleon, but there were at least no guilds to stifle commerce, and no revolutionary commissioners to engineer atrocities. Coblentz and Bonn might regret a luxurious Court and an expensive nobility, but charity was better organized, public works more actively undertaken, and roads multiplied and improved. It was the intention of Napoleon to make Mainz a great centre of commerce. 'We will cause the merchandise of the Mediterranean,' he said to the mayor, 'to come here by the Rhine Canal, and the great merchants of Frankfort will bring us their money [3].' But though the city was declared to be a free port, and a stone bridge was projected over the Rhine, the continental

---

[1] Sepp, *Görres und seine Zeitgenossen*, 54; Spach, *Comte Adrien de Lézay-Marnesia*.

[2] Lévy-Schneider, *Jean Bon St. André*; Perthes, *Politische Zustände und Personen in Deutschland*.

[3] Michel Nicolas, *Jean Bon St. André*, 135-6.

blockade was fatal to any real development. A German who travelled down the Rhine in 1812 has described the unnatural calm caused by the almost entire cessation of traffic, the poverty and decadence of the small places on the banks, and the long line of huts, set at regular intervals of a thousand paces, in which the customs officers of the French Empire kept their sterilizing vigils [1].

On the other hand, France now freely opened her markets to Rhenish wares, a concession which we might think would have compensated for the fiscal barrier which severed the Rhinelander from Germany, or for the continental blockade which deprived him of the produce of the tropics. But the natural movements of commerce can seldom be affected permanently and never beneficially by the fiat of the legislator, and the efforts of the French government to withdraw the left bank from its economic dependence upon Germany resulted in failure. In a report of October 31, 1810, to the Minister of the Interior, the prefect of Mont-Tonnerre speaks as follows: 'Our commerce with the interior is almost zero ; . . . we buy nothing and we sell nothing. All our wines, our grains, our oils, our hemp, our rape-seed, and nine-tenths of our tobacco are exported abroad either to Holland or to Germany [2].' And the big traders still kept their balances at the bank of Vienna.

The police of the Empire, always strict and efficient, nowhere achieved a more signal triumph than in the *départements réunis*. During the miseries of the revolutionary period a well-organized gang of criminals, commanded by a wretch named John Buckler (better known under the nickname of Schinderhannes), and admirably served by a force of Jewish spies, kept this region in a continual state of alarm. Houses were broken into on dark nights; men were knocked over in country lanes; and a series of villainous crimes, unredeemed by a single touch of chivalry, called loudly for punishment. A lucky accident delivered Buckler into the hands of justice in 1802, and the ingenuity and patience of the police succeeded soon afterwards in discovering his accomplices. When the guillotine had done

---

[1] *Annalen des hist. Ver. f. den Niederrhein*, 1867, 172, and Eilers, iii. 4, 5, on the decay of Coblentz, once the seat of the Court of Treves.

[2] Quoted by Lévy-Schneider, *Révolution française*, Feb. 1902, 160.

its work, it was again possible to travel in security over country roads[1].

Unlike the other German territories of the Empire, the four departments were spared the direct visitation of war until 1814. They were, of course, frequently traversed by French armies, not always under the best control, but these military movements were not without compensation, for the French soldier spent his money freely, and the tradesmen of the Rhineland were the first to profit from the plunder of their German neighbours.

It would appear that the conscription was not seriously felt, for it was always easy to obtain a substitute for payment, and even to raise volunteers. The men liked their comfortable quarters in Germany, the life, the loot, the stir, the glory, and for many a farm-labourer of the Rhineland there was no higher thing than to die in battle for the great Emperor[2]. The marriage of Napoleon with Marie Louise seemed to conciliate the new with the old loyalty, and was greeted with genuine enthusiasm by a population which had always regarded Vienna with affection and Berlin with dislike[3]. In 1810, when the Emperor toured through the Rhine provinces with his newly married wife, all hearts were won. It was not till 1813 that old memories began to revive, and an active spirit of discontent, mainly caused by military requisitions, manifested itself in the country[4]. But the inhabitants had no burning desire to change their political allegiance, for upon the whole they had prospered under the rule of Napoleon.

These provinces, whose acquisition was the dream of centuries, and the most precious trophy of the revolutionary arms, passed away from France in the cataclysm of the Empire. The Congress of Vienna, careless here as everywhere of the deeper affinities, carved the region into three segments, of which the largest, extending between Bingen and the Dutch frontier, became Rhenish Prussia. A slip of territory south of this,

---

[1] A curious account of these brigands is contained in *Causes criminelles célèbres du xixe siècle*, 1827, ii. 58 ff.

[2] Neigebaur, 280 ff.   [3] Id. 283.

[4] Bockenheimer, *Geschichte der Stadt Mainz in den Jahren* 1813 *und* 1814.

from Bingen to Worms and including the city of Mainz, was given to the Grand-Duchy of Hesse-Darmstadt; while the country still further to the south, which lay between Worms and the northern border of Alsace, passed into the hands of Bavaria as a recompense for her assistance in the war, and became known as the Bavarian Palatinate. The change was viewed by the inhabitants with indifference, if not with active dislike, and grateful memories of the Napoleonic epoch lingered far into the nineteenth century [1]. It was here, indeed, that the system of the Empire was seen at its best, repairing material waste, obliterating senseless divisions, driving into a torpid populace its keen and vital energies, and in the ordered structure of French law bequeathing one of the most splendid legacies which a conqueror has ever left to a vanquished province.

[1] ' *On sait encore le Code Napoléon à Mayence, ainsi que dans toute la partie du Palatinat dépendant du Grand-duché de Hesse-Darmstadt: et même sur la rive droite du Rhin, où l'ancien droit germanique s'est maintenu, la législation financière repose encore sur celle de la France, modifiée seulement par quelques ordonnances du Duc régnant. Bien d'autres travaux de notre influence y subsistent.*'—Lerebours, *Napoléon et les Mayençais*, 1858.

CHIEF AUTHORITIES: The French laws (1792–1814) are most conveniently consulted in Bormann und Daniel's *Handbuch der für die Königl. Preuss. Rheinprovinzen verkündigten Gesetze, Verordnungen und Regierungsbeschlüsse aus der Zeit der Fremdherrschaft*, Köln, 1834, 8 vols.; Perthes, *Politische Zustände und Personen in Deutschland*; Rambaud, *Les Français sur le Rhin*; Görres, *Politische Schriften*; Neigebaur, *Darstellung der provisorischen Verwaltung am Rhein von 1813 bis 1819*; Ennen, *Zeitbilder aus der neueren Geschichte der Stadt Köln*; Eilers, *Meine Wanderung durch's Leben*; Lévy-Schneider, *Les habitans de la rive gauche du Rhin* (*Révolution française*, Feb. and March 1902); id., *Jean Bon St. André*; Bodmann, *Annuaire statistique du département de Mont-Tonnerre*; Spach, Comte Adrien de Lézay-Marnesia; van Alpen, *Geschichte des frankischen Rheinufers: was es war und was es itzt ist*.

CHAPTER XVII

CONCLUSIONS

The working faith of the best men of the French Revolution was the legacy of eighteenth-century philosophy, belief in scientific progress, in growing material comfort, in natural rights, in religious toleration, and in the ultimate triumph of good sense throughout the world. It was a philosophy which took little heed of the various temperaments and idiosyncrasies of men or nations, regarding humanity as something homogeneous through place and time, capable of being nourished by the same food and rescued by the same medicines. It paid scant attention to historical conditions, believing that in politics, as in physics, there was a mathematical art of discovery and scientific certainty of truth. The Christian religion it despised as superstitious, vulgar, and degrading to human dignity.

Napoleon brought France to earth. We may call him the first of the Romantics for his love of Ossian and his haunting dreams of oriental enterprise, or else the last of the Classics, remembering the lapidary style of his correspondence, his passion for Corneille, the studied and unstudied Caesarism of his politics. But the thing which made the Consulate great was Napoleon's realism, his close and comprehensive grasp of facts. He saw men as they were, gauged their characters, flattered their vanities, and in his political calculus allowed for vulgar foibles as well as for science and good sense. He had the strong dash of cynicism which the enthusiasts lacked, and this, though often repulsive in its excess, was valuable in an age of hyperbolic expectations. There has been no greater master in the art of using, driving, and inspiring men. He found great disorder and demoralization; he created a bureaucracy more competent, active, and enlightened than any which Europe had seen. But as the Consulate passed into the Empire, and as the growing palsy of despotism spread over France, the quality of the work declined. The best men hated the never-ending wars, and saw insanity written in large tokens over their master's schemes. The blockade, the conscription, the arrangements for the cantonment and provisioning of troops, the supervision of the press, consumed their most valuable energies, and the Emperor, growing ever more impatient of contradiction, cared for little else. All criticism, all independent political thought expired. Resolutely closing his eyes to unpleasant facts, Napoleon insisted that his servants should be blind also, and being despotic and irritable, he was able to exact a constant supply of nutriment for his illusions. The men who spoke the truth and thought justly were dismissed or scolded, and as compliance came to be rated more highly than ability, the most precious qualities were excised from public life.

Insensibility to bribes was not the strong point of the eighteenth century, and neither English nor German politics have much to boast in that respect. But the accusation levelled in Germany against the French and also against the Germans who helped to work the French system is, not that they trafficked in opinions, but that they blackmailed the helpless. Napoleon was a strict disciplinarian and reprobated private plunder, and from time to time an official of the Empire was compelled to disgorge ill-gotten gains. To his lasting credit it must be said that he was free from the slightest taint of pecuniary ambition, that he never lost an opportunity of denouncing the meanness of fortune-hunting, and that by his strict system of national accounts, no less than by his personal example, he did much to correct the singularly loose code of pecuniary morality which prevailed even among the most distinguished public servants of the French State. On the other hand, the spoliation of foreign countries inaugurated under the Directorate, and systematized by Napoleon, must have set the worst of examples to those French officers and civilians who were employed abroad. It will always be difficult to persuade public officials that the State has any monopoly of a tempting vice. Consequently we seem to hear two voices, distinct, sincere, and contradictory, in the French administrative correspondence of this epoch. 'It is our mission,' says one voice, 'to spread the light of our splendid civilization, to base government on human reason, to create model constitutions, in which administrative efficiency shall be combined with the representation of learning and substance, and to sweep away the absurdities of privilege and superstition. Under our rule the rights of man will be restored, and all the obstacles to material progress raised by the selfishness of prince or noble, of priest or guild, will crumble at a touch. Roads and aqueducts, gardens and promenades, canals and quays, an improved system of education, these we will make, and there is no burgher taking his afternoon stroll, or peasant bringing vegetables to market, who shall not find cause for grateful memories of our care. The conquests of science shall be applied to the common arts of life, and shall enrich agriculture and industry, and ward off disease. Germany, indeed, is a confederation of States formed under our protection, and some of these States are ruled by Frenchmen. But it is for no ignoble end that we exercise our political authority. We are practical, and the Germans are idealists; we are emancipated, and the Germans are enslaved. Each of these little States ruled by us is to be a model of reasonable contrivance, a seed-plot destined to refine the whole political vegetation of Germany.'

But side by side with this idea of beneficence there is the idea of exploitation. 'This country,' says another voice, 'these patient tobacco-smoking, beer-drinking Germans, exist for us and for our ambitions. We have destroyed their own constitution which was comic, and given them another which is convenient. By this means our military operations are aided by a considerable German army, which, although prone to plunder, possesses the soldierly qualities of courage and steadfastness. We have carved out from Germany certain reserved domains, from which we can assist our own taxpayers, and endow our successful generals. The management of these estates is often a source of profit to French agents. Owing to our war with England, we are compelled to enforce a continental blockade which damages German commerce, but the inconvenience is temporary, and may in the end be more than counterbalanced by the extraction of sugar from the beetroot, and the discovery of agreeable substitutes for coffee. Meanwhile it is unfortunately impossible to compensate the injured manufacturers by throwing open to them the French or even the Dutch market, for such a course would expose us to foreign competition of a most odious kind, and recall the dark days of Pitt's commercial treaty. It would be foolish to allow the Germans, who understand so little, to express opinions adverse to our system, and so we muzzle the press, police the universities, and "shadow" all vigorous and intellectual persons. The German princes we bully and exploit. We do not much care how they govern, so long as they provide their quota of troops, and provision our forces when they happen to be quartered in their territories. It is, on the whole, to our interest that they should be despotic, for if they were hampered by refractory Estates, how could they supply us punctually with our tribute of soldiers? And thus we have everywhere encouraged the most absolute autocracy. We do not expect to rule the Germans for ever. Indeed, we have taken the precaution of removing the most valuable pictures from their galleries. The Bavarians, with a promptitude which might almost be termed discourteous, anticipated us at Düsseldorf, where our Commissioner found little or nothing deserving his attention. Our generals were also disappointed with Hanover, a poor and insipid province, from which they were able to remit only the most inconsiderable trifles—some fine horses and a manuscript, the *Consilium Ægyptiacum* of Leibnitz. It is best that these and other treasures should be concentrated in Paris, where they will be accessible to civilized mankind.

'A great many of our young men have made fortunes out of Germany, not only as generals—a most lucrative profession—but also as police agents, customs officers, and administrators of domains. They will return satisfied to their parents. Others have been less fortunate through wounds and death. The Westphalian army has proved to be convenient, offering as it does higher rank and better pay to French officers who have been left behind in the race for promotion, or have other reasons for desiring a change. Indeed, it will be found that the applications for Westphalian service generally come from those who have in some way been crossed in their careers. Our soldiers have often been enabled to surround themselves with comforts, even with luxuries, when quartered in German cities, and it is well that there should be some compensation, however illicit, for the perils and hardships which they are called upon to endure. But Germany is always exile. We are never at home in this strange country. Fortunately a knowledge of the language is quite unnecessary for administrative posts.'

Thus the Napoleonic system, albeit containing many elements of splendid promise, became the despair of its best servants. Men of high aims and unquestioned integrity were made accomplices in a suspicious and restless despotism. They had dreamed the dream of an '*Allemagne française*.' They saw their work shattered before their eyes, the ideal of exploitation conquering the ideal of beneficence, the enthusiasm of the governed passing into acquiescence, and the acquiescence into concentrated hate.

The Nemesis of this spirit of exploitation was that in the reaction the good perished with the bad. In Hanover, in Hesse-Cassel, in Brunswick, the old governments returned, popular, unrepentant, and uninstructed by calamity. The reaction was particularly violent in Hesse-Cassel, where the Elector actually annulled all the alienations of the royal domain which had been made under the preceding government, but it was also clearly marked in every other portion of Germany which had been ruled by the French [1]. The Code was swept out of Posen and Hesse-Cassel, Brunswick and the Hanseatic departments, and Savigny had no difficulty in explaining to a learned and sympathetic audience that it was founded upon discussions which were trivial, perfunctory, and ignorant [2]. Yet some fragments of the Napoleonic system survived the cataclysm. Though the Elector of Hesse restored the old *corvées* and feudal dues, he found it convenient to maintain the abolition of patrimonial jurisdiction. The Jews, whose pecuniary assistance was always valuable to a miserly monarch, were allowed to preserve some of the privileges accorded to them under the French rule; and the religious disabilities, abolished by Napo-

---

[1] Wippermann, *Kurhessen seit dem Freiheitskriege*; Heinemann, *Geschichte von Braunschweig und Hannover*.

[2] *Vom Beruf unsrer Zeit für Gesetzgebung*.

leon, were never reimposed in the Electorate of Hesse or in the Grand-Duchy of Fulda, which was united to it upon the conclusion of the peace [1]. When the project for the German Civil Code came before the Reichstag in 1900, it was stated that seventeen per cent. of the fifty million inhabitants of the German Empire were still ruled by French law [2]. In the Prussian, Hessian, and Bavarian Rhine provinces, and in Alsace-Lorraine, the Code Napoléon was administered in its original tongue; while a German translation, only slightly differing from its French prototype, was current in Baden [3]. That the Code should have persisted in any portion of Germany, when all the circumstances of the War of Liberation are taken into account, is a remarkable tribute to its merits. We may admit that its preparation was hurried, that the discussions in the Council of State were often unsatisfactory, and that it is based upon an imperfect survey of practical contingencies. There is doubtless great weight in Savigny's contention that Germany was not ripe for a Code, and that the legal system of a country should be the natural result of its historical development. But the choice in 1807 and in 1815 did not lie between pure German and pure French law. It lay between the Code Napoléon on the one hand, sketchy no doubt, and over-simplified, but lucid, intelligible, and portable, and 'an endless waste of contradictory, conjectural, and motley ordinances . . . calculated to make it impossible for judges and advocates to obtain a thorough knowledge of the law, and so imperfect that ninety out of a hundred cases have to be decided by Roman, canon, or received foreign law [4].' We cannot wonder that in comparison with this hybrid miscellany the French Code seemed to many Germans to be the utterance of Reason herself [5]. The separation of contentious from non-contentious jurisdiction, the organization of the

---

[1] Treitschke, *Deutsche Geschichte*, iii. 523-34.
[2] Mugdan, *Die gesammten Materialien zum Bürgerlichen Gesetzbuch*, i. 847-8. I owe this reference to the kindness of Professor Maitland.
[3] Holtzendorff, *Encyclopädie der Rechtswissenschaft*, 296. Schröder gives a useful map showing the diffusion of the Civil Code in 1894; *Lehrbuch der deutschen Rechtsgeschichte.*
[4] Thibaut, *Ueber die Nothwendigkeit eines allgemeinen bürgerlichen Rechts für Deutschland*, 7.
[5] Stobbe, *Geschichte des deutschen Rechts*, 484 ff.

notariat, the sharp distinction between judicial and executive functions, the introduction of oral pleading and of the jury, the abolition of the *Carolina* wherever it survived, the stricter definition of judicial competence, these were felt in many quarters to be unmixed benefits flowing from the French rule[1]. That there should have been some opposition to these innovations need cause no surprise, for lawyers are as wedded to the law which they practise as are professors to the law which they teach. But, on the whole, the French legal system met with remarkable acceptance, and it was a grave misfortune that it should have been abolished in Brunswick and Hesse when it was working well and had given satisfaction[2].

The agrarian reforms of the Revolution, the Consulate, and the Empire had scarcely had time to take full effect save in the Rhenish provinces. Elsewhere, French domination had been short-lived, and French legislation tentative and respectful of vested interests. Indeed, save for one circumstance, in itself connected with the career of Napoleon, there is no doubt that the French land settlement would have been overthrown throughout Germany after the War of Liberation. That circumstance was the agrarian legislation of Stein and Hardenberg in Prussia. That the reforms of these two great statesmen, undertaken to repair the Prussian disaster of 1806, were complete or fully satisfactory it would be absurd to pretend, for they left untouched the patrimonial jurisdiction of the lord, and provided no adequate machinery for the commutation of labour dues. But they were the first attack upon a system defended by one of the hardest and most stubborn aristocracies in Europe, and in the general reaction which followed the battle of Leipzig, the work of Stein and Hardenberg was not undone. It may, indeed, be argued that it was not until then that its full value for Ger-

---

[1] Grolman, *Ausführliches Handbuch über den Code Napoléon*, Giessen und Darmstadt, 1810.

[2] The following is a list of the territories on the right bank of the Rhine which received the French law:—Danzig (Nov. 19, 1807); Westphalia (Nov. 15, 1807); Arenburg (Jan. 28, 1808); Grand-Duchy of Warsaw (1808 and 1810); Baden (July 5, 1808); Frankfort (Sept. 15, 1809); Berg (Jan. 1, 1810); Lippe department (May 29, 1810); Hanseatic departments (Dec. 10, 1810); Duchy of Köthen (Dec. 28, 1810); Duchy of Nassau (Feb. 1 and 4, 1811).

many was disclosed, since but for the fact that Prussia had taken in hand the reform of her own land-system, there would have been little chance of any part of the French settlement surviving. As it was, Prussia obtained the Duchy of Posen, the Duchy of Berg, and part of the Rhenish provinces in 1815, and the Prussian administrators were strong enough to disregard the appeals of the nobility for the restoration of the feudal system. In these provinces, therefore, the hand of the clock was not set back. On the contrary, the Prussian government zealously exerted itself to repair the ravages of war and to promote material prosperity; and though many passages in Prussian history are more illustrious, there is none more truly honourable than the great work done by the Prussian administrators in the districts ceded to the Hohenzollerns by the Congress of Vienna. Elsewhere, the reaction was both furious and stupid, and a worse pair of rulers than Duke Charles of Brunswick or William II of Hesse it would be difficult to find in the whole range of modern history. Cassel was to witness scandals far uglier than any associated with the merry days of King Jerome. The most elementary rights had to be extorted by popular force, and in the risings of 1830 there was a substratum of thought derived from the recollection of all that was modern and enlightened in the Westphalian kingdom.

The influence of Napoleon upon the general political structure of Germany is more easy to determine. He reduced the number of sovereign princes, simplified the political geography, secularized the ecclesiastical States, built up Bavaria, Würtemberg, and Baden, and abolished the Holy Roman Empire.

The elimination of Austrian influence from Germany was not permanent, though it was never again destined to be exercised in ways so various, intricate and subtle: and the Confederation of the Rhine perished when Bavaria signed the Treaty of Ried in 1813. But though the nineteenth century witnessed the revival of Roman Catholic influence in the Rhenish bishoprics, none of the work of 1803 has ever been undone; and many of the results of the victory of Austerlitz are still marked upon our maps. Indeed, without the great winnowing-fan of the Napoleonic wars to scatter the chaff and sift the grain, who knows if the political unity of Germany would ever have been attained?

Whether it was to the advantage of France to clear the floor of Germany of its mediaeval rubble is another question. Napoleon thought one thing in 1797, and in 1803 and 1806 he did another. Yet the mediation of 1803 and the abolition of the Empire in 1806 were dictated by interests which at the time seemed imperative, for while the one settled the questions arising out of the French conquest of the Rhine frontier, the other drove Austria out of Germany and placed Napoleon at the head of a Germanic Confederacy. Such a Confederacy had been formed by Mazarin in 1658, and followed the lines of an old tradition, nor was there any reason founded on national sympathies or antipathies why it should not have been permanent, if the terms had been equitably framed, and if the league had been directed against the Hapsburgs alone. Neither of these conditions was observed. By the terms of the act of the Confederation of the Rhine, the princes of Germany were bound in strict vassalage to France, and the war with Prussia in 1806 promptly revealed the extent of their liabilities. If the Emperor of the French had been prudent, he would have spared no effort to avert this contest. The Germanic States from 1740 to 1805 had grouped themselves round the two contending forces of Austria and Prussia, and this dualism was not only thoroughly engrained in German politics, but was also the foundation of French influence in Central Europe. Napoleon eliminated Austria from the Germanic system in 1805, and left Germany divided between Frederick William and himself. A long passage of patient, delicate, and conciliatory diplomacy might have secured the stability of this new political equilibrium. But at this supreme crisis the attitude of France was provocative, and Prussia, tormented by accepted indignities and legitimate fears, rushed into war. We know the sequel, the French arms crowning the heights of Auerstädt and Jena, the imperial eagles in Warsaw and Danzig, the Baltic coast watched for English smugglers from the Trave to the Vistula, and Jerome gaily masquerading in Westphalian palaces. For six years Northern Germany was crushed under the heels of the French legionaries, and German blood was freely poured in an alien quarrel. The new equilibrium was shattered as soon as formed, and Germany found herself under the single mastery of Napoleon. No greater misfortune could have befallen France, for out of Jena and Auerstädt sprang the resurrection of Prussia, the War of Liberation, and the ultimate modern German Empire.

The main strength of the Napoleonic position in France was derived from the support of the peasantry, from the fact that the Empire was pledged to uphold the agrarian revolution of 1789. But in Germany, Napoleon was primarily allied not with the peasants but with the princes. 'The Confederation of the Rhine,' wrote a French envoy, who possessed a long experience of German affairs, 'will never be consolidated until the majority of the inhabitants of each of the confederate States have acquired Church property and national domains, or have redeemed their real and personal servitudes at a low price, as well as the greater part of their feudal and seigneurial dues [1].' If Napoleon's main object had been to create an atmosphere favourable to the diffusion and the maintenance of French institutions in Germany, some such an appeal to the appetites of the lower classes might conceivably have borne fruit. But in view of the unquestioned popularity of the ruling German dynasties, the step would have been full of hazard. It might have alienated the princes and failed to win the peasants. The authority of Napoleon in Germany therefore depended not upon the interested support of the populace, but upon personal prestige, the force of arms, and the alliance of the ruling dynasties. The clergy who had been secularized, the sovereigns who had been mediatized, the nobles who had lost or feared to lose dues and services, were the natural foes of the new order. Only the princes had been unquestioned gainers, and their gains were solid and permanent. At the expense of ignominy, they had purchased power. But the alliance of Napoleon with the princes, though admirably adapted for its immediate purpose, the control of the military forces of Germany, was directly opposed to the cause of liberty, and to all the feelings and tendencies which the French Revolution had encouraged in the thinking class. Thus, although the Emperor was able to fascinate some of the older intellects of Germany, the 'retired robber-captains' of the storm and stress period, the heart and brain of younger Germany were ranged

[1] Bacher to Champagny, June 11, 1811 ; *Affaires étrangères, Corr. Pol.: Allemagne*, 744.

against him. The War of Liberation was a movement of peoples rather than a coalition of princes, an outburst of the old passion for political liberty which France had been the first to stir, and Napoleon had so ruthlessly attempted to extinguish. The most zealous guardian of this great tradition was Görres, who hailed the dawn of freedom in 1789, preached the crusade against Napoleon in 1814, and five years later passionately denounced the governments of Germany for their despotism and breach of faith.

With no patience, with no sense of human dignity, with no feeling for the pathos of the common lot, Napoleon lacked the sound and noble gifts which sweeten and inspire public life. The woman of genius whom he had exiled from France had a truer and more generous, and therefore a more statesmanlike vision of the people whose destiny had been so harshly deflected by the legions of the Empire. The *Germany* of Madame de Staël is an ideal picture, and the authoress has been taken to task for the clouds of sentiment and sympathy with which she has enveloped her theme. But it is not thus that we should approach these eloquent discourses. Rather we should see in them the fine protest of a generous French heart against the subjection of a simple and laborious people; an appeal from force to conscience, from the mailed tyranny of the later Empire to the ideals of human brotherhood which France had once preached, and which a cruel destiny had caused her to forget.

INDEX

Abel, 77.
Aix-la-Chapelle, 81, 353, 354, 356, 361.
Albini, Baron d', 85, 122, 314.
Alexander of Russia, 40, 75, 99, 105, 125, 129, 144 ff., 148.
Alkmaar, capitulation of, 38.
Amiens, breach of the Peace of, 43, 48, 49.
Artlenburg, Convention of, 57.
Artois, Count of, 67, 69.
Aschaffenburg, 43, 112, 312, 317, 324, 329.
Auerstädt, 131, 137, 138, 382.
Augusta of Bavaria, 96, 109.
Austerlitz, 103, 106, 126, 129, 142, 161, 175, 176, 334.
Austria, policy of, at Campo-Formio, 29; views as to secularization, 39; power in Empire weakened, 43, 44; declines to intervene in d'Enghien affair, 75; Empire of, 81, 123; recognition of French Empire by, 81; alleged aggression of, 102; losses of, by Treaty of Pressburg, 107; aids revolts in Westphalia, 253, 254; influence of, on Germany, 381; eliminated from Germanic system, 382.

Baden, Napoleon's courtesy to, 32, 101; enlargement of, 42, 44, 45, 107, 381; required to expel *émigrés*, 72; territory violated, 73; submission of, 74, 75; tempted with Breisgau, 87, 88; gains of, by Treaty of Pressburg, 108, 168; negotiates for Concordat, 169; treatment of Jews in, 329; Code Napoléon in, 379, 380.
Baden, Grand-Duke of: *see* Charles Frederick.
Basle, Peace of, 24, 29, 49, 124.
Bavaria, backwardness of, 9; enlargement of, 44, 45, 107; expels Drake, 77; drawn into French alliance, 95, 96; gains of, by Treaty of Pressburg, 107, 108, 168; desires special Concordat, 113, 167 ff.; objects to French protectorate, 121; booksellers arrested in, 129, 130; cedes Berg in exchange for Anspach, 176; treatment of Jews in, 329.
Bavaria, Elector of: *see* Maximilian Joseph. Electress of: *see* Caroline of Bavaria.
Bayonne, Treaty of, 153, 190, 191; Murat summoned to, 187.
Belgium, cession of, 27.
Berg, Murat becomes Grand-Duke of, 111, 177; territory of, augmented, 145, 182; constitution of, 155, 183 ff., 197; Beugnot made Imperial Commissioner in, 191; Prince Napoleon Louis, Grand-Duke of, 194; educational and religious policy in, 195, 209, 211; legal administration in, 196 ff.; abolition of serfage in, 203; trade and manufactures of, 205; conscription in, 215; fiscal policy of, 217; Grand-Duchy of, comes to an end, 221.
Berlin, Treaty of, 297.
Bernadotte, 60, 64, 89, 90, 97, 156, 337.
Berry, Duke of, 67, 69.
Beugnot, Count, 183, 191, 195 ff., 210, 213, 219, 221, 235, 237, 246.
Beust, Count, 77, 85.
Blücher, General, 125, 135, 335.
Bonaparte, Jerome: *see* Jerome.
Bonaparte, Joseph: *see* Joseph.
Bonaparte, Louis: *see* Louis.
Bonaparte, Napoleon: *see* Napoleon.
Bremen, 43, 50, 54, 61, 62, 64, 333, 335–7, 347.
Brunn, Treaty of, 107.
Brunswick, Elector of: *see* Charles Ferdinand.
Brunswick-Oels, Duke of, 251, 253, 303.
Bülow, Baron von, 237 ff.

FISHER

Cadoudal Plot, 68-71.
Cambridge, Duke of, 12, 54.
Cameral Science, 20.
Campo-Formio, 25 ff.
Caroline of Bavaria, 95.
Cassel, projected League of, 47; Jerome's entry into, 235; first parliament in, 241; German language in, 247; French adventurers in, 248; alarmed at revolts, 253; von Strombeck at, 260; schools in, 286; financial condition of, 298.
Charles Ferdinand of Brunswick, 125; character and career of, 137; deposed and exiled, 139, 289; his son leads a revolt, 253, 254.
Charles Frederick of Baden, frees serfs, 23; is made an Elector, 45; his character, 73, 74; comes to Mainz, 82; sends his son and grandson to imperial coronation, 87; forced to abandon Bavarian match, 96; signs Treaty of Ettlingen, 97; is aggrandized and promoted, 107, 108.
Cisalpine Republic, 26, 94.
Cisrhenane Confederation, 79, 80.
Cisrhenane Republic, 24, 352, 356.
Cleves, Duchy of, 176, 178, 180; Diet of, 186; territory of, 187; town of, 350; *and see* Berg.
Code Napoléon, 188 ff., 197, 232, 241, 257, 260, 285, 328, 378, 379, 380 *n.*
Concordat, German, 87, 109, 113, 163 ff., 171.
Condé, Prince of, 67.
Confederation of the Rhine, seeds of, 45, 47, 81, 86, 88; Treaty of, signed, 117; German princes join, 118; purposes and provisions of treaty, 120; ratification of treaty, 121; joined by Saxony, 135; fundamental statute for, 163, 171; Diet of, 164, 172.
Consulate, brilliance of, 48.
Continental blockade, 63, 125, 142, 154, 206, 236, 298, 319, 333 ff.
Cuxhaven, 63, 125, 255, 336.

Dalberg, Baron von, 74, 75, 80.
Dalberg, Karl Theodor von, an Electorate designed for, 42; given Bishopric of Ratisbon, 43; expresses through envoy indignation with Drake, 77; character and career of, 82-5; discusses Concordat and scheme for Federation, 87, 88; submits schemes of reform to Napoleon, 112; proposes Fesch as coadjutor, 113; is given Frankfort, 119; signs Treaty of the Confederation of the Rhine, 122; draws up constitution for Rhenish Confederation, 163; aims at Patriarchate, 164, 168, 170; his rule in Frankfort, 312 ff.; appeals for an organization, 317; loses Ratisbon, 318; his educational policy, 328; forces Jews to buy civic rights, 330.
Danzig, 145, 146, 302, 344.
Davoût, Marshal, 148, 151, 154, 156, 305, 343, 348.
Didelot, 78, 99.
Dörnberg, Baron von, 240, 250.
Drake, 76, 77.
Dresden, Convention of, 148, 149.
Dumouriez, 71, 73.
Durbach, C. F., 59.
Düsseldorf, 177, 184, 193 ff., 210.

Elbe, Convention of, 57.
Ems *Punktation*, 10.
Enghien, Duc d', 71-3, 125.
England, her opposition and its consequences, 49; excluded from Elbe and Weser, 127; Napoleon's animosity towards, 141, 142; trade with Germany prohibited, 319, 320, 334, 337; annexes Heligoland, 339.
Éphémérides du citoyen, 20.
Estates: *see* Landstände.
Eugène, Prince, 96, 109, 175, 319.
Eylau, 144, 147.

Febronius, 10.
Fersen, Count, 34.
Fesch, Cardinal, 112 ff., 168, 319.
Fichte, 277.
France, ignorance of German literature in, 3, 4; ignorance of German language in, 4, 246; intellectual supremacy of, in Europe, 5; Revolution, influence of, in Germany, 22, 53, 203, 352, 364, 366, 383; war with England, 49, 62, 68; foundation of Empire in, 80; war with Prussia, 124; Concordat in, 167, 171; drifts into war with Russia, 306, 348; ruins commerce and manufactures in Berg, 206, 209, 219; establishes free trade with Rhine departments, 371; effects of Napoleonic system on, 382, 383.

Francis II, 43, 75, 81, 96, 123.
Frankfort, town of, 43, 119 ; union of, 47 ; *émigrés* at, 70 ; Diet of, 118, 164, 165 ; Grand-Duchy of, 312 ; treatment of Jews in, 313 ff., 330 ; English trade in, 319, 320 ; French army in, 321 ; German officials in, 322 ; local government in, 323, 324 ; French law in, 325 ff. ; education in, 328 ; serfdom in, 330 ; conscription in, 331.
Frankfort, Grand-Duke of : *see* Dalberg.
Frederick Augustus, Elector of Saxony, 130 ; receives Grand-Duchy of Warsaw, 148 ; makes ruinous bargain with Napoleon, 153.
Frederick II of Würtemberg, made an Elector, 45 ; quarrel with son, 87 ; character and aims of, 98 ; contract of, with Napoleon, 103–6 ; becomes King, 107.
Frederick William of Prussia, 17, 36, 51, 91, 125, 127, 131, 135, 145, 147, 382.
Free towns, 42, 43 ff., 61, 65, 334 ; *and see* Hanseatic towns.
French Empire, foundation of, 80.
Frère, General, 50, 90.
Friedland, 144, 147.
\:da, 128, 140, 154, 157, 158, 318, ?1, 324, 329, 379.

:orge II, 51.
.eorge III, 52, 79.
.ierman Catholicism, 9, 10, 11, 134, 140, 166, 170, 212, 318, 324, 351, 362.
German Empire, constitution of, 6, 7 ; injured by Campo-Formio, 27–9 ; views of Napoleon on, 31 ; changes in 1803, 43, 44 ; changes in 1806, 116 ff. ; French law in (1900), 379 ; rise of the modern, 383.
German Princes, greed of, 8, 120, 164 ; their zeal for Napoleon, 103 ; Napoleon's views on, 115 ; fifteen join the Rhenish Confederation, 118 ; attitude of, towards the Church, 170 ; in ecclesiastical principalities, 351 ; vassalage to France, 382 ; power of, increased by alliance with Napoleon, 383.
Germany, intellectual emancipation of, from France, 2, 3 ; Hellenism in, 2, 277 ; knowledge of French in, 4, 5 ; difference of, from France, 6 ; constitution of, 6, 7 ; political divisions in, 8 ; religious divisions in, 9 ; *Sturm und Drang* in, 14 ; militarism of, 15 ; administration in, 17 ; political life in, 19 ; Cameral Science in, 20 ; physiocratic theories in, 20 ; poverty of, 21 ; submissiveness of, 21 ; piety of, 23 ; rearrangement of territory in, by provisions of the Rhine league, 119 ; Northern, after Jena, 130 ff. ; Napoleon master of Northern, 141, 382 ; organization of Western, 154 ; Universities of, 275 ; philosophical thought in, 277 ; intellectual supremacy of, in 1810, 282 ; War of Liberation in, 379, 384 ; agrarian reforms in, 380 ; Napoleon's influence on political structure of, 381.
Goethe, 23, 351.
Görres, 357, 360.
Göttingen, 51, 226, 240, 259, 277, 279, 282, 284.
Grimm, Jacob, 240, 292, 324.
Gustavus IV, 75.

Halle, 12, 133, 226, 254, 259, 276, 284.
Hamburg, 43, 61, 62, 64, 70, 89, 90, 333 ff.
Hanover, 44, 49–65 ; neutrality of, 49 ; description of, 51 ; constitution of, 52 ; social conditions in, 53 ; French invasion of, 54–8 ; French views of, 58 ; patience of, 59 ; French occupation of, 60–1 ; English spies in, 70 ; given to Prussia, 126 ; offered to England, 128 ; second military occupation of, 155, 159 ; financial condition of, 159 ; ceded to Westphalia, 297 ff. ; exploitation of, by French generals, 377 ; reaction from Napoleonic system in, 378.
Hanoverian Legion, 57.
Hanoverian loan, 61, 160.
Hanoverian Regency, 61.
Hanseatic towns, compelled to advance money, 61–5 ; trade with France, 65 ; express through envoy indignation against Drake, 77 ; refused to Prussia, 128 ; Marshal Brune in, 159 ; annexed by Napoleon, 298, 344 ; Napoleon's control of, 333 ff. ; reduced to misery,

388 INDEX

342; French systems introduced in, 345; education in, 347; taxation in, 348.
Hardenberg, Prince of, 125, 380.
Haugwitz, 126, 127.
Hegel, 162, 277.
Heine, 220, 285.
Heligoland, 338.
Herder, 3, 279, 280.
Hesse, Landgrave of: *see* William VIII.
Hesse-Cassel, 30, 42, 45, 76, 78, 80, 82, 134; Electoral family of, deposed, 136; military government of, 156; condition of, in 1807, 226, 245, 289; the army of, 226, 250, 289; reaction from Napoleonic system in, 378.
Hesse-Darmstadt, Landgrave of: *see* Louis.
Heyne, 277, 281, 285.
Hohenlinden, 38.
Holland, annexed by Napoleon, 344; trade with France, 348.
Holland, King of: *see* Louis Bonaparte.
Holy Roman Empire, 44, 81, 94, 111, 123, 163, 168, 381.

Imperial Knights, claims of, disregarded, 44, 102, 103; domains of, mediatized, 107, 119.
Italy, crown of, 94; republic of, founded, 175.

Jena, 132, 161, 335, 382.
Jerome Bonaparte, 14, 146, 148, 195; character and career of, 228 ff., 231, 292, 308; chosen King of Westphalia, 228; his Court, 235; and ministers, 236; opens the Reichstag, 241; defeats Austrians at Waldheim, 254; his extravagance, 293, 299; his military policy and ambition, 300-3; his fear of Prussia, 303; takes part in Russian campaign, 304, 306; returns in disgrace, 309.
Jews, treatment of, in Grand-Duchy of Warsaw, 150, 152; Westphalia, 264, 304, 329; Frankfort, 313 ff., 330; Fulda, 329; Baden and Bavaria, 329; Rhine departments, 368.
Jollivet, 236, 248, 310, 360.
Joseph Bonaparte, 94, 128, 175, 177.

Kant, 277, 278, 351.
Katte, Friedrich Wilhelm von, 249.

Lagrange, General, 156, 235, 237.
Landstände, or Estates, 19, 53, 56, 63, 99, 101; in Hanover, 159, 160; in Cleves and Berg, 177, 180, 182, 222; in Westphalia, 232-3, 234, 240, 288; in Frankfort, 324.
Leibnitz, 225, 377.
Leipzig, 209, 331, 380.
Lessing, 3, 62, 226, 351.
Louis, Landgrave of Hesse-Darmstadt, 82, 87, 97, 107.
Louis Bonaparte, 94, 128, 177, 181, 194, 310, 335.
Louise, Queen of Prussia, 125, 146.
Lübeck, 43, 61, 335, 337 ff.
Lucchesini, 85.
Lunéville, 38-47, 72, 358.
Lutheranism, servility of, 12; rationalism of, 12, 13; in Saxony, 134; of Prince of Orange, 140; in Hanover, 264; in Rhine departments, 362.

Magdeburg, 146, 226, 230, 231, 237, 249, 253, 306.
Mainz, reforms of Karl Joseph von Erthal in, 11; cession of, to France, 28, 35, 36; gathering at, 81, 82; See of, 167; Court of, 351; the tricolour in, 352; bishopric founded in, 361; consistory created in, 363; schools in, 364; commerce of, 370.
Malchus, Karl August, 238, 239, 295.
Marburg, 157, 227, 252, 271, 282-4.
Marengo, 38.
Maximilian Joseph, Elector of Bavaria, 96, 97, 166.
Mecklenburg, 42, 128, 146.
Mehée de la Touche, 69, 71, 76, 78.
Melzi, 175.
Metternich, 130, 165.
Military governments, Napoleon's system of, 155 ff.
Mirabeau, 8; remarks on Prussian clergy, 13; and on Charles Ferdinand of Brunswick, 138.
Modena, Prince of, 29.
Moniteur, 71, 74, 76, 92, 178, 282, 283, 310, 368.
Montgelas, Baron von, 17, 77, 95, 167.
Moreau, 68, 70, 71.

Mortier, General, 50, 54, 55, 56, 60, 136, 155, 160, 335, 336.
Möser, Justus, 23.
Moser, Karl Friedrich von, 15, 16.
Müller, Johann von, 22, 157, 235, 236, 248, 283.
Münchhausen, von, 51, 160, 240.
Munich, 76; Austrians in possession of, 97, 103; Napoleon in, 109; ratifications of Treaty of the Confederation of the Rhine exchanged at, 121, 129; negotiates for Concordat, 167, 169; picture galleries of, 184.
Murat, Prince Joachim, becomes Grand-Duke of Cleves and Berg, 111, 116, 129; joins Rhine league, 118; appearance and career of, 173 ff.; takes possession of his duchy, 177; provokes war with Prussia, 181; his territory increased, 182; is summoned to Bayonne, 187; his municipal regulations, 189; resigns his duchy, 190.

Napoleon Bonaparte, conquests in Italy, 24; makes Peace of Campo-Formio, 28; travels through Switzerland, 30, 31; arrives at Rastadt, 31; appearance and conversation of, 32, 33; learns Germany, 32, 46; insults Count Fersen, 35; signs convention with Austria, 35; leaves Rastadt, 35, 37; conversations with Sandoz Rollin, 35, 36; leaves Paris for the East, 37; overthrows Directory, 38; intervenes in the affair of compensations, 39–47; gives counsel to Bavaria, 40; his German policy, 42, 108, 383; his northern scheme, 47; provokes hostilities with England, 49; intervenes in Hanover, 50; suspends ratification of Convention of Suhlingen, 56; reinforces Mortier, 57; orders Mortier to disarm Hanoverian army, 57; accepts Convention of the Elbe, 57; policy in Hanover, 61; views on the Hanoverian loan, 63; his suspicions of Hamburg and Bremen, 64, 65; regards war as essential to his power, 65, 66; determines to exclude English emissaries and goods from the continent, 67; intrigues in Ireland, 67; instructs Mehée, 69; orders seizure of d'Enghien, 71; and of other alleged conspirators, 73; protests against Drake, 76; orders Drake's expulsion, 77; orders expulsion of Taylor, 80; ambition of, 80; tour in Rhine provinces, 81, 82; conversations of, at Mainz, 86, 87; discusses a German Concordat, 87; promotes discussion of subversive schemes in Germany, 88; orders seizure of Rumbold, 88–92; provokes war with Austria, 93–5; forms alliance with South German powers, 95–103; his Germanic Confederation scheme, 97, 109, 382; visits Frederick of Würtemberg at Ludwigsburg, 101; his official justification of Austrian campaign, 102; correspondence with Frederick of Würtemberg, 103–6; defeats Austrians at Austerlitz, 106, 126; concludes treaties at Brunn and Pressburg, 107; quarrels with the Pope, 109, 319; his dealings with Dalberg, 109 ff.; schemes for the settlement of Germany, 115 ff.; enforces continental blockade, 125, 142, 208, 319, 336; treaty with Prussia at Schönbrunn, 126, 127; offers Hanover to England, 128; becomes master of Prussia by victories of Jena and Auerstädt, 130; takes Saxony under his protection, 133; abolishes Houses of Hesse-Cassel, Brunswick, and Nassau, 136–41; his views on, and animosity towards, Great Britain, 141, 142; his attitude towards Poland, 143; treats with Alexander on the Niemen, 144 ff.; signs Treaties of Tilsit, 145; drafts constitution for Grand-Duchy of Warsaw, 149; organizes Western Germany, 154; his system of military governments, 155; his views on Diet for Rhine Confederacy, 164; his opinion of Dalberg, 165; intervenes with the Curia for Bavarian Concordat, 167; writes to the Pope, 169; marries his sister Caroline to Murat, 174; decrees the Duchies of Cleves and Berg to Murat, 176; instructs Murat on organization, 179, 180; reproves his avidity, after Treaty of Bayonne, 190; makes his nephew, Prince Napoleon Louis, Grand-Duke of Berg, 194; visits

Berg (1811), 194, 220; receives petition from peasants of Berg, 204; introduces French methods of administration in Berg, 221; appoints Roederer to correspond with Beugnot, 221; makes Jerome King of Westphalia, 228; receives Westphalian deputation, 229; his views on religion, 229; advises Jerome on constitution of Westphalia, 234, 236, 295; converts Johann von Müller, 235; criticizes Jerome, 295, 299; ruins Westphalia by his financial and military policy, 295 ff.; writes to Jerome on military organization, 301; his reception in Frankfort, 314; nominates Eugène to the succession of Frankfort, 319; his last visit to Frankfort, 332; his treatment of Hamburg, 337; threatens to vanquish England, 345; annexes the Rhine departments, 358; settles territorial dues at Mainz, 368; legislates for the Jews, 368; his marriage with Marie Louise, 372; visits the Rhine provinces, 372; his realism, 374; and moral ideals, 375; the merits and defects of his system, 378; and its results, 378 ff.; his influence on the political structure of Germany, 381.

Nassau, 136, 154, 162, 181, 185: *and see* William Frederick, Prince of Orange.

Nimeguen, 50.

Orange: *see* William Frederick.

Otto, 95-7.

Pichegru, 68, 70 ff.

Piedmont, annexation of, 49.

Poland, French army in, 142; Grand-Duchy of Warsaw created in, 147 ff.; condition of, in 1807, 152.

Posen, Treaty of, 133, 134; Duchy of, 381.

Press, censorship of, 17, 18; in Warsaw, 154; Berg, 223; Hamburg, 346; the Rhineland, 361.

Pressburg, Treaty of, 107, 109.

Prussia, unwise legislation in, 21; reaction in, 24; territories on left bank of Rhine, 27; makes treaty with France, 29; promised indemnity, 30; jealousy of Austria, 39; indemnity of, 44; occupies Hanover in 1801, 49; fails to prevent French occupation of Hanover in 1803, 51; acquiesces in d'Enghien affair, 75; King of, protests against seizure of Rumbold, 91; condition of, in 1806, 124; war with France, 124 ff.; alliance with Russia, 125; receives Hanover by Treaty, of Schönbrunn, 127; army defeated at Jena and Auerstädt, 130; humiliation and losses of, by Treaty of Tilsit, 145, 146; deprived of Cleves, 176; loses territory to Murat, 182, 183; agrarian legislation in, 380; acquires territory in 1815, 381.

Prussia, King of: *see* Frederick William.

Prussia, Queen of: *see* Louise.

Rapp, General, 343.

Rastadt, 27-37; French troops in, 101.

Ratisbon, Diet of, 6; prohibits students' associations, 24; represented at Rastadt, 31; discusses compensations, 39; change of balance of power in, 43; declares itself neutral, 103; period of suspense in, 110; consents to the abolition of the Empire, 123; negotiates for Concordat, 168.

Ratisbon, town of, 85, 109, 112; Dalberg, Archbishop of, 113; ceded to Bavaria, 318.

Régnier, 69, 72, 76, 77, 80.

Reich, Baroness von, 72, 73.

Reinhard, 65, 234, 239, 244, 250, 297, 308, 310, 340.

Remscheid, 185, 206 ff.

Rhine frontier, conquest of, by France, 24, 26, 382; ceded at Campo-Formio, 28; ceded at Lunéville, 38, 86.

Rhine provinces, alleged conspiracy in, 79; ecclesiastical principalities in, 351; influence of French Revolution and French government on, 352; departments organized in, 354; views of Görres on, 357, 360; union of, with France, 358; send deputation to Napoleon, 358; van Alpen's description of, 359; condition of, under Napoleonic régime, 361 ff.; primary education in, 365; French codes introduced in, 366 ff.; development of, hindered by continental blockade, 370; French

customs line abolished, 371 ; conscription in, 372.
Roederer, 192, 208, 213, 221.
Rosey, Captain, 78.
Rousseau, influence of, 279.
Rudler, 354, 357, 360.
Rumbold, Sir George, 88–92, 125.
Russia, mediation of, 40–2 ; alliance with Prussia, 125 ; defeat of, at Friedland, 144 ; signs Treaty of Tilsit, 145 ; war with Napoleon (1812), 307, 308, 348.
Russia, Emperor of : *see* Alexander.

Sailer, 9.
Salzburg, 28, 107.
Savary, 70.
Saxony, treatment of, by Napoleon after Jena, 133 ; joins Rhenish Confederacy, 133, 145, 162 ; Lutheranism in, 134 ; education in, 278.
Saxony, Elector of : *see* Frederick Augustus.
Schill, Major, 252.
Schiller, 3, 351.
Schlözer, 18, 20.
Schönbrunn, Treaty of, 126, 127, 177.
Secularization, idea of, 8, 29, 35, 37, 39, 85, 139, 168, 298, 366.
Semler, Johann, 12.
Serfs, liberation of, in Austria and Baden, 23 ; views of Goethe and Möser on, 23 ; in Osnabrück, 53 ; liberation of, in the Grand-Duchy of Warsaw, 149 ; in Berg, 183, 201 ff. ; in Westphalia, 230, 232 ; in Frankfort, 330.
Silesia, 145, 147.
Siméon, 234, 238, 242, 243, 256, 260, 270, 275.
Smith, Adam, 20.
Spain, war with, 187, 193.
Spencer-Smith, 76, 78.
Stein, 380.
Strombeck, von, 260 ff., 292.
Students' clubs prohibited by Diet, 24.
Stuttgart, 76, 100, 121, 169.
Süssmilch, 20.
Swabian League, prospect of, 47.
Sweden, claims to take part in Congress of Rastadt, 34.
Sweden, King of : *see* Gustavus IV.
Switzerland, Napoleon in, 31 ; act of mediation, 49.

Talleyrand, settles German indemnities, 41 ; receives bribes, 62, 117 ; demands expulsion of *émigrés* from Baden, 72 ; demands Bavarian alliance, 95 ; continental policy of, 108 ; devises schemes for settlement of Germany, 116 ff. ; his views on constitution of Rhenish Confederacy, 164 ; his scheme for Bavarian Concordat, 167 ; is appealed to by Murat, 178, 181.
Taylor, 76, 78, 80.
Teschen, Treaty of, 40.
Tilsit, Treaties of, 145, 161, 169, 191, 226.

Ulm, 103.
Universities, control of, 24 ; in Berg, 195, 210 ; their place in the national life, 275 ; in Westphalia, 282 ff. ; in Aschaffenburg, 329 ; in Hanseatic towns, 347 ; in Rhine departments, 364.

Venice, spoliation of, 27 ; in Talleyrand's scheme, 108.
Verden, 54.
Vienna, Peace of, 248 ; Congress of, 372, 381.
Villers, Charles de, 2, 4, 5, 227.

Wagram, 249, 254, 303.
Wallmoden, Johann Ludwig von, 55.
Warsaw, Grand-Duchy of, 145, 147 ; offered to King of Saxony, 148, 153 ; Napoleon's constitution of, 149–51 ; fiscal affairs in, 153 ; wretched condition of Poles in, 154 ; military governments in, 154.
Wesel, 128, 179, 182, 190.
Westphalia, King of : *see* Jerome Bonaparte.
Westphalia, kingdom of, 146, 155, 189, 199, 202, 224 ff. ; constitution of, 231 ff. ; German officials in, 240, 248 ; parliament of, 243, 294 ; military affairs in, 248, 300 ; revolts and conspiracies in, 249 ff. ; feudalism abolished in, 256 ff. ; French codes in, 259 ; religious toleration in, 264 ; conscription in, 264, 300 ; position of the Church in, 265 ff. ; poor relief and charities in, 267 ff. ; local government in, 269 ; vaccination in, 274 ; the 'high police,' 274 ; educational problems in, 278 ff. ; fine arts in, 287 ; fiscal affairs of, 289 ff. ; ruined by Napoleon's financial

policy, 295; Hanover ceded to, and withdrawn from, 299; hatred of the French in, 307; final collapse of, 308-10.

Wetzlar, imperial Chamber of, 7; town of, 43, 83; enclave of, 317, 318; courts of law in, 327; law school in, 329.

Wieland, 23.

William VIII, Landgrave and Elector of Hesse-Cassel, 134, 135, 227, 252, 254.

William Frederick, Prince of Orange, 28, 29, 44, 128, 136, 139.

Wolfenbüttel, library of, 225.

Wolffradt, 239, 247, 248, 292.

Würtemberg, flattered by Napoleon, 32; Napoleon's policy of strengthening, 42, 44; enlargement of, 45; subjection to France, 78; pillaged by the French, 102; indemnities of, 107, 108; gains of, by Treaty of Pressburg, 108, 168; objects to French protectorate, 121.

Würtemberg, Duke of: *see* Frederick of Würtemberg.

Zürich, victory of, 38.